Full Stack JavaScript Strategies
The Hidden Parts Every Mid-Level
Developer Needs to Know

Milecia McGregor

Full Stack JavaScript Strategies

by Milecia McGregor

Published by O'Reilly Media, Inc., 1005 Gravenstein Highway North, Sebastopol, CA 95472.

O'Reilly books may be purchased for educational, business, or sales promotional use. Online editions are also available for most titles (*http://oreilly.com*). For more information, contact our corporate/institutional sales department: 800-998-9938 or *corporate@oreilly.com*.

Acquisitions Editor: Amanda Quinn	**Indexer:** Ellen Troutman-Zaig
Development Editor: Virginia Wilson	**Interior Designer:** David Futato
Production Editor: Christopher Faucher	**Cover Designer:** Karen Montgomery
Copyeditor: Shannon Turlington	**Illustrator:** Kate Dullea
Proofreader: Vanessa Moore	

January 2025: First Edition

Revision History for the First Edition

2025-01-09: First Release

See *http://oreilly.com/catalog/errata.csp?isbn=9781098122256* for release details.

978-1-098-12225-6

[LSI]

Table of Contents

Part IV.   Deploying the Full Stack App

Preface

My goal with this book is to give you a reference—kind of a sanity check—for when you're working on either greenfield or legacy projects across the frontend and backend and handling deployments. Some questions are relevant for both types of projects, like how you'll handle testing, performance, and security. Many applications have core commonalities that you can use regardless of the industry you work in. When those moments come where you find yourself questioning why you've never heard of something, hopefully this book will make you feel more confident asking those "simple" questions.

Who This Book Is For

If you are trying to figure out how senior devs seem to magically know how everything works and how they understand complex concepts so quickly, I'm going to show you how.

At this point in your career, you've probably been working as a software developer for a few years. You know how to complete your tasks with solid code regardless of whether it's on the frontend or backend. While you may have some knowledge across the full stack, it's likely you focus on one part of the stack over the other. On the frontend, you should be familiar with making responsive layouts, fetching data from APIs, and using some of the frameworks, such as React, Astro, or Svelte. On the backend, you've done some database migrations, built some APIs, and handled some basic authentication flows.

You also have skills like using Git with any of the repo hosting services, such as GitHub or GitLab, and using different tools to test your changes. You may have worked on one project for years, or you may have hopped around projects, but the scope of your work has typically fallen under some of the concepts mentioned.

Now you're ready to move to the next level in your career. That means learning how the whole system works and why technical decisions are made. That's what will be covered in this book.

What You Will Learn

At the highest level, what you're going to learn in this book is everything it takes to create a full stack web application hosted on a cloud platform. You're going to learn how to find where the business logic for every app comes from. You're going to gain some intuition for how to decide between different architectures, third-party services, and tools to create a maintainable application. You're going to learn the subtle yet deep skills it takes to become a senior developer. This book is going to give you strategies for working with different teams and understanding how product decisions are made. You'll also deepen your existing skills to cover the full stack confidently.

Regardless of whether you start on the frontend or backend, you're going to learn about design and development principles and when to apply them. You'll learn all these things as you go through the software development lifecycle (SDLC) of a project in this book and build a production-like application.

Think of this book as a reference you can pick up at any point in the SDLC and use as a checklist. You will learn all the essential parts that need to be considered for app development so that you know exactly what to do when a question comes up. By the time you finish, you'll know how, why, and when to make technical decisions and how the business requirements evolve.

What This Book Is Not

This book is not a deep dive into any specific set of tools, and it will not teach you general JavaScript programming. A large range of topics will be covered in this book, with accompanying examples to demonstrate senior-level considerations, but it is expected that you know how to read code, debug issues, and find additional learning resources.

Since so many topics are covered, strategies will be discussed along with the code. These strategies are meant to be tools you can bring to any project you work on, although they may not work on *every* project. There isn't a single approach that would work for any two projects because everything has its own nuances. So the goal is to give you a number of options you can choose from as needed.

Some parts of the book will need a much deeper explanation than a chapter or section can provide. No book can adequately cover all the topics presented here, and I want to make sure you get all the information you need. So while some topics will be light on the full implementation details, there will always be links to complementary resources.

How This Book Is Organized

Part I, "Starting Your New Project", will be relatively short and will cover how you translate designs into tasks and questions that you'll have to ask the Product team and other teams. This is when you'll get your first introduction to where the business logic comes from.

Part II, "Building the Backend", focuses on creating the backend of this project. You'll work with NestJS (*https://nestjs.com*) as we walk through a number of considerations, like security and third-party services, for development.

After you have the backend ready, you'll switch over to Part III, "Building the Front-end", where you'll work with a React project. You'll build the UI for this project and cover concerns associated with frontend apps, such as responsiveness and performance.

Finally, in Part IV, "Deploying the Full Stack App", you'll dive into the details of connecting the frontend, backend, and other systems to build and deploy a full stack app to production. By the time you finish this book, you should feel comfortable jumping into any part of a project and asking questions that will help clarify tasks as well as provide technical advice.

You'll notice that each part of the book varies in length. That's because it's supposed to help break down where a lot of time really gets spent during development. Some parts of a project take more time than others or have different feedback cycles. This book is trying to reflect real-world conditions as closely as possible.

To add to the real-world feel of this book, I've incorporated some opinions and thoughts from other software engineers throughout the chapters. Ethan Brown is the founder of OptionLab and author of *Learning JavaScript*, 3rd Edition (O'Reilly) and *Web Development with Node and Express*, 2nd Edition (O'Reilly). Jeff Graham is the Head of Engineering at Proxima AI and previously worked in financial technology (fintech), education technology (edtech), media, and ecommerce.

Conventions Used in This Book

The following typographical conventions are used in this book:

Italic

Indicates new terms, URLs, email addresses, filenames, and file extensions.

`Constant width`

Used for program listings, as well as within paragraphs to refer to program elements such as variable or function names, databases, data types, environment variables, statements, and keywords.

`Constant width italic`

Shows text that should be replaced with user-supplied values or by values determined by context.

This element signifies a tip or suggestion.

This element signifies a general note.

This element indicates a warning or caution.

Using Code Examples

Supplemental material (code examples, exercises, etc.) is available for download at *https://github.com/flippedcoder/dashboard-web* and *https://github.com/flippedcoder/dashboard-server*.

If you have a technical question or a problem using the code examples, please send email to *support@oreilly.com*.

This book is here to help you get your job done. In general, if example code is offered with this book, you may use it in your programs and documentation. You do not need to contact us for permission unless you're reproducing a significant portion of the code. For example, writing a program that uses several chunks of code from this book does not require permission. Selling or distributing examples from O'Reilly books does require permission. Answering a question by citing this book and quoting example code does not require permission. Incorporating a significant amount of example code from this book into your product's documentation does require permission.

We appreciate, but generally do not require, attribution. An attribution usually includes the title, author, publisher, and ISBN. For example: "*Full Stack JavaScript Strategies* by Milecia McGregor (O'Reilly). Copyright 2025 Milecia McGregor, 978-1-098-12225-6."

If you feel your use of code examples falls outside fair use or the permission given above, feel free to contact us at *permissions@oreilly.com*.

O'Reilly Online Learning

 For more than 40 years, *O'Reilly Media* has provided technology and business training, knowledge, and insight to help companies succeed.

Our unique network of experts and innovators share their knowledge and expertise through books, articles, and our online learning platform. O'Reilly's online learning platform gives you on-demand access to live training courses, in-depth learning paths, interactive coding environments, and a vast collection of text and video from O'Reilly and 200+ other publishers. For more information, visit *https://oreilly.com*.

How to Contact Us

Please address comments and questions concerning this book to the publisher:

O'Reilly Media, Inc.
1005 Gravenstein Highway North
Sebastopol, CA 95472
800-889-8969 (in the United States or Canada)
707-827-7019 (international or local)
707-829-0104 (fax)
support@oreilly.com
https://oreilly.com/about/contact.html

We have a web page for this book, where we list errata, examples, and any additional information. You can access this page at *https://oreil.ly/full-stack-javascript*.

For news and information about our books and courses, visit *https://oreilly.com*.

Find us on LinkedIn: *https://linkedin.com/company/oreilly-media*.

Watch us on YouTube: *https://youtube.com/oreillymedia*.

Acknowledgments

First, I'd like to thank my grandma, Carol Matthews, for listening to me endlessly rant about writing this book for the past 2 years. Any time I needed to vent, she was always there.

I want to thank all of the people I've worked with at O'Reilly that have made this experience so smooth. Virginia Wilson, I couldn't have made it through all of the edits and feedback without you! Amanda Quinn, thank you for handling all of the behind-the-scenes things and coordinating with everyone! A big, big thank you to Ethan Brown for all of the very thoughtful, thorough feedback you gave me over the course of writing this book. I learned a lot from your comments and resources you showed me. Another thank you to Adam Scott for all the feedback and suggestions throughout the book.

I also want to thank my sister, Soleil Gibbs, and close friends for listening to me talk about this book when I was low on energy or I ran into a difficult section. They helped me push through when I really didn't want to. Another huge source of motivation was my husband who gave me the time and space I needed to get through this journey.

This definitely wasn't a solo process and I couldn't be more thankful for everyone that was a part of this journey, in big and small ways.

## PART I

Starting Your New Project

## CHAPTER 1

Kicking Off the Project

Welcome to the team! If you're like most readers of this book, you're a frontend or backend developer, but you would like to be a senior-level full stack developer. Now imagine fast-forwarding to that point in your career: you're a new, senior, full stack JavaScript developer. That means you're responsible for helping drive the technical direction of the project and coordinating efforts across different teams to get software to users. Your task is to start a *greenfield app*, a project you get to build from scratch with no existing code, based on designs and conversations with a number of teams.

Let's break down what you'll learn in this chapter:

- How to work with several other teams to fully define features
- How to take a design and break it into small, actionable tasks
- How to determine the data you'll need to work with

The Project You'll Build

The project you'll be building as you work through the book will be an ecommerce platform that has access to a lot of user data, including some personally identifiable information (PII), and that connects with multiple third-party services. You and your team have been tasked with creating a user dashboard so that customers can make purchases, see information about their order history and other actions they have taken, and interact with their digital purchases, like ebooks. They'll also be able to take different actions based on their permissions within the app.

You're starting with a fresh Product team and a Design team that you'll work with to make this dashboard a reality. The Product team will be responsible for talking with different stakeholders to decide what features should be built. The Design team will be responsible for making the UI for those features and doing the first pass at the user experience.

The first part of the project will likely involve the Product and Design teams working closely together to make some mock screens for you and some behavioral docs. These mocks will be shown to you and discussed in a project kickoff meeting.

Project Kickoff Meeting

The kickoff meeting typically involves the Product team going through the mocks the Design team has made. It's very likely that these mocks will change as you go through development, but they should be about 80% of the way there. They'll take you through the user flow, show you how users interact with the app, and give you an idea of the data you need. At this point in the project, get comfortable asking a lot of questions. Usually, you'll think of things when you start looking at the designs from a technical perspective that the Product or Design teams haven't considered.

 Make sure that in this initial meeting you do some introductions so that everyone knows who they're working with. It's easy to dive into the work immediately, but remember that it's just as important to get to know your coworkers.

Remember, this whole process is very collaborative. Asking questions early and often will make things go more smoothly as the project moves forward. Right now, only two screens need to be built for a proof of concept, although Product has told you that the functionality will expand over time. Let's take a look at these screens and go through the user flow.

The screenshots are from a commonly used design tool called Figma (*https://www.figma.com*). There's usually a design somewhere that visually describes how the app flows. As you move through the engineering process, you'll focus on one of these views at a time, like the user info screen in Figure 1-1.

Figure 1-1. User info screen design in Figma

Figure 1-2 shows a screen where users can see their information, such as orders, suggested products, and other details. This is also where users edit their information, such as their address, and where they can cancel orders and see their digital purchases.

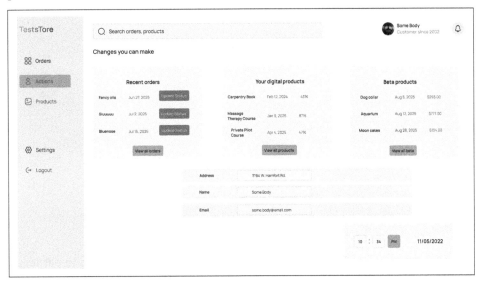

Figure 1-2. User actions screen design in Figma

The design in Figure 1-3 shows how these views should look on mobile devices. Most projects that interact with external users will have mobile designs. If you don't see these designs, make sure you ask about them!

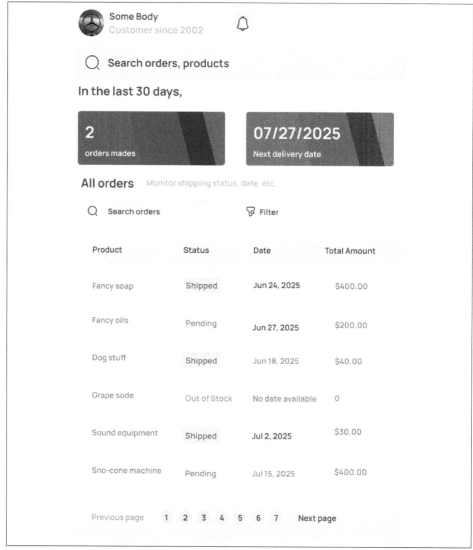

Figure 1-3. App designs with mobile view in Figma

A lot of designers use Figma when they create the mocks for an app or a particular feature. Some other tools you might run into include InVision (now Miro) (*https://miro.com*) or the newer alternative, Penpot (*https://penpot.app*). The Figma designs also have the HTML and CSS in them, so they can be useful for developers when they want to check dimensions while arranging elements on the page. Although the CSS is there, it's not always completely accurate. You can use them as a starting point, but make sure to modify the styles to meet the requirements.

By the time you see these mock designs, Product and Design will have had several meetings to iron out as much detail as they can. That doesn't mean they'll have everything figured out, and that's where you come in. Based on these designs and the explanations of how a user will interact with the app, you have to work with your team to decide the technical approach you want to take.

Let's walk through these designs just as you would with your Product team. On the first screen (Figure 1-1), there are:

- A navigation bar on the side of the page with links to other areas in the app
- A search bar at the top of the page to help find products
- A featured products section, along with the user's most recent order
- A sortable, paginated table with several columns that displays all the user's orders

Several sections on the second screen (Figure 1-2) have fields that the user can interact with. Users can toggle a few settings, update fields, and take actions based on their purchases. This screen has more complexity than the first screen, so you'll want to take the time to really go through this with the team. Product and Design will often turn to you as the senior developer on the team for the final say on technical decisions.

 Never make promises without talking to your team first, no matter how hard you get pushed. The Product team may pull you into a meeting to try to get an idea of how complicated it will be to implement a feature they have in mind. This can lead to them expecting a quick commitment on a timeline, which is something you'll have to get comfortable handling as you become a more senior-level dev. You have to firmly state that you can't give an accurate estimate until you talk to the rest of the team. The other devs will be able to bring up concerns that you might not realize, and they'll be working on the feature eventually anyway. Stand your ground and simply don't commit if the Product team keeps pressing for a date. That way, *you're* not the one who put the team on a tight deadline.

With these designs in hand and a few documents on how the screens are supposed to work, it's time for you to develop an understanding of the business logic before you go to the team. Having a solid understanding of the business decisions behind the designs is a huge help when you're trying to explain them to other developers.

As you go through this information, you'll need to consider several things based on the designs you have.

Design Considerations

At this stage, you'll find yourself asking a lot of questions, and that's totally normal. Now is the time to really dive into the details and get nitpicky. One of the ways you can gain more experience with evaluating designs for technical purposes is by getting exposure to different design sets. For example, the Design team you're working with is likely doing design work for other apps in the organization.

If you have questions about how a drop-down feature is supposed to behave, ask if there are other designs you can use as a reference. Often there are, and you should take the time to thoroughly understand how they work. Some of the best questions come from experience with different implementations. Another way to get more exposure to different designs is to start paying close attention to the apps you use. Have you ever *really* thought about the user flow for your bank app or an exercise or meditation app? These are all examples of product designs in production that you can make comparisons with.

It can be a little tricky finding time to do exploratory work. One way is by writing a ticket that details what you'll be researching, some of the thoughts you've had about the issue so far, and some open questions. Go ahead and add points to the ticket, too, to make it more official.

Think about how designs look for other products and how interfaces behave when you're breaking them down into the details. As you think of differences, take notes about the questions they bring up.

A word of caution for when you're compiling your list of questions: as you think of a question, look through the documentation you were given. Sometimes the answers are already there, and it saves everyone time when you read the docs first. Take about an hour to go through any engineering docs the team has for other projects. Also read through the docs on third-party services that are being used as well as for any packages you're thinking about using.

You might be wondering what some good questions are. That always depends on the designs and the business logic.

Here are some questions that can get you started as you look at the screens you have available for this example project:

- Are there translations to other languages that you need to account for?
- What are the brand guidelines, such as colors, fonts, and responsive sizes, that should be used throughout the app?
- What permissions do users need to see their information?
- What permissions do users need to take actions in the app?
- How many different types of users will there be?
- How long do we expect users to be active, so we know how long an access token should live?
- What is all of the data we expect to handle for users?
- Do we want to show this data for different time ranges?
- Should the table be sortable by each column or only specific columns?
- How do we know which orders should be featured?
- What type of data do the input fields accept?
- When a user saves changes, what should we show them?
- If there's an API error on the client side, what should the user see or be able to do?
- Does the user need to enter more credentials before taking sensitive actions like changing PII?
- Should input errors be shown inline with the field or by the Submit button?
- Do we need to consider tablet-sized and other mobile devices?
- Will the backend of this app be used by any other apps?
- Will the frontend need to be integrated into another app?
- Are there any compliances or regulations this app falls under or will get audited by?

You can see that this list of questions can get very long, and I'm sure you thought of other questions as well. Don't worry if the list is long. It'll be hard to get all these questions addressed in one go, so you should definitely prioritize this list based on the feature. It's better to ask as many of these questions as you can in the beginning compared to halfway to the deadline. If there are small things, then you can probably use your experience to make judgment calls, such as with form handling.

The questions can be all over the place, but the Product or Design team should be able to answer them. There isn't anything technical in here yet, although the answers to all these questions will drive technical decisions. Getting answers to these sorts of questions early is why senior developers tend to deeply understand the business logic.

To make the best technical decisions you can, you have to understand the purpose of the app's functionality and how it fits in the overall business. This can give you some foresight into how to build the app in the most maintainable way because you see the direction the business is going. Some of this foresight will come from the data you know you're going to work with.

Data-Driven Design

Data drives design. Everything the designs do is built around how to best deliver data and let users interact with it. Take the table screen, for example. The data doesn't have to be displayed as a table. It could be a collapsible list or a graph. That's why you have to dig into these questions about the business logic and what you will be working with. It's one of the reasons that frontend development is usually dependent on backend development. We'll talk about this more in Chapter 2.

As you go through the designs, it's a good idea to take notes on the data that you see you'll need for each screen. On the settings screen, you can see that you'll need the user's name, shipping address, and language preference in one section. Take notes on potential variable names and data types for these that you feel comfortable sharing with the team. That can help spark the initial conversations around how to approach the project.

Also confirm with the Product team that these values are correct and what's expected by the app. Always check with the Product team that you have the correct data and relationships between the data. They won't explain it in technical terms, but they'll walk you through different scenarios so that you can paint the big picture.

This is like the discovery phase of the project for your development team. Once you've gone through the designs and you have your questions and notes, get ready to talk about specific features.

Breaking Down Designs into Tasks

You've made it through the first round of refinement for the project! In this next round, you can assume that Product has answered all your team's questions and you have updated designs. Now you'll be working with Product to carve features out of this info. This is when you'll first use a ticket system, such as Jira (*https://oreil.ly/ qmodA*), Trello (*https://trello.com*), ClickUp (*https://clickup.com*), or Shortcut (*https:// www.shortcut.com*). Figure 1-4 is an example of a ticket system in Trello.

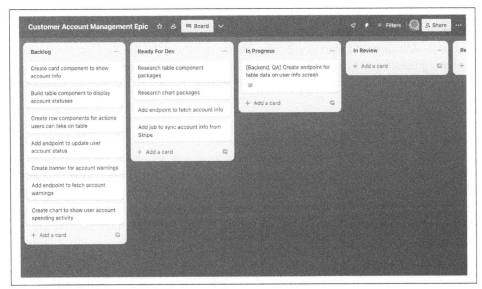

Figure 1-4. Example of a backlog in Trello

The tickets you make here are going to go through refinement once you start bringing in more developers and other teams. The goal at this stage is to make action items for parts of the designs. The user info screen, for example, has several pieces that can be broken out into features, such as the featured section and the table. You're trying to get people thinking about how the designs will actually work, and you'll start bringing in that technical perspective.

You might try to group features based on data relationships. This will help make it easier for backend changes to be made and deployed as the frontend is being built. This is also a stage when you can still point out any big issues you run into as you start thinking through the tech stack. Any time you have a thought for a feature or technical requirements, make sure a ticket gets made. If there isn't a ticket, the work won't get prioritized.

Refining Tasks from Feature Requirements

You're at the point in the project where Product should have some user stories written for you to refine with technical details. These user stories are part of the documentation you get that define the features you're developing. They are typically written from the perspective of the user to give you some of the hidden context behind how the user will interact with the functionality. This doesn't happen all the time, though. Often, you'll be working with Product to fully define features, but they'll have some details to get started with from the previous round.

You can assume that your team follows a normal Agile process with two-week sprints and the standard meetings like daily stand-up, backlog grooming, sprint planning, and retro. At this point, start going through the tickets in the Jira backlog in a backlog grooming meeting. This meeting should include the development, quality assurance (QA), Design, and Product teams so that everyone can ask or answer questions and bring up concerns. Feature tickets should be broken down into the smallest pieces of work a developer can do.

This is one of the times when you have to use some art versus science. The "smallest" piece could mean having a ticket to write an endpoint with all the tasks associated with it and having a separate ticket for triggering events. One way to think about it is from a QA testing perspective. What is the smallest grouping of work that makes sense to test together? Entire books and numerous resources have been written about Agile and these kinds of project decisions. One resource you might look at are the Atlassian articles on Agile (*https://oreil.ly/chgWf*).

To keep expectations aligned with what the team can output, estimates are usually made on every ticket for how complex the task is. When you're going through tickets during backlog grooming, don't hesitate to slow things down. If you spend the entire time on one ticket, then that shows Product where they need to improve, which can be brought up in the retro meeting.

Make sure every ticket has acceptance criteria agreed on by Product, QA, and your team. If the ticket has UI elements, make sure you have access to the designs for both desktop and mobile. Every ticket should also have background information on how the functionality fits in the overall app so that the developers have context. All the developers should be in agreement on estimates for each ticket.

This might seem like a lot of fuss over tickets, but doing all of this up front saves your team time. Getting everyone on the same page at the very beginning helps keep your team unblocked. With this level of documentation for each ticket, there shouldn't be much ambiguity in the task when anyone on the project gets to it. Here's an example of info you will find in a well-defined ticket:

Title: [Backend, QA] Create endpoint for table data on user info screen

Description: As a user, I need to see a table with my purchase info. This info should include the product name, price, estimated arrival date, and quantity in each row on the table. This table should also be sortable by clicking on the column headers. It should have pagination so that I can go through my purchase history for the previous 12 months. It should match the designs attached. (See Figure 1-1.)

Acceptance criteria:

- Update data schema to include purchase history definition: product name, price, estimated arrival date, and quantity.
- Run migration on database.
- Create endpoint that responds with user purchase history for past 12 months.
- Ensure authentication is working correctly.
- Implement validation on request data.
- Write tests for new endpoint.
- Write docs for how the endpoint works so frontend can use it.

Points: 5

It should be very clear to any engineer what needs to be done, although the ticket shouldn't tell them how to implement it. That's something they can decide after the team has discussed it. Having tickets written out like this will spark deeper technical discussions that will help drive the overall architecture of your project.

This is when you start to take the tasks from Product and refine them even more as a development team. It's always a good idea to include any highlights that come out of team meetings in the tickets, so everyone remembers why things were done a certain way. You might learn that one of your third-party services only accepts data in a certain format, which leads to you needing to write some utility functions. But you absolutely have to have this because of a product requirement. That will be important context to have for code review and testing.

It may seem like this is a long process, but usually you can define the tickets for the upcoming sprint in a few days. Then once the sprint starts, you can jump in. But before you get to pick your own tickets and start coding, there are a few more conversations you'll need to have.

Discussing Timelines with Product and Other Teams

At this point in the project, you can assume you have well-defined tickets and the details are as ironed out as possible. Now it's time for one of the higher-level conversations. After all the tickets have been estimated, Product will be ready to set a launch date.

Sometimes Product will come to you with a launch date before you've had a chance to estimate tickets. If you find that their timeline is shorter than what Engineering needs to adequately get through the tickets, push back. Always speak up when timelines are tight. This will save everyone from unnecessary stress.

This discussion is going to involve more than just your team. You might need to coordinate with developers on other projects, the DevOps team, the Support team, and the QA team. It just depends on how far the reach of your changes goes. Don't commit to a launch date until you've talked with these other teams. You'll want to see how your goals fit with theirs and what you can do to make the process easier for them.

Talking to Other Development Teams

Your project might depend on another team implementing something in their code that your app consumes. You'll need to give them plenty of heads-up and details so that they can include this in their sprint. Development teams aren't always aware of when feature releases for one app cross over into their app. Talk to them about what you need and keep it as simple as possible. Mention what your target launch date is and see if that's something they can help you reach.

On the other hand, the new features in your app might cause breaking changes for other teams, and you need to let them know what updates they need to make and by when. Don't hesitate to reach out to any teams you think will be affected just to double-check. As you find out which teams are affected, update the team docs to show them as consumers of your app.

Here are some things you'll need to have ready before you talk to them:

Well-defined technical requirements
> Give them a task that's just as defined as if your team were doing it. Also give them time to ask questions if they need more information.

A general idea of where in their code the changes need to be made
> You don't have to go in their code and implement the changes, but having a clue of where to get started helps.

Context behind the change you're requesting
> A change that seems small to you could change the functionality of something important in their app. Make sure they understand why this change is needed.

A deadline
> Of course, you'll ask how long it'll take them to get to it, but have a flexible date in mind.

Willingness to do the work
> If it would be faster for you to implement the change and the team to review it, be open to that.

When you know you have everyone across the development teams on the same page, then you can talk to the next set of people. These discussions don't need to happen in this order, but they do need to happen. Whoever is available to talk first can be the first conversation you have.

Coordinating with DevOps

When it's time to release to different environments, you'll need to check in with the DevOps team. That's assuming there *is* a DevOps team. Sometimes at smaller companies, you will also be responsible for handling deployments. This book assumes that you're working with at least one DevOps engineer who handles infrastructure and pipeline changes for you.

Since this will be a completely new app, you'll need the infrastructure to be set up for QA to do testing, for production, and for any other environments. You may be able to help set up the continuous integration and continuous deployment (CI/CD) pipeline using tools like CircleCI (*https://circleci.com*), Jenkins (*https://www.jenkins.io*), or GitHub Actions (*https://oreil.ly/bX9eg*), although when it comes to provisioning resources and handling infrastructure concerns, that will be completely up to the DevOps team.

The DevOps team will provide important information, such as which cloud provider the app will be hosted on. You'll give them important information, like the programming language and frameworks being used. The goal for both teams on a new project is to have at least a few environments up for testing before prepping for production releases. Getting DevOps involved early is going to make things go more smoothly as development progresses.

Remember, all these teams that you're interacting with already have their own priorities. So you have to take into account that they may not get to you right away. That's why you want to coordinate with DevOps as soon as you have a technical direction. The last thing you want is to put DevOps in a crunched position right before an important deadline. Be ready to jump into a call to go over the project with them so that they understand what performance and usage are expected from this app. During your call, there are several things you'll want to cover:

Work on developing playbooks—the strategies and steps you implement to resolve issues —for outages and other issues in production
> When an issue happens, it can be hard to figure out the best steps. That's why you and DevOps need to think about this ahead of time.

Determine the right number of environments for the app
> Some projects can have three environments while others have an environment for every Git branch in existence. Find the right balance of environments that is maintainable on the infrastructure side and flexible for testing and other uses.

Figure out the best deployment strategy
> It's important for DevOps to know when they need to trigger scripts to run and how often they will run. Some parts will be automated, and others will need to be run manually. The best strategy is one that works for both teams.

Decide how to handle CI/CD maintenance
> Most CI/CD tools use YAML files to define the configurations for a pipeline, and these config files live in the project's repo. Sometimes developers make the changes, sometimes DevOps makes the changes, or both can feel comfortable making changes. Just get everyone on the same page.

Agree on the versions of the JavaScript runtime, like Node, Deno, or Bun, that will be supported
> Servers aren't always running the latest version of your runtime, and that can cause weird bugs in your app. Know the oldest version of the runtime your project will work with, just in case.

Find out when credentials are cycled
> Some apps are dependent on keys and secrets that are maintained as part of the infrastructure, such as npm tokens. Add a reminder ticket to the backlog so that you can plan to update them before they expire and cause production issues.

Choose a location to store assets
> For some apps, this will be included as part of the cloud provider, and for others, a third-party service will be used. Even if you don't come to an absolute answer right now, make another ticket to come back to this.

Set up time to test the app together before deploying
> You know how the app should behave, so DevOps will lean on you to handle some of the environment testing. They can usually get the app running, but you have to verify it's in the correct state.

Reserve some time for after the initial app deployment
> Things always come up with the first few deploys that need to be fixed. Go ahead and put that meeting on the calendar. If nothing happens, you just reserved celebration time for everyone.

One thing to remember while you're talking to DevOps is that you won't understand everything they're talking about and you don't need to. You'll start to pick up on things as you work with them, and it wouldn't hurt to pair with them a few times to see what they do. If you don't want to dive into the DevOps world, that's fine. They'll handle everything on their side from here.

Now you need to talk with the QA team.

Working with QA

While developers, especially seniors, are expected to thoroughly check their work, sometimes bugs slip through. That's why QA teams exist: to make sure those bugs don't reach production. Weird integration issues happen, pull requests (PRs) over-write functionality, edge cases are found, and a number of things cause bugs that developers don't catch. Getting new features and bug fixes to QA in a timely manner is important for staying on time for releases. You need to get the new code to them, give them time to test and report back defects, and then give yourself time to fix the defects and send the code back to QA.

 There is a chance that you might not work with a QA team at all. It really depends on the company. In some early-stage startups, you won't have a dedicated QA team. It'll just be you and the other developers, maybe even the CEO. In other companies, you might see the Product team do some manual QA on features. Regardless of whether there's a QA team, you can use the steps in this section to help do your own QA more thoroughly.

You see, this loop can take quite a while. To shorten that time and make sure the highest-priority tickets are tested first, include QA in many of your development calls. They will have questions about features and bugs from a QA perspective that need to be understood. All the test cases they write are basically like the history of the app. Many features will have test coverage, whether it's automated or manual. These tests will exist even when the feature doesn't, so QA keeps a record of changes in a different way than other teams do.

Set up a call between the QA team and your dev team, and make sure you've discussed:

Automated integration tests
> This is a responsibility that's usually owned by QA, but since the tests live in the project's repo in many cases, developers can write these tests as well. Also make the distinction between integration tests and unit tests. Developers should always be the ones writing unit tests.

Level of detail in reproduction steps
> There's a balance between not enough detail and way too much. Discuss what works best for the developers and the QA engineers so that everyone knows what

to expect. You'll end up working with a QA engineer to home in on the issue anyway, but it helps to have a starting point.

Including QA in relevant calls, such as backlog grooming and stand-ups
This ensures that QA will be up to date on any upcoming deadlines, shifted priorities, or releases and that they can give updates if they're running into issues. Try to put any updates for them at the beginning of these calls, such as tickets they can test, so they can use their time best.

Make it clear that QA should feel comfortable reaching out to the developer who worked on a ticket they're testing. Developers should be willing to pair with QA to help them determine if an issue is a bug or something else, like an environment difference.

QA is everybody's best friend because they find a lot of bugs that would have caused issues on production. It's not good for anyone when there are issues on production. QA is not there to tell the developer they're wrong or that their code is bad. They just want to make sure that absolutely nothing makes us bring out those playbooks for production fires. Be patient with them as they report defects because they're just doing their job.

You'll interact with a number of teams once you're ready to deploy changes; that will really depend on the company. You might interact with the Sales team to help them understand what the product is capable of so that they can set realistic customer expectations.

There's also the integration or customer success team. These teams usually work with customers one-on-one to help them integrate the product into their systems. They definitely need to be aware of any breaking changes or new features.

Some companies have a dedicated Security team as well, especially if the product is in fintech, health care, ecommerce, or manufacturing. This team may come in right after QA to run security tests, and continuous security scans might also be happening on the app throughout your development pipeline.

One team that will be around in some form or another is the Support team. This is the next and probably the last team you need to talk with.

Planning with Support

Support are the people who are in direct contact with users who are experiencing problems. Some of the bugs you will fix come directly from Support. They might even link their support ticket to your bug ticket so that they can keep users updated. The Support team is also a source of inspiration for new features. If they keep getting the same requests from different users, it's worth looking into a solution.

Support does a difficult job of dealing with upset customers. You want to make sure that happens as little as possible. When you're talking with Support about an upcoming feature release, they need to know how it affects users. Product should have already discussed timelines with them. You're trying to see what they need from the development team.

Keep in mind that Support team members usually don't have highly technical backgrounds. They understand how the app works from a user perspective and as an app admin, but they don't necessarily understand the weeds of the technical details. Knowing where they are coming from will help your communications exponentially. Your job with Support is to translate the technical stuff into the information they need.

Here are some things you can do that will help:

Have documentation Support can refer to for using a feature
> Describe anything that has changed compared to existing functionality. Highlight values users will need to enter since user input causes many of the issues they receive.

Listen when Support brings up complaints with the app
> Take in the feedback they give you from bugs or other requests and work with Product to prioritize that. This doesn't mean you implement everything that Support asks for, but it does mean you do a little research into why they're asking about it and how hard it would be to fix.

Always sync up on release dates and times
> Support will sometimes set aside special time around releases because there are going to be more user questions. They need to know exactly when changes are going out so that they aren't blindsided with an increase in issues.

Do a demo of the finished feature right before release
> After the changes have been approved for release, do a quick live demo with Support (and really everybody else). That way, they can see how the app is supposed to work and ask any questions.

Dedicate extra developer time to Support around release days
> If Support starts getting overwhelmed with issues, you might need to roll back the changes. Just be ready to pay close attention to them.

Discussing these things with Support is another way to bring up issues that can be addressed early in the process. It's also a great way to build a relationship between the Engineering and Support teams because you work closer together than it seems. This is the last team you need to coordinate with. Now it's time to bring back all your findings and notes to make a cohesive plan.

Conclusion

You've made it to the final step of project kickoff. You have your notes from the different team meetings, and it's time to distill it all and give the highlights to Product. All these conversations will help you come up with a reasonable deadline.

This is when some negotiations will start. One thing to keep in mind with deadlines is that something in development will go wrong. Give yourself and your team room to breathe and possibly overdeliver. Remember, underpromise and overdeliver. Unless the feature you need to implement is time sensitive, such as a third-party service being updated, add a few days of padding to account for weird happenings. After you've settled on a date with Product, taking all of the other teams' concerns into account, summon everyone together for one final, short call.

 It's important to understand that setting deadlines is extremely tricky in software development. Any number of things can pop up at any time and derail everything. If someone gets sick or a natural disaster takes out someone's electricity for a week, some tickets aren't going to get done. You might get deep into development and realize that a tool you're trying to integrate with is way more complex than you accounted for. You might be waiting to receive work from another dev team and they fall off schedule, putting you behind as well.

All of that is OK. The best thing you can do is communicate these issues with everyone as soon as you find out about them. Then you can start making plans for what to do next. Life happens, and you have to try your best not to let this stress you out every time—because it will happen a lot!

This call will have someone from all the teams you've talked to. The only things you want to confirm at this point are everyone's action items and deadlines. Having this call is about establishing accountability and triple-checking that everyone is on the same page. As prep for this meeting, take all this info out of your notes and make a short doc that everyone can reference leading up to the release.

At this point, you have many of the tickets you'll be working on and they're well defined. You've documented the cross-team connections. Project kickoff is complete. You have everything you need to finally get started writing code. In the next part of this book, you'll build a scalable backend in TypeScript using the NestJS framework.

## PART II

Building the Backend

## CHAPTER 2

Setting Up the Backend

You've got all your tickets ready to go, and you can assume you've been tasked with building the bones of the backend. The framework of choice at your company is NestJS (*https://nestjs.com*). Don't worry if you've never seen NestJS or even heard of it before. The docs for it are good, and you'll have other code you can reference. Reach out to othruer developers to see why certain architecture and design decisions have been made on existing backends.

In this chapter, you'll learn about:

- Making architecture decisions for the backend
- Checking the app to make sure it runs after initial setup
- Writing the initial documentation

These tasks are all crucial to ensuring that development is able to run smoothly as both the Product and the dev team grow and change over time. Everything that you build on the backend will start from the foundation you set here, so take your time to thoroughly discuss options with your team.

Why NestJS?

Before we dive too deep into the weeds, let's discuss why NestJS is a solid choice. It's basically like a backend architecture in a box. As soon as you initialize the app, you immediately have access to validation, authentication, routing, controllers, data schema, and a lot of other functionality. Instead of you having to piece everything together, NestJS gives you everything you need to make a scalable backend from the beginning. That does mean it's a little less flexible in how you organize it, but that's the trade-off for all the up-front scaffolding.

This is when you get to have some fun as you set up the initial repo for the backend. The decisions you make here drive the direction for the future of this project. As you come to questions that have options, ask your team for their technical input. They might be aware of something you don't know about. Not only does this help you build a better app, but it also helps everyone on the team learn.

There are so many considerations for building a backend that having other input will help you make decisions faster and more confidently. It will also help to keep architecture decision records (ADRs). These keep track of why and when important architectural decisions were made. You can see some examples in this GitHub repo (*https://oreil.ly/C78GT*).

It can be a little overwhelming being the one to open the empty terminal and bootstrap a completely new project. There's nothing to build on except examples and boilerplate code. It will go in whatever direction you and your team decide to take it. This is a fun time because you can really set up the codebase to be clean to update, test, and expand.

Choosing a Project Approach

This project will be a monolithic backend with a few serverless functions. This will allow you to build and deploy quickly, and you'll get to work with a hybrid backend architecture. You could have also decided to take a microservices approach. Then all your APIs could be serverless functions, for example. Your choice of backend architecture depends on how the app is going to grow over time.

Microservices can take more resources and more engineers to maintain compared to monoliths, but they can be great if you go with a domain-driven architecture, which you'll learn about in Chapter 30. On the other hand, monoliths can make it more difficult to make larger changes as quickly as you can with microservices.

You'll also be using TypeScript (*http://typescriptlang.org*) to build the full stack. The reason you're starting the project off with TypeScript is to help make debugging easier because it's harder to write incorrect code. By strictly enforcing typing, you'll catch some errors before you even run the code. TypeScript also makes it easier to see what fields and data types you're working with and where they come from, which is wonderful for keeping types consistent across the frontend and backend. Having typing in place is like having documentation for how things are connected, and it lets you see all the parameters you have available.

Setting Up NestJS

You'll walk through all the steps to bootstrap this whole project. To start, you need to have a few environmental things in place. You can follow along with the demo repo (*https://oreil.ly/-Czox*). You'll need to install the NestJS CLI. The current version of NestJS as of this writing is 9.2.0. Open a terminal and run the following command:

```
npm i -g @nestjs/cli
```

You can create a new NestJS project with the command:

```
nest new <your-project-name>
```

For this project, you'll use this command:

```
nest new dashboard-server
```

NestJS will ask you which package manager you want to use. Select npm and hit Enter:

```
? Which package manager would you ♥ to use? (Use arrow keys)
> npm
  yarn
  pnpm
```

Keeping track of package versions is something a senior dev might do silently. As we go through building this app, I'll introduce you to some leadership best practices, such as keeping docs updated and making sure everyone's local environment is running correctly. You'll also have to consider things like linting with something like ESLint (*https://eslint.org*), formatting rules with a common tool like Prettier (*https://prettier.io*) for the repo, and any number of environment configs to keep everything consistent in the code for everyone.

After that, the installation will start, which might take a few minutes. This process includes installing all the project dependencies, scaffolding the entire architecture, adding boilerplate code, and more. It even comes with TypeScript preconfigured. Take some time to go through this repo before you start making changes. Whether you're working on a brand-new app like this one or a legacy project, always take time in the beginning to get a high-level understanding of how everything works.

Key things to look at are:

- The *package.json* so you can see which packages are used in the project
- All the config files so you know how things work under the hood
- The test files because these give you a good idea of the major functionality of the app
- Some of the actual code to see how developers are expected to write things and if anything can be improved

After you've poked around a bit, go ahead and run the app with these commands:

```
cd dashboard-server
npm start
```

You'll see an output in the terminal like this that will let you know the app is running successfully:

```
> dashboard-server@0.0.1 start
> nest start

[Nest] 20891  - 03/03/2023, 8:18:46 PM     LOG [NestFactory] Starting Nest
  application...
[Nest] 20891  - 03/03/2023, 8:18:46 PM     LOG [InstanceLoader] AppModule
  dependencies initialized +11ms
[Nest] 20891  - 03/03/2023, 8:18:46 PM     LOG [RoutesResolver] AppController
  {/}: +5ms
[Nest] 20891  - 03/03/2023, 8:18:46 PM     LOG [RouterExplorer] Mapped {/, GET}
  route +3ms
[Nest] 20891  - 03/03/2023, 8:18:46 PM     LOG [NestApplication] Nest application
  successfully started +1ms
```

This is where one of your first senior decisions comes up. How exactly are you going to test this backend? Having a consistent environment for development will change how quickly you can test code and how much frustration the team experiences as the product grows and the team grows, too.

A standard choice is to use Docker (*https://oreil.ly/iMG1T*) because you can set up everything from a Postgres database instance to the server that the app will run on in a container (or two). These containers can hold the exact same data and versions and be set up on any local environment, regardless of the operating system (OS). Another option would be using some functionality in VS Code called Dev Containers (*https://oreil.ly/c4Bck*). Depending on the team and the project, this can be a good choice.

Testing the Backend Locally

Some popular testing tools you'll see include Postman (*https://oreil.ly/17Yn0*) and RapidAPI (*https://paw.cloud*). You'll work with Postman in this book (and many times in real life) because it has a free version. This is how you'll be able to make requests to your endpoints with different headers, body values, and other values and see what responses you get. That's typically how you test the backend before a UI is available.

Remember, tools like these are here to help you move faster. Don't get caught up in all the tool options. At the end of the day, it doesn't matter what you use for your local development as long as you're able to make meaningful progress. Now that you have Postman available, make a GET request to *http://localhost:3000*. You should see `Hello World!` as the response, like in Figure 2-1.

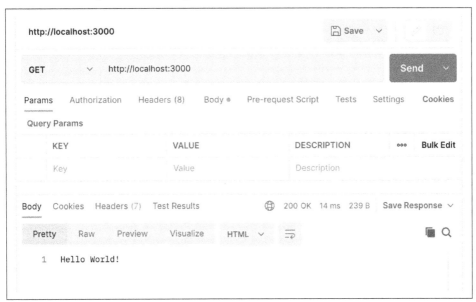

Figure 2-1. GET request and response in Postman

Everyone will have a different preference for the tools they like to use for backend testing, and it typically doesn't matter. However, it's easier to troubleshoot when all the devs on the team are in agreement on this particular tool. You can share your endpoint tests with other devs, which helps everyone find issues faster and more consistently. Eventually, your backend tests can serve as some of the documentation for the frontend. This will be something worth making a ticket for so that you can get it included in a sprint.

Now that you know the app is working, you can start making changes to get it ready for the team.

Updating the README

Start by updating the *README.md* with specific instructions for how to set up and run the app. There's already a lot of good stuff in there, so you can trim it up a bit and add a few things. A basic update can look like this:

```
# Dashboard Server

## Description

Back-end to support customers built on [Nest](https://github.com/nestjs/nest)
  framework TypeScript starter repository.

## Installation

```bash
$ npm install
```

Running the app

```bash
# development
$ npm run start

# watch mode
$ npm run start:dev

# production mode
$ npm run start:prod
```

Test

```bash
# unit tests
$ npm run test

# e2e tests
$ npm run test:e2e

# test coverage
$ npm run test:cov
```
```

This doesn't have to be a huge doc that expounds on your philosophical thoughts about code and the project. Give enough guidance that any dev could clone this repo and get it running. Other docs for the project will be stored somewhere else. As the repo grows, adding more details to the README will be helpful. This is a living document that everyone should feel comfortable updating as part of their PRs when needed.

Adding a CHANGELOG

As a best practice, it's good to include a *CHANGELOG.md* file in your repo. This will keep a close record of everything in each release over time. Having this record will help you determine which version of the app contains which updates; this comes in handy when there are issues with production. Here's what the start of this file can look like:

```
# CHANGELOG

## Guide

- Major releases include breaking changes and the version number will be
  incremented like, `x.0.0`
- Minor releases include new features, but no breaking changes and the version
  number will be incremented like, `0.x.0`
- Patch releases include bug fixes and performance enhancements and the version
  number will be incremented like, `0.0.x`

### 0.0.1

- Initial release
```

You might consider setting specific rules on commit messages. If you prefer a certain format, set up a tool like commitlint (*https://commitlint.js.org/#*) to enforce it early. This means your commit messages can include details such as whether it's a fix or a chore. It can include ticket numbers if needed. You can also make it enforce things like the message starting with a verb to state what the change does.

The commit message might look like this:

```
fix: update modal to send API call once
```

You might be responsible for preparing the release PRs, so it's important to make sure that updating this file gets included in that process. A good way to remember is when you update the app version in *package.json*, update this file, too.

In many projects, you may need to set up ESLint, Prettier, and TypeScript config files. This app comes with a lot of configs set by default, so you should go through them and add or remove values as needed. That's all for the initial app setup. Now you can turn your attention to building the data schema.

Monolith and Microservice Architectures

This is a crucial point in the project because you're setting the foundation for how everything will be built for the foreseeable future. You'll need to think about the future of the project, how it might grow, and what blockers that growth might run into.

Take some time to make an architecture diagram. It doesn't have to be fancy, but it does need to represent how the backend interacts with different pieces of the entire system. This includes everything the app touches, ranging from the frontend to cron jobs. *Cron jobs* are tasks that run in the background of your system on a schedule. They can be written in TypeScript as well.

The backend is like your control center. It drives the development of everything else because it interacts with a number of parts in the overall system. That's why it's so important to take your time and make this calculated decision. The two common architectures you'll run into are monoliths and microservices. I'll cover the differences here. Think of this as a guide to help you choose one or the other.

A *monolith* is when all your backend functionality is contained in a single codebase. You'll see this a lot with enterprise apps. There's one database and one server for the application. It gets deployed as a single unit that is connected to all the services you work with. All the endpoints, maybe some cron jobs, and some third-party integrations will be handled here.

With a monolith, you get the benefit of all the code being in one place. That way, you can get exposure to how the entirety of the system works and where changes need to be made. Setting up the infrastructure is straightforward because you'll be deploying only one app. Debugging is also easy because you can check the backend holistically.

Building a monolith is a simpler approach, but it comes with drawbacks. For example, if a bug gets released to production and causes errors at runtime that didn't happen locally, the whole app is down for users. It can also be hard to scale the app appropriately. You might have only one endpoint that gets a large amount of traffic, but with a monolith, you have to scale the whole backend, which can cost a lot. Figure 2-2 shows an example of what a monolithic backend can look like.

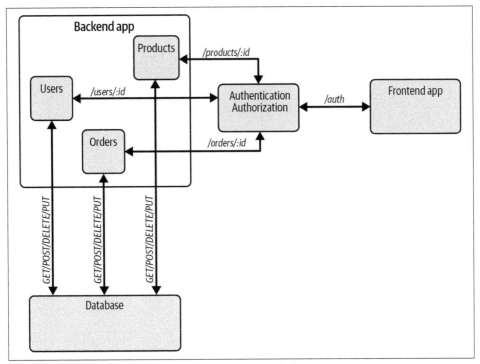

Figure 2-2. Architecture diagram for a simple monolith

A *microservice* is the complete opposite of a monolith. If you have a directory or set of files dedicated to one piece of business logic in your monolith, it becomes its own API in the form of a microservice. With microservices, all the backend business logic is split into different chunks based on functionality. Each microservice has its own codebase, database, and server.

One of the biggest benefits of microservices is scaling. Since all the business logic is separated into specific entities, you can ramp up resources for one endpoint while keeping the others the same. A unique thing you can do is use different programming languages for different microservices. You might have a microservice written in Rust for concurrency handling, a microservice written in Python to serve a machine learning model, and a microservice written in TypeScript because that's the dominant language used by the team.

Microservices give you more flexibility throughout development and deployment. There are a few drawbacks, though. Debugging microservices can get tricky. It may be hard to figure out the source of an issue when you have to sift through all the microservices you have running. The issue of data integrity may also come up if you have references to the same data across multiple microservices. Figure 2-3 shows an example of what a microservices backend can look like.

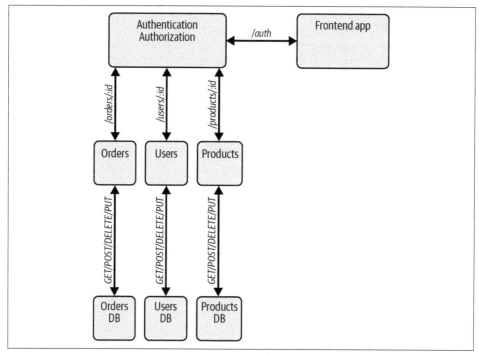

Figure 2-3. Architecture diagram for simple microservices

Alternative Architectures to Consider

Another architecture you'll hear about is *serverless architecture*. This can be used to handle all the backend functionality, but you have to be aware of the differences because it can make a huge difference in your cloud provider bills. If you need a few lambda functions, for example, to handle very specific behavior, this could be a good addition to your backend design. You might see serverless and monolithic architectures used together as the product grows.

Before microservices became a thing, there was *service-oriented architecture* (SOA). The main difference is that with SOA, all the separate services are sharing the same database. This can still be a good approach if your app gets complex enough that it's a good idea to break out functionality into smaller chunks code-wise to keep things maintainable. I'm not going to dive into the details of SOA (*https://oreil.ly/lYFoW*), but you can consider if it should be used as part of your architecture.

The beautiful thing about architecture is that you can take the bits and pieces that work for your use case and put them together. As you work with microservices, you might hear about service meshes, too. I encourage you to learn more about service meshes (*https://oreil.ly/e5cGC*) and how they are implemented, but I won't cover them here.

Remember that the process of designing a backend will take time. This isn't something that should be rushed through, and you should seek out as much feedback as possible from the other developers and teams you work with. Selecting any combination of these approaches cements the future development of the project because it's not an easy task to switch the entire architecture to something else later.

Selecting an API Design Pattern: REST and GraphQL

There's something else you need to decide on during this phase of setting up the project: are you going to go with REST APIs, GraphQL, or something else? This will determine how the frontend and other services are able to interface with your backend as well as how you extend your code as new roles, permissions, and other features are added over time.

REST is the standard in backend development at the moment, and GraphQL has become a close second. There are other options, like Simple Object Access Protocol (SOAP) APIs, but hopefully you won't have to work with those.

The main difference between REST and GraphQL is that GraphQL uses a single endpoint to handle all requests while REST uses multiple endpoints for requests. You may hear people talk about these paradigms like they're very different, but they really aren't. It's more a difference in the way you can build the APIs and consume them. One thing to highlight is that GraphQL comes with subscriptions built in. The only way to handle that with REST is with WebSockets (*https://oreil.ly/_vq7K*) or a similar technology.

With REST APIs, you typically have one type of resource per endpoint. Take the `orders` endpoint in your project, for example. You have GET, POST, and PUT requests for the different ways you need to interact with your order data. If this were a GraphQL API, the endpoints would become your GraphQL schema like this:

```
type Order {
  id: ID
  name: String
  total: Number
  products: Product[]
  createdAt: Date
  updatedAt: Date
}

type CreateOrderInput {
  name: String
  total: Number
  products: Product[]
}

type UpdateOrderInput {
  name: String
```

```
    total: Number
    products: Product[]
}

type Query {
  order(id: ID!): Order
  orders: Order[]
}

type Mutation {
    create(input: CreateOrderInput): Order
    update(input: UpdateOrderInput): Order
}
```

With GraphQL, you can specify the operation you want with the `query` or `mutation` keyword instead of an HTTP method. There's no difference in the data that you'll receive compared to your HTTP requests. The GraphQL response will still be in JSON format with the same values as an HTTP response. The difference is in how you manage the code.

When you write HTTP requests in REST, you specify an endpoint path, a method, and any data you need to send in the request. With GraphQL, you have more flexibility with your requests. Using queries and mutations, you can write resolver functions instead of endpoint paths. Here's an example of what resolvers might look like for your orders functionality:

```
{
  Query: {
    order: (root, { id }) => find(orders, { id: id }),
  },
  Order: {
    products: (order) => filter(products, { orderId: order.id }),
  },
}
```

So when you're ready to make a request, the query would look like this:

```
query {
  order(id: 'fejiw-f4wt301-4tfw2g-g4t24') {
    name
    products {
      name
      price
    }
  }
}
```

This is where some of the power of GraphQL comes in. You can query for the exact data you want without returning values you don't need. When you make REST requests, you can't ask for one or two values to be returned. You get all the data from that endpoint every time. GraphQL can save on response times for systems that handle massive amounts of interrelated data because you can ask for exactly what you need.

This book isn't going to do a deep dive into GraphQL, but I wanted to make sure that you know this option is available and it's widely used across the tech industry. You can think of GraphQL as the next evolution after REST. It's like when TypeScript came along to become the standard over JavaScript. It's worth taking some time to learn more about it, so check out some GraphQL resources directly (*https://graphql.org*)—you'll find all kinds of communities, classes, tools, and docs.

Conclusion

In this chapter, you learned about the NestJS app you'll be setting up to handle your backend. You learned about a few different architectures and API paradigms and their trade-offs. Now that you've done the initial setup for the NestJS backend and you know why each decision was made, it's time to turn your attention to the data schema.

## CHAPTER 3

Building the Data Schema

The data layer covers a lot, so it's awesome that we have so many good tools to work with. Regardless of the tools you choose, you do need to understand what's going on beneath the surface. When you start building your data schema, take your time to really write it out. The data schema drives everything for the app and any of its dependencies. Over time, it can become hard to update the schema without breaking everything.

Since you've already decided what kind of backend architecture to go with, you probably have an idea of how data will be related and what that data looks like. Making a diagram of how the data will be connected is going to help you and the team a lot because you'll see the relationships.

That's why this chapter is going to cover:

- Initial considerations for setting up the data schema
- Setting up a database
- Using object relational mapping (ORM) tools
- Writing data migrations in your database
- Seeding the database with initial data

You want to be as detailed as you can and document as much of the business logic as possible. You'll also want to get feedback from the team in small intervals because the schema can get complex as the app grows. Make sure everyone understands how and where data is being stored and why. By the time you finish this chapter, you'll have a good foundation for how to build out your data schema.

Initial Considerations

To build out your data layer, you'll go through these basic steps:

1. Make a diagram for a data schema. This should include the entities, their columns and data types, and their relationships.

2. Set up the database connection in the app. This example will use Prisma (*https://oreil.ly/i7lYw*) to connect to a PostgreSQL (*https://postgresql.org*) database, but there are other popular tools you can use, such as Knex.js (*https://knexjs.org*) or Drizzle (*https://oreil.ly/5ye9-*). Some reasons to use Postgres are because it is open source and has a long history of reliability. You'll find it behind huge, complex apps that have been in production for decades as well as newer apps that have just been released.

3. Write the data schema in the app by translating your diagram into code.

4. Add seed data. This is to ensure that your database has the essential data it needs from the beginning. This is also a good way to add data to test in different environments.

5. Run migrations. After the connection is established and the schema and seed data is ready, you need to run a migration to get these changes to the database.

6. Test the database with simple SQL queries. Check that the tables are creating, updating, and storing data as expected. Double-check the relationships between tables by looking at primary and foreign keys.

Some apps will have a more complex scenario than this, but you'll see a process similar to this across all projects. You already know what data you're expecting based on your conversations with Product, so now it's time to make a good diagram for the dev team.

 We're not going to discuss nonrelational databases in this book because we're going to work with relational databases. Relational databases enforce strict rules between data whereas nonrelational databases don't. Choosing between the two depends on the type of project you're working on. If you want somewhere to store any format of data that comes in, such as with events that may have constantly changing information, nonrelational databases can give you more flexibility. Nonrelational databases have specific use cases, but many apps are fine with a normal relational database.

Diagramming the Data Schema

A diagram is a great visual reference for developers and QA to understand what values to expect and why. It's a good tool to spark discussions between the frontend and backend developers and to document relations between data in a noncode way. Again, these diagrams don't have to be anything fancy. Developers tend to get hung up on little details in places that don't matter, such as diagramming tools and image formats. You have to be self-aware enough to notice when you start diving too deep on a task that doesn't need that much attention.

Your diagram can be simple as long as it has the tables, columns, data types, and relationships between tables. When possible, you want to use a tool that connects directly to the database to create the visualization, such as DBeaver (*https://oreil.ly/GRPz9*). That way, you can see the exact relationships you've defined. Or you can continue using Miro to keep all your architectural documentation in one place. The important thing is that it's in a format that everyone can understand.

Figures 3-1, 3-2, and 3-3 show what some of the documentation for different tables can look like and how they can relate to one another.

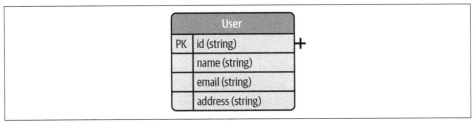

Figure 3-1. User table columns

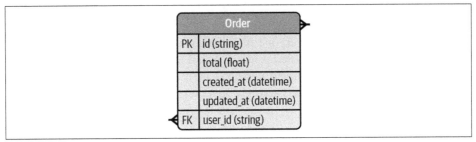

Figure 3-2. Order table columns

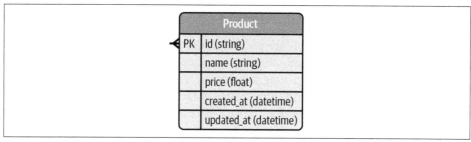

Figure 3-3. Product table columns

In Figure 3-4, you can see how all the tables are related to one another.

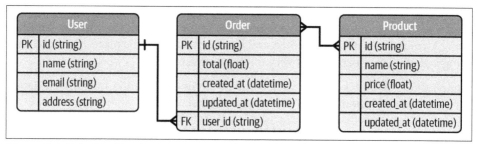

Figure 3-4. Relationships between users, orders, and products

Now that you have documented the data schema, you'll take this to the team, walk through what your thoughts are, and ask for feedback. The frontend devs may have specific data-format requests based on how they have to render elements. When it comes to the frontend, you typically shouldn't plan the schema around it. It's important to make sure that the queries the frontend makes, like searches and sorts, are thought of in the endpoint response, though. Other devs may bring up security considerations.

When you open this up for everyone to think about, you end up with a stronger schema than if one person handled it alone. You'll learn how to be more confident with sharing your ideas and getting others to share theirs. Don't be afraid to be wrong during these discussions because that might spark an idea for someone else.

This can be an uncomfortable place for a while because it feels like everyone is heavily scrutinizing your code and your technical skills when they aren't. You have to get used to receiving constructive feedback; that's what will help you and the team build better code. The more you present your code and thoughts to the team, the quicker you'll be able to improve things for everyone.

With the data schema diagrammed and agreed on by the frontend and backend devs, you can start work on connecting the backend to the database to create the tables.

You'll be working with a Postgres instance locally, but this can also be hosted on a server in the cloud.

Setting Up Postgres

You need to set up Postgres so that you can get the connection information for your app. This will normally be handled by the team that manages the infrastructure for your production and nonproduction environments. You'll still need your own local instance to make sure the changes that you and the team are making work as expected. This is something you'd include in a Docker container (*https://oreil.ly/beu9J*) if that's how you want to keep the local environments consistent. Something else you're responsible for thinking about is how to make onboarding smooth for new devs. Getting the local environment set up is one of the biggest hurdles for anyone joining a new team, so doing this will pay off as the team and the product grow.

You can download Postgres for free (*https://oreil.ly/qZocC*). Follow the documentation to get everything up and running and set a master password. Doing some basic database security locally can help reveal potential issues early because you'll already be thinking about a production environment. Once pgAdmin has finished installing, open the app to create a new database. Then click the PostgreSQL 14 drop-down menu and right-click Databases. This will give you the option to create a new database that you'll name *dashboard*. It will look similar to Figure 3-5 when you're done.

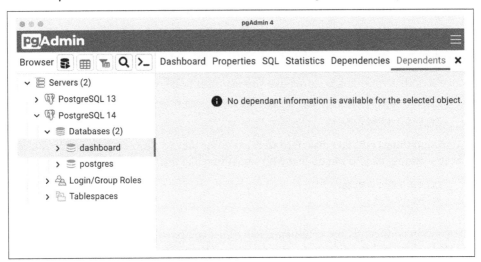

Figure 3-5. Dashboard database in local Postgres

After you have the new dashboard database, you'll need to remember the database name, database password, port number, and database username to set up the connection to the backend. Unless you choose something other than the default values, some of your credentials will be the following:

- Database username: postgres
- Database port number: 5432

Now you're ready to start creating the tables you diagrammed earlier. You can move on to using an ORM tool to connect the backend to the database and make sure everything's set up correctly.

Basic SQL Queries

It's good to know some basic SQL commands. You don't have to get super in-depth with things like views and indexing, but knowing enough to do create, read, update, and delete (CRUD) operations goes a long way. One way to get started is by writing a statement to insert a new row into a table. You can do that with the following SQL:

```
INSERT INTO table_name (column1, column2, column3) VALUES (value1, value2,
    value3);
```

Change *table_name* to the table you want to insert the data into. The *column1*, *column2*, and *column3* fields represent the column names you want to put the data into. Finally, *value1*, *value2*, and *value3* are the values you want to add to the respective columns. For testing purposes, you can add new row entries like this:

```
INSERT INTO Orders (id, name, total)
VALUES (4, 'Mark', 25.99)
RETURNING id;
```

To check that your data is stored like you expect it to be, you can query the data like this:

```
SELECT * FROM Orders;
```

To round things out, you may need to delete some data to clean up an example you've been working on. You can do that with something like this:

```
DELETE FROM Orders
WHERE id = 4
RETURNING *;
```

If you can confidently use commands like these, you have enough SQL knowledge to double-check values directly in the database. Of course, you can dive deeper into SQL with resources like SQLBolt (*https://sqlbolt.com*) or LearnSQL.com, but you don't need to.

Deciding What ORM to Use

Aside from choosing the framework for your backend, choosing the ORM tool is one of the big decisions you'll make for the future of your project. It's not an easy task to switch to a different ORM tool once you've started building. NestJS comes with Type-ORM (*https://oreil.ly/LdFeM*), Sequelize (*https://sequelize.org*), and Mongoose (*https://mongoosejs.com/docs*) built in if you don't have a preference. Other common ORM tools that you'll be using include Knex.js (*https://knexjs.org*) and Prisma (*https://prisma.io*).

All these tools essentially do the same thing but with a different flavor. Choosing the one you and the team use will come down to everyone's experience and comfort level as well as any limitations the tools may have. For this project, you've decided to go with Prisma because it's the tool everyone on the team has used before, the documentation is well maintained, and tech teams across different projects in the industry use it. There's a built-in ORM for NestJS, but Prisma has more support and a bigger community, and it works really well with Postgres. These reasons make it a strong candidate, which is why you and the team have selected it.

Now you'll need to install Prisma and TSX as dev dependencies in your project with the following command:

```
npm install prisma @prisma/client tsx --save-dev
```

 There are some finer details you need to be aware of, especially concerning dependencies. When you're adding a dependency to your project, make sure you understand what type of dependency it needs to be. There are three types of dependencies: dependencies (regular), development (dev) dependencies, and peer dependencies. *Dependencies* are the packages your app needs to run after it's been built for production. *Dev dependencies* are the packages you need to do development work, like testing and linting, but they aren't required for the app to work. You'll learn more about *peer dependencies* if you work on a project that needs to be published as its own package, but they are the packages that your package expects to be installed in a container app.

With Prisma installed in your project, you need to set up some configs to connect the app to your Postgres database. As with any ORM, you have to initialize it in your project. With Prisma, you can run the following command to do that. Remember, this output is an example of what you might see, and it could have changed with the latest version:

```
npx prisma init --datasource-provider postgresql

✓ Your Prisma schema was created at prisma/schema.prisma
```

You can now open it in your favorite editor.

warn You already have a .gitignore file. Don't forget to add `.env` in it to not
  commit any private information.

Next steps:
1. Set the DATABASE_URL in the .env file to point to your existing database. If
   your database has no tables yet, read https://pris.ly/d/getting-started
2. Run prisma db pull to turn your database schema into a Prisma schema.
3. Run prisma generate to generate the Prisma Client. You can then start
   querying your database.

More information in our documentation:
https://pris.ly/d/getting-started

 Always read the console output after you run commands. It usually
gives you useful advice!

This will create the *prisma* directory and a *.env* file in your project. Make sure the *.env*
file is in your *.gitignore* first. Then, inside the *prisma* directory, you'll find
schema.prisma, which is where you'll set up your database connection and the models
for the app. The *.env* file has a URL to your database, which is the connection string
that will contain the database credentials. Update the value for DATABASE_URL in
the *.env* file with your local credentials. It might look something like this:

    DATABASE_URL="postgresql://username:password@localhost:5432/dashboard"

Any values in your *.env* should be handled in your CI/CD pipeline. Work with the
DevOps team to get this in place depending on the infrastructure setup. Here's a simple example of what that might look like with GitHub Actions (*https://oreil.ly/R4d_u*):

```
name: Node.js CI

on:
  push:
    branches: [ "main" ]
  pull_request:
    branches: [ "main" ]

env:
  DATABASE_URL: ${{ secrets.ProdDatabase }}

jobs:
  build:
    runs-on: ubuntu-latest
...
```

Now you can move over to the *schema.prisma* file and start writing your model. You've already done the hard part of thinking out how everything relates, so now you can confidently start coding. You'll notice this is where you can see one of the biggest differences between the ORM tools. Prisma has its own flavor that you'll have to get used to, and you should refer to the docs often.

In your *schema.prisma,* you can start adding pieces of your model. Add the following code to the end of the file:

```
// schema.prisma
…
model User {
  id        Int       @id @default(autoincrement())
  email     String    @unique
  name      String
  address   String
  orders    Order[]
}

model Order {
  id          Int         @id @default(autoincrement())
  total       Float
  createdAt   DateTime    @default(now())
  updatedAt   DateTime    @updatedAt
  products    Product[]
  userId      Int?
  User        User?       @relation(fields: [userId], references: [id])
}

model Product {
  id          String      @id @default(uuid())
  name        String
  price       Float
  createdAt   DateTime @default(now())
  updatedAt   DateTime @updatedAt
  orders      Order[]
}
```

These models represent the three tables you diagrammed earlier and their relationships. Building models with Prisma is similar to writing objects or type definitions with TypeScript. These models use special Prisma syntax for the types, but they match closely to the common types you work with. The most important thing to note is how relationships are defined between tables. On the Product table, there's an associated userId. On the User table, we have an array of orders. This is how Prisma defines relationships between tables, and I highly encourage you to look through the documentation to learn about building more complex relationships.

You might also want to consider using the Prisma VS Code plug-in (*https://oreil.ly/ cKsig*) to help make development smoother. For this app, though, these few models will get you moving.

This completes the data schema for your app so far. Now it's time to get this schema onto the database with a migration.

Writing Migrations

Migrations are the SQL queries made by the ORM based on your schema definition. When you connect to the database to run a migration, you're essentially executing SQL statements. That's what makes ORM tools so useful. Instead of having to manually write the SQL for multiple tables, you can write the query in TypeScript, and the ORM will translate it to SQL. JavaScript developers use these tools so that they don't have to learn all the details of SQL and database quirks. Running a migration is also how you will check that your database is connected to your backend correctly. To run a migration with Prisma, you'll open your console, navigate to the root of the project, and run this command:

```
prisma migrate dev --name initialize_dashboard_db

Environment variables loaded from .env
Prisma schema loaded from prisma/schema.prisma
Datasource "db": PostgreSQL database "dashboard", schema "public" at
  "localhost:5432"

Applying migration `20230318132006_initialize_dashboard_db`

The following migration(s) have been created and applied from new schema changes:

migrations/
  └ 20230318132006_initialize_dashboard_db/
    └ migration.sql

Your database is now in sync with your schema.
```

After the migration is successful, check your Postgres instance. You should see these tables and their columns populated in your dashboard database. Check that the tables have the columns you defined in your models. You should also see a new table called _OrderToProduct that defines the relationship you created between the Order and Product tables in your model. This is the fastest way to determine if your database connection is established. The migration would have failed if the connection didn't exist, but looking directly at the database lets you know everything is fine.

Anytime you update your schema, you'll need to make a new migration to update the database. Make sure to give it a descriptive name so that you can quickly understand what happened in the database history. This is super helpful if you run into data issues on the backend because it's easier to see what changes have been made and when. Every migration will automatically generate the timestamp at the beginning of the folder name in Prisma. The timestamp is important for the database to know in what order to run the migrations when someone is trying to set up the database initially.

Other tools will handle migrations a little differently. Knex.js, for example, lets you write migrations in pure SQL if you want, and it generates migration files instead of folders. If you look in your project's *prisma* directory, you should see a *migrations* folder with a subfolder. This is where the generated SQL for your migrations are. That's the beauty of an ORM. You can write in syntax you're familiar with, and it will generate the SQL for you. Take a look at the *migration.sql* file in the migration folder. You'll see something like this:

```
-- CreateTable
CREATE TABLE "User" (
    "id" SERIAL NOT NULL,
    "email" TEXT NOT NULL,
    "name" TEXT NOT NULL,
    "address" TEXT NOT NULL,

    CONSTRAINT "User_pkey" PRIMARY KEY ("id")
);
...
```

This is just the initial setup migration for the database. You'll be adding more tables and columns and changing names as the app grows. When you run into issues with a migration, you can roll it back; turn to the Prisma docs (*https://oreil.ly/PogrK*) to learn how to do that. For now, you have what you need to add some seed data to the database so that you can start working on the rest of the app.

Seeding the Database

Since this is your local database, you'll eventually need some test data to play with. You can add that as part of the dev *.env* setup and have it as part of the setup for the real database. To start, create a new *seed.ts* file in the *prisma* directory. This is where you'll use the Prisma Client to create some records. In your *seed.ts* file, add the following code:

```
// seed.ts
const { PrismaClient } = require('@prisma/client');
const db = new PrismaClient();

const main = async () => {
  const orderData = [...Array(10)].map(() => ({
    id: faker.number.int({ min: 10, max: 170 }),
    total: faker.number.float({ min: 7, max: 15657, precision: 0.01 }),
    createdAt: faker.date.anytime(),
    updatedAt: faker.date.anytime(),
    userId: 5,
  }));
```

```
const productData = [...Array(10)].map(() => ({
    id: faker.lorem.word(),
    name: faker.commerce.productName(),
    price: faker.number.float({ min: 35, max: 1055, precision: 0.01 }),
    createdAt: faker.date.anytime(),
    updatedAt: faker.date.anytime(),
}));
...
```

The complete *seed.ts* file can be found on GitHub (*https://oreil.ly/sb7vL*).

This code allows you to connect to the database and insert the new rows into their respective tables. Then, it disconnects from the database. To run this with Prisma, you need to add the **seed** config to your *package.json* like this:

```
...
"collectCoverageFrom": [
    "**/*.(t|j)s"
  ],
  "coverageDirectory": "../coverage",
  "testEnvironment": "node"
},
"prisma": {
  "seed": "tsx prisma/seed.ts"
}
}
```

This tells Prisma where to look for your seed file and how to execute it. With the configs and some data ready, you can run this command to actually insert the data into your Postgres instance:

```
npx prisma db seed

Environment variables loaded from .env
Running seed command `ts-node prisma/seed.ts` ..

🌱  The seed command has been executed.
```

If you look in your Postgres tables (see Figure 3-6), you should see the values you wrote in *seed.ts*. This should be everything you need for your data concerns right now. Just to double-check, here's a quick checklist you can go through when you think you're finished setting everything up:

- Does the schema match the designs and functionality explained in the behavioral doc?

- Have you had at least one other dev look at it?

- Have you checked to make sure the schema works for all the apps consuming data from this database?

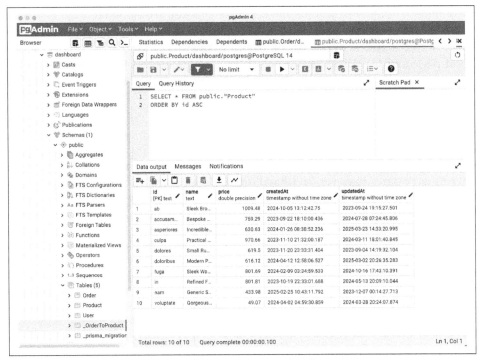

Figure 3-6. Dashboard database with seeded data in local Postgres

There are more advanced things to consider as well that are out of scope for this book. Here's a list of some of them and links to more resources:

- Does your schema give room for the app to grow?

  Software Architecture: The Hard Parts by Neal Ford, Mark Richards, Pramod Sadalage, and Zhamak Dehghani (O'Reilly)

- Is there a way to audit actions and the users who triggered them?

  "What Is an Audit Trail? Everything You Need to Know" (*https://oreil.ly/W0s-P*) (Auditboard)

- Have you considered different user-role levels for table operation access?

  "Role-Based Access Control (RBAC)" (*https://oreil.ly/XNcZv*) (Imperva)

These advanced topics could have their own chapters or even entire books dedicated to them. There are a wide range of questions you can ask here, but to keep things moving forward at this stage, don't get too deep into the details. If you can answer these questions, explain the schema decisions to another dev, and demo it to the Product team, you're good to go for now.

Take notes and make tickets for any optimizations you see along the way. That way, you can come back and actually work on the details because it's documented in a way that Product considers during sprint planning. You've decided that the schema is in a good place and the tickets regarding different endpoints can be unblocked. This is when you'll start working on the API that different apps will interact with to get data from the database you just set up.

Conclusion

In this chapter, you went through the process of drawing diagrams for your data, setting up a Postgres instance, and handling some initial setup with your ORM. You should feel pretty good about expanding your data schema from here because you've already answered a lot of questions about the future of the app.

## CHAPTER 4

REST APIs

With the data schema defined, it's time to get into the details of exposing that data. You'll build an API with multiple endpoints that perform various operations, such as getting all the orders or submitting new ones. This is one area of the backend where we'll get very into the details.

To create an API that can be maintained by different developers as the team changes, you need standard conventions for the team. Standard conventions are usually outlined in a document that defines the way the team agrees to approach code implementation, ranging from everything to naming conventions to the error codes and messages used in responses.

This set of conventions will make it easier to check for deviations in PR reviews for any code changes. Your PRs are changes you submit for other developers to review before they get merged with the central code and deployed. Since there may be multiple PRs for a piece of functionality, this rule enforcement is important for maintaining code consistency across codebases.

This chapter will go over how to address this convention while actually building an API, covering these areas:

- Working through data formatting with the frontend and other consuming services
- Writing an example of code conventions
- Writing the code for the interface, service, and controller for the API
- Tracking errors with logs and custom error handlers
- Ensuring that validation is in place

These are some of the concerns that will come up as you build out your API and the different endpoints. You'll run into a lot of different approaches to API development and architecture decisions, and most of them are valid. As with everything else, it depends on the needs of your project and the team's preferences.

For this API, we're going to follow these conventions:

- It will send and receive data in JSON format.
- Endpoint logic shouldn't reference other endpoints to keep separation of concerns.
- Use endpoint naming to reflect relationships of data and functionality (e.g., /orders/{orderId}/products).
- Return standard error codes and custom messages.
- Version the endpoints to gracefully handle deprecation.
- Handle calculations, pagination, filtering, and sorting on the backend.
- All endpoints receiving data should have validation.
- Endpoint documentation should be updated with all changes.

Making Sure the Frontend and Backend Agree

There is always a partnership between the frontend displaying data and the backend processing it. When the frontend has to make multiple calls to fetch data, that can make the view render more slowly for a user. When the backend sends more data in responses, that can lead to unnecessary information being gathered and sent, which makes the response take longer. This is a trade-off you have to balance.

Typically, any type of pagination, filtering, sorting, and calculations should happen on the backend. This is because you can handle the data more efficiently on the backend compared to loading all the data on the frontend and making it do these operations. It's very rare that you'll ever want to load all the data for an app on the frontend. Generally, the engineers work together to come up with a way to handle data that provides a good UX.

This might mean introducing a microservice into the architecture to help both the frontend and backend performance. If there's a specific endpoint that is called much more than the others, it's worth researching if it makes sense to separate it out into a microservice and what type of work that would involve.

One area where you might have to push back is how endpoints send data to the frontend. For the frontend, it may make more sense for multiple pieces of data to get sent back on the same endpoint to help with performance and reduce the number of calls made. If it crosses data boundaries, then you need to double-check if the data should be combined. Data boundaries are how we keep a separation of concerns between different functionalities Figure 4-1 is an example of keeping a boundary between any products and orders calls.

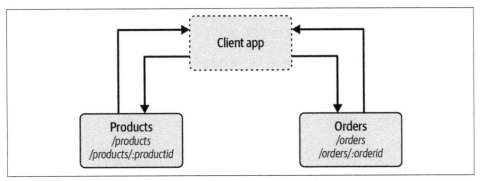

Figure 4-1. Example of data boundaries and how they don't cross

Remember, the frontend can filter the data out in the view, but anyone can check the developer tools in the browser to check the network response. It's always the responsibility of the backend to enforce security when it comes to data handling. The frontend can have some security implemented, but users can bypass the UI and use the endpoints directly. We'll address some security concerns in Chapter 8, but this is one reason why you want to enforce data boundaries.

Now that the engineers understand the expectations of the frontend and backend, let's work on the conventions doc for the backend.

Creating a Document for Conventions

You can tighten up your code conventions even more with a doc that you share with the team and use to help new devs onboard with the team's code style. This doc will evolve over time as you encounter new scenarios. It serves as a resource for the team when a new endpoint or even a new API needs to be created. That way, everyone knows how to build the code so that consistency is maintained everywhere.

Tools like Prettier (*https://prettier.io*), ESLint (*https://eslint.org*), EditorConfig (*https://editorconfig.org*), and Husky (*https://oreil.ly/qYeav*) can help you automatically enforce the conventions with every PR. Sometimes, nitpicks like spacing, tabs, quotation marks, and tests can get tedious to check for manually. Using these types of tools requires devs to meet the conventions before a commit can even be made. Now every PR will have these little checks, which makes reviews faster and code more consistent.

The following are examples of some conventions:

- Microsoft Azure: RESTful Web API Design (*https://oreil.ly/uSDNu*)
- Google JavaScript Style Guide (*https://oreil.ly/CMYVk*)
- Airbnb JavaScript Style Guide (*https://oreil.ly/M8GTl*)

Docs like these can be starting points for your in-house conventions that you extend to match team preferences. For example, your conventions doc might contain an additional section like the following:

```
For pagination, responses should return this structure:
{
  "page": [
    {
      "id": 4,
      "first_name": "My first name",
      "last_name": "My last name",
      "email": "myemail@server.com"
    },
    {
      "id": 5,
      "first_name": "My first name",
      "last_name": "My last name",
      "email": "myemail@server.com"
    },
    {
      "id": 6,
      "first_name": "My first name",
      "last_name": "My last name",
      "email": "myemail@server.com"
    }
  ],
  "count": 3,
  "limit": 3,
  "offset": 0,
  "total_pages": 4,
  "total_count": 12,
  "previous_page": 1,
  "current_page": 2,
  "next_page": 3,
}

For error handling, responses should return this structure:
{
  "errors": [
    { "statusCode": "111", "message": "age must be an int" },
    { "statusCode": "112", "message": "email is mandatory" }
  ]
}
```

This is another way you can get feedback from others and make the convention doc the best it can be for everyone.

 Some things that you'll set in your conventions will be annoying to stick to sometimes, especially during a time crunch. That's why it's important to implement a few features and see how things go in practice before you really enforce conventions through linting and other scripts. Once your conventions are in a good place, though, don't deviate from them unless there's a significant change to the direction of the project. The consistency throughout your codebases is what will make projects easier to maintain over the long term.

Making the API and First Endpoint

As discussed in Chapter 2, NestJS is the framework you'll build with. We won't go through writing all the code tutorial-style here. I'll address underlying reasons for why functionality is implemented a certain way. This is the type of thinking that spreads to any framework. I'll leave it up to you to look through the NestJS docs to understand the syntax of the code.

There are so many things to consider when you start coding on the backend. The secret is to just pick an area and focus on it first. You'll come back through and address security, performance, and testing concerns. For now, though, you need to get some endpoints working, so the frontend can start connecting the UI to the API. You'll start by writing the basic CRUD operations you know the app will need. In this project, you'll need CRUD endpoints for:

- Managing products
- Managing orders
- Administrative functions

The first two sets of endpoints are based on what you already know about the app. The last set of endpoints will come from other discussions with Product. There will be actions the Support team will need access to that no user should ever be able to touch. You'll learn how to handle these different user permission levels and access control in Chapter 8. Remember, these endpoints will likely change. The main thing is that you have to start building somewhere.

You can delete some of the boilerplate files, specifically *app.control-ler.spec.ts, app.controller.ts*, and *app.service.ts*. Also go ahead and update *app.module.ts* to remove the references to those files. This is to keep things as clean as possible as you start to make changes and add new code. Those files are just there as examples of how to implement endpoint functionality. It's normal to remove some of the example files when you use a scaffolding tool so that you only have what you need. This is something that will come from experience as you work with scaffolding tools and start to understand which files can be removed and which ones are useful starting points.

Creating the Orders Endpoints

You can start by working on the functionality for orders. In the *src* directory, make a new subfolder called *orders* and add the files to handle the types for this endpoint, the tests, the service, and the controller.

The *orders.controller.ts* file is where you define all the endpoints for this specific feature. You can learn more about how controllers work (*https://oreil.ly/X_2ET*) in the NestJS docs. So anytime you need to fetch orders or make changes to them, the frontend will reference the endpoints here. This is a great place to do your initial validation on data received in requests. Here's an example of an endpoint:

```
// orders.controller.ts
…
@Get()
  public async orders(): Promise<Array<Order>> {
    try {
      const orders = await this.ordersService.orders({});
      return orders;
    } catch (err) {
      if (err) {
        throw new HttpException('Not found', HttpStatus.NOT_FOUND);
      }
      throw new HttpException('Generic', HttpStatus.BAD_GATEWAY);
    }
  }
```

Here you can see some custom error handling, and it sends a message and status code like you defined in the conventions. The controller shouldn't contain any business logic because that will be handled in your service. Controllers are just there to handle requests and responses. This makes the code more testable, and it keeps the code separated based on what it should do.

Controllers will also do some of that validation I mentioned. Let's take a look at an endpoint that will update orders:

```
// orders.controller.ts
…
@Patch(':id')
public async update(
  @Param('id', ParseIntPipe) id: number,
  @Body() order: UpdateOrderDto,
): Promise<Order> {
  try {
    return await this.ordersService.updateOrder({
      where: { id },
      data: order,
    });
  } catch (err) {
    if (err) {
      throw new HttpException('Not found', HttpStatus.NOT_FOUND);
    }
    throw new HttpException('Generic', HttpStatus.BAD_GATEWAY);
  }
}
```

Note how the `try-catch` statement is used for both the endpoints. This is a clean way of making sure your errors are handled. The code in the `try` block is always run first. If any errors happen in this block, the `catch` block will be triggered. Then, you can focus on how to handle the errors that are caught. This is something that can get overlooked when devs are in a hurry, so it's a prime candidate to include in your code conventions.

The validation here is happening through the `UpdateOrderDto`. Here's what it looks like in *orders.interface.ts*:

```
// orders.interface.ts
…
export class UpdateOrderDto {
  @IsNumber()
  total: number;

  @IsNotEmpty()
  products: Product[];

  @IsNotEmpty()
  userId: number;
}
```

 DTO means *data transfer object*. DTOs are used to encapsulate data commonly used by the service layer on the backend to reduce the amount of data that needs to be sent between the backend and frontend. In a Model-View-Controller (MVC) framework like NestJS, these are also useful as the models for application. They mainly define the parameters passed to the methods on the backend.

NestJS handles validation under the hood with the `class-validator` (*https://oreil.ly/bbyFa*) `package` (*https://oreil.ly/A2p_f*), so if the `userId` is empty or the `total` isn't a number, an error will be thrown to the frontend telling it the body data was in the wrong format. Sending proper validation messages to the frontend will help the devs know what to do and give users helpful information.

Working on the Orders Service

The last file is *orders.service.ts*. This is where the business logic for the orders functionality is handled. Refer to the NestJS for more details on service files (*https://oreil.ly/s2jZ6*). Any calculations, sorting, filtering, or other data manipulation is going to happen in this file. Here's an example of a method to update an order:

```
// orders.service.ts
…
public async updateOrder(params: {
  where: Prisma.OrderWhereUniqueInput;
  data: Prisma.OrderUpdateInput;
}): Promise<Order> {
  const { data, where } = params;
  this.logger.log(`Updated existing order ${where.id}`);

  try {
    const updatedOrder = await this.prisma.order.update({
      data: {
        ...data,
        updatedAt: new Date(),
      },
      where,
    });

    this.logger.log(`Updated for existing order ${updatedOrder.id} successful`);

    return updatedOrder;
  } catch (err) {
    this.logger.log(`Updated for existing order ${where.id} failed`);

    throw new HttpException(err.message, HttpStatus.CONFLICT);
  }
}
```

Now you're adding even more backend best practices and following the conventions because you have error handling and logging (*https://oreil.ly/k3F8n*) happening here. There will also be errors that come from the service level, which is why you have the `try-catch` statement to bubble those errors back up to the controller.

You should also add logging like this in your controllers. One thing you'll find is that logs are invaluable when you're trying to debug the backend. Make your logs as descriptive as you need to in order to track values across your database and other endpoints or third-party services.

Regardless of the framework you decide to use on the backend, you've seen the core things you need to implement: validation on inputs, logging for the crucial parts of the flow, and error handling for issues that may arise. As long as you remember these things and keep the code conventions in mind, your team is on the way to a strongly built codebase.

It's time to look at some other parts of the backend that will ensure that the endpoints and services work as expected.

Checking the Database Connection

Many projects have a folder called *utils* or *helpers* or something similar. You'll need to create one of those folders to hold the service you're going to use to instantiate Prisma Client and connect to the database. This was discussed in Chapter 3, so now you're expanding on that base you already have. In the *src* folder, make a new folder called *utils*. In this folder, create a file called *prisma.service.ts* and put this code from the NestJS documentation (*https://oreil.ly/CzD1B*) in the file.

You don't have to worry about writing everything from scratch most of the time if you spend a few minutes reading and looking through docs. That's a thing you'll find senior devs doing all the time. Also, don't be afraid to add more things to this *utils* folder! When you see small functions that are repeated in numerous parts of the app, like data formatters, move them here so that they are easy for other devs to find and use.

If you haven't stopped to make a Git commit, this is a good time to do so. Now you have the backend in a state where other devs can come in and add more functionality or configurations. One of the hardest tasks is to set something up that others can improve. That's what you're doing right now.

As you build on this application throughout the book, you'll start to add calls to third-party services, handle data from different sources, and work on security concerns. All of these will involve endpoints and other service methods that you'll add on as you move through the tasks on your sprint.

It's important to get some practice in, so try to add error handling, logging, and validation to the remaining endpoints in the orders controller. Of course, you can always check out the GitHub repo (*https://oreil.ly/tbcvR*), too.

Conclusion

We covered a lot in this chapter, and we will dive even deeper in Chapters 5 through 10! The main takeaways from this chapter are making an agreement with the engineers working on the frontend, setting up strict conventions for your API as soon as possible, creating some initial endpoints to get the frontend devs moving, and error handling, validation, and logging. Now that you have a few endpoints up, you can start building on top of them.

## CHAPTER 5

Third-Party Services

There will come a point in developing a product when you'll need to use a third-party service. Third-party services offer complex or proprietary functionality that exists outside your codebase and your company. The third-party service is usually managed by another company; you pay a fee to use it and have access to support when things go wrong.

Third-party services come up when you need functionality that would take a significant amount of time to implement, would be difficult to maintain, and would likely need its own team, such as payment systems, authentication/authorization, and monitoring and logging for your app.

In this chapter, I'll go over:

- Choosing third-party services
- Implementing a third-party service in your system
- Managing errors, outages, and upgrades

Working with third-party services is going to come up at some point, so it's best to go in with an idea of what you're getting into. Usually, the third-party service provides an API or software development kit (SDK) as an npm package that you install in your app, but you'll need to provide some type of credentials to access the full functionality. There are also some SDKs that exist without a service just to give you specific functionality.

Keep in mind that there's a chance that something on the service's side could change and break without letting you know. It's all interface code that you'll be working with, so it won't be any different in that regard.

We'll be adding Stripe as the third-party service to handle the payment part of the app. First, I'll go over some things you should consider for third-party services. Then, you'll implement the controller, service, and other code to get Stripe working in the demo project.

Choosing a Third-Party Service

There are numerous services to handle payments, authentication, data processing, tax handling, logging, working with other company's data, and any other functionality you can think of. That can make the task of choosing a service seem daunting because you have to decide what to build and balance that with costs. In reality, this is pretty similar to the process of selecting a package to use in your code.

The most important difference between selecting a third-party service and a package is that the services cost money. There's nothing wrong with selecting a paid service over a free package if it's going to save you development time and get features out faster and with more confidence that the app will work as expected. Getting locked into a great product with a good pricing structure is something to hope for compared to the opposite.

Here are some things you might look into as you research services you need:

- Does it have good documentation that is regularly updated?
- How are new version releases handled?
- Is responsive support available?
- Is the pricing structure clearly defined, even if you have to get on a call with a sales rep?
- Are there other options for the functionality you need?
- Is the company mature and stable?
- How easy would it be to add the solution to your existing architecture?
- How does this solution compare to other popular solutions for this service?
- Is there a good sandbox environment for testing?
- How much effort would it take to switch to a different tool from this one?

These are all things to consider, and there will be some interesting trade-offs. You might even get into more industry-specific questions around legal compliance and regulations. Once you've done a thorough business analysis of a service, take it for a spin in your codebase. See how long it takes to add the smallest working integration to your code. That'll be a good early test run to see what it would be like working with the service.

When you're doing this testing, don't forget to share your findings with the team as well as with management. Do some quick demos to show how things are going in the code. This is one way you can help others on the team level up. It'll also help you understand the service at a deeper level because you'll be answering questions that the team has.

While you're checking out how the integration works, look into the reputation of the product and company. It's important to know the experiences other developers have had with any service you're considering paying for. If the service seems awesome and has great support, see if anyone else had that experience after they signed a contract. It may seem cynical, but it's good to check these things out before you are deeply integrated with a product.

You also need to consider the country of origin of the service. If you develop software for any government, there will likely be countries that you have to avoid selecting software from. This is something you might not initially think about depending on what industry you're in, but geopolitics affects the tools we use to develop software. On the other side, if your company wants to show its support for a country, you can evaluate services for good geopolitical reasons.

As you continue to research third-party services, consider looking at the GitHub repo for the service if there is one. You'll be able to see other developers' experiences with it and how the third-party service company handled any bugs or questions. You'll probably find the most common issues everyone runs into before you're too deep into the implementation.

One more thing to check for is how third-party services interact with one another. You may need to use multiple services through another service like Zapier (*https:// zapier.com*) or your cloud provider's services, which can complicate things. See if any of the services complement the other tools and services you're using.

List of Potential Services

It can be hard to know what to even look at when you figure out you need a third-party service. These are some options to start with:

Payment handlers
- Stripe (*https://stripe.com/docs*)
- Square (*https://developer.squareup.com/docs*)
- Clover (*https://docs.clover.com/docs*)
- PayPal (*https://developer.paypal.com/home*)
- Paddle (*https://www.paddle.com*)

Logging/monitoring
- DataDog (*https://docs.datadoghq.com*)
- New Relic (*https://docs.newrelic.com*)
- Splunk (*https://docs.splunk.com/Documentation*)
- Sentry (*https://docs.sentry.io*)

Third-party apps
- Meta (*https://developers.facebook.com/docs*)
- Instagram (*https://developers.facebook.com/docs/instagram*)
- YouTube (*https://developers.google.com/youtube/v3*)
- Google Workspace (*https://developers.google.com/workspace*)

Ecommerce
- Shopify (*https://shopify.dev/docs/api*)
- Amazon (*https://developer-docs.amazon.com/sp-api*)
- Etsy (*https://developers.etsy.com/documentation*)
- BigCommerce (*https://developer.bigcommerce.com/api-docs/overview*)

Authentication
- Auth0 (*https://auth0.com/docs*)
- FusionAuth (*https://fusionauth.io/docs*)
- Amazon Cognito (*https://docs.aws.amazon.com/cognito*)
- SuperTokens (*https://supertokens.com/docs/guides*)
- Clerk (*https://clerk.com*)

Email services
- SendGrid (*https://docs.sendgrid.com/for-developers*)
- Amazon Simple Email Service (SES) (*https://docs.aws.amazon.com/ses/latest/dg/send-email-api.html*)
- Mailgun (*https://documentation.mailgun.com/en/latest/quickstart.html*)
- Postmark (*https://postmarkapp.com/email-api*)
- Brevo (*https://www.brevo.com*)

Geolocation
- Google Maps (*https://developers.google.com/maps/documentation/javascript*)
- Mapbox (*https://www.mapbox.com*)
- Esri ArcGIS (*https://developers.arcgis.com/javascript/latest*)
- Radar (*https://radar.com/documentation*)

You may run into some very niche services out there depending on what your product needs. These services can be challenging to integrate, so make sure you are clearly communicating what you're finding and ask others to join in the search, too.

Always check the data structure that you'll get from the API responses because some of them won't be as well documented as others. Do some initial exploration between services you're considering to see what you will get back. This is another good way to evaluate how well a service is going to fit into your infrastructure. You'd be surprised at the response structure you'll get back from some of the services you'll use over the years.

Since the app you're building will require the ability for users to make payments, you'll need to implement a third-party service to handle this: a service that has Payment Card Industry Data Security Standard (PCI DSS) compliance built in and has lots of security in place to keep users' financial and personal information secure. For this part of the project, you'll get to work with Stripe.

Integrating Stripe

The reason you'll use Stripe in this project is because it has great documentation (which you'll refer to often), a large community of developers uses it, and there's a pretty good testing environment for it. I still encourage you to take a look at some of the other options and compare the trade-offs you see.

I won't go through setting up a Stripe account because it gets pretty in-depth, and you will need to add your personal information. If you don't feel comfortable doing that, it's OK. This information will be provided by your organization anyway. I'll go over the programmatic implementation so that you can follow along with the code to see what you would do after the account is set up.

The first thing you need to do is decide how you want to handle third-party services in your app. When you're thinking about this, keep in mind that you will likely have other integrations as the product grows and needs more capabilities. The approach you'll take in this project is adding a new folder called *integrations* in *src*. Inside the *integrations* folder, you'll add a subfolder called *stripe* with a few files in it. This will make your folder tree look like this:

```
|__ prisma
|__ src
|____ integrations
|_____ stripe
|_____ stripe.controller.spec.ts
|_____ stripe.controller.ts
|_____ stripe.interface.ts
|_____ stripe.module.ts
```

```
|_____ stripe.service.spec.ts
|_____ stripe.service.ts
|____ orders
|____ app.module.ts
|____ main.ts
|__ test
```

This is also a great time to update your architecture diagram to show how this new service integrates with your overall app, as in Figure 5-1. Docs are never really finished, so remember to update relevant docs as you add new functionality. The way third-party services will work with this app includes some event handling with your cloud service using tools like Amazon CloudWatch (*https://oreil.ly/16lJQ*) and Event-Bridge (*https://oreil.ly/2rJzv*) as well as directly interfacing with your own APIs.

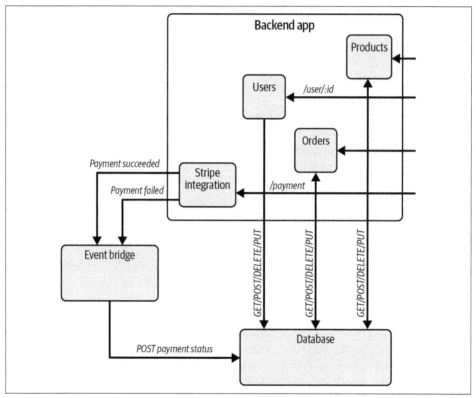

Figure 5-1. Updated architecture diagram

You'll follow the same programming pattern here as you did with the orders functionality. The endpoints your frontend will call are defined in the controller. The interactions directly with the Stripe API will be in the service. Keeping this separation of concerns is what helps make your code modular and easier to test. You'll want to keep that up even as you add other third-party code.

You can start by updating the new *stripe.module.ts* file to import and use the new service and controller because this is a quick win:

```
// stripe.module.ts
import { Module } from '@nestjs/common';
import { StripeService } from './stripe.service';
import { StripeController } from './stripe.controller';

@Module({
  exports: [StripeService],
  providers: [StripeService],
  controllers: [StripeController],
})
export class StripeModule {}
```

 Starting with a quick win is a way to build up momentum when you're facing something big. It can make the problem feel more approachable. As you write out functionality, see if you like to write code in a specific order. It can help you get to the more complex details faster. Throughout this book, I'll typically start with the initial module imports, move on to the controller, and finish with the service. I'll update the interface as we go and save the tests for last. But I tend to jump around files *a lot* during real development.

You need to add a new environment variable to *.env* to use the Stripe API. You'll get this value from your account, but there's a test one you can use that's found in the docs. So in your *.env*, add the following line.

```
STRIPE_SECRET_KEY="sk_your_stripe_account_secret_key"
```

Writing the Controller

From here, you can jump into your Stripe controller and start writing out endpoints you'll use. You'll need an endpoint to take user payments and an endpoint to update your products in Stripe's system. Open *stripe.controller.ts* and add this code to start making the endpoints:

```
// stripe.controller.ts
import {
Body,
Controller,
Headers,
HttpException,
HttpStatus,
Post,
Res
} from '@nestjs/common';
import { StripeService } from './stripe.service';
import { CreateStripePaymentDto } from './stripe.interface';
```

```
@Controller('/v1/stripe')
export class StripeController {
  constructor(private readonly stripeService: StripeService) {}

  @Post('/payments')
  public async createPayment(
    @Body() payment: CreateStripePaymentDto,
    @Headers() headers,
    @Res() res,
  ) {
    try {
      const paymentInfo = await this.stripeService.createPayment({
        payment,
        res,
        origin: headers.origin,
      });

      return paymentInfo;
    } catch (err) {
      throw new HttpException('Something happened', HttpStatus.NOT_FOUND);
    }
  }
}
```

In this controller, you've defined one endpoint. The endpoint is how you can handle payments through Stripe. This one is a little different; you'll need to do a redirect in your service method because the user will be sent to Stripe's checkout page through the payment request, and you need a way to send them back to your app after the payment has been made. You can check out why you do the redirect by looking at the diagram on how Stripe handles checkouts (*https://oreil.ly/WuKg-*).

Keep in mind you have the CreateStripePaymentDto in this controller, so you need to double-check that the interface meets the exact data requirements. As the app grows, you will also have some nested validation so that you can ensure you're sending the correct values to Stripe's API:

```
// stripe.interface.ts
import { IsNotEmpty, MinLength } from 'class-validator';

export class CreateStripePaymentDto {
  @IsNotEmpty()
  priceId: string;

  @MinLength(1, {
    message: 'quantity has to be at least 1',
  })
  quantity: number;
}
```

This validation functionality can be done with other packages like Joi (*https://joi.dev*) or Zod (*https://oreil.ly/tXs42*) in your middleware if you aren't using NestJS. `Stripe PriceData` is something you may use multiple times throughout your service implementation as it grows. A good practice is to mirror the types and requirements from the service docs so that you know you're sending exactly what they expect. Sometimes you can simply use the types that come directly from the SDK.

There are also times when you know that you'll be using only certain fields from the types and you'll be adding other fields that don't come from the SDK. You'll have to determine if it's worth the time to fit the SDK types into what you need or if you should write your own. When you know that you'll use the response exactly how it comes to you, go ahead and use the SDK types. If you know that you will have some new combination of fields or the SDK types need to be in a different format, consider mirroring the types to build your own interface.

 Not every service is as developer friendly as Stripe. If you aren't sure what types the request expects or what the response will be, just test the service and see what you get back. Sometimes, third-party services require a discovery phase so that you know what you're working with and how you can add the correct types to your app. You might use tools like mitmproxy (*https://mitmproxy.org*) or even Postman to see what you'll be working with.

Writing the Service

Now that you've written out the bulk of the code for the controller, turn your attention to the service where you'll work directly with Stripe. Stripe has a nice npm package that will let you use the API.

Let's implement the ability to make payments in Stripe. As you write the code, you can reference the docs for the checkout API to handle payments (*https://oreil.ly/M-6g5*). In *stripe.service.ts*, you'll do some file setup like importing packages and adding your constructor and logger. Then you can add the method to handle the request to the Stripe checkout API for your payments:

```
// stripe.service.ts
…

@Injectable()
export class StripeService {
  private readonly logger = new Logger(StripeService.name);
  // Keep the version string like this because Stripe said so
  private stripe =
    new Stripe(process.env.STRIPE_SECRET_KEY, { apiVersion: '2023-08-16' });

  public async createPayment({
    payment,
```

```
        origin,
        res,
      }: {
        payment: CreateStripePaymentDto;
        origin: string;
        res: any;
      }) {
        this.logger.log('Started payment in Stripe');

        try {
          // Create Checkout Sessions from body params.
          const session = await this.stripe.checkout.sessions.create({
            line_items: [
              {
                // Provide the Price ID (for example, price_H5ggYwtDq4fbrJ) of the
                // product you want to sell
                price: payment.priceId,
                quantity: payment.quantity,
              },
            ],
            mode: 'payment',
            success_url: `${origin}/?success=true`,
            cancel_url: `${origin}/?canceled=true`,
          });

          res.status(303).redirect(session.url);
        } catch (err) {
          throw Error('Something happened with Stripe');
        }
      }
    }
```

One of the biggest things to note here is the logger that's been initialized in the service. The logs you write will be invaluable when you're debugging issues because you can create a record of every action that happens. When you combine this with another third-party service like Datadog, the insights you get will help you fix issues with precision.

Between the logs and the error handling is the heart of third-party service integration: making sure that your code can handle any issues that come up from the third-party code. One thing to note is that third-party code might break some of your conventions, but that's one of the trade-offs of using the service.

Something else to keep in the back of your mind are any edge cases you can think of. What will your app do if the service you need is down? It's important to have this conversation with the Product team as you find out the quirks of the service through all your testing, which you'll get into in Chapter 7.

You'll see there's a new field that needs to be added to the database: stripeProduct Id. You want to keep track of some third-party data in your system so that you can perform actions through the API and validate any changes. That means you'll need to update the *schema.prisma* and run a migration. I'll leave that to you to do, but you can check your *schema.prisma* against the version in the GitHub repo (*https://oreil.ly/ 4mlvc*).

Conclusion

This chapter focused on getting comfortable researching and using third-party services in your code. The most important thing to remember when working with these services is that sometimes they just don't behave the way you expect. Weird race conditions can happen, data can come back in inconsistent formats, and request parameters can change. This is where error handling and logging will be your best friends. Issues will pop up with third-party services from time to time, and that's OK. It's nothing you can't handle with some communication among the dev and Product teams and a willingness to try different code strategies.

## CHAPTER 6

Background Jobs

Once you have some third-party integrations, it's likely that you'll end up needing automated ways to keep the company's data in sync with the third party's data and to trigger other events like sending emails. That's where background jobs and cron jobs come in.

A *background job* executes code or actions that need to run outside the flow of an API in a systematic way. This will include tasks like sending emails or doing complex calculations after a user has made an update. Background jobs are going to work alongside your server-side application code and are typically triggered directly from an endpoint call. These jobs are usually defined at the service level because they typically have business logic around them.

A *cron job* is a task that is executed on a schedule. It will run at some time interval you set based on the business needs. Syncing data from or to a third-party service on a schedule is a prime example of using a cron job. Cron jobs can be in your application, but it's more common and better practice to have them handled somewhere else, like an Amazon Elastic Compute Cloud (EC2) instance or just another server. That way, you won't use up resources that your application is running with.

One of the hardest things about working with background jobs or cron jobs is that, since they run on their own schedules, they can affect the state of the whole system in unexpected ways. That's where your senior dev skills come in.

In this chapter, you'll dive into:

- Incorporating background and cron jobs into your app architecture
- Setting up alerts, monitoring, and logging for background and cron jobs
- Handling data-sync issues with third-party services and cron jobs
- Handling task-execution issues with background jobs
- Future-proofing your background and cron jobs

The first thing to note is that your jobs can be written in any programming language. So you aren't doing anything drastically different, you're still going to use TypeScript. This is just code that gets run somewhere aside from your endpoints or service logic. This is why understanding the overall architecture of the app is important because jobs can get lost over time as developers come and go and the product changes.

You'll be expected to be able to make and document those architecture changes and explain how they will affect resource allocation. You may even be responsible for the initial research around the tools that work best with your infrastructure. This is where it's great to talk to the DevOps team or whoever manages the infrastructure.

Find out what cloud providers are used to handle all the apps for the company. This will give you an idea of the tools you have available and how you should approach writing the code for your jobs. The tool you use will have a direct impact on your implementation because you have to use its SDK to interface from its resources to your code. You'll learn more about this as we go through this chapter, but let's start with the architecture before going too deep.

Updating the Backend Architecture

For this project, you'll implement a background job to send emails and a cron job to sync data from Stripe to your database. To make sure you and everyone else understands where these fit into the backend, you need to update the architecture diagram. Whenever there is a question about how things go together and why resources are used a certain way, the architecture diagram should be the source of truth. It's essential for you to make sure this document is maintained. This is also a good place to see if there are any initial concerns with how a new feature will get integrated into the backend. Figure 6-1 shows what the diagram will look like now.

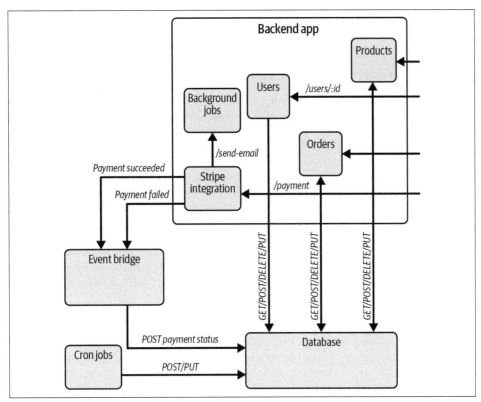

Figure 6-1. Updated architecture diagram with background and cron jobs

Updating docs is an incredible opportunity for you to really see if you know what you're talking about. An important skill for you to have is being able to mentor more junior devs; this is so important that it can't be overstated. Take architecture updates as a way to introduce new concepts to the team and make sure everyone, including you, remembers how this whole product works. You might even run into some areas you need a refresher on!

Now you have a visual representation of the flow of the jobs. The background job to send emails will get triggered only when something happens in the Stripe integration. The cron job to sync Stripe data, like products, with your database will happen on a schedule.

A Different Opinion on Structuring Your Cron and Background Jobs with the App Code

Ethan Brown has some great advice about this. What follows is from Ethan:

> Increasingly, I'm preferring monorepos, and on most of my projects, I do colocate cron/background code with my application code. It's organized in appropriate folders, of course, but it's not in a separate repo or project, and it's certainly not a microservice. The way I like to think about it is that it's all application code.
>
> Some of it is invoked as a direct response to user requests, some of it is invoked on a schedule (cron jobs), and some of it is invoked directly or indirectly from a user action, but long-running enough to have a push mechanism for informing interested parties that the job had completed (background jobs).
>
> In general, I think this approach offers a powerful paradigm that can demystify cron/background jobs. Think about it all as part of the problem domain (i.e., application code), which is primarily event driven: the bulk of the events may be direct user requests (HTTP, XHR, WebSockets, usually), but some events are driven by schedules and some are driven by queues (Amazon's SQS [Simple Queue Service] or SNS [Simple Notification Service], in my case).
>
> I'd be more inclined to make an exception to this paradigm for read-only background jobs like analytics or reporting. If this job isn't changing system state, just monitoring or doing business intelligence work, that can be a microservice or separate app.
>
> But if a job changes system state, it is application code, regardless of how it was invoked.
>
> I extend philosophy to system diagrams: they show not only the application endpoints but what kind of events trigger them.

Since you have an idea of how these jobs will work within the existing architecture, it's time to take a glance at the infrastructure.

Using Cron Jobs

This is where things get really specific, so make sure you have input from the DevOps team. For this project, we'll assume that your infrastructure is built on Amazon Web Services (AWS). You won't get a deep dive into the services in this book other than some quick implementation. If you want to learn more about a specific cloud provider, I suggest starting with their docs, blog posts, and free training materials.

Cron job scheduling is often handled through the cloud configurations, which you usually won't touch. You'll be responsible for the code that runs the job, though, and you should know the schedule it runs on. The example cron job you'll implement to sync the Stripe data will be in the repo with the rest of the project for now. This is a good way to test that it works as expected before you start updating the infrastructure.

Just to see what a cron job can look like, here's a code snippet from the project you're working on (you can find the complete file on GitHub (*https://oreil.ly/a6zxC*)):

```
...
onModuleInit() {
  this.addCronJob('sync_stripe_orders', '5 00 * * *',
    this.cronSyncStripeOrders.bind(this));
}
...
async cronSyncStripeOrders(syncDate: Date) {
  this.logger.debug(`Stripe orders sync started at ${new Date()}`);

  const previousDate = syncDate.setDate(syncDate.getDate() - 1);

  // Set params to get the invoices that have been created since yesterday
  const params = {
    created: {
      gte: previousDate,
    },
  };

  // Get invoices from Stripe
  const { data: latestInvoices } = await this.stripe.invoices.list(params);

  // Check that there are new invoices to process
  if (latestInvoices.length === 0) {
    this.logger.debug(`No new Stripe invoices since ${previousDate}`);
    return;
  }

  // Loop through invoices and create new DB records
  for (const invoice of latestInvoices) {
    const orderRecord = {
      name: invoice.account_name,
      stripeInvoiceId: invoice.id,
      total: invoice.total,
    };

    try {
      const doesOrderRecordExist = await this.prisma.order.findUnique({
        where: { stripeInvoiceId: invoice.id },
      });

      if (!doesOrderRecordExist) {
        await this.prisma.order.create({ data: orderRecord });
      }
    } catch (error) {
      this.logger.debug(`Something happened with invoice ${invoice.id}:
        ${error}`);
    }
  }
}
```

```
    this.logger.debug(`Stripe orders sync finished at ${new Date()}`);
  }
```

Let's break down some of the key things. The first is the cron expression `'5 00 * * *'` that defines the schedule for your sync job. You can play with different values on the Cronitor cron expressions site (*https://crontab.guru/#5_00_*_*_**). The expression is set to run the code at five minutes after midnight every night. That way, your data syncs when you can get the most info with the least impact on your users. Keep time zones in mind here because that can have a surprising impact on your system. If you have the code running on a server in UTC-5 and the user lives in UTC-8, that can cause some issues with data syncing on time. You can see the full code in the repo (*https://oreil.ly/Bs9Hs*).

More to Note on Your Cron Jobs

Jeff Graham has some additional insights on what to watch for with your cron jobs:

It's common that cron jobs encounter issues as your traffic or usage increases. You might find it takes longer and longer for a job to complete, which can lead to time-outs, long queries, and failures. Worst case, your job can't complete its list of tasks, but restarts at the beginning over and over throughout the day. Disaster!

Monitoring your jobs to prevent these situations is crucial. This way, you will see the problem coming, and you can implement changes ahead of time. All jobs are inherently different: some may run quietly in their original form, while others will need improvements and maturation.

Alerts and Monitoring

There's another almost-hidden thing happening with this cron job. As any errors are being logged, certain ones may be more urgent than others. That's where your monitoring tools will come in. This is probably something that the DevOps team will handle because they are responsible for resource management and infrastructure-level incidents. When programmatic issues come up, though, it's on your dev team to solve them and figure out the root cause.

You're watching for things like a number of errors being thrown in a specified time range, a specific type of error that occurs, or something else you and the DevOps team have agreed on. Monitoring can be used to trigger alerts, which help the team address issues as soon as they come up. Monitoring usually involves agreed-upon metrics, and it can also help establish baselines for how the app should perform.

Most of the time, alerts will be configured in the infrastructure. If you have a job that starts to trigger a lot unexpectedly, the DevOps team may have an alert that lets them know when a certain resource-utilization level is reached. Or if you start seeing a lot of 403 errors in your monitoring tool, that could indicate an attack on the system.

There are also alerts that the dev team will need, such as code continuously throwing errors. You'll go into more depth on monitoring and alerts in Chapter 12.

Between logging, monitoring, and alerts, you should be able to start triaging an issue as soon as it comes up and have the info you need to find a root cause.

Logging

The next important thing to note is the logging that's in place. When jobs are running automatically, they will have errors from time to time. Debugging scheduled jobs can be hard for a number of reasons. Issues like the service throwing errors or being down, records getting skipped, errors happening only at a certain time of day, or database issues happen.

Sometimes you can't replicate the errors because they occur under very specific conditions. That's where going through logs comes in; we'll get to that in Chapter 9. There are a number of logging lines in here because these are the places in the job where errors may happen and cause other issues. As you think about what to log, think about the info you might need to debug errors. IDs, statuses, names, and the like are all things you can look up across different parts of the system.

Something else that can help is to put specific searchable terms in your logs. As the product grows, a ton of logs will be generated every time an endpoint is called. So being able to quickly filter the logs down to a specific event is essential for concise debugging.

Issues with Data Sync and Task Execution

Once you have a *root cause*, or the source of the error in the code or environment configs, and you've figured out the fix, you need a way to retrigger the job that failed. It's good backend practice to have a retry mechanism for any cron or background jobs. When you run into data-sync issues, usually retrying to fetch the records will fix them. In your retry function, you might do a quick count to see how many records were updated so that you know the impact of the issue before fixing it.

I'm not going to walk through the code for the background job that will send emails, but you can find it on GitHub (*https://oreil.ly/oR5sA*). For jobs that are time sensitive and communicate important info to the customers, your alerts will be helpful for the dev team. This can involve an automated response to the customers or the dev team that also lets the Support team know something has happened. You may even get to the point where your monitoring metrics can be used to trigger retry events automatically. Most of the time, you'll work closely with the DevOps team to debug issues with jobs because of the way they integrate with the infrastructure.

Future Considerations

More errors will occur as the number of jobs and the amount of data they handle increase with the number of users. You're at a great point in the project to build a stop mechanism for your jobs. Sometimes jobs just execute unexpectedly, and you need a way to stop them quickly. You can have stop mechanisms for each job or for specific jobs that are more impactful on the overall system. If you start by building this functionality into your first job, when it inevitably gets copy-pasted to create a new job, it'll already have this handling baked in.

When you create jobs, there's a chance that the code won't get updated as often as it should as long as the jobs run successfully. To prevent the code for your jobs from becoming legacy code, always have a ticket somewhere in your backlog to update the packages and do refactors for the jobs. Doing this at least once a quarter should be often enough to keep the code maintainable.

Conclusion

In this chapter, you were able to write a cron job to handle syncing your Stripe data to the company database and a background job to handle sending emails to users for orders. This is where having a solid understanding of the architecture becomes important so that functionality doesn't get lost or forgotten about. You also can see how much the dev team and the DevOps team work together.

You don't have to be a DevOps engineer to get a basic understanding of how the infrastructure works and how to use the tools that have been set up. You may feel like you should know how to do everything. You don't. Learn how to lean on other teams for their expertise to help your team get things done more efficiently.

## CHAPTER 7

Backend Testing

At this point in the project, you've got quite a bit of code. There are services, controllers, and integrations. While you and the team will do your best to not introduce code *regressions* (where previously working functionality is broken from an unrelated change), that will happen at some point, and it's normal as the code grows. That's why you write tests for the major functionality of the app.

On the backend, you'll test for things like errors being called in the correct scenarios, data being returned in the correct format, and the correct methods being called with the correct parameters. Writing unit tests like these will help keep you from making regressions, understand the way the code should work, and make the code maintainable because you are writing more concise, modular code.

In this chapter, I'll cover:

- Trade-offs between having tests and not having them
- How to write tests using Jest
- The importance of mock data

Regardless of whether you are starting a project from scratch or inheriting one, tests can be a great help. This is also a great time to collaborate with the Product team on the current and future state of the product. Writing tests will often bring up more detailed questions about exactly what is expected from some functionality.

Why Spend the Time on Tests

You'll find that developers have differing views on how tests should be implemented. Some strong opinions can come up here because, just like with everything else, there are trade-offs. A major consideration is the level of test coverage for a project. I've seen many projects where getting close to 100% test coverage on the backend isn't far-fetched, but aiming for 90% or higher is more reasonable. There comes a point when you and the team have to decide if more tedious tests are worth writing by looking at the value they add compared to the amount of time they take to write.

When you take the time to write tests, it does slow release cycles initially. Tests can take a while to run in your CI and take time away from feature development or refactoring. I think that the benefits outweigh the costs, but you have to maintain a balance between them. While you may sacrifice some speed in the beginning, tests can prevent a lot of headaches and give the team more confidence in their code as the app grows. Having tests improves the developer experience for the team because you all can make changes without as much worry about regressions and things breaking in unexpected places.

Tests give you a chance to think through and document the way the code should work. They can even bring up more product-related questions. You may run into cases where tests lead to questions that shake up your architecture. Having automated regression tests in place also helps you keep preventable bugs from getting to production.

This is a good place to pair with the QA team, if you have one. If you don't, then you're building in some level of QA for your team. Most of the time, the dev team will be focused on writing unit tests. *Unit tests* are what you use to make sure the code is implemented properly and running as expected for different use cases. The QA team can come in and write some automated end-to-end (e2e) tests to run against your development environment. An *e2e test* is more focused on testing the user flow than the code. Some good tools for this are Postman (*https://www.postman.com*) and Thunder Client (*https://www.thunderclient.com*). You can write collections of tests to hit your development environment to make sure endpoints are really working as expected.

Having a way to validate that your endpoints are manipulating data correctly becomes a necessity as the product grows and new business rules come up. Sometimes things can slip through manual testing as people come and go. Having test cases set up for both unit tests and e2e tests is a form of documentation that is kept up to date consistently.

Whenever a new change breaks a test, you can see what the initial assumptions were and then double-check with the dev or Product team that those assumptions are still valid. Again, writing tests with this level of thoroughness can slow releases because you have to account for the time it takes to write the tests *and* get them to pass. So it's important to consider how long this takes in your ticket estimates.

Implementing code and deploying it without tests can be useful when you need to get features and bug fixes out really fast. The trade-off is that you don't have the assurance that you didn't break something seemingly unrelated. For example, you may update the data schema for products and rename a field. This can break things you wouldn't expect, like functionality for retrieving orders.

You may think you can come back and add tests later as long as you get this next release out on time. This is a risky assumption to make. It's best to write the tests along with the implementation so that you don't miss anything before releasing. Plus, tests tend to get pushed to the backlog as bugs and new features come along.

Work with the Product team to help them understand why writing tests is helpful for getting a better product to the end user. Show them how it will help prevent the need to do hotfixes for unexpected regressions. Once they see the value that tests add, they will start asking about different scenarios that will help you write even better test cases.

How to Approach Test Writing

Although approaches like test-driven development (TDD) or behavior-driven development (BDD) can be helpful, you don't need to follow them. The important thing is to make sure you know what to write tests for. That's a big part of testing that tends to get left out in most courses or blog posts. When you write unit tests on the backend, you're checking for specific functionality.

When you make a request to an endpoint, what exactly is supposed to happen? You may need tests for the potential errors that could be returned in the response. It also helps to make sure that the functions you expect to get called actually do, they get called with the correct parameters, and they return the expected data.

Go through your code line by line. Is an error being thrown? Write a test for it. Is a function being called? Write a test to see if it gets called with the correct parameters. There's a balance between knowing when to mock functions or letting the actual function be tested. If you find that you're trying to test a package you've installed, then that's a good case for mocking the functionality. If it's internal code that you and the team have written, it's usually OK to let the tests call the actual code. By having these tests to start with, you can save yourself a lot of debugging time when you and other devs start adding new functionality and code gets refactored.

Any time a change is made that makes the tests fail, that will help you get to the root cause faster. This also helps you think through the way the code should work as it grows over time. You may even find areas where the logic can be improved as you handle failed tests and think about how the code should really work. Your tests should focus on where the logic is, such as conditions in your code, when HTTP status codes will be returned, how user permissions affect the results of API requests, and anything else that will change the outcome a user or service receives.

Let's take a look at the create method in *orders.controller.ts* and see how you would write unit tests for this:

```
@Post()
public async create(@Body() user: User, order: CreateOrderDto): Promise<Order>
{
 if (!user) {
  throw new HttpException('Unauthorized', HttpStatus.UNAUTHORIZED);
 }
 if (!user.permissions.includes('create:orders')) {
  throw new HttpException('Forbidden', HttpStatus.FORBIDDEN);
 }
 if (!order) {
  throw new HttpException('No order data', HttpStatus.BAD_REQUEST);
 }
 if (order.products.length === 0) {
  throw new HttpException('No products in order', HttpStatus.CONFLICT);
 }
 if (!order.total) {
  throw new HttpException('No order total', HttpStatus.CONFLICT);
 }

 try {
  const newOrder = await this.ordersService.createOrder(order);
  return newOrder;
 } catch (err) {
  throw new HttpException('Something happened', HttpStatus.NOT_FOUND);
 }
 }
}
```

You can see the errors that may get thrown before making the call to the service method. If any of those conditions are met, then an error will be sent to the frontend in the response. You can be explicit in the error message or leave it more generic. As long as you aren't revealing any PII data or anything specific enough to give attackers useful info, you can say just about anything.

It's a good practice to keep the message short and send the associated status code. Now you can look at this from a testing perspective and go through the method line by line. By reading the code, you can identify five test cases from the errors being thrown, a test case for a successful service call, and a test case for an error being thrown from the service. Let's look at how you would write these seven tests with Jest:

```
import { Test, TestingModule } from '@nestjs/testing';
import { OrdersV1Controller } from './orders.controller';
import { OrdersService } from './orders.service';

const user = {
  id: 1001,
  email: 'tester@rest.com',
  name: 'Tester Rest',
  permissions: ['get:orders', 'create:orders'],
```

```
};

const order = {
  name: 'Biggest order',
  total: 125.99,
  stripeInvoiceId: 'stripeInvoiceId',
};

describe('OrdersController', () => {
  let controller: OrdersV1Controller;
  let ordersService: OrdersService;

  beforeEach(async () => {
    const module: TestingModule = await Test.createTestingModule({
      controllers: [OrdersV1Controller],
      providers: [OrdersService],
    }).compile();

    controller = module.get<OrdersV1Controller>(OrdersV1Controller);
    ordersService = module.get<OrdersService>(OrdersService);
  });

  it('throws unauthorized error if the user is undefined', async () => {
    await controller.create(undefined, order);

    expect(controller.create).toThrowError('Unauthorized');
  });

  it('throws forbidden error if the user does not have correct permissions',
    async () => {
    const badPermissionsUser = {
      id: 1001,
      email: 'tester@rest.com',
      name: 'Tester Rest',
      permissions: ['get:products],
    };

    await controller.create(badPermissionsUser, order);

    expect(controller.create).toThrowError('Forbidden');
  });

  it('throws bad request error if the order is undefined', async () => {
    await controller.create(user, undefined);

    expect(controller.create).toThrowError('No order data');
  });

  it('throws conflict error if products are missing from the order',
    async () => {
    const orderWithoutName = {
      total: 125.99,
```

```
      stripeInvoiceId: 'stripeInvoiceId',
    };

    await controller.create(user, orderWithoutName);

    expect(controller.create).toThrowError('No order name');
  });

  it('throws conflict error if the order total is missing', async () => {
    const orderWithoutTotal = {
      name: 'Biggest order',
      stripeInvoiceId: 'stripeInvoiceId',
    };

    await controller.create(user, orderWithoutTotal);

    expect(controller.create).toThrowError('No order total');
  });

  it('successfully creates a new order', async () => {
    controller.create(user, order);
    const newOrder = await ordersService.createOrder(undefined);

    expect(ordersService.createOrder).toBeCalledWith(order);
    expect(ordersService.createOrder).toReturnWith(newOrder);
  });

  it('throws not found error if something happens in the service', async () => {
    try {
      controller.create(user, order);
      await ordersService.createOrder(undefined);
      expect(ordersService.createOrder).toThrowError();
    } catch (e) {
      expect(e.message).toBe('Something happened');
    }
  });
});
```

This is a great time to mention some popular AI tools currently
available that could help you write tests, like Copilot (*https://
oreil.ly/s6glK*) or ChatGPT (*https://openai.com/chatgpt*). Tools like
these can help speed up your process for writing tests or generating
scenarios.

All these tests came from scenarios described in the controller code. When you're
writing tests in general, you typically don't need to worry about testing the implementation for things like helpers and service functions because they will have their
own unit tests. That's one of the benefits of a modular approach like this. It makes
writing tests clearer because you have a separation of responsibilities.

For each scenario, you have test data, and you have the expected response. This is a good way to ensure that you get the main cases. While you should try your best to anticipate edge cases when you talk with Product and QA, you can also add edge cases to these tests as you find them.

One thing that helps me a lot when writing tests is to have the test file and the code file open side by side. That way, I can see if I've tested each line of code as I move through the file.

There are a few ways to approach e2e API testing. You can use a tool like Postman because it's friendlier to work with for nondevs. Or you can use a tool like Cypress (*https://www.cypress.io*) or Playwright (*https://playwright.dev*). Figure 7-1 shows what the tests would look like in Postman. You can import the JSON file for these tests (*https://oreil.ly/Eerfp*) into Postman and check out the tests yourself. In Chapter 24, I'll go over running e2e tests in your CI/CD pipeline.

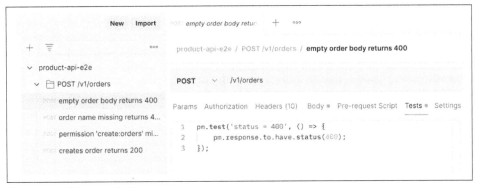

Figure 7-1. E2e tests in Postman

E2e testing is an ambiguous term—it depends on whom you talk to about it. Some would argue that e2e tests are only when you test both the frontend and backend together. Others will say that e2e tests can be divided between the frontend or backend if they focus on functionality instead of code implementation, similar to unit tests. Just keep in mind that there isn't a specific definition for e2e tests that's more correct than another. You have to understand that the distinction may depend on the organization.

If you decide to go the programmatic way with something like Cypress, the tests will look something like this:

```
it('/v1/orders (POST)', () => {
    return request(app.getHttpServer())
        .post('/v1/orders')\
        .expect(200)
        .expect(order);
});
```

So the syntax is comparable to what you'll be writing your unit tests with. With the programmatic approach, make sure to factor in the time it will take for the team to get ramped up on how to use a particular library. But the scenarios will be very similar across your unit and e2e tests. The unit tests will check code implementation and data manipulation, and the e2e tests will check for the flow of the data at a higher level similar to what the frontend or another service would do. You'll learn more about e2e testing in Chapter 24.

Mock Data

You may have noticed that there was some mock data in a few of those test cases. Your mock data should account for different scenarios that can happen with the project. For the highest level of documentation, it helps to have the mocks in separate files with very specific names, although sometimes the difference between one test case and another is a single field. This is where some of those code conventions might need some updates. As long as the team agrees on the best approach for the scenario, then that's what works.

You can get the mock data directly from your database or by using a tool like Faker (*https://fakerjs.dev/guide*) or Falso (*https://github.com/ngneat/falso*). This is a great time to double-check your types as well. As you make this mock data, work with the Product team to decide what should happen in different scenarios. It's OK to make assumptions, but verify that they are valid for what's expected of the product.

Something else you should consider with your mock data is creating test data in your database. This is how you can have mock data available for your e2e tests, which is great for demos to the Product team and any other stakeholders because you can go through the entire flow without having to do code hacks. It also gives them a chance to test things for themselves and see if anything needs to be changed.

Here's another great tidbit from Ethan Brown:

> I think having a robust mock data infrastructure is an underrated principle in software development. Most real-world applications deal with all these very specific data types, and developers are always spending time reinventing the wheel of test data for every little thing they do. Having robust and realistic test-data factories—indeed, building it into the very process of class/type creation—can be a game changer for productivity.
>
> For example, if I have a dev starting on some piece of functionality involving a "user" object, I don't want them to either (a) create a bare-bones user object that might miss something that would break in production or (b) spend a lot of time mocking up user objects. I'd rather they just call `FakeUserFactory.create(10)` to get 10 users as if they had been created in the real world. This also has follow-up benefits for product demos, trial accounts, or simulations.
>
> It also helps having some robust test data to choose from that covers several real-world situations. Even if you just have a file with a list of 10 or 15 fictitious users and devs get to pick which one(s) they want to use for testing, it may remind them to handle messy real-world data.
>
> In the case of users, I would have a user with a ridiculously long name ("Sir Charles Xavier Tester Testalot III"), one-word names ("Prince"), and names with non-Latin characters ("Dvořák"). As a junior dev looks through that list, even though they were just looking for some test data, they might think, for example, "Oh shoot, I just did something that'll break if there isn't a last and first name."

A good way to start mocking data is to make a complete object for each model. For example, you made the user mock data here:

```
const user = {
  id: 1001,
  email: 'tester@rest.com',
  name: 'Tester Rest',
  permissions: ['get:orders', 'create:orders'],
};
```

This has everything you need based on the user schema. Now if you need to modify fields, you can just update this object in the test to account for that specific case. You have an example of how this works in the user permissions test case where the `permissions` field is modified.

Another good way to start mocking data will actually be from your database seed data! This is a good time to note that your database seed data should be updated along with any schema changes. That way, when you need to set up the project on a new computer, you won't run into missing data or incompatible types.

Conclusion

In this chapter, we covered testing on the backend and why it's important. You'll run into some developers who haven't written tests with this much detail before, and they might push back. Just keep in mind that every time you deploy a bug and it gets found, you cause a mini panic within the organization and create the need for hot-fixes. Tests help you avoid that even if they do take extra developer time. We'll get into deployments and integrating tests there in Chapters 24 and 25.

We also covered several different ways to test your code. Unit tests are there for the details in the code implementation, and e2e tests are there to make sure the flow works as expected from a user standpoint. You can even say that any testing done by the Product team counts as user-acceptance testing because they are the ones checking functionality from a user perspective. Testing is a group effort, so a lot of discussion with the Product team and any other stakeholders may be necessary to make sure everything makes sense.

## CHAPTER 8

Backend Security Considerations

The security of your app is going to be one of the top concerns for the dev team, the Product team, and the whole organization. You never want an unintended entity to gain access they aren't supposed to have. That's why you'll need to look at the app from all angles, such as authentication, authorization, validation, common attacks, and external dependencies.

Security is a topic with so much depth and breadth that entire books are dedicated to it. I'm going to keep this chapter focused on what you can do on the backend specifically, but there are far more areas covered by security. You may be lucky enough to work with a Security team. They go through every part of the company's technical infrastructure, all the way down to what you can install on your laptop.

In this chapter, you will learn about:

- Authentication methods and when to use them
- Authorization for users to give them different levels of access to the functionality and data in the app
- Why you should typically go with an out-of-the-box solution
- The parts of the Open Web Application Security Project (OWASP) Top 10 that apply to the backend
- Best security practices, regulations, and where to learn more about different areas of security

I'm just touching the surface of this topic in this chapter, and I'll leave you with plenty of resources to learn all the details. But you will see how to implement some good, practical security practices here. Then you can build off that based on any regulations your product falls under, such as the Health Insurance Portability and Accountability

Act (HIPAA) (*https://oreil.ly/uLXpC*) for health care apps, PCI DSS (*https://oreil.ly/nALD1*) for fintech apps, or the General Data Protection Regulation (GDPR) (*https://gdpr.eu/checklist*) for almost every app. Let's start with how users log in to the app with authentication.

Authentication

Authentication (AuthN) is how the user's identity is validated by the app. This happens through some method of login. Some of the common authentication methods (*https://oreil.ly/65NI_*) you'll work with are:

- Password authentication
- Multifactor authentication (MFA)
- Token authentication
- Biometric authentication
- Open authorization (OAuth)
- One-time password (OTP)

Depending on the app you're working on, you may use some combination of these methods to give users more login options. You can expect to use at least one or two of these methods on any given app, though.

Ensuring a user is who they claim to be is a complex task. There are many ways a malicious user can try to impersonate a real user. They might try brute force attacks, phishing scams, or hijacking a user's session token. What you're trying to do is keep the wrong people out.

The most common method you'll implement is some form of password authentication. The user's password will be securely stored in your database, and only their username and password combination will let them log in. Some of the deeper topics behind security will include how salted password hashing (*https://oreil.ly/JKRfu*), encryption (*https://oreil.ly/TVMX3*), and decryption work for sensitive user info, such as Social Security numbers or banking information. These topics are out of the scope of this chapter, but I encourage you to do more reading on them to get a better understanding of how and when they are used.

Password authentication can be made even more secure when you add password requirements like a length and specific characters. One of the biggest risks with this authentication method lies with the user. If they have the same password across multiple systems, there's not much you can do about that with the username-password method alone.

That's where methods like MFA (*https://oreil.ly/vS_7a*) and OTP (*https://oreil.ly/xYoyP*) come in handy because they add another layer of identification on top of the password login. This brings in other tools the user needs access to, such as an email, a phone number, or a special app like Google Authenticator (*https://oreil.ly/LpaC_*) or Okta Verify (*https://oreil.ly/wff9u*). The user typically gets a code they need to put in the app to finish the authentication process. Adding this extra step prevents malicious users from logging in even if they have the password credentials.

I briefly mentioned some of the services you can use for authentication in Chapter 5, but it's worth mentioning them again here: Auth0 (*https://auth0.com/docs*), FusionAuth (*https://fusionauth.io/docs*), Amazon Cognito (*https://oreil.ly/06RmU*), SuperTokens (*https://supertokens.com/docs/guides*), and Clerk (*https://clerk.com*). You also have the option of working with open source options like Passport.js (*https://www.passportjs.org*), NextAuth.js (*https://next-auth.js.org*), and the built-in functionality in NestJS (*https://oreil.ly/FIRPN*). It's usually a good idea to go with one of the third-party services for authentication when you know you need a higher level of security because of industry regulations.

You will also get into details around how you store tokens for a user session and how to handle it when they expire. This will bring up topics like authorization code flow (*https://oreil.ly/UCB28*) and Proof Key for Code Exchange (PKCE) (*https://oreil.ly/Kdzeg*). Or maybe you decide it's better to log the user out and make them log in again after a certain amount of time.

Something to keep in mind as you weigh options is the user experience. Sure, it's more secure to require biometric authentication, but is it something your users will do? There's going to be a balance between user comfort and authentication methods that you'll need to discuss with your team and the Security team.

Once the user has successfully been identified, you need to tell the system the level of access they have. Not all users will have the same functionality level; that's based on what they need to do in the app.

Authorization

Even if a user can log in, that doesn't mean they should have access to everything. So now you have to handle *authorization* (AuthZ): when you give users a set of permissions they use after authentication. AuthZ is what defines the difference in user roles. For example, a customer support user will have access to many different accounts whereas a customer should be able to access only their account.

Authorization is one of the reasons strong authentication is so important. If a malicious user gains access to one user's account, that's bad. If they gain access to an admin user's account, that's *really* bad. Now you have to decide which access control model you'll work with. A common and very basic thing to implement with authorization is the principle of least privilege (*https://oreil.ly/HNLFe*).

Least-privilege access ensures that users have only the access they really need to perform the tasks for their permission level. For example, someone who manages the docs for an app doesn't need the same access as someone who onboards users. This should be the base level for any other access control you implement.

You'll most commonly see role-based access control (RBAC) (*https://oreil.ly/PfS9v*). RBAC gives you a way to assign users to different roles based on the level of access that role has. Many services you can use for authentication provide some kind of RBAC functionality. You can also build this functionality internally, but keep in mind that you'll likely end up building frontend features to support internal users updating the roles and users.

Here's a small example of an RBAC implementation that you can use to build your own functions to check user roles and give access to different parts of the app:

```
export const rbacConfig = {
  rolesConfig: [
    {
      roles: ['Customer'],
      permissions: ['get:order', 'create:order', 'get:product'],
    },
    {
      roles: ['Support'],
      permissions: ['get:order', 'update:order', 'delete:order', 'get:product'],
    },
    {
      roles: ['Store'],
      permissions: [
          'get:product',
            'delete:product',
            'create:product',
            'update:product'
      ],
    },
  ],
};

const canCreateOrder = (user: User) => {
  if (user.roles.includes(Roles.Customer)) return true;
  return false;
}
```

There's also attribute-based access control (ABAC) (*https://oreil.ly/MTLH_*). ABAC lets you have extremely fine-grained control over what users can do based on their roles, the resources they want to access, the actions they want to take, and the environment they are in. This gives you a more flexible way to implement security because you can keep access very specific based on the exact things a user needs to do. You can expand existing roles to do more or use them as templates for new roles. You'll find ABAC in action if you ever work with AWS Identity and Access Management (IAM) entities because that's what they use.

Another Perspective on ABAC and RBAC

Ethan Brown has some good insights into how different types of authorization are implemented. Here are some of his thoughts:

> I think there are different pitfalls in both RBAC and ABAC that can compromise security, and I wouldn't call ABAC inherently more secure. The danger I see with ABAC is that with such fine-grained access controls, roles can have dozens or hundreds of rules, which makes it harder to reason about and validate specific authorization scenarios. Very often, vast lists of ABAC policies will get copied from one role to another just to save time, but it's easy to miss policies that were accidentally included but shouldn't have been.
>
> RBAC is better in this regard—there are just fewer places for security vulnerabilities to hide in a simpler authorization framework—but RBAC won't be robust enough for every system. The value of ABAC is that it's less rigid and allows you to craft new roles and access patterns in the future, ones that you haven't yet anticipated. If you can envision an application having increasingly complex authorization rules, ABAC in addition to RBAC (I rarely see ABAC without it) may be a better choice.

The biggest drawback to ABAC is that these systems can be complex to set up. Making sure you have the right attributes assigned to the correct roles is the most important part. It's tedious to initialize, but over time the payoff can be worth it if your application has complex permission requirements. You'll be able to copy-paste a lot of things for new attributes as roles change over time. Be careful with copying roles when you use ABAC because you could accidentally give a role more permissions than it needs.

Here's a small example of an ABAC definition:

```
export const abacConfig = {
  attributesConfig: [
    {
      action: 'CreateOrder',
      attributes: {
        user: {
          type: ['customer'],
        },
        resource: {
          type: 'order',
        },
      },
    },
    {
      action: 'GetOrder',
      attributes: {
        user: {
          type: ['customer', 'support'],
        },
```

```
            resource: {
              type: 'order',
            },
          },
        },
        {
          action: 'GetProduct',
          attributes: {
            user: {
              type: ['customer', 'support', 'store'],
            },
            resource: {
              type: 'product',
            },
          },
        },
      ],
    };

    const canGetOrder = ({ user, resource, action }: GetOrderProps) => {
      if (acceptedOrderUserTypes.includes(user.type) &&
        resource === 'order' &&
          action === 'GetOrder') {
        return true;
      }
      return false;
    };
```

The last model I'll cover is policy-based access control (PBAC) (*https://oreil.ly/Hrl2R*), which is very similar to ABAC. Both are referred to as *fine-grained access control* (FGAC). The main difference between the two is that PBAC uses the policies you define compared to the attributes you define in ABAC. It's just a different way of defining how you want to restrict access. This is another access model that your cloud provider might have available.

Many times, access control is managed by the Security team or a user support team once the dev and Product teams have documented how different users should be able to interact with the app. Other times, you will be able to directly add new attributes or roles and change existing permissions. A good rule to follow is granting all users the least privilege they need to get started and then adding more permissions as they need them.

All of these access models have trade-offs. RBAC is probably the fastest to implement, but managing all the roles over time can get messy. If you foresee the app growing to a level where RBAC will get unwieldy, then it's time to consider adding ABAC or PBAC. These models will take more time to set up, but they will be easier to manage over time. When you have to decide which model to use, here are a few questions you can ask:

- What are the different types of users and the access level for each type?
- Do any of the services you use offer any access control functionality?
- What level of granularity do you need when it comes to access?
- How flexible or dynamic do access levels need to be?
- What information do you have available to determine a user's access level?

This barely scratches the surface of how deep you can go into authorization. I encourage you to check out some of the resources in this section. These are some different strategies you can choose from; you'll work with the Security and Support teams to fully implement them across the company.

With this background on AuthN and AuthZ, you can move on to some of the most common security risks online and how your work helps prevent a lot of them.

OWASP Top 10

Regardless of whether you're familiar with the OWASP Top 10 (*https://oreil.ly/4QqBE*), you should look at all of them in detail to understand the security side of your code. A few of these in particular fall under what we've covered in this chapter. Broken access control is the number-one vulnerability on the list, so you know it's an area worth spending time on.

Broken access control (*https://oreil.ly/1tkhr*) is something that can easily slip through the cracks as roles and users change. One of the most common ways this becomes an issue is not following the principle of least privilege. It can get to the point where you or someone on the Security team is constantly having to update permissions, so eventually they give everyone the same permissions to make it easier. This can lead to people who should only be able to read data also having the ability to write data, whether they know it or not.

Another really common way that access control can be bypassed is by not having access control on certain resources. You might remember to put access control guards on POST endpoints, but maybe you leave them off PUT or DELETE endpoints. This is a way users can work around the permissions you think you have in place. One way to avoid this is to deny access by default. That way, you have to explicitly allow users to have access to resources.

Another Top 10 issue is injection (*https://oreil.ly/-eyJe*) due to not validating inputs. You need to validate all the inputs you receive from the frontend or direct endpoint calls. Some devs make the mistake of thinking frontend validation will cover them, and that's incorrect. Anytime an endpoint receives a request where the user passes parameters, those values should be validated and sanitized to prevent things like SQL injection attacks and cross-site scripting attacks.

Authentication failure (*https://oreil.ly/1Ctrq*), another Top 10 security issue, happens when you have any weaknesses in your authentication process, such as allowing weak passwords, putting credentials directly in the URL, or even having weak reset-password flows. Some of these weaknesses come from wanting to cater to user comfort. This is part of those trade-offs you have to consider when you decide what type of authentication to use.

Some ways you can avoid authentication failure are by enforcing strong user passwords, adding MFA, and limiting the number of logins a user can attempt. These aren't foolproof, and there are still ways for a determined attacker to try to manipulate your authentication. But when you have these things in place along with all the other security layers involved, you have a higher likelihood of preventing attacks.

One vulnerability that often gets overlooked is vulnerable and outdated components (*https://oreil.ly/oN47F*). Once security vulnerabilities have been discovered and patches have been released, any outdated versions of packages or tools will have well-documented attack vectors. Keeping your packages up to date is just as important for security as it is for code maintenance. Making sure your infrastructure is using the most up-to-date version of services is another way to keep everything as secure as possible.

The last vulnerability from the Top 10 that I'll go over is insecure design (*https://oreil.ly/7b8xU*) because it's an interesting one. Sometimes your app can be insecure by design or a lack of design. You should consider doing some threat modeling (*https://oreil.ly/q8XOv*) to address this. This modeling should involve a four-step process:

1. What is the feature we are working on?
2. What can go wrong with it?
3. How are we going to handle it?
4. Did we do a good enough job addressing the concerns?

A scenario where this can happen is when placing orders. Is there a way for users to bypass the number of items you actually have in stock? Can they change any order details from an email link? Is there a chance that users might see the wrong information based on conditional checks you have in the code?

It can be harder to spot these vulnerabilities because sometimes they're part of the feature requirement. This is where you have to look at a feature from every angle you can think of. If you need to bring in other teams to get an idea of how something would work, set up a call. Point out any security issues you see when a product owner is explaining how they'd like a feature to work. It might lead to a completely different path for a feature.

Make sure you take a look at the remaining vulnerabilities in the Top 10. Some of these will be discussed later in the book when we get to Chapter 19 on frontend security. But there are a few general security practices you can add to your toolbox that don't fall under a specific topic.

Other Noteworthy Practices

Regardless of the industry regulations your product falls under, you should always implement some kind of audit trail for any data changes or event triggers. At the bare minimum, include fields like the updated date and the ID of the user who made the update. This can help you identify users and services that are causing issues with things like unexpected data access, and you can determine when the attack started. You might even consider adding audit trails on your GET requests if you want to track who accessed data across time.

Using a tool like Snyk (*https://snyk.io*) or Veracode (*https://www.veracode.com*) is a way to automatically scan your code for most known security vulnerabilities. You'll include these kinds of tools in your DevOps pipelines; that will come up in Chapter 27. These tools will even point out dependencies that have vulnerabilities in them. When you get reports on the app's vulnerabilities, take some time to go through them and think about the best approach to handling them. You may decide to replace packages or use other services.

It's important to note that there are a few different types of security testing going on. One of the first you should implement is Static Application Security Testing (SAST) (*https://oreil.ly/USD_5*). This will analyze your code for known vulnerabilities and insecure code patterns. This is how you can check your code before you run it. To check your code while it's running, similar to how an attacker would, you can use Dynamic Application Security Testing (DAST) (*https://oreil.ly/UeAJ-*). You'll work with the DevOps team to add this to your pipeline.

Advocate for things like regular penetration testing (pen testing) (*https://oreil.ly/m2X7l*). This is usually when a team of ethical hackers are contracted to try to find weaknesses in your system. They write up reports with their findings and some potential solutions. This might also fall under the tasks that the Security team handles. Some companies even put out bug bounties (*https://oreil.ly/3QWN2*) for anyone who can find legit vulnerabilities in their live apps. Apps need to be attacked from as many angles as possible so that you can proactively harden them against real attacks.

Real attacks usually come from black-hat attackers (*https://oreil.ly/3QWN2*). They are the opposite of white-hat attackers, who only use their skills to help identify and resolve vulnerabilities. Black-hat attackers are who you're trying to keep from getting unauthorized access to different parts of your app. There are also grey-hat attackers (*https://oreil.ly/6_65O*), who usually find vulnerabilities without permission but don't exploit them with malicious intent.

Do regular industry-specific audits to make sure the app still meets all the required regulations. Likely, a legal team will be involved somewhere in the background to make sure everyone remembers this, but if not, go through your code and make sure it's compliant. Encrypting user PII and giving users access to their data are examples of things you should check for.

Update your dependencies as often as you can so that you don't miss any security patches. A tool like Dependabot (*https://oreil.ly/LBdN5*) will help you with this. You'll find that some apps are several major versions behind on certain packages, even though the vulnerabilities are well known and documented. This is one of those tech-debt things you'll want to work with Product to prioritize in the backlog. It's much easier to do updates incrementally than trying to update when there have been several breaking changes.

Something else you need to consider with your dependencies is supply chain security. We often use open source software, which has its own dependencies that could have vulnerabilities. These vulnerabilities could be intentional, such as if a package causes distributed denial of service (DDos) attacks on your server (*https://oreil.ly/S1Bld*). Or they could be accidental, such as if someone on the team installs a copycat version of a package (*https://oreil.ly/-rKKg*). You can use this supply chain security framework (*https://oreil.ly/gzXlO*) to help watch out for any vulnerabilities introduced from third-party dependencies in your app.

You also need to rotate any access tokens or credentials you use with your third-party services or other tools. I've seen companies that have had the same tokens for years and then had to take days to figure out why the system is broken because the service they used finally expired the token. Rotate them a few times a year at least, but see if the Security team has any rules.

Considering Developer Experience with AuthZ Testing

Here are more great insights about working on real-world projects from Ethan Brown:

> The DX of AuthZ is something that often gets overlooked. I worked on a large project that had extensive AuthZ requirements. At first, all the developers just gave themselves a "superuser"-type policy so they could get features done. The problem is, when we started doing user acceptance testing with actual users with restricted permissions, a lot of functionality was broken because developers hadn't "role-played" as they were developing; they just did everything as a superuser. This led us to introduce a "Developer" policy, which didn't directly provide any elevated authorization except the ability to assume any role with a handy "role switcher."

> This got development moving more smoothly. Once devs could easily switch roles without logging out and in or having multiple user accounts or multiple browsers, role-based feature development got a lot easier. Not only does it make development less painful, it subtly keeps roles in the front of developer's minds, so they're more aware of AuthZ considerations.

Take some time to learn how to do some basic attacks yourself! This falls under ethical or white-hat hacking (*https://oreil.ly/2oF2I*), where you can use hacking skills to find and document vulnerabilities so that they can be remedied. PortSwigger's Web Security Academy (*https://oreil.ly/ZzNSw*) has great resources on the different types of attacks that commonly come up. You can also look up some of the tools attackers commonly use, such as sqlmap (*https://sqlmap.org*), Wireshark (*https://www.wireshark.org*), John the Ripper (*https://github.com/openwall/john*), or even the whole Kali Linux OS (*https://www.kali.org*). You don't need to be an expert, but it's cool to see how things work from an attacker's perspective. It'll help you learn ways to better defend your code because you know what attackers will be trying to do.

Conclusion

This chapter was more of a discussion on security than going over any code implementation. That's because the things you need to look out for can be less obvious than the code you'll write. Security concerns slip into places you may not originally look at, such as logging and monitoring or feature requirements. We'll go over logging in detail in the next chapter because it also helps with debugging.

The goal of this chapter is to make you aware that you should consider security at every point of development, from discussions with other teams to the code you write. There are already a lot of questions to ask as you develop, but one that should stay at the top of your mind is this: is this secure? If you can show a vulnerability in it, then someone whose specialty is security can probably find even more. Your knowledge of security can go as deep as you like, but you don't need to know the details of hashing math and encryption to understand how to effectively use the tools.

## CHAPTER 9

Backend Debugging

No matter what you do, you'll have to have solid debugging skills and processes. Being able to sort through possible issues quickly is going to get you to the root cause efficiently. There's not a strictly right or wrong way to perform your debugging, although there are some things you should definitely check for.

Debugging is an art of persistence with the discipline of a systematic approach because it's going to take some twists and turns and lead to some dead ends. Often, the code causing the bug isn't very complex. It might be a one-line change, but the path to finding that one line can take days. I'm going to give you some tools and strategies that will hopefully get you to the root cause as fast as possible.

In this chapter, I'll cover:

- Detailed log messages
- Environment configurations
- Tools you can use
- Strategies for tracing bugs
- How to help others find bugs

Debugging is one area where you will be looked up to for help. When some of the less experienced developers run into issues with their code, you'll be one of the people they turn to. This is a great opportunity to mentor another developer as well as learn from them. Some bugs are just too big for one person to track down because of how complex a system gets. Over time, all the team members will develop expertise in specific parts of the app, which means you'll get farther faster when you help one another.

Detailed Log Messages

One way you can start helping the team is by writing log messages with useful information. There isn't a limit to the number of logs you can include in a method, so you'll have to decide what information is most important for everyone to see. Let's take a look at some of the log messages already in the project and see how you can strengthen them.

The *stripe.service.ts* file is a good place for more logging. This time, we'll go through the `createProduct` method because it has quite a few moving parts. You're making a database update and calling different endpoints from a third-party service. If something happens in this chain of calls and updates, how will you be able to trace what happened? Let's add some logs and improve the existing ones:

```
public async createProduct(product: CreateStripeProductDto) {
  this.logger.debug(
    `Started product creation in Stripe with product data:
        ${JSON.stringify(product, null, 2)}`,
  );

  try {
    const productResponse = await this.stripe.products.create({
      name: product.name,
      description: product.description,
    });
    this.logger.log(
      `Response from stripe.products.create sdk:
          ${JSON.stringify(productResponse)}`,
    );

    this.logger.log(
      `Add price info for product id: ${
        productResponse.id
      }, unit_amount: ${1009}, currency: ${'usd'} with stripe.prices.create sdk`,
    );
    const priceResponse = await this.stripe.prices.create({
      product: productResponse.id,
      unit_amount: 1009,
      currency: 'usd',
    });
    this.logger.log(`Response from stripe.prices.create sdk:
        ${JSON.stringify(priceResponse)}`);

    const productRecord = {
      stripeProductId: productResponse.id,
      name: productResponse.name,
      price: priceResponse.unit_amount,
    };

    this.logger.log(
```

```
        `Create product table record with productRecord:
            ${JSON.stringify(productRecord)}`,
    );

    try {
      const [dbProduct] = await this.prisma.$transaction([
        this.prisma.product.create({ data: productRecord }),
      ]);
      this.logger.debug(`Created product id: ${dbProduct.id} in product table`);
    } catch (err) {
      this.logger.debug(
        `DB rollback for product record: ${JSON.stringify(
          productRecord,
        )} with error: ${JSON.stringify(err)}`,
      );
    }
  } catch (err) {
    this.logger.error(
      `Stripe failed with status: ${err.status} and error:
          ${JSON.stringify(err)}`,
    );

    throw new Error(`Stripe failed with status: ${err.status}`);
  }
}
```

There are nine log messages here, and you could add more if you want. You'll notice that each one that passes an object in the message is stringified. Without this, you end up with a lot of instances of [Object object] in your logs, and that's not going to help you debug. You might even include the environment in your log messages specifically, but many tools like Datadog (*https://www.datadoghq.com*) or Sentry (*https://sentry.io/welcome*) have something like that built in. If you want to see all this information at a glance, it doesn't hurt to include it, though. You'll learn more about the specifics of monitoring tools in Chapter 12.

You can also see that different log levels are being used. The common log levels are trace, debug, info, warn, error, and fatal. The *debug* level is used for diagnosing issues or when you're working in a test environment to make sure everything is running correctly. The *trace* level is like a more verbose form of the debug level. Trace logs give you all the info about what's happening in your app and in third-party dependencies you use. These aren't commonly used and typically come up only when you need granular visibility into a specific part of the app.

How to Determine an Adequate Amount of Logging

Here's some more advice from Jeff Graham on logs:

> Determining the "right" amount of log messages can be tricky. You'll want as much info as possible to debug, but it can be cumbersome to scan through a long list of log entries. It's good to test logs locally: could you diagnose a problem with your API by only reading the logs? There are also products to manage and search logs: Cloud-Watch, Splunk, Datadog, New Relic, and many more.
>
> Logs can also unexpectedly contain PII or other secure details: credit card numbers, API tokens, addresses, etc. It's important to make sure these details are removed or obfuscated from production logs.
>
> Lastly, don't be the engineer who doesn't read their logs until the first production issue occurs. You'll likely find yourself wishing you had better details to use in debugging.

The *info* level is very commonly used in logs to show that something happened. This is how you can see authorization requests, determine what parameters were used in an API call, and keep an eye on the state of the app. Info logs shouldn't contain important details that would be needed if an issue arises with the app.

The *warn* level is used to show that something unexpected happened in the app, but it didn't stop the app from running. This could happen if data is parsed incorrectly, for example.

The *error* level should be used whenever something stops the app from functioning as expected. This typically includes 4xx errors and 5xx errors. An example of an error log would be if Stripe were down but a user could still try to place an order through a backup service or if one of the user's login methods isn't working. A *fatal*-level log is reserved for when a core piece of business functionality is down, such as if your users are trying to get their order info but can't because the database is having issues or if a user can't log in to the app because all the login methods aren't working.

It helps to use logging at the correct level. Being able to quickly distinguish between error logs and debug logs will help you get answers faster than if everything is at the same level. Check for things like the API version in the request, any parameter issues, the source of the traffic, and the times and dates logs are generated. These are some quick-start points to figure out what's happening. That way, you can catch patterns like certain errors being thrown when specific values are sent. This can also help you find concurrency issues because you'll be able to see when a request call started, when it returned, and anything that happened in between.

Another thing to be cautious of is having nested `try-catch` blocks. Pay close attention to how you handle errors because it could lead to a case where errors are unexpectedly suppressed through these blocks.

Something to keep in mind is that when you log errors from somewhere else, you need to pass that original error within your log. It's easy to hide the real error message when you might catch the error with custom handling. Anytime you use a third-party service, it will help to log the requests you make as well as the responses you receive. Here's a snippet to highlight this from the previous example:

```
try {
    const productResponse = await this.stripe.products.create({
      name: product.name,
      description: product.description,
    });
    this.logger.log(
      `Response from stripe.products.create sdk:
          ${JSON.stringify(productResponse)}`,
    );
} catch (err) {
    this.logger.error(
      `Stripe failed with status: ${err.status} and error:
          ${JSON.stringify(err)}`,
    );

    throw new Error(`Stripe failed with status: ${err.status}`);
}
```

Since you have custom error handling here to log the error, you should be intentional about preserving the original error response that comes directly from Stripe and triggers the `catch` part of this block. That's what the error log does in the example.

 This is a place where testing can really shine because ideally, you should have a unit test written for each possible path the code can take. That can help you catch bugs during development, too. You should have a test case for each error scenario, which can help you find if messages are suppressed under custom error handling.

When you go through these logs, you'll get all kinds of good info. You'll be able to filter logs based on the time when issues happen, which gives you insight into how code was executed. For example, if there are errors creating products on Stripe, you'll be able to see when calls were made and what data was sent to cause the errors. You might find things like multiple calls happening at the same time, leading to race conditions that then lead to data inconsistency.

If you have a bug and nothing in the code looks wrong, go look in the logs. Here's an example of what some log entries might look like:

```
[Nest] 90322  - 06/19/2024, 1:43:22 PM   DEBUG [OrdersService] Create order
called with: {"user":{"id":5,"roles":["Customer"]},
"order":{"total":23.54,"userId":5,"products":[{"id":"aperiam"},{"id":"ipsa"}]}}
[Nest] 90322  - 06/19/2024, 1:43:22 PM   ERROR [ExceptionsHandler] Cannot read
properties of undefined (reading 'includes')
```

```
TypeError: Cannot read properties of undefined (reading 'includes')
    at OrdersV1Controller.create (/Users/milecia/Repos/dashboard-server/src/
        orders/orders.controller.ts:29:21)
    at /Users/milecia/Repos/dashboard-server/node_modules/@nestjs/core/router/
        router-execution-context.js:38:29
    at processTicksAndRejections (node:internal/process/task_queues:95:5)
    at /Users/milecia/Repos/dashboard-server/node_modules/@nestjs/core/router/
        router-execution-context.js:46:28
    at /Users/milecia/Repos/dashboard-server/node_modules/@nestjs/core/router/
        router-proxy.js:9:17
```

Figure 9-1 shows an example of logs from Google Cloud Platform (GCP) so that you can see a different tool, but don't worry about the details of what's in the screenshot. You'll get a better look at logging tools later in the book.

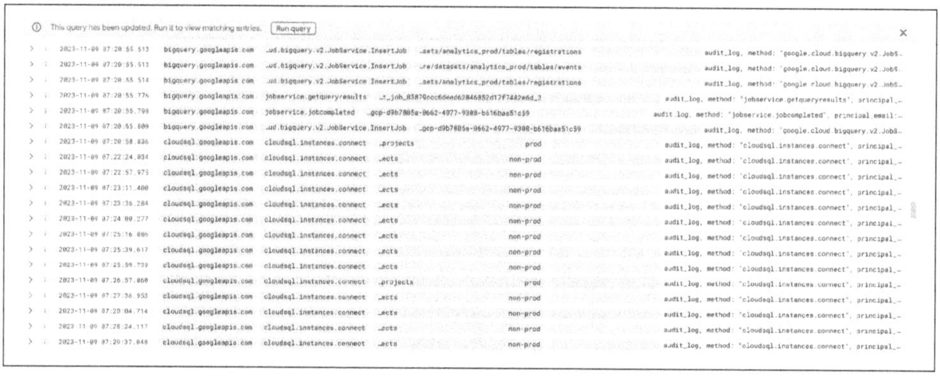

Figure 9-1. Logs in GCP

Here's what the details of one of these logs might look like:

```
{
  "protoPayload": {
    "@type": "type.googleapis.com/google.cloud.audit.AuditLog",
    "status": {},
    "authenticationInfo": {
      "principalEmail": "customersync@customerstore.iam.gserviceaccount.com",
      "serviceAccountDelegationInfo": [
        {
          "firstPartyPrincipal": {
            "principalEmail": "service-309022651100@serverless-robot-prod.iam.
                    gserviceaccount.com"
          }
        }
      ],
      "principalSubject": "serviceAccount:customersync@customerstore.iam.
          gserviceaccount.com"
    },
    "requestMetadata": {
      "callerIp": "2600:1900:2000:a5::1:400",
      "requestAttributes": {
```

```
        "time": "2023-11-09T15:09:16.934724Z",
        "auth": {}
      },
      "destinationAttributes": {}
    },
    "serviceName": "cloudsql.googleapis.com",
    "methodName": "cloudsql.instances.connect",
    "authorizationInfo": [
      {
        "resource": "projects/customerstore/instances/customer-non-prod",
        "permission": "cloudsql.instances.connect",
        "granted": true,
        "resourceAttributes": {
          "service": "sqladmin.googleapis.com",
          "name": "projects/customerstore/instances/customer-non-prod",
          "type": "sqladmin.googleapis.com/Instance"
        }
      }
    ],
    "resourceName": "projects/customerstore/instances/customer-non-prod",
    "request": {
      "instance": "us-central1~customer-non-prod",
      "project": "customerstore",
      "@type": "type.googleapis.com/google.cloud.sql.v1.
          GenerateEphemeralCertRequest"
    },
    "response": {
      "ephemeralCert": {
        "kind": "sql#sslCert"
      },
      "@type": "type.googleapis.com/google.cloud.sql.v1.
          GenerateEphemeralCertResponse"
    }
  },
  "insertId": "-sae16ve1degi",
  "resource": {
    "type": "cloudsql_database",
    "labels": {
      "project_id": "customerstore",
      "database_id": "customerstore:customer-non-prod",
      "region": "us-central1"
    }
  },
  "timestamp": "2023-11-09T15:09:16.909393Z",
  "severity": "NOTICE",
  "logName": "projects/customerstore/logs/cloudaudit.googleapis.com%2Factivity",
  "receiveTimestamp": "2023-11-09T15:09:17.392870312Z"
}
```

You're going to check the time that the logs occurred, the services they came from, and what information is contained in them. If you're debugging, focus on the logs that are from the endpoint or service you're troubleshooting. Check the status codes that are returned because that can take you to the exact location of the bug in the code. Look for any auth messages to see if that's where the problem is. From there, see if any missing or invalid parameters have been passed. Also check the frequency of the bug in the logs and see if you can trigger the action that creates the log yourself. That'll help you figure out how to resolve it with a systematic approach.

Environment Configurations

I'll go into way more detail about things like CI/CD pipelines, deployment tools and strategies, and other related infrastructure topics starting in Chapter 25. For now, I'll focus on specific environment configurations that may be in your codebase or somewhere that you have easy access to, like CircleCI (*https://circleci.com*). The following code snippet is an example of an environment config file, and Figure 9-2 shows these environment variables in CircleCI:

```
# .env file
DATABASE_URL="postgresql://your_username:your_password@localhost:5432/dashboard"
STRIPE_SECRET_KEY="your_secret_stripe_key"
```

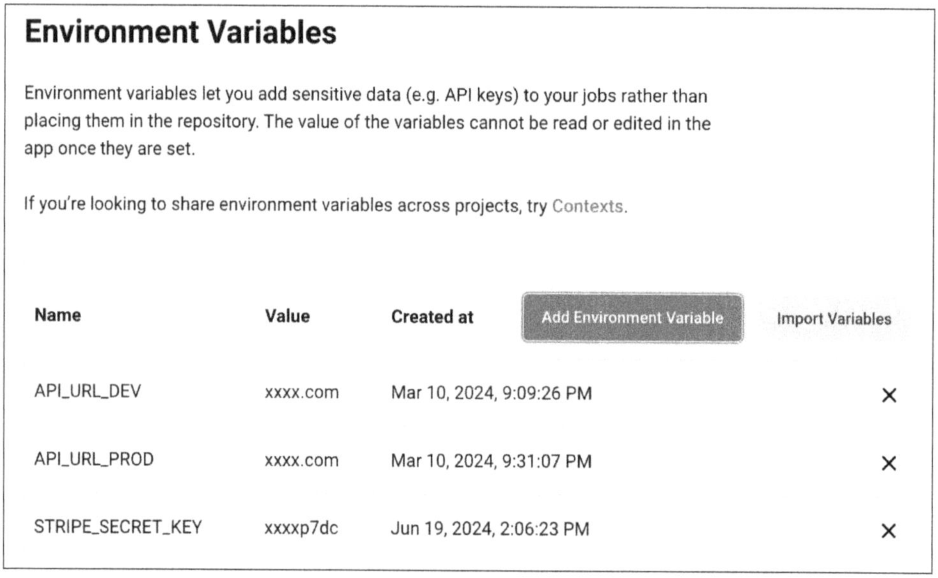

Figure 9-2. Environment variables in CircleCI

When you add new third-party services or need new environment variables, make sure that they actually get added. This is an easy step to overlook in the process of getting everything else out. These types of errors will usually come up quickly in your CI/CD pipeline, and you can add the values in the correct places. This is a good place to make a technical ticket so that everyone on the team remembers it needs to be done, not just you.

See if any roles are missing from the request based on the access token. This might be something a little trickier to pin down, depending on how your logs and error handling are set up. Ask around and see if any new permissions were added based on security updates or new features. Also check that your services have the right roles and permissions being passed to in their requests.

Make sure your changes are getting deployed to the correct environment. This is especially true the first few times you do any deployments in new environments. Check out the deployment artifacts and see if file hashes match what you expect. A *deployment artifact* is the actual build with all the bundled code and metadata that is produced when your code is compiled to what gets run on the server. You can see these in your cloud platform in a service like an Amazon S3 bucket. The *file hash* is the unique string identifier for each artifact. Sometimes you might see that an artifact has been deployed, but when you check the hash, you find out it's the same version as a previous artifact.

When you don't see the changes you pushed, it becomes harder to debug the issue because it's not related to your change. This happens occasionally, and it can take some time to dig through and get to this check.

If you have a complex deploy pipeline that moves your application across different parts of the infrastructure, check each stage. You might find success messages that still have errors being thrown by the infrastructure service. Go through the logs in each stage to ensure that no unexpected errors are sneaking through silently.

 As you get deeper into debugging issues, you will inevitably end up looking at some part of the infrastructure. That's where some lines of responsibility can get blurred between the dev team and the DevOps team. Both should look through infrastructure logs to see if a command or something didn't execute as expected and determine if that's a code issue or an infrastructure issue. That will help decide who handles the issue and makes the updates.

This brings up another reason to make and maintain a system architecture diagram: you know exactly how everything fits together, and you can see where things might have gotten tangled. Seeing the architecture will remind you of things like having an updated access token for your background and cron jobs. It'll also help you consider other parts of the system that could be causing the issue, which you wouldn't have initially thought about.

Strategies for Tracing Bugs

When you've been digging through logs and code for a while, it's easy to get stuck in a certain place. You may have been looking at the same few files for hours, maybe even days. Go for a walk or work on something else for a while. It always surprises me how fast I can figure out a bug once I've had some time away from it.

If you can't break out of the weeds, then shift your focus to another part of the app that might cause the issue. Ask a teammate for a few minutes to talk through the problem with them. A rule of thumb I've found useful is to try debugging on your own for about 30 minutes, and if you haven't gotten past the initial error, reach out to someone else. Giving yourself distance and getting help from someone not as close to the problem give you a different perspective to approach debugging with. You could consider using online forums like Stack Overflow or a Discord server to help you get going. Just remember to make your code generic so that you aren't leaking organization info. Try all of these to make your debugging super effective.

 Debugging is definitely an area where AI tools like ChatGPT can help. Sometimes you can type your question into the chat box, and the output it gives you is similar to talking with another dev. Depending on the rules your organization has around protecting the code, you may even be able to copy-paste a snippet in the tool and get some really good feedback on things to try.

Use *console.log*! This is the simplest debugging tool you have available. You can log every line of code if it helps you figure out what's happening. Using console messages can show you any unexpected calls or data transformations as they happen. Also don't be afraid to try some hacky code to reproduce the issue and test out a theory or a potential fix. When you're looking for the root cause, you don't have to keep code PR-ready. Test out your thoughts, and then you can clean it up.

Here's an example of how you might write hacky code to figure out if an endpoint is working. You can slowly uncomment code and manually update the user and order inputs to see if one of those is causing the error to throw:

```
// if (!user) {
//    throw new HttpException('Unauthorized', HttpStatus.UNAUTHORIZED);
// }
// if (!user.roles.includes('Customer')) {
//    throw new HttpException('Forbidden', HttpStatus.FORBIDDEN);
// }
// if (!order) {
//    throw new HttpException('No order data', HttpStatus.BAD_REQUEST);
// }
// if (order.products.length === 0) {
//    throw new HttpException('No products in order', HttpStatus.CONFLICT);
// }
// if (!order.total) {
//    throw new HttpException('No order total', HttpStatus.CONFLICT);
// }
```

```
try {
  // const newOrder = await this.ordersService.createOrder(order);
  const newOrder = {
    id: 35354252,
    total: 1342.24,
    createdAt: new Date(),
    updatedAt: new Date(),
    products: [],
    userId: 7,
  }
  return newOrder;
} catch (err) {
  throw new HttpException('Something happened', HttpStatus.NOT_FOUND);
}
```

Knowing the tools to help you test your hypothesis will give you more confidence in checking more things. If you think there's an issue with a request or response, try using Postman (*https://postman.com*) to make the request like a client would. When you want to check if data has been updated correctly, use a tool like pgAdmin for Postgres (*https://oreil.ly/LsJrb*). It gives you a quick, graphical way to interface directly with the database, which can help in pairing sessions.

Make some fake data right there in the code and run it locally. Sometimes you just need to hack together some code to reproduce a bug. In the process of reproducing the bug, you may solve the problem. You can find some really interesting third-party bugs this way as you start seeing what the actual response is. You might even be surprised by some unexpected data transformation happening because of a bad function call.

Debugging the backend will take you into the infrastructure occasionally. You'll run into cases where data didn't get deleted because an event threw an error silently two days ago. This is a large process that touches many parts of the system, which can take more time to debug. Get comfortable with it and look through the services as you develop features and fix other bugs. That way, when a big bug comes up, you're comfortable with what you see in the infrastructure.

Double-check the business logic. Sometimes the system is working exactly like it's supposed to, but there are some business conflicts. As you talk through the issues with the Product team, confirm that the business rules are written in the code as expected. This one can be more subtle because it means that you have to have some intuition about how the product works; that's why you need to truly understand what's a bug and what's a feature.

I'll go over incident handling more in Chapters 12 and 23, but it's worth mentioning a bit about it here. Keep people up to date with what you've checked out so far. This will be especially important for large production-level bugs that are affecting users. Communicate your findings as you rule out things. This will help you keep track of what you've done, let the stakeholders know what is going on, and give everyone an idea of how things are going and who can help.

Helping Other Devs Debug

Knowing how to help others debug their issues is a huge skill to have. This is where you can bring in a few approaches. First is the scientific method, where you come up with a theory about what the problem is, create a test, and then run the test. A good example of this is a forbidden error like the following:

```
if (!user.roles.includes('Customer')) {
  throw new HttpException('Forbidden', HttpStatus.FORBIDDEN);
}
```

You and the other dev could form a hypothesis that the user doesn't have the Customer role. Then you could test it by calling the endpoint locally with Postman and passing user data with the correct role. After you run the test, you can check the terminal the app is running in to see what errors or messages come up. Then you can repeat this process with a different hypothesis to try something else. Or you can both come up with several hypotheses, try them individually, and report back with your results.

Another method is to construct a specific flow diagram that shows the exact sequence of events and code touched in the pathway of the bug. You and the dev can use a tool like Miro or even just a Google Slide to quickly diagram what's happening. Figure 9-3 is an example of a flow diagram for the same bug as in the previous example.

The next approach is to start breaking down the problem space. See if you can trace the bug to the controller or service. If it's in the controller, then you can stop breaking things down. If it's in the service, see if you can break it down to either service code or something with the database or a third-party service. Keep breaking down the path of the bug until you reach the part of the app it's most likely coming from.

Another approach you can take when helping someone else debug is "rubber-ducking" with them. *Rubber-ducking* (*https://oreil.ly/1i554*) is when you talk through each line of code with an inanimate object or another developer. Just let them talk through the issue while they have your attention. It's surprising how many bugs are resolved just by talking it through with someone else. The act of explaining a bug to someone in normal language can trigger a new thought or reveal something that becomes really obvious when it's said aloud. This can be done on a call or even through messages. The key is to get them to describe the bug and what they are trying to do. Sometimes you don't even need to say or do anything, and they'll figure it out in a few minutes!

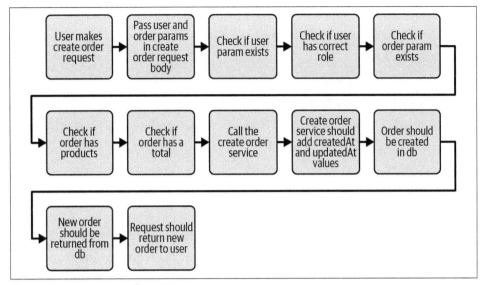

Figure 9-3. Debugging flow diagram

The last approach I'll cover is helping them use tools like ChatGPT (*https://chat.openai.com*) or Copilot (*https://oreil.ly/y0kZy*). These tools can act as automated rubber-ducking because they can analyze your code for inconsistencies. They also make you think about how to describe the issue so that you *can* get help from them. AI tools like these can help simplify the issue for them and give them a blurb about what's going on with the code.

Debugging Checklist

This isn't an exhaustive list of every possible thing to check for when you're debugging the backend, but it is a pretty long one. Mainly, I wanted to point out the specific things you're looking for at each check. It's like cutting into a cake with precision. Hopefully, you can use this checklist as a good starting point if you get stuck in your debugging process:

- Check the application logs
  — Are there any errors? If so, where are they coming from?
  — Is there a certain time when the issue started happening?
  — Can you find any helpful stack traces?
  — Did you go to the line of code highlighted in the errors if there was one?
- Check the access token
  — Is it expired?

- — Does the requester have the correct permissions?
- — Is the token malformed like someone tried to edit it?
- Check the request
  - — Are the correct parameters present?
  - — Do the parameters have the correct types?
  - — Is it a CORS (*https://oreil.ly/cVGm5*) (Cross-Origin Resource Sharing) issue?
  - — Have you checked the headers?
- Check the response
  - — Did it send the expected error?
  - — Was the data in the right format?
  - — Are data transformations happening before the response is sent?
  - — Are any third-party services being called before the response is sent?
- Check the database
  - — Have the expected fields been updated or queried?
  - — When was the last update for the data?
  - — What happens when you run a raw SQL query compared to the query made from the app?
- Check the environment
  - — Did you add the new environment variables?
  - — Have you updated existing environment variables?
  - — Did you add the environment variables to all the infrastructure tools and code that use them?
  - — Has a third-party service rotated values?
  - — Are you deploying to the correct environment?
  - — Can you check the artifact version?
  - — Have you asked someone on the DevOps team to pair with you?
- Check your third-party services
  - — Have any new versions been released?
  - — Did any fields change their names or types?
  - — Can you go through the docs and check the request and response types?
  - — Has anything changed in the dashboard?
  - — Do you need a new API key?

- Check the code
  — Are all your package versions up to date?

  — Have you gone through the methods line by line?

  — Did you try breaking the code down to its simplest form, like in the hacky example, and slowly add code back?

  — Are there any `try-catch` blocks that might suppress errors?

  — How are database errors handled?

  — Does the business logic make sense?

  — Are there other parts of the code that touch this one?

As you go through your career, you can build your own personal debugging list. I have something like that, and it helps me cross things off a lot faster without taking as much mental energy. It's tedious checking all these areas, but it's a thorough way to rule out root causes.

Conclusion

Debugging is going to be one of the areas of development that will require persistence. There may have been times when you wondered how another dev fixed a bug in 30 minutes that you've been looking at for days. It's OK to ask for help because it means you understand how others can help you eliminate potential sources of the bugs.

As your app grows, so will the complexity of your debugging. There's no perfect way to find bugs. Sometimes you'll need to hack together some code, use a lot of console messages, or even change data directly in the database. Remember that this is one of the artistic parts of being a dev. Any approach is valid as long as it doesn't break other things!

## CHAPTER 10

Backend Performance

Now that you've got an app that's ready for production, it's time to look at some performance improvements you can make. This is where you start looking at metrics and tweaking your infrastructure and configs. Making changes to the code can also improve your performance, so never underestimate a good refactor.

How you handle performance updates will vary greatly depending on your app. Deciding where and how to make performance improvements will take insight into how the app works, what's currently happening, and how it's expected to grow. Once you get these data-driven answers, you can start looking at trade-offs among the options you have. I'll go over a few things you might research as your app is used by more people.

In this chapter, you'll learn about:

- Metrics
- Alerts and monitoring
- Caching

- Product considerations
- Other ways to speed up performance

Taking care of performance enhancements can be an exciting time because it means the product is being used. This is one time when having meetings can be helpful because this is going to involve costs to your organization. Stakeholders see the product from a different perspective, and that can help you make decisions about the best approach.

Metrics

To determine if you need to look at performance enhancements, figure out what brought up the topic in the first place. Were users reporting slower load times, or was the server crashing under a certain load? The enhancements can also be a preventive measure. If you know you're releasing an app that users have been waiting for, your servers can hit a utilization level you didn't think was possible.

That's why you turn to the data if you're unsure or you need to explain the reason for new engineering costs to someone. Look through your logs to see if there are any general trends. You might notice one endpoint getting a significantly higher number of requests than the others. You could see that a particular set of endpoints are used the most during a certain time of day. This type of business analysis can guide what enhancements will be most beneficial.

Some backend metrics you'll see include:

- The application's average latency (amount of time the app needs to respond to a request on average, excluding processing time)
- Standard deviation of the latency for responses
- Minimum and maximum latency
- P90 latency (the slowest response in the 90th percentile of the fastest requests)
- Number of requests per second
- Data I/O ratio (the data input metric is the size of the request payloads coming in, and the data output metric is the size of the response payloads going out)
- Peak response time (PRT; finding the longest response times out of all requests coming to the server)
- Hardware utilization, such as RAM and disk space usage
- Number of threads being used across all requests (determines how many concurrent requests are happening at the same time)
- Server load (measures the average number of threads currently running or waiting for CPU time during a specified time range)
- Server uptime rate (percentage of time that a server is available to use)
- HTTP server error rate (how often certain errors occur)
- Apdex (an open standard for aggregating user satisfaction into a weighted average score)

More Insights into Performance Metrics

The metrics we discussed in this section have a lot under the hood. So I got some input from Ethan Brown.

Regarding the P90 latency:

> The P90 latency is the value that partitions your requests into the 90% that are at or above a specific latency threshold and the 10% that are slower than that. For example, if the P90 latency is 100 ms, 90% of your requests are completing in under 100 ms, and 10% are completing more slowly.

Regarding PRT:

> "Latency" is explicitly referring to transport latency (excluding processing time), and peak response time includes processing time. Max latency and PRT are not the same.

Regarding number of threads:

> Node is, by default, a single-threaded server. Unless you explicitly build it to use worker threads, it'll be single-threaded. A server configuration may have multiple Node processes running and do some kind of load balancing, but the usual configuration is scaling instances out, not up. Of course, a single-threaded Node process can handle concurrent requests by using an event loop, but that won't show up in OS threading statistics.

Depending on the focus of the business, there will likely be a subset of these metrics that you'll consider. You'll need to be comfortable using multiple services and finding this type of information in your cloud platform dashboards. The Splunk dashboard examples at logit.io (*https://oreil.ly/sH3wF*) are good examples of what you might look for as you go through your product. They highlight specific metrics that matter most to the users, such as severity errors and network performance. You are doing something similar for your product as you decide which metrics are important. Figures 10-1 and 10-2 are examples of some metrics you may find on a GCP dashboard.

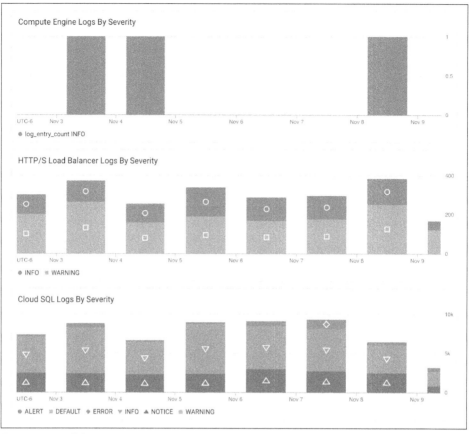

Figure 10-1. GCP metrics

Since these metrics have the most meaning from a production app, it will help you to actually see the numbers in tools being used at your organization or on any project you're working on. If you can make time this week, look through all the server tools you use. If you don't know where to find things or what different metrics are being measured, make sure to ask someone. Get comfortable digging into the areas you might be less familiar with. You don't have to become an expert, but you do need to know enough to be effective.

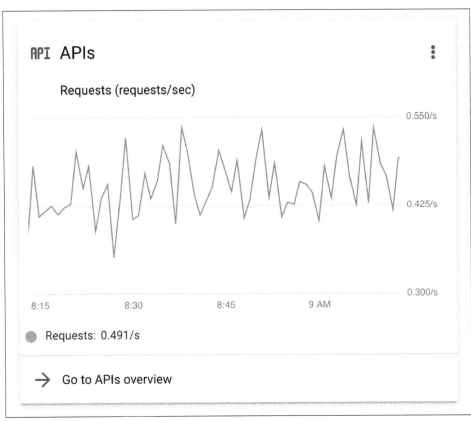

Figure 10-2. API requests per second in GCP

A couple of other optimization improvements you might consider include algorithmic performance and database query optimization. *Algorithmic performance (https:// oreil.ly/EEEIz)* is usually best suited to apps that are computation intensive, such as data-processing apps or apps that handle real-time calculations like in video games. Then you'll consider metrics like time complexity and space complexity. *Database query optimization (https://oreil.ly/_XTON)* is when you refine SQL queries for performance and efficiency in your database. That can include decreasing read or write times or finding ways to target specific data and exclude what you don't need.

I'm not going to go into detail on these last two because they can lead to prematurely optimizing your app. As you start to see patterns and trends over time, keep everyone up to date. That way, you can prevent performance issues before they become a big thing. Tracking metrics will give you other insights you can use to make operations run more smoothly.

Alerts and Monitoring

Since you'll already be measuring your metrics, you might as well add some automation in the form of monitoring and alerts. Monitoring will help you find when your metrics reach a certain threshold, and alerts will notify you when those thresholds are exceeded. By setting thresholds for your metrics, you can see how often they get close to the max, which will tell you which parts of the app need adjustments.

By monitoring your metrics over the long term, you'll see trends that happen throughout the months and years. This can help you make decisions that can save the organization a lot of money on cloud expenses. You'll be able to see what times of the year require more resources than others, and you can scale up and down accordingly.

 Something cool you can do for your team is to have a quarterly or semiannual meeting just to talk about these metrics. It's a good way to expose more junior developers to things that happen behind the code and give everyone an idea of where technical improvements can be made. You might even include the Product team in this meeting so that they can see where users are interacting with the app the most from a technical side.

Something else you can do with monitoring is trigger events when a metric is within a certain range. You can always use the monitoring and alerts services that come with your cloud platform, such as Amazon CloudWatch (*https://oreil.ly/goYNU*), Azure Monitor (*https://oreil.ly/8ig8-*), and Google Cloud Monitoring (*https://oreil.ly/Nt7vi*). Zapier (*https://zapier.com*), n8n (*https://n8n.io*), and Make (*https://www.make.com*) are other widely used services that integrate with a number of tools. They can help you trigger complex events automatically when your metrics reach a limit. For example, you could have an automation that scales up the resources, sends an email and Slack notification to the dev team, updates a message displayed on the website, and updates a value in a database. No matter what your automation flow looks like, you need to know what's happening.

Alerts are going to help you in a few ways. The biggest is that in production, you can find out about issues as soon as they happen with messages in specific chats or channels with relevant team members. This gets into the practice of ChatOps (*https://oreil.ly/Tn7Lw*), where you use tools to help automate communication between resources and people (Figure 10-3). Alerts help spread the responsibility and awareness of issues across the team. One thing you should stay on the lookout for is how you can enable the team to do more. Make sure that everyone knows how the automations work and what metrics are being monitored.

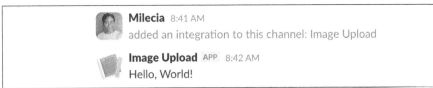

Figure 10-3. Bot integration into Slack

Once you understand where the metrics are and you have some monitoring and alerts set up, write some docs and do a quick call with the team to explain everything. This is a quick way you can level up your team as you learn new things. Your team will also help you level up with the questions they ask. Questions are always good for you because they help you figure out where you can deepen your knowledge.

There's another art involved with alerts. Make sure you send only the most important ones, or else they all tend to get ignored. You'll have to make updates to keep alerts relevant as metrics change. Set aside some time to go through the current alerts, see which ones are happening most often, and make updates accordingly. Also consider having alerts delivered to different places depending on the severity. You might have production alerts sent to a Slack channel and emailed to the team. Other alerts might go to a different Slack channel or skip the email part. You'll learn about all this in detail in Chapter 12.

Once you have all of this in place and it's been through a few weeks of testing, you can start trying out more performance enhancements.

Caching

A few metrics are likely to get monitored at every organization, such as latency. You usually want this number to remain low so that users have the fastest experience possible. Server-side or database caching is one of the enhancements you can add to help with this. Database caching usually involves having a storage location to retain responses from the servers it sits in front of, which reduces the latency by reducing the number of database requests.

Load is another metric you might measure, but it's more complex than latency. If you're using a serverless technology, the load metric probably doesn't matter, or there may be different metrics you would care about. If you're provisioning your own servers to handle your aggregate load, the objective is to find a balance. You don't want load to be routinely low because that would mean you're paying for resources you're not using, and you don't want your servers at high load all the time. So you have to reserve capacity for spikes in usage, which can be difficult to anticipate.

When you use a server-side cache, the server will make a request to the cache first, if possible. The cache contains the responses for the most requested endpoints. This set of endpoints will usually be determined by your monitoring efforts. The cache gets the response values either at a set time interval or when a request is made for the first time within a certain time period. That way, users are getting up-to-date information and not stale data.

If the request data is found in the cache, then the server will never hit the database, which saves time on sending the response. That's how caches are used to improve the server performance. They make sure the database server only gets called when it's necessary and not every time a request is made, as shown in Figure 10-4. This type of caching is also called *database caching* because it reduces the number of queries made.

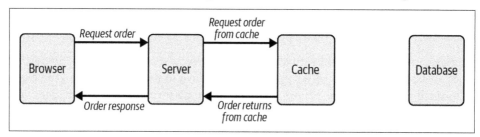

Figure 10-4. Cache hit

 When you are using a cache, it's very important that you don't store PII in it. This is a security vulnerability because there's always a chance someone can attack the cache instead of the server if they figure out what is being used. Cache poisoning (*https://oreil.ly/ 7A7zh*) is a vulnerability attackers can take advantage of by forcing malicious content into the cache that is referenced by users. Users will continue receiving the malicious content until the cache is purged.

Sometimes you will have requested data that isn't in the cache, or the responses in the cache become stale and get removed. When that happens, it's usually a cache miss, like in Figure 10-5. That means the request goes through the cache and hits the database. The server response gets stored on the cache and then sent to the browser.

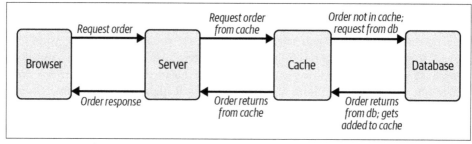

Figure 10-5. Cache miss

Cache Strategies

You can use several cache strategies to maintain the balance of fresh data with fast responses. Some of these strategies include read-through, write-through, write-back, and cache-aside.

With *read-through* (shown in Figure 10-6), the cache is always checked first for data. If the data isn't available on the cache, the request is made to the backend to fetch that data from the database. It's then stored on the cache. There isn't a mechanism to update the data in the cache, so this strategy is best used in situations where the database isn't updated often or the requests are really slow. This doesn't affect how update or create requests are handled. They still go straight to the server and database.

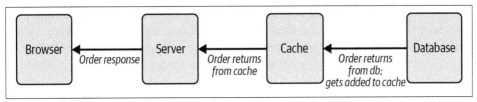

Figure 10-6. Read-through cache strategy

The *write-through* strategy (shown in Figure 10-7) lets you write data to the cache and the database from the requests. This ensures that you always have the most up-to-date data, but it can slow the initial write operation because it's waiting for the database write operation to finish. You'll usually see this strategy implemented along with the read-through strategy to get the best performance.

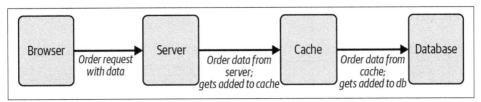

Figure 10-7. Write-through cache strategy

You can also use the *write-back* or *write-behind* strategy, like in Figure 10-8. This is similar to the write-through strategy except you make multiple writes to the cache before the database gets updated. This lets you process user input a lot faster, and you can handle database updates in batches, although you have to be careful to avoid massive data inconsistencies or data loss in case something happens to the cache before the database is updated. Write-back is useful for high write performance when you don't need data immediately in your database, like with image or audio processing.

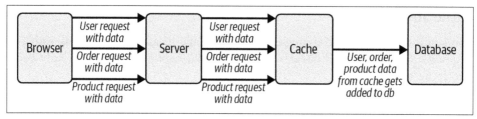

Figure 10-8. Write-back or write-behind strategy

A final strategy is the *cache-aside* approach, shown in Figure 10-9. In this case, the application has to manage the cache. When data is requested, the application will check the cache first. If the data isn't in the cache, then you'll get it from the database and store it in the cache. This approach is a pretty well-rounded one. The main concern here is keeping the cache data up to date. This is a strategy to consider when your resource demand is unpredictable so that you can load data on demand. You can also use this strategy when the cache doesn't have read-through and write-through operations.

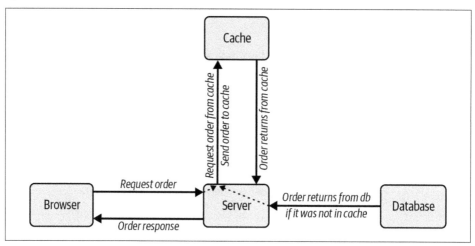

Figure 10-9. Cache-aside strategy

Types of Caching

There are different types of caching, such as caching you build yourself and caching tools; both are typically in-memory. Caching in-memory stores data on the server's RAM. This approach can be useful when you have a large amount of data that rarely changes, such as a product list. This product list might get loaded the first time the user visits the site and then is cached in-memory. Implementing in-memory caching is usually fast, and it provides quick response times. One of the biggest downsides to this type of cache is that the data is gone whenever the system is restarted or the RAM is cleared.

Some common caching tools include Redis (*https://redis.io*) and Memcached (*https://memcached.org*). With a caching tool, you don't have to worry about implementation details. If you're working on an app that has users around the world, this type of cache makes sense. You can have cache servers in different regions so that they can get fast response times with a distributed cache system.

Having distributed cache servers with these tools is a cost-effective way to make data available all over the world. Some drawbacks are that data consistency can become a problem and the system can become complex to manage. When there are data-consistency issues, some users might see a different set of data than others. Once the distributed system is large, it can be hard to trace issues and manage configs.

There's also client-side caching, but I'll come back to that in Chapter 20. Once you've figured out how to add caching to your architecture, take a break and step back to look at it from a different angle. Figure 10-10 shows an example of how you can add Redis caching to your architecture.

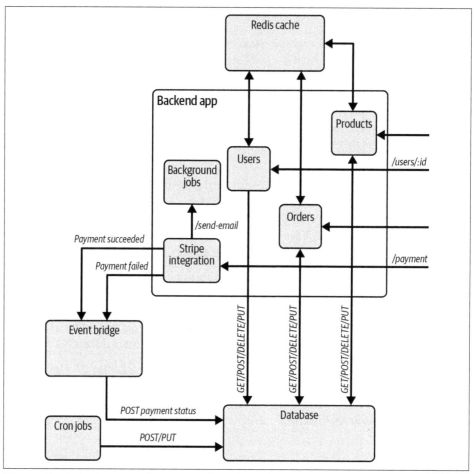

Figure 10-10. Architecture diagram with Redis cache

Cache Implementation with Redis

Just so you have an idea of how the code would look to work with Redis, here's an example with the products controller in the project. First, you'll need to configure the app to use caching with your Redis server. You can experiment with a Redis instance in Docker (*https://oreil.ly/7mukL*). Once you have your Redis credentials, you'll need to install a few packages and then update the `imports` in your *app.module.ts* file:

```
// app.module.ts
…

@Module({
  imports: [
    AuthModule,
    OrdersModule,
```

```
      StripeModule,
      ProductsModule,
      UsersModule,
      ScheduleModule.forRoot(),
      // makes cache available to all modules in the app
      CacheModule.register({
        isGlobal: true,
        store: redisStore,
        host: process.env.REDIS_HOST,
        port: process.env.REDIS_PORT,
        username: process.env.REDIS_USERNAME,
        password: process.env.REDIS_PASSWORD,
      }),
    ],
    ...
```

The `CacheModule` has all the values you need to connect to your Redis instance. You can check out the full code in this file (*https://oreil.ly/XbVM2*) to get the details; for example, `redisStore` is an imported package. All the environment variables are values that you will get from your Redis dashboard.

Now you have to update your endpoints to actually use this cache. Let's look at the products controller and see how you can cache the response for fetching all the products:

```
// products.controller.ts

...
  // Automatically cache the response for this endpoint
  @UseInterceptors(CacheInterceptor)
  @CacheKey('products')
  @CacheTTL(30) // override TTL to 30 seconds
  @Get()
  public async products(): Promise<Array<Product>> {
    return await this.productsService.products({});
  }
...
```

This involves some imports, so I encourage you to look at the full code in this file (*https://oreil.ly/tASkx*) so that you have all the context. There are three big things to note here regardless of the framework you use:

- The response from this endpoint is automatically being cached. That's something you want to happen on the busy endpoints so that the user experiences those speed improvements.

- Define the cache key. Your cache stores data in key-value pairs, so this cache key tells you where to look for the data.

- The cache time-to-live (TTL) value dictates how long the value will remain on the cache before it's declared stale.

You can do more advanced things with your cache, like storing responses from third-party services you use to speed up your responses. No matter what your framework is or even if you write your backend in straight Node, as long as you have a way to implement the three things I just mentioned, you can implement an efficient caching strategy.

Now that you've implemented your first attempt at caching, it's time to take a look at your performance enhancements from a different perspective.

Product Considerations

It's easy to get caught up in the technical details of your enhancements to the point where you lose sight of what the original problem was. At every step of your enhancement implementation, stop to ask how it affects the product you're building. Does it make things faster and easier for a user, or is there a level of trade-off that needs to be considered? While your caching strategy will decrease latency, how confident are you with identifying and debugging cache issues? Is this something that needs to be considered for team velocity because it needs to be maintained? These are a few questions that may come up as you think about performance improvements from the product side.

 You also want to consider the image of your dev team and the engineering department as a whole within the organization. This is especially true when it comes to monitoring and alerts. Be careful with what you agree is important to report on because it will influence how other teams view you. It shouldn't be this way because of the dynamic nature of software, but how the team is perceived does make a difference in the level of autonomy and trust you have.

Think about performance from a user's perspective and actually test it out. You might try throttling the response rate to compare the difference in latency before and after caching to make sure it has the impact you wanted. Also think about how this can grow in the future. The service you decide to use for caching will help you determine future costs and maintenance.

You should also consider other ways to speed up your app. Maybe you can increase the RAM on the server to handle more requests or bigger loads, or you can increase the number of concurrent requests allowed programmatically. Remember, there's always a trade-off with the time it takes to implement performance enhancements compared to implementing new features. You can start with a quick approach to test a hypothesis and then add some tickets to research and plan a long-term solution. Some things you might consider to determine if an optimization is worth the time include preventing customer churn due to slow responses or comparisons to competitors.

Conclusion

In this chapter, you learned how to find areas for performance improvements. Turn to the metrics you're going to use to measure performance so that you can figure out what improvement means. Look at your monitoring to see where your app consistently crosses the threshold for your metrics.

Once you know which endpoints need to be addressed from your metrics, you can decide how to make your improvements. This might be implementing a caching strategy, increasing resources, or doing something differently in the code. Many of the other strategies you can use start to get into scaling, which we'll cover in the next chapter.

## CHAPTER 11

Scalability Considerations

You've covered everything from the architecture down to the endpoint logic and all the way through security and debugging. You've made some performance updates to ensure your app is running smoothly, so one of the last touches you can make is getting it ready to scale for more users. That means your backend application is "done." You'll add more features, make optimizations, and change things as the product develops and matures, but it's in a state where the core functionality is stable.

Scaling is something that will start costing your company more money because you'll need different tiers of third-party services and maybe even more team members. You know it's time to start considering scaling when your performance enhancements aren't enough to keep up with usage.

In this chapter, you'll get more insight on:

- Types of scaling
- Scaling strategies

Deciding to scale is a huge undertaking because you might need to split existing data or significantly change resources and services. Take a considerable amount of time to research your options and verify what you have available as well as any business limitations you have. The decisions you make for scaling are an important part of how your systems will work going forward because migrations are harder at scale.

Types of Scaling

There are a few different ways you can tackle scaling a backend app. You can scale *horizontally*, which is when you increase the number of instances your app runs on. In an AWS environment, this could mean adding more EC2 instances. Or you can scale *vertically*, which is when you increase the power or size of a resource. That would be like increasing the number of CPU cores or RAM for a single EC2 instance. Or, you may use a combination of these two methods. Let's look at each of these in more detail.

Vertical Scaling

Vertical scaling is usually the more straightforward option if your app isn't already written in a distributed manner because you don't have to change anything in your code. It's the same server you already have with better resources. Many companies will go with this type of scaling first because it usually means changing some configurations quickly. It's also generally a cheaper option because you're still only paying for one resource.

There are some trade-offs with vertical scaling. Since you can have multiple servers that get vertically scaled, this can increase your cost and possibly your susceptibility to points of failure. If something happens to a server, a part of your application can be down with no other resources for the app to try to run on. If you do run into any downtime, that means you don't have anywhere else to divert traffic to. With vertical scaling (shown in Figure 11-1), you also have to consider upgrades because they can become more tedious and lead to required downtime.

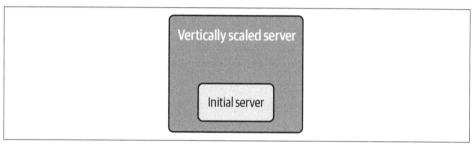

Figure 11-1. What vertical scaling looks like

Horizontal Scaling

With horizontal scaling (shown in Figure 11-2), you have more resilience and a higher guarantee that your app won't experience as much downtime. You'll usually take the current resource settings for your server and duplicate them across multiple instances. With this approach, you'll need to configure a load balancer so that you can spread the traffic across the instances. This makes upgrades easier because you can divert traffic as you make the upgrades. It's usually a more sound solution for commercial products.

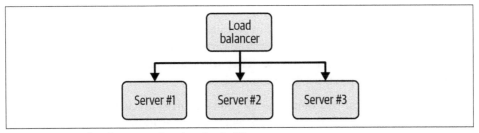

Figure 11-2. What horizontal scaling looks like

However, it will take longer to implement horizontal scaling compared to vertical scaling. This is where a DevOps or infrastructure team would come in to manage and orchestrate all the resources. This is one of those areas where you get to decide how much depth of knowledge you want to gain. You can learn all about provisioning resources and scaling tools (like Kubernetes clusters (*https://oreil.ly/fdpY7*), Docker Swarm (*https://oreil.ly/CUw99*), or Rancher (*https://www.rancher.com*)), or you can stick to a higher-level understanding, which will still help you converse with the DevOps team.

Look at Your Cloud Provider's Scaling Options

Jeff Graham offers additional tips when it comes to horizontal scaling:

> Depending on your app, most cloud providers have ways to manage horizontal scaling for you. Often called "auto scaling," these services can monitor traffic or resource usage and add/remove servers (or other resources) as needed. This can save you both time and cost—you won't need to manage your clusters as often, and it will remove unneeded servers during low-traffic hours (at night, for example). A version of this is usually available for other cloud services too: databases, queues, containers, etc.

Hybrid Scaling

As you learn more about your needs, you may choose to implement a hybrid of vertical and horizontal scaling. There may be some instances that need more resources because of the region where they're hosted. Load balancers can help you avoid downtime by distributing the requests across the different server instances you have. If you know this is going to be a highly utilized app, then it's best to include a load balancer in your initial architecture.

Resource Scaling

Scaling isn't just for your API requests. You might need to scale resources to handle the jobs you run in your queues. A sign that you need scaling here is when data isn't available after the jobs have been running at their normal time. If you check your queues and see that jobs are still waiting, it's time to start looking at scaling. In some cases, that means your jobs may need to be split out to a separate repo. Then you can run them on a separate server and see how vertical scaling works. Another resource you can try scaling is your database. That will allow you to support higher data throughput or accept more database connections.

You have to consider if you want to scale your resources manually or automatically. Typically, autoscaling is the way to go when you're working with cloud services. Something to keep in mind is that when you use autoscaling, it's referred to as *elastic scaling*; that's when your resources increase and decrease in response to the number of requests or events. Elastic scaling is usually for horizontal scaling, but you might find a rare instance of this with vertical scaling.

This is worth exploring if you know your traffic spikes at certain times of the year. This happens a lot on ecommerce and financial platforms during the holidays because people are shopping more than usual. Then after a few months, the traffic goes back to normal. Or services will experience large spikes in usage after a major event happens. Any website that has gone viral unexpectedly could probably benefit from cloud elasticity more than scaling because the increase is short term. When you're scaling an app, there's been long-term consistent usage at this higher level, so you know it's not temporary.

Scaling Best Practices

Once you've made a decision on how to approach scaling, it's time to actually do it. By now, you should have done at least a few performance improvements to make sure scaling is really the route you need to take. Here are some steps you can take to scale your apps.

Make a Plan

I have a template that I've created from doing different scaling projects, which you can find in the project repo (*https://oreil.ly/y_P7T*). This is a good starting point if your company doesn't have a procedure for how scaling should work. Hopefully, it will help you ask some good questions as you start to make a plan with all the other teams you'll work with. A big question that comes up early is if you should stay with your current cloud platform or migrate to another. Scaling is something that should be considered before you fully commit to a cloud platform.

The platform you choose usually depends on a combination of the DevOps team's experience, the tech stack you've chosen, how well the platform works with your suite of external services, and the services it has available. When it comes to scaling, you should be able to implement the type you want with ease in your cloud platform. So consider what you have available before migrating becomes a serious option.

I worked on a project where we had to migrate from Heroku to AWS because of some changes Heroku made. That was honestly a painful process that took about a year and a half and involved multiple teams. In another project, we migrated from GCP to Azure because the parent organization switched over to Microsoft products for everything else. This took almost two years. Think about the big, long-term picture when deciding on the cloud platform because if you need to migrate for any reason, it's a massive undertaking.

After you know that your cloud platform is what you want, then you can decide on the metrics you want to measure and monitor to determine when to scale your apps; we discussed many of those metrics in Chapter 10. You'll need to decide which teams are involved and responsible for handling and testing the scaled app. There will be a rollout plan and a rollback plan to ensure that all teams are expecting the update, that they know what they can expect, and that there is a way to undo the changes if anything goes wrong. There will also be a test plan to double-check that the app is still functioning correctly and meeting the new performance requirements.

Finally, there will be a cost analysis to make sure the type of scaling you choose isn't creating a large cloud bill. In almost every case, you'll go with a horizontally scaled, automated approach, but you may find that a scheduled approach will keep your bill lower or more manageable if you only want to ramp up resources during a specific time.

Document the Plan

Document the details and decisions for the scaling choice. The question of why this approach was chosen will come up a few times throughout the process, so have the architecture diagram and research readily available. You should update that diagram to show your expected changes as in Figure 11-3, which is a detailed view of Figure 11-2.

As you share the updated architecture diagram, document the questions that come up and the discussions around them. This will help everyone keep track of each decision point as well as help you keep the whole process organized. Don't be afraid to include comments directly in the diagram because that can give you more context when you come back to discussion points later. Also encourage others on your team to contribute to the docs because that will help distribute the knowledge and give everyone a deeper understanding of what's happening.

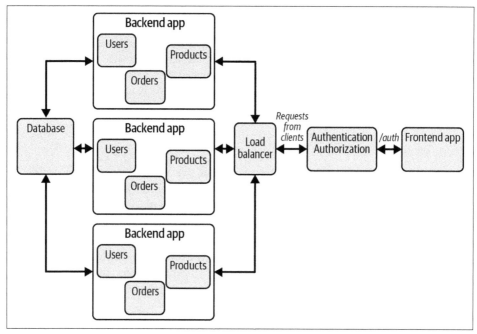

Figure 11-3. Current architecture with horizontal scaling

Run Tests

You'll usually need to have automated tests ready so that some initial checks can be done with the new resources. The first round of app testing with the new scaling in place should be done by you and the dev team. You have deep product knowledge, and you know how the code is supposed to work. You can find those little bugs that no one else will notice. After you've checked everything out programmatically and you see the app is running, double-check the deploy pipeline.

The app should be running on the expected version of Node, and there shouldn't be any issues with dependencies. It's also good to check the logs to see if any errors are being thrown from the new resources. Spend some time with the team going through all the endpoints to make sure they work as expected. This is where your unit and e2e tests will really show their value because you won't have to do as much manual testing. It's still good to run some manual tests, though, so choose some of those high-traffic endpoints to call first. This kind of testing can take anywhere from a few weeks to a few months depending on the complexity of the system.

When you have your scaled approach in place, it's important to perform some stress testing to see how your backend app performs as the number of user requests fluctuates. This ensures that you have scaled your resources appropriately and the system doesn't crash under extreme conditions. It gives you a chance to analyze performance under a great load so that you can determine if your system can handle sudden surges in traffic, see how the system works under unusual conditions, and see how prepared the system and teams are for any unusual conditions.

A few steps are involved with stress testing:

- Planning the test
- Creating automation scripts
- Executing the scripts
- Analyzing the results
- Making any optimizations and tweaks

Planning the test means that you evaluate how the system currently performs and then define a stress-test goal. This could be something like handling 25,000 requests per minute without crashing, maintaining a three-second response time, and showing appropriate error messages. Your automation scripts will simulate user actions that trigger these requests and generate test data to use in the requests.

Then you'll run the scripts and check your logs as you gradually increase the load on the system. At this point, you'll see if you can find any bottlenecks where the system slows down. After all your scripts have been run and you've tested the system under peak load, you'll analyze your results and look for metrics like response times and error rates. Finally, you'll take those results and fine-tune the system to optimize your scaling settings to give you the best balance of cost and expected performance.

Do small tests as you start shifting toward the new resources. Check that the code still runs as expected. You'd be surprised how a change in resources can make the capitalization in filenames matter. So double-check *everything*.

Communicate Progress

Communicate what's happening as you do these small tests. Include other dev teams because they may be doing this one day. Include the Product team so that they understand why feature development is slower than usual during this testing period. Let the Support team know when any testing is being done that affects users so that they can prepare for an influx of messages.

Keep in mind that each team has its own expertise in this process. Your dev team is going to be expected to know the ins and outs of how your code works, the systems it interacts with, and why everything does what it does. The DevOps team is going to take charge of all the infrastructure changes, but they'll have questions for you. The most useful thing you can do as a senior dev is make yourself available to coordinate with the DevOps team. The work that you'll do tends to blur with their work, especially on smaller teams.

Depending on the timeline for the scaling effort, you should bring a more mid-level dev into these conversations so that they can learn how things work behind the code.

The more people who understand how the project is being scaled, the better. This is another way to spread the responsibility for handling bugs and new features. For example, if the app hasn't been containerized until now, the DevOps team will need your help figuring out if the app is running like expected.

Be prepared to have a lot of conversations with the Product team and any other business stakeholders, such as the Support team. They won't need the technical details, but they will need to know timelines and what they should expect as far as performance changes and any downtime. Keep a consistent flow of communication with them so that they know when things are being done and why. This will keep their stress levels down and raise their confidence in what you and your dev team can do.

There will probably be interaction with other dev teams as well because their code might be dependent on your app working. Let them know when changes are expected so that they can plan their feature development around that. If you're really lucky, you'll be the first dev team to go through this process. Then you'll become an expert that other dev teams will call on for help during their scaling processes.

I've worked on projects that have gone through this scaling process a few times, and the biggest thing is always communication. Unexpected technical issues will always pop up, but communication is what helps get everyone through them. Let people know when you've hit a blocker so that the effort doesn't get delayed. Also push back when you know you need more time to test things so that you catch as much as possible before switching to production.

Start Shifting Traffic

Many times, you can work with the DevOps team to trigger automatic scaling so that resources and costs are managed in the most optimal way for user reliability. This is really where the DevOps team should take over and handle everything on the cloud platform. It's another area where you can decide to deepen your knowledge with the cloud platform or learn just enough to do what you need to do.

 Choose your scaling approach as early as possible. I worked on a project once where the decision to implement hybrid scaling was made at the mid-stage in the company. The product was mature enough that the user base was growing quickly and consistently. It took about a year for that effort to finish, and there were so many bumps in that road. Scaling is a huge undertaking that will involve multiple teams across the company, both technical and nontechnical. That's why it's better to think through your scaling approach during the initial phases of the project so that you don't end up in this situation.

You never want to immediately switch all your traffic to freshly scaled resources because there's a chance something can go wrong. A gradual transition to the new resources is a safe approach.

Have rollback plans in case something doesn't work out with the current phase of scaling. During this time, it's not uncommon to have your production server along with your new server resources. This way, you can ensure that users don't experience much downtime as the changes are made.

Slowly shift traffic over to the new resources and see what happens. Stay vigilant as you watch the logs and look for any new errors or messages. It may help to have a separate alert for this new traffic so that you quickly know which part of production to check. It also helps to do this during nonpeak hours, so if something happens, it affects the least number of users.

Once you've completed these steps, you're ready to go over everything with all the teams affected by the changes just to make sure it's all working as expected.

Conclusion

In this chapter, you learned some ways to extend your performance enhancements into a deeper part of your architecture. This is a complex process no matter which scaling approach you choose, and it'll practically cement you into your current cloud platform. That's not a bad thing, but it is something to be aware of, especially if you're using platforms other than AWS, GCP, or Azure. I've worked on migrating across cloud platforms, and it's not the most fun process.

Keeping communication flowing is essential. That doesn't mean you're responsible for overseeing this whole effort, though. It just means you do your part to make sure your dev team isn't blocking anyone or being blocked. Do what you can to document changes and decisions, and be available to help out when you need to. Now you can set your attention on everything with the frontend.

## CHAPTER 12

Monitoring, Logging, and Incident Handling

Now that you have built your backend, it's time to take a deeper look into your monitoring and logging tools. This is where you'll get the info you need to figure out what's happening in your app across different environments and decide how to handle it.

You've set up logging throughout your code, so you already understand what to log and have plenty to test and check for. The goal now is to get meaningful insights from what you're already logging, such as figuring out when incidents are occurring and resolving them.

In this chapter, I'll go over:

- Multiple uses for logs and monitoring data
- How different tools work
- Incident plans for production based on logs and monitoring

Monitoring and logging aren't there just for when something goes wrong. They tell you the story about what is going on across your full stack app and even on the infrastructure level. If you know exactly what happens with the app and when it happens, then you can find out why it happens. This gives you a chance to exercise some creativity and take part in the direction the product goes.

Uses for Logs and Monitoring

Let's start by defining what logging and monitoring are. If you remember in Chapter 9, we talked about logging for debugging purposes. *Logs* are messages that are sent as events happen in your app. These are typically created when an action is triggered so that you have a record of the events that happen. Your logs can initially be sent to a text file somewhere in your system, but you'll move on to more robust logging tools so that you can easily search for messages associated with particular events.

This is where monitoring comes in. *Monitoring* gives you real-time insight into key events and metrics so that you notice errors, unusual activity, and downtime immediately. Monitoring can make your logs more actionable because it will highlight the activities and messages that are the most important. This is crucial for your apps that are in production and actively being used by customers. It's one of the first ways you can determine that an incident is occurring. Before we discuss incident handling, let's go over some of the practical uses of logging and monitoring.

Use Logs for Debugging

As you know, debugging is an important use of logs. Whenever you get a bug or you're looking to see if a job has run, see if you can find it in your log messages. A quick way to figure out where in the code an error is coming from is to search for the log message in the repo. That will take you to the exact line of code where the message is being sent from, and you can start your debugging efforts from there. Take a look at the log messages to see if there are any other errors that occur higher in the call stack (*https://oreil.ly/1BqA1*). That's another way to quickly get to a root cause if you aren't finding anything in the first file you check.

You may find out that you have bugs in production that you can't replicate in staging or locally. Or you may find bugs in staging that don't occur in production. That's when you can debug the differences in your environments to see if there are resource issues or if it's something like a limitation of the test accounts you have for third-party services or in your database.

Sometimes, your logs will show that errors consistently happen in staging, and you need to address them just to keep the messages clear for real errors. Other times, your logs can show you warnings for your code that don't seem to cause issues. Always take a look at the warnings regardless of whether they cause any side effects. Just because the app still runs with a variable being undefined doesn't mean that this is an issue you can ignore. A warning can still lead you to a root cause for an error, but be selective about the warnings and errors you report. Sometimes they create noise you have to sort through, which can lead to everything being ignored, even the important errors.

Another useful thing is tracking bugs through the full stack of log messages. The frontend will often give you a good starting point for where issues are happening because the app will stop functioning there. With your logs, you can look for any backend errors that happened at the same time as the frontend error. That could lead you to the source faster than if you dig through the frontend code. This is one approach that can save you time when the true issue is something with the backend anyway.

Your logs should also be the first place you check when you notice any discrepancies with jobs running. Data sync issues can be tricky to track down because they are dependent on so many layers. By going to the logs, you can find out if your next step should be checking the database for inconsistencies or if there's something in your queue that isn't being executed because there are errors with the infrastructure. You can also use your logs to cross-check if any issues from third-party data coincide with downtime from those services.

Another thing you can do with logs is add more as you debug. You might find that you track down a bug to a certain point but you can't see it unless you deploy to staging. You can add more logs and open small PRs for them that give you more insight into what happened before or after the original log message in your code. It's not uncommon to wrap data-fetching functions with logs that capture parameters that were sent and the data that gets returned. Throw in as many log messages as you need to figure out what's happening. You could also use different log levels like we discussed in Chapter 9, coupled with environment variables to turn log messages on and off.

 Something I mentioned in an earlier chapter is being mindful of how you pass data in log messages. The main reason why is because seeing [Object object] in your messages isn't helpful. If you do run into this, modify your log message to use JSON.stringify or something that extracts the data out of the object because these messages are going to be converted to strings every time.

Logs can be used for more than debugging because they give you actual, real-time insights into how users interact with your app. They also show where you might need to invest in your staging-environment resources or limits you're running into with your third-party services. It can take time to get the most use out of your logs because it's a lot of data to sort through if you don't have a specific goal. Logs can answer a lot of questions, so this is your chance to exercise real technical creativity and come up with interesting questions to find answers to.

Use Monitoring to Inform Your Actions

While the logs will give you plenty of information, monitoring gives you aggregated info that you can act on immediately. Monitoring lets you set up metrics and thresholds for how your app behaves in production or any other environment. You'll have metrics regarding how often endpoints are called, when certain errors are triggered, and other activities that you and the different teams decide are important. These are usually coupled with alerts so that you and the team are aware when unusual activity is happening in the app.

Monitoring gives you actionable information from all of your logs. You and the infrastructure team can take actions based on the metrics you get over time. Monitoring happens in your environment in real time, so you can be aware of when resources need to be scaled up to accommodate more traffic. You can also quickly determine if someone is trying to perform a DDoS attack (*https://oreil.ly/TCcY7*) on your app based on the number of calls and frequency of those calls being made to the backend. Since you know the errors you may encounter, you should set up a metric for the number of errors the app runs into so that you and the dev team can better address them.

The metrics you have from Chapter 10 and upcoming in Chapter 20 can give you other important app data to monitor. These metrics track when your page loading time changes, how long API responses take, and your cumulative layout shift. With monitoring, you'll get graphs and statistics based on these metrics, and you'll have a threshold set for all of them. If that threshold is passed, then alerts will be triggered so that the teams can figure out what the issue is and resolve it. Alerts help make sure that a team will be responsible for addressing issues.

Monitoring and alerts also help make incident response more manageable because the team gets a notification when thresholds are passed. This might seem like something that should be in place by default, but I've worked in places where they didn't set up any monitoring or alerts until the app had suffered DDoS attacks a few times. So whenever we were on call, we had to manually dig through the logs to figure out which endpoints were getting flooded with traffic. That made the process much more stressful compared to after we had monitoring in place. Then when issues came up, the root cause was clearly presented to us, and it was a matter of either working with the infrastructure team or making a quick code update.

Monitoring and Logging Tools

Now let's take a look at some popular logging and monitoring tools so that you have an idea of how they work. I'll go through some logs and show monitoring examples in Datadog (*https://oreil.ly/4bK-m*) because it's one of the more commonly used tools I've seen across organizations. Sentry (*https://oreil.ly/cLJN9*) and LogRocket (*https://logrocket.com*) are also great products that are widely used, and I've worked with these as well. I'll implement logging and monitoring on the backend so that you can see how Datadog works, what its dashboards look like, and some of the features you have access to. Remember that while some of these tools have free trials, they do have a price for production apps.

 Just as a mention, Sentry can be self-hosted for free if you want to test out features more before committing to a purchase. Or you might find that the self-hosted option is perfect for what you need. Do some research to see if the monitoring and logging tool you want to use has a self-hosted option. All the tools mentioned in this chapter offer both logging and monitoring since the functionalities are closely coupled.

Datadog has a 14-day trial so you can test it out. For these examples, you'll work in the backend and trigger errors on endpoint requests and info logs. You'll need to create an account and then set up an agent (*https://oreil.ly/WQ2E4*) to try Datadog. Figure 12-1 shows an example of the output I got running the agent on macOS after following the setup docs.

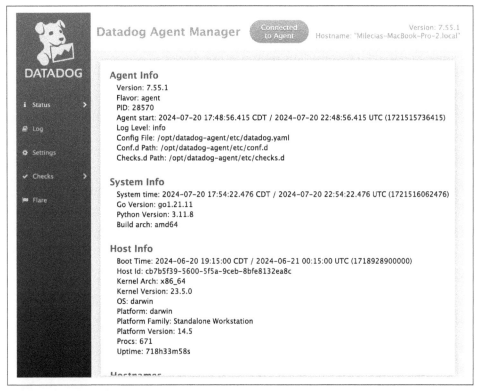

Figure 12-1. Datadog agent running

Validate that your agent is running and then install Datadog's recommended logging tool, Winston (*https://oreil.ly/J7Dcr*):

```
npm i winston
```

Create a utility file called *datadog.ts* in the *utils* folder that will initialize an instance of the Datadog logger with all of the setup from the Datadog docs (*https://oreil.ly/i3POE*):

```
// datadog.ts
import { createLogger, format, transports } from 'winston';

const datadogLogger = createLogger({
  level: 'info',
  exitOnError: false,
  format: format.json(),
  transports: [new transports.File({ filename: './logs/server.log' })],
});

// Example logs
datadogLogger.log('info', 'Testing Datadog logs...');
datadogLogger.info('This is an info log with a blue color', { color: 'blue' });

export default datadogLogger;
```

Then you can add the `datadogLogger` in any controllers or services you want. For this example, you'll add it to the orders controller like this:

```
// orders.controller.ts
…
import datadogLogger from 'src/utils/loggers/datadog';

@Get()
public async orders(@Param() user: User): Promise<Omit<Order, 'products'>[]> {
  if (!user) {
    datadogLogger.error(`unauthorized user: ${user}`);
    throw new HttpException('Unauthorized', HttpStatus.UNAUTHORIZED);
  }
  if (!user.permissions.includes('get:orders')) {
    datadogLogger.error(`forbidden user: ${user}`);
    throw new HttpException('Forbidden', HttpStatus.FORBIDDEN);
  }

  datadogLogger.info('GET /v1/orders requested');

  try {
    const orders = await this.ordersService.orders();
    datadogLogger.debug(`orders: ${orders}`);
    return orders;
  } catch (err) {
    if (err) {
      datadogLogger.error(`orders: ${err}`);
      throw new HttpException('Not found', HttpStatus.NOT_FOUND, { cause: err });
```

```
    }
    throw new HttpException('Generic', HttpStatus.BAD_GATEWAY);
  }
}
...
```

Now if you go to your Datadog dashboard and check out the logs, you'll be able to see whenever a request to GET /orders is made and any associated errors. The dashboard will give you a list of all of the logs that have happened in the past 15 minutes by default, which in production can be thousands of logs, as shown in Figure 12-2.

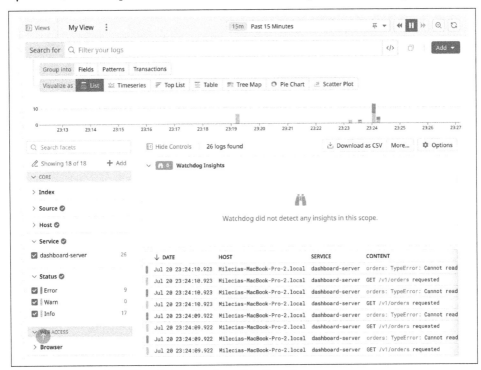

Figure 12-2. Live list of logs being monitored in Datadog

This is one way that monitoring works. You're able to see the events that are getting triggered in real time with some statistics around how often errors are occurring, when they happen, and what they are. By monitoring your services this way, you can use your logs to figure out when incidents happen and start getting to the root of what's causing them. You'll also be able to set up alerts that trigger when certain threshold limits in your monitoring are passed.

You can look through all the logs over a certain time period, or you can filter by log type, service, or some other parameter. Once you find the log you're looking for, you can click on it to get a more detailed view, as shown in Figure 12-3. This will give you info like what was sent in a request or the error thrown for the response. A cool feature with Datadog is that you can send any type of logs to it. It also helps you track stats for how often users trigger certain functionality.

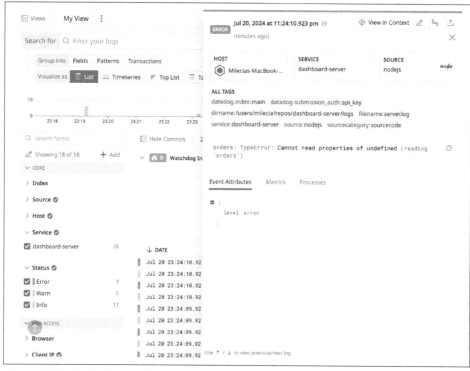

Figure 12-3. A detailed look at a log in Datadog

Datadog has a lot of information available, so you have to learn how to use the filters effectively. If you're logging more than errors, it can take some time to get used to sorting through all the logs. Once you start adding all the backend logs to the dashboard, it will become even more important to have detailed log messages so that you know what data was used for different requests and how that connects to what was sent from the frontend.

Keep in mind that Datadog is just one tool, and the others I mentioned earlier are definitely worth researching more. You may discover that you like another tool's interface better or that it has features you find more useful. Now that you know how logging and monitoring are connected, let's move on to how you can use them to notice and handle incidents that happen.

Incident Playbooks

Despite your best attempts to keep everything free of bugs and errors in production, there will be new and surprising ways the app will mess up. No matter what you do, users will always find ways to break the app unexpectedly, services will go down, and tools will have glitches. That's why you have to have an incident playbook ready to quickly and procedurally address production issues. You need to work with the infrastructure team to create this playbook because they will be involved in the process as well.

Playbook Stages

Several stages go into an incident playbook:

1. Detect an incident
2. Set up incident communication
3. Determine the impact and severity
4. Notify users
5. Notify the right teams
6. Delegate the incident responsibilities
7. Resolve the incident

Let's take a look at each.

Stage 1: Detect an incident

To get started, you have to know what an incident is for your app. This can tie into the metrics you're monitoring, especially around security breaches and downtime. That's why it's important to get your logging and monitoring tool set up in a way that everyone understands and is familiar with. Remember, you can't resolve an incident if you don't know what it is. Once you have defined a list of incidents, when one actually occurs, you and the team won't spend time arguing over what is happening.

Stage 2: Set up incident communication

Once you know what your incidents are, you can move on to setting up the communication channels for them. Something I've seen work is having a designated Slack channel or Teams chat for each incident type. Then you can add the relevant people for each of those incidents to the specified channel. These initial channels are small, sometimes with fewer than 10 people. This keeps the communication more focused, and you all can give updates to others after you figure things out.

Stage 3: Determine the impact and severity

After you have the appropriate group of people in a designated channel, you all will need to assess the impact and severity of the incident. As you look into the severity of the incident, note things like the number of users affected, which services are down and what functionality that affects, whether it's something that can be fixed quickly, and how much the initial research reveals about the problem. This will give you an idea of how much the organization will be affected during the incident. It will also help you figure out how many people should be dedicated to working on the incident and where they should focus. After you and the incident team have determined the impact and severity, check in with the stakeholders and give them this information.

Stage 4: Notify users

Start communicating with users about what is happening. If there's a customer support team, they should be included in the stakeholder communication because they will be talking directly with customers; they need accurate information so that they aren't blindsided. Once user communication has gone out, you can focus on the incident resolution.

Stage 5: Notify the right teams

By now, the teams that need to be included should know they are going to have a role in fixing the incident. Based on the initial research, there should be a direction for all of the involved teams to move in. This is likely going to be some combination of the dev and infrastructure teams working together.

Stage 6: Delegate incident responsibilities

Now you're in the midst of searching for the root cause. Something I've seen work is having an incident call with everyone on it. That way, you can do quick screen sharing when someone finds something, and it makes teamwork more effective because you can throw out ideas as they come up so that no one is silently spinning their wheels. It also helps when you're working with multiple teams on the same call because you can trigger something programmatically and have the infrastructure team see what happens or vice versa. This helps with the optics of your team and the engineering department as a whole, which is under scrutiny at this point no matter what.

Frequently Communicate with Stakeholders During Incidents

Always keep stakeholders up to date with everything you discover during an incident. Since they don't have the same technical knowledge as you or the other teams involved, they won't necessarily understand what is happening. This will help manage anxiety around the incident as well. Every organization wants to have a reliable product for its customers, so when something is wrong, emotional responses can be expected.

Keep the heat off you and the incident group by checking in regularly with updates. Even if the update is that you are still looking into the matter, that's better than

---

absolute silence. A rule of thumb I've found useful is to send updates every 10–15 minutes. This shows that you are treating the matter with urgency and it's your highest priority to get things fixed, which gives stakeholders confidence in all the technical experts involved.

Stage 7: Resolve the incident

Once you think you have a resolution, do some testing among the teams involved before you announce that everything is fixed to the stakeholders. Sometimes it seems like everything is fine until you click a different button. Have multiple people test the resolution in as many ways as you can as quickly as you can. You can update stakeholders and let them know you're working on the resolution, but don't tell them it's ready until there has been some level of testing. Let them know to wait to communicate with users until the resolution has been deployed to production and the teams have done a little more testing there.

Incident Response Template

Now that you know the main stages in an incident response, here's a general template of an incident playbook you can use based on incident response playbooks from Google (*https://oreil.ly/SDfus*); just remember to update it with the details for your organization:

- Identification (Stages 1 and 2)
  - Become aware that an incident is happening through monitoring and alerts.
  - Report the issue to the correct incident response team.
- Incident coordination (Stages 3, 4, and 5)
  - The incident response team triages the incident.
  - The impact and severity are determined.
  - Facts around the incident are gathered.
  - Relevant teams are notified to investigate the incident.
  - Stakeholders are notified with the current findings.
- Resolution (Stages 6 and 7)
  - The facts around the incident are researched.
  - Consistent communication is sent to key stakeholders.
  - Any steps to mitigate damage are taken.
  - The underlying issue is resolved.
  - The resolution gets tested.

— Any affected systems and apps are restored to normal operations.

- Postmortem
    - Have a retrospective meeting on what happened.
    - Make a report that outlines timelines and actions taken.
    - Find areas that can be improved.
    - Plan for any processes or tools that need to be improved or maintained.

Blameless Postmortems

After everyone is sure the incident has been resolved and users have been notified, it's time to do a blameless postmortem (*https://oreil.ly/i7tVn*). This is as crucial as every other part of incident management because it's going to help find places where your playbook can be strengthened and where you can add resilience to your other processes. This is not a place to point fingers or assign blame to anyone.

Incidents don't typically happen because of one person. Usually, multiple things happened leading up to the incident, and understanding what they are and how they all contributed is the purpose of the postmortem. One nice thing about having a dedicated channel to handle the incident is that you get timestamps for everything, so you can see how long the incident lasted and how well the team worked together toward the resolution.

Here's a general template for some things you should cover when you're doing a postmortem:

- Set a meeting time
    - Avoid placing blame on anyone.
    - Focus on the issues that happened in the process leading to the incident.
- Share everyone's findings
    - The incident team should have notes on what they did during the resolution process.
    - Each team member can give the details from the part they reviewed.
    - No detail is unimportant.
- Write a formal report
    - Include everyone's findings.
    - Highlight key actions that happened over the course of the incident.
    - Create takeaways for improvements.
    - Share the report across the organization.

- Praise people for doing things right
  - Consider having a meeting with teams across the organization based on the scale of the incident.
  - If someone made a mistake and owned up to it, publicly praise them for it to encourage a culture of this.
- Review the postmortem a few days later
  - This will give everyone time to take a step back and see if the report is good.
  - Do some role-playing through the steps that happened during the incident.
  - Accept feedback on what could have made the postmortem more effective.

Keeping postmortems blameless gives everyone more confidence to report issues rather than sweep them under the rug. If the first thought someone has when they become aware of an incident is that they might lose their job, that incident could last much longer than it needs to. It can't be emphasized enough that no one person is the point of failure leading to an incident. There had to be, or should have been, multiple checks to go through in a release process. So focus on the process failure, not an individual failure.

You will eventually become an important point of contact when incidents arise. Since you've been involved with setting up much of the core functionality of the app and you've already worked with all the teams that could be involved in an incident, you have a broad view of how things work. This is a time when all your documentation and planning will shine because you won't have to dig through code to find some of the connectivity answers quickly.

The main thing is to keep a calm attitude and approach the situation systematically. Others may be highly anxious because there's an issue in production, so your level-headedness will be a true asset. There's a balance you have to maintain to keep those emotional responses tempered as you and the team work to resolve the issue as quickly as you can. When you look at large-scale incidents, such as the CrowdStrike incident (*https://oreil.ly/w9_zD*), you can see that potentially millions of dollars are at stake and the impact could affect critical services like health care, transportation, and finance. You absolutely have to make sure everyone involved is in constant communication with stakeholders, even as high as the CEO.

Conclusion

In this chapter, I went over the reasons why logging and monitoring are useful and some of the tools you can use. Your team, along with other engineering teams, will look at the logs and monitoring dashboards to help debug issues and get to root causes for incidents. You can debug any errors and get insight into what's happening with your app more efficiently than if you were just looking through code and PRs. It can take some time to set up dashboards and figure out what the relevant data points are. It also takes some digging into the features of your tools because some of them can help you decipher all the data you get from your logs.

The logs and monitoring tools give you an understanding of the life of your app as it continues to grow in production. Make sure you have monitoring in place so that you can set up alerts when anything interesting starts happening in any of your environments, such as resources reaching their limits or endpoints being called an unusual number of times. Any of these could indicate that an incident is occurring. This will save you, the team, and the organization from situations that could have major impacts on revenue and user experience.

## PART III

Building the Frontend

## CHAPTER 13

Setting Up the Frontend

The core functionality of the backend is in place, so now it's time to focus on building the frontend. This is how your customers will be able to use the product and interface with all the backend functionality you have. The frontend is the face of the product your company is building and growing. No matter how cool your data is or how fast your APIs are, if the user experience is bad, then it will be hard for customers to want to use the product.

The frontend requires a different type of thinking from the backend because some user research is involved to see how designs and layouts make people feel about the product. Usually, the Product team or other stakeholders will get the direct user feedback and help translate it into designs, which get passed to you. Then it's time for you to start your magic.

In this chapter, I'll cover:

- How to choose a frontend framework
- How to choose other packages for your framework
- Some long-term decisions you can make now
- Why this frontend project will use React

As you start thinking through how you want to set up this new frontend repo, study the designs you have and ask about the Product roadmap so that you can consider the direction in which the app is intended to grow. Ask every little question that comes to mind as you go through the designs and look at them from a user perspective. You'll be surprised how many conditions you can come up with!

Just like with every project, though, you have to get started somewhere. Before you dive into the code, take a look at some of the framework options you have. This is a huge decision for the lifetime of this product because the framework you choose will lock you into the packages and services you can use. Migrating frontend frameworks usually means completely rebuilding the app in a different framework, so do *a lot* of research.

Frontend Architecture Decisions

The decisions you make on the frontend will have to be consistent because if there are differences, your users can *see* them. Just like you did on the backend, you'll create code conventions with your team. On the frontend, those little differences can directly affect the UX because they are visual and interactive.

Take a look at the designs for the app you'll be building in this Figma file (*https:// oreil.ly/gt0yx*). Note where you'll need to handle data and API calls, what parts of the UI might be reusable, and any other patterns you can find. This will give you some initial thoughts on how to separate parts of the app and what architecture pattern you should go with.

Patterns to look at before you dive into the project include Model-View-Controller (MVC) (*https://oreil.ly/fJ0P7*), Model-View-View Model (MVVM) (*https://oreil.ly/ xpRea*), component based (*https://oreil.ly/qJqTd*), and micro frontends (*https://micro-frontends.org*). No one architecture is better than any other; it just depends on the approach you want for the app and the tools you're going to work with. For this project, you'll go with component-based architecture.

The reason we're using a component-based architecture is because it's a common architecture for large-scale apps; you're building the app with React, which encourages component usage. We'll also use the atomic design methodology (*https://oreil.ly/ fnBe9*), but don't get too caught up on the terminology. Use names that make the code structure make sense to the team. This methodology breaks down the frontend into the smallest pieces and then slowly builds the pages from there. You'll likely see some version of this implemented in different projects, so familiarize yourself with it. It may even give you some ideas for refactors you can currently do.

 This is a great teaching moment! As you research the different architectures and make decisions based on the designs and road-map, share what you find with the team. You don't have to make a fancy presentation to share your findings. You can just talk through the tabs and editors you have open from your research. That way, the team can see some of your thoughts behind how you make decisions, which will give them insight into what they can look for in making their own decisions.

On all the projects I've worked on, the PR review process for frontend changes has taken longer than for the backend. It can also get a little nitpicky. Things like naming conventions matter because variables get passed around different components in different states, and you need to make sure you're referencing the right values. Make a template for things to check in PR reviews, especially on the frontend. Here's one that I made in the frontend repo (*https://oreil.ly/pU70I*), and here's one from the Google engineering practices docs (*https://oreil.ly/bJ4tI*).

Technical history gets lost as developers come and go, so unexpected breaking changes can happen. I've seen this a lot with style changes breaking mobile designs and props getting changed in one component while breaking 11 other components. Having a PR review template will make the team aware of what needs to be checked without having to remember it every time.

Security is going to be huge on the frontend, and I'll go over that in detail in Chapter 19. I mention it now because that's going to be a driver behind some of the decisions you make for architecture patterns. For example, you need to decide what tools you'll use to validate inputs and user tokens. You'll also need to know how to prevent common attacks. This will get repeated numerous times throughout your app, so it will have lasting impacts on how you build forms and make API requests.

As far as how you create and organize components, you can do anything you can imagine. That's why you need to be strict about code conventions in the beginning. (Sound familiar?) Here are a few things you need to consider as you start building components:

Follow a modular approach and keep business logic separated from components when possible.
> Having modular components helps you keep track of the different business areas and lets you reuse code across the app. That might look like having files or custom hooks that call endpoints instead of doing it directly in components.

Work with the Design team on building a standard for components and the terminology you use to refer to elements.
> Using the same phrases will help everyone understand what's being used and where changes need to be made. In a more mature organization, the Design team will likely have a design system (*https://oreil.ly/QNDLe*) in place, so you need to take that into consideration.

Implement separation of concerns and single responsibility principles as soon as you start building.
> Keeping a separation of concerns separates design and business logic so that components are truly reusable. With single responsibility, you keep components from having too much code bloat. If a component manages a lot of props, it's probably responsible for too many things, which makes it harder to work with.

Since you know what architecture you'll be building the app with, it's time to make an architecture diagram based on the designs. This will help you figure out how to break down the design into your components and views in a reusable way. Figure 13-1 shows what the skeleton of the architecture might look like based on the designs (*https://oreil.ly/_zOyJ*) you got at the beginning of the project.

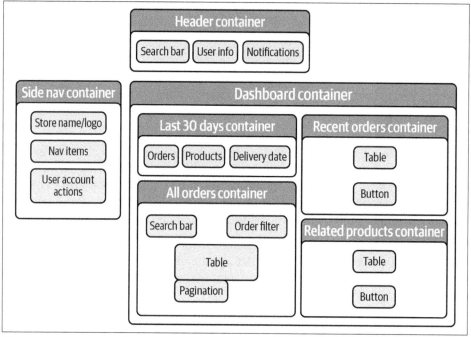

Figure 13-1. Project architecture diagram

As you fill in more details as you work on the app, you can include where API calls will be made and how state should flow between components. This diagram gives you an idea of how you might break the pages up into different containers and the components that go in those containers. This will let you find some of those common components, like the tables, search bars, and buttons.

Once you have this rough draft of the architecture, you can share it with the team and get their input on if the app should be broken up in a different way. Encourage some of the mid-level devs to take a container and add details like states, API calls, and conditional rendering. Now you and the team have a path forward so that you can start making code decisions.

Choosing a Frontend Framework

The frontend landscape is constantly and rapidly changing. I remember when jQuery used to be the closest thing we had to a JavaScript framework. Then at some point, the number of frameworks exploded. You have React (*https://react.dev*), Angular (*https://angular.io*), Vue.js (*https://vuejs.org*), Astro (*https://astro.build*), SolidJS (*https://www.solidjs.com*), Svelte (*https://svelte.dev*), Next.js (*https://nextjs.org*), Remix (*https://remix.run*), and a ton of other frameworks to choose from now.

 Because new frameworks are constantly coming out, it can be easy to get caught up in the hype. Be careful with choosing newer frameworks over existing ones. There are some great new tools out there, but not everything is ready for production. Some developers have been burned by investing their time heavily into a new tool just for it to lose community interest and support. Sometimes the best way to try out new frameworks is on smaller, personal projects rather than full production apps.

It can be daunting to look through all the possible frameworks and choose one, so here are some key things you should look for during your evaluation:

- Look at community support and how issues are handled on GitHub and Stack Overflow.
- Go through the documentation to see how quickly you can find answers.
- Check how often the framework is updated.
- Check how long the framework has been around.
- Research if any companies support, sponsor, or own the framework.
- Research accompanying packages, such as data visualization, bundling, and state management, as well as third-party service SDKs.
- Check developer surveys like State of JavaScript (*https://stateofjs.com*) or Stack Overflow's Annual Developer Survey (*https://survey.stackoverflow.co*) to see what people are using in production and what the trends are.
- Read through job descriptions to find out what tech stacks companies are using in production.
- Find out if there are any geographical restrictions on where the framework is developed due to world politics.
- Check the license type for the framework.
- Make sure security vulnerabilities get patched regularly and quickly.

- Check if there are docs on how your cloud platform handles deployments for your framework.

- Look at the tools other projects in your organization are using.

Pick no more than five frameworks and decide on your five minimum requirements from this list. Five is an arbitrary number, and you can choose more or less, but this will give you a good breadth and depth to explore. As you go through your evaluation list, start eliminating the frameworks that are falling behind. There's no need to keep researching them if they don't meet your minimum requirements.

Then you can take deeper dives into the frameworks' details with more of the items from the list. It does get hard to decide between the top two, so bring in the team and see what everyone feels the most confident with. This might not be the same as what everyone's the most interested in, but you have to keep the product's maintainability as the top priority. Keep in mind what everyone's expertise is because this will be a huge factor in the final decision. If you have several engineers who work with React, it could be difficult to get adoption of Vue or Astro even if they make sense for the product.

There's nothing wrong with using the tried and tested frameworks that are out there. For production apps, that's usually a better choice because you know there's support as you add features. It's tempting to pick up the shiny new thing for a greenfield project. To help strike a balance, you can build a prototype in the more stable framework and the same prototype in a newer framework. Let the team test-drive them and see which one gets developed faster and with a better DX.

This project will use React and TypeScript because these are tried and tested tools for production apps. React checks many of the boxes on the list, making it a solid choice. The market currently still heavily favors React, but doing all the research will ensure that you're using the most up-to-date production framework.

Just because React is currently the most used framework doesn't mean it's necessarily the best choice. Other frameworks I mentioned earlier, like Svelte and Solid, have great DX and are just as good—if not better in some cases—than React. I very much encourage you to try some of these frameworks and try to get them adopted at your organization. The only way our profession evolves is when people bring in changes and others start to see how good they are. Be one of those people who helps keep us moving forward to a better future!

App Setup Options

Regardless of the framework you choose, you need a way to run the frontend app. You'll need to do some initial setup that will determine how the app is built and where and how it can run. This is when you'll start looking into build tools like Vite (*https://vitejs.dev*), Rollup (*https://rollupjs.org*), esbuild (*https://esbuild.github.io*), and Webpack (*https://webpack.js.org*) (if you have to). The build tool you use will affect the bundle size, other tools you can interface with, app performance, and how fast you can deploy the app.

Common Components

Every frontend app has some similar functionality. Your project will include error handling, modals, tables, forms, search, filtering, and toast messages. Go to any website you use and see how many of these features you can find on each one. Do a walkthrough of the designs and start looking for common functionality across pages. If you have some questions about UX, bring them up early and often. Making design changes as the app grows gets tricky because that could have unintended side effects on page layouts and consistency across functionality.

Choosing Packages

There's a trade-off between having total control over your code through internally developed packages and speeding up feature development by using existing packages from npm (*https://www.npmjs.com/*). The other thing you have to watch with packages is bloat. This is another art form for you to get comfortable with. You need to be able to make a call on when it's worth developing an internal package over using an existing one to balance bundle size and load time.

Here are some common tools for all kinds of frontend functionality:

Data visualization
- Chart.js (*https://www.chartjs.org*)
- D3 (*https://d3js.org*)
- Three.js (*https://threejs.org*)
- Recharts (*https://recharts.org/en-US*)
- VictoryChart (*https://formidable.com/open-source/victory/docs/victory-chart*)
- Highcharts (*https://github.com/highcharts/highcharts-react*)

Form handling
- React Final Form (*https://final-form.org/react*)
- React Hook Form (*https://react-hook-form.com*)
- Formik (*https://formik.org*)

Component library

- Material UI (*https://mui.com/material-ui*)
- Chakra UI (*https://chakra-ui.com*)
- Materialize (*https://materializecss.com*)
- Semantic UI (*https://semantic-ui.com*)
- Mantine (*https://ui.mantine.dev*)
- React Bootstrap (*https://react-bootstrap.netlify.app*)
- Radix UI (*https://www.radix-ui.com*)

State management

- Redux (*https://redux.js.org*)
- MobX (*https://mobx.js.org/README.html*)
- Zustand (*https://github.com/pmndrs/zustand*)
- XState (*https://xstate.js.org*)
- Jotai (*https://jotai.org*)
- Valtio (*https://valtio.dev/docs/introduction/getting-started*)

Data fetching

- TanStack Query (*https://tanstack.com/query/latest/docs/react/overview*)
- SWR (*https://swr.vercel.app*)
- Apollo Client (*https://www.apollographql.com/docs/react/get-started*)
- RTK-Query (*https://redux-toolkit.js.org/rtk-query/overview*)
- React Router (*https://reactrouter.com/en/main/guides/data-libs#loading-data*)

Styling

- styled-components (*https://styled-components.com*)
- Emotion (*https://emotion.sh/docs/styled*)
- CSS Modules (*https://github.com/css-modules/css-modules*)
- Tailwind CSS (*https://tailwindcss.com*)

Accessibility

- i18n (*https://github.com/mashpie/i18n-node*)
- React Aria (*https://react-spectrum.adobe.com/react-aria*)

Utilities

- Lodash (*https://lodash.com*)
- date-fns (*https://date-fns.org*)
- Day.js (*https://day.js.org*)

- jwt-decode (*https://github.com/auth0/jwt-decode*)

Linters/formatters
- ESLint (*https://eslint.org*)
- Babel (*https://babeljs.io*)
- Prettier (*https://prettier.io*)
- js-beautify (*https://github.com/beautify-web/js-beautify*)
- Biome (*https://biomejs.dev*)
- dprint (*https://dprint.dev/overview*)

Package managers
- npm (*https://www.npmjs.com*)
- pnpm (*https://pnpm.js.org*)
- Yarn (*https://yarnpkg.com*)

Testing
- Jest (*https://jestjs.io*)
- Vitest (*https://vitest.dev*)
- React Testing Library (*https://testing-library.com/docs/react-testing-library/intro*)
- Mocha (*https://mochajs.org*)
- Cypress (*https://cypress.io*)
- Puppeteer (*https://pptr.dev*)
- Playwright (*https://playwright.dev*)

Now that you have an outline of how the app works and the tools you want to use, take some time to think through the architecture pattern you want to follow.

 Keep in mind that these package options are current suggestions. The ecosystem changes fast, so it's important that you do your due diligence and find the latest and greatest tools being used. At some point, all tools get replaced with newer, hopefully better versions. So don't stop learning and looking for what different teams are using for their production apps.

Working with Other Teams

As you review the designs, you and your team will have questions about functionality and UX. Go through the designs as a team and write up some tickets for each screen. Write out the acceptance criteria (*https://oreil.ly/PzyJC*) in terms of how the screen should work. Think about how inputs should look and how they should handle errors and validation. You also have to consider what happens when a user submits a form or pushes a button that triggers an API call or a UI event.

Look for a few edge cases and add all questions to the tickets. This is a great way to work with the Product team to help guide them from the technical side. The questions you ask will have an impact on the way Product thinks about features and other ideas they have in mind. You'll go through plenty of iterations with questions as development starts, but it's good to get an initial round in before starting.

There might be a QA team you need to work with as well. Even if there isn't, you should still get a test plan in place. You'll work with QA to decide the scenarios that should be tested and which environments will be used to test different states of deployed changes. You can bring up any new questions to the Product team. If you don't have QA, this can also be a group activity for the dev team to get a different perspective on the app.

Talk with the DevOps team to start getting deployment pipelines set up for multiple environments. This can be something they work on in parallel with you as you get the codebase ready. You'll probably need some type of storage for assets, like images, so make sure that's a part of their setup. We'll get into some of the operations (Ops) tasks you'll handle as a full stack dev starting in Chapter 27, so for now we're not going to worry about pipelines and the tools to integrate with the DevOps infrastructure.

Conclusion

In this chapter, I went over some considerations you should have as you start building your frontend. The type of complexity you'll run into will make you think about implementation details differently than the backend. Your changes can propagate in unintended ways without this first round of thinking about the architecture. As the app grows, you'll be able to add things and adapt, so don't feel like you have to have it all figured out now.

This project is built with React because it is one of the most popular, well-supported frameworks at the time of writing, but please try out some of the others! I'd encourage you to at least initialize this project in two other frameworks to truly see the differences between them. While React may be the common go-to, the others are also very popular and well supported by their communities. Go through some of those differences with the rest of the team as a teaching moment.

## CHAPTER 14

Building the React App

Now that you've done your research and know the tools you're going to use, it's time to initialize your frontend project! You'll set up the React app and all the tooling you need to build your frontend.

By now, you've reviewed the designs multiple times, had discussions with the Product team and your dev team, and talked to the DevOps team about getting the infrastructure for the frontend ready. You have a few diagrams and documents to guide you and the team through building all the components. You also have plenty of tickets to split up among the team. When you're starting a greenfield project, though, you'll be looked to as the person who will initialize the repo and make the structure of the project. That way, your team can start working on different parts of the app, and everyone has confidence that development can proceed without issues.

In this chapter, I'll go over:

- Setting up the React app with some of the packages
- Building the first feature
- Writing the first test

You don't need to have everything in place, just enough for the team to start work. You may be tasked with background development while the rest of the team does feature work. This is one way you act as a multiplier for the team: by working on conventions, docs, and implementing tools that help others get up to speed and get through their tasks more smoothly.

Set Up the Initial React App

First, initialize Git in a new repo or connect it to a remote repo so that you have version control in place at the very beginning. Then initialize the app with Vite (*https://vitejs.dev/guide*). Run the command below and follow along with the prompts. Keep in mind that the following example has the current prompts, which may be different when you run the command. Make sure to choose the React and TypeScript options when they appear:

```
npm create vite@latest

? Project name: › dashboard-web
? Select a framework: › - Use arrow-keys. Return to submit.
    Vanilla
    Vue
❯   React
    Preact
    Lit
    Svelte
    Solid
    Qwik
    Others
? Select a variant: › - Use arrow-keys. Return to submit.
❯   TypeScript
    TypeScript + SWC
    JavaScript
    JavaScript + SWC
```

Your project is called `dashboard-web` and will be scaffolded with some files to get you started. One of the convenient things about Vite is that it's not very opinionated. So you can set your file structure up for the components and screens any way you like. For now, it's good to finish installing and configuring some of the core developer tools you need.

Set Up Linters and Formatters

As the team commits code and pushes changes when deadlines get tight, you might write code that doesn't stick to the conventions for the sake of time. This leads to messy code that's hard to read and manage. That's why you're implementing a linter and a formatter. The formatter will be Prettier (*https://oreil.ly/nPbYC*) to ensure that the code format stays consistent. It will check for things like spacing, commas, and line lengths.

The linter will be ESLint (*https://eslint.org*) to make sure you don't let bugs in like unused variables, deeply nested ternaries, or magic numbers. These tools are usually paired with husky (*https://oreil.ly/nr5fo*) to plug in to your Git hooks (*https://oreil.ly/ibGXC*), such as commits and pushes. ESLint was configured as part of the Vite initialization, so you can leave that config file as is for now, but you can check out some of the rules in their docs (*https://oreil.ly/g52M_*). Install the other packages with this command:

```
npm install --save-dev husky prettier
```

 Make sure you don't have conflicting rules in your Prettier and ESLint configs. I've seen this be a problem for Git hooks and CI pipelines. Just be sure to run the `lint` command a few times to ensure that you've handled any issues before committing the changes. You won't implement this, but if you need to run linters on specific files or in a specific order, lint-staged (*https://oreil.ly/8S75r*) is a great tool to get Prettier and ESLint to work well together.

Now you'll need to add a new file to the root of your project called *.prettierrc*. Remember, the configurations that you're setting up are a matter of opinion and will reflect the formatting preferences of the team. There will be some formatting that everyone agrees with and some that people disagree with, but eventually, the team gets used to it. In the *.prettierrc* file, you can add the following code, which are some of my preferences:

```
{
    "arrowParens": "always",
    "bracketSpacing": true,
    "trailingComma": "es5",
    "tabWidth": 2,
    "semi": false,
    "singleQuote": true
}
```

This is some basic formatting you may want to keep consistent in your codebase—the little things that can keep a codebase tidy and readable. You can check out all the options available in the Prettier docs (*https://oreil.ly/L6OAB*). You'll also need a way to ignore files that don't need to be formatted, like your *package-lock.json* or some of the other config files. So add another file to the root of your project called *.prettierignore* to handle this:

```
# Ignore artifacts:
build

# Ignore all HTML files:
**/*.html

# Ignore other config files:
**/*.json
.prettierrc
.eslintrc.cjs
src/vite-env.d.ts
vite.config.ts
```

This is similar to how your *.gitignore* file works. You put the files that you don't want Prettier to format in here. A good practice is to add a command to automatically format the code when a developer wants to. This will edit the code directly in the file to make it meet the formatting rules. So in your *package.json,* add the following code to the scripts section:

```
"scripts": {
  ...
  "format": "prettier . --write"
},
```

You can also encourage the devs on the team to enable formatting on save in their code editor. VS Code has this in its settings (*https://oreil.ly/IfATs*), so no one has to deal with last-minute formatting changes when they're ready to push a commit. Now you can set up husky to run different commands when you get ready to commit changes or push to the remote repo. To do that, run the following command:

```
npx husky-init && npm install
```

Take a look in your repo; you should find that a *.husky* directory has been created. This has the husky script needed to interface with the different Git hooks you target. It also has the first Git hook script for pre-committing a change. You'll need to create another file in this directory called *pre-push*. This is where you'll put commands to run before code can be pushed to the remote repo. Update the *pre-commit* file with this code:

```
#!/usr/bin/env sh
. "$(dirname -- "$0")/_/husky.sh"

npm run lint
npm run format
```

Then add the following code to the *pre-push* file:

```
#!/usr/bin/env sh
. "$(dirname -- "$0")/_/husky.sh"

# npm test
```

This is a personal preference, but I like to do the linting and formatting for precommit and save the testing for pre-push. You can do any combination of these things if you like something better. See if anyone on your team has strong opinions about linting and formatting rules. That way, you are including everyone in these initial decisions. Do a test to see if your husky configs are working by committing and pushing your changes so far. Note that the test command is commented out right now. We'll set that up a little later.

That's all for the linters right now. So you can turn your attention to how the app is actually built with Vite as your bundler.

Set Up the Build Configs

This is important because it will determine how the project is compiled into the code that gets run in the browser. This can change the way you import packages and components, the syntax you use, and how big your bundles are. You usually make this choice based on the environments your app will run in. Not every browser supports the latest features in JavaScript.

First, to compile your TypeScript to JavaScript, take a look at the *tsconfig.json,* where you'll find the `target`, `module`, and `lib` values. This is one of those files that just gets copy-pasted across new projects, but it's good to at least understand what the values do for your build. These determine the way your TypeScript code gets compiled to JavaScript.

The `target` value determines the versions of ECMAScript (*https://oreil.ly/NY9cC*) your app will be compatible with. This is important because it determines what browsers and Node versions the app can run on. This can affect things like the Node version your server needs to use. The `lib` value tells the compiler which JavaScript features are available when the compiled code is executed. This is usually the same as the `target` value because it affects the output of your build. You might have a different `lib` value if you are working in a polyfilled environment (*https://oreil.ly/gsWX5*). The `module` value is how the compiler resolves the modules in your app. For example, using import statements will fail in old versions of Node. This value affects how the modules in your project are found, so that's what makes it important.

You can leave the config values unchanged for now since the defaults should run in most modern browsers. I encourage you to glance through the TSConfig docs (*https://oreil.ly/DkYfN*) to learn more about these values and deepen your knowledge about builds.

> Choosing the values for `lib`, `target`, and `module` will make a huge difference in your bundle size and how you write your code. The values you choose will affect how you import functionality in different files and how your code interacts with other code. This is usually more noticeable when you're making packages that are used by other projects, but it's something that you should be aware of for all projects you work on.

When you're ready to bundle all your code into the build artifact that gets deployed to servers, you can change the build options in your *vite.config.ts* file. Vite uses Rollup (*https://rollupjs.org*) under the hood to create builds, and the default options are usually good enough. If you need to do anything more specific to change the bundle size or work with browser compatibility, you can add build options (*https://oreil.ly/Zmlc0*) to your Vite config.

Set Up Styles

Let's move on to the styles. To handle any custom styling and avoid inline styles, you'll use styled-components (*https://styled-components.com*). When you have a component for your styles, you have more control over how the styles work, and you can do things like conditionally update styles with props.

You'll also be using Material UI (*https://mui.com/material-ui*) (MUI) for the component library. This will make it easier for you to focus on functionality because your components will already have accessibility and responsiveness built in. Combined with styled-components, MUI can be customized to have any theme you want. MUI can also be extended to include its Material Icons (*https://oreil.ly/8Yznl*) if you know you'll need these for buttons or other visuals.

Be Careful When Using Component Libraries

I've been on a number of teams across organizations of different sizes, and I never really saw any of them implement a custom component library well unless they had a team dedicated to that. It always starts out with the best intentions, but over time an internal component library becomes hard to maintain without a dedicated team, especially if it's used by multiple frontend teams with different component needs.

Ethan Brown also had a few things to say about this:

> I think component libraries are changing thanks to projects like Tailwind UI, Headless UI, shadcn/ui. The downside of traditional component libraries is that they're great until you need to do something slightly different. If you're using MUI, and you need to do something that isn't the "MUI way," it can be incredibly time-consuming and frustrating.
>
> I personally feel the future lies in something like shadcn/ui and Headless UI where you say, "Generate a button component for me," and it drops a button component into your project, which you then control and customize. Time will tell. I will say that every UI library I've used—including my favorite, Mantine—is eventually as much hindrance as help. It's a real "choose your poison" decision.

Often, the organization will already have a preferred choice for how to handle styles and components because the Design team will have created a design system to have a consistent look and feel for apps across the organization. So regardless of the component library you work with, there will be scenarios where you have to override the existing styles.

To get started, go ahead and install the packages you need with this command:

```
npm install @mui/material @mui/icons-material @emotion/react
    @emotion/styled styled-components
```

Now you can import MUI components and icons and create your own components with styled-components. The next thing you can do is initialize the theme for your app. Every app will have custom colors, spacing, fonts, and other details. To prepare for this, you can delete *App.css*, *index.css*, and the *assets* folder from the *src* directory. You'll need to update the *main.tsx* file by deleting `import './index.css'` from the file. Then create a new file called *theme.tsx* and add the following code:

```
import { createTheme } from '@mui/material/styles';
import { blue, orange } from '@mui/material/colors';

const theme = createTheme({
  palette: {
    primary: {
      main: blue[900],
    },
    secondary: {
      main: orange[400],
    },
  },
});

export default theme;
```

This sets a couple of colors in the theme object. This theme will definitely change as you start building views and getting the colors you need from the Figma designs, but you have a good starting point here. You should take a look at the MUI docs on theming (*https://oreil.ly/ygc00*) to understand all the values you can set, including dark mode.

For the theme to be applied throughout your app, you need to add a `ThemeProvider` to *App.tsx*. A *provider* is a common pattern in React development to provide top-level functionality that should be available to all the components in your application and is commonly used for functionality like themes, modals, and state management. It's usually based on React Context (*https://oreil.ly/0LmlB*). Open the file and update the contents with this code:

```
import { useState } from 'react'
import { ThemeProvider } from '@mui/material/styles';
import theme from './theme';

function App() {
  const [count, setCount] = useState(0)

  return (
    <ThemeProvider theme={theme}>
      <h1>Vite + React</h1>
      <div className="card">
        <button onClick={() => setCount((count) => count + 1)}>
          count is {count}
        </button>
```

```
      <p>
        Edit <code>src/App.tsx</code> and save to test HMR
      </p>
    </div>
    <p className="read-the-docs">
      Click on the Vite and React logos to learn more
    </p>
  </ThemeProvider>
 )
}
```

```
export default App
```

You've imported the `theme` you just created and applied it with the `ThemeProvider` component. Now every MUI component inside this provider will have the theme you defined. This sets the foundation for all your styles, so you can move on to the other tasks to get this repo developer-ready.

Set Up Testing

Frontend testing, just like backend testing, is going to save you from regressions all across the app. It gets trickier on the frontend because you have dynamically rendered components and API requests happening, which changes how you have to write and think about tests. Since you're using Vite as the tool to run and build the app, you'll use Vitest (*https://vitest.dev*) and React Testing Library (*https://oreil.ly/kRvDD*) to write the unit tests for the app. You'll need to install them in your project with the following command:

```
npm install -D jsdom vitest @testing-library/react
```

Then in your *package.json,* you need to add the following script to run the tests:

```
...
"scripts": {
    ...
    "test": "vitest"
  }
  ...
```

You also need to update the *vite.config.ts* file so that your tests will run correctly. You can overwrite all of the code in this file with the following:

```
/// <reference types="vitest" />
/// <reference types="vite/client" />

import { defineConfig } from 'vite'
import react from '@vitejs/plugin-react'

// https://vitejs.dev/config/
export default defineConfig({
  plugins: [react()],
```

```
  test: {
    globals: true,
    environment: 'jsdom',
  }
})
```

Now when you write tests for the components you build, you'll have the packages and script ready. This will also be used in your CI pipeline, and when you try to push changes, husky will run the tests for your pre-push Git hook. We'll go into deeper detail on tests in Chapters 21 and 24.

You now have the core of the app set up. There are just a couple more things to do to make sure you set the code up for long-term maintainability.

Set Up CHANGELOG and README

The README and CHANGELOG files are some subtle files that will really help over the lifetime of the project. Think of the README as the how-to file for the project. This should tell any developer how to set up the project, any environment variables, and any quirks that you know exist. The CHANGELOG keeps the history of all the changes in each release. Changes should be recorded so that you always know what's been released in each version. It's good to link tickets in the CHANGELOG so you can refer to them later.

Another View on CHANGELOGs

Depending on the release process at your organization, you will run into different ways to document changes. Here's another view on them from Ethan Brown:

> My thinking on CHANGELOGs has shifted. I used to use this approach where there's just a Markdown file that you update as you make changes. The problem with that is that it usually just duplicates work done in the release process. The release process usually involves examining all PRs merged since the last release and writing a summary for the release. And yes, the CHANGELOG can help facilitate this, but it can also introduce confusion and be one more thing that has to be maintained and referenced as part of the release process.
>
> I've found it to be a much better approach to focus on issue/PR documentation. If the description of each PR contains all the relevant information (as it should), constructing release notes becomes much easier, and it concentrates the documentation effort where it belongs, on well-defined issues and PRs.

You can find an example of the project README (*https://oreil.ly/2EPK7*) and CHANGELOG (*https://oreil.ly/1Or-2*) in the GitHub repo. This is something you'll want to discuss with the team because keeping these files up to date is the only way they stay relevant. Work with the team to incorporate these updates as part of your normal PR reviews so that you don't miss them when you have a breaking change.

Run the App Locally

You've set up all the tools, so now it's time to make sure this app runs with all your configs! Start by checking the version of Node you're using. I'll be running this app locally with Node 20.10.0 (*https://nodejs.org*). If you don't have a way to switch between Node versions, try out nvm (*https://oreil.ly/IguE3*), Volta (*https://volta.sh*), or n (*https://github.com/tj/n*). Once you have the correct version ready in your terminal, navigate to the project directory and install all of the packages with this command:

```
npm i
```

Then you should be able to run the app with this command and get the same output as follows:

```
npm run dev

VITE v5.0.5  ready in 174 ms

→ Local:   http://localhost:5173/
→ Network: use --host to expose
→ press h + enter to show help
```

When you navigate to the localhost URL, you should see something like Figure 14-1 in your browser.

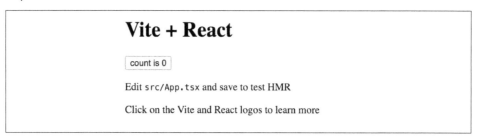

Figure 14-1. UI app running locally

Next, you need to try out all the other commands for your build, tests, linting, and formatting. They should all run without errors. The test script won't execute because there aren't any test files right now. The build script should generate a new *dist* directory in the root of the project. Double-check that this directory is in your *.gitignore* since you don't want to commit builds. The lint and format scripts should run and not generate any errors.

With all these checks complete, you should commit the changes you have so far because this is a good foundation for the app. Anything you add after this will be feature work or some improvements or additions to the tools the project uses. But you have the bare bones to get started on the first feature.

Build the First Feature

With this repo set up and ready for development, it's time to add some functionality! You can start with any part of the designs you want, but I like to pick something relatively small yet big enough to highlight potential issues. In this example, you'll get the folder structure in place, set up the initial routing, and build the container for the different app pages.

Project Structure

We'll go with a take on the simple React approach. In your *src* directory, add two new folders named *components* and *pages*. The *components* folder will have the smaller, reusable functionality, like search bars and shared styled components, as well as things like the navbar and header. The *pages* folder will have the larger functionality that makes up a whole page, like the user info and user actions pages.

 This is some info you should add to the README. It tells future devs how the code is organized so that they can quickly figure out where to look for things. When you get the README in a good place, you should have the team test out the steps and add more details when they run into issues.

Add some boilerplate code in the *pages* folder for the user info page. The folder structure will look like this:

```
...
|__ pages
|____ UserInfo
|_____ index.tsx
|_____ UserInfo.Container.tsx
|_____ UserInfo.Container.test.tsx
...
```

For now, you can put the following code in the *UserInfo.Container.tsx* file:

```
import styled from 'styled-components'

const Container = styled.div`
  background-color:
  height: 100vh;
  width: 100%;
`

const UserInfo = () => {
  // Fetch user info from the backend here

  return (
    <Container>
```

```
    <div>
      <div>Search bar</div>
      <div>User notification</div>
    </div>
  </Container>
  )
}

export default UserInfo
```

Then you can add code in the *index.tsx* file in the *UserInfo* directory to create the module for this directory. The reason you're using this module file is to streamline imports and exports across the app. That way, you don't have to import all your functionality from separate files as the app grows. Take a deeper dive into how modules work in this MDN doc (*https://oreil.ly/k4jh-*) because it's something you should know about and be able to help others on the team understand. Here's the code to handle the module:

```
import UserInfo from './UserInfo.Container'

export default UserInfo
```

The last thing to do is write at least one test to make sure tests aren't overlooked during development. This sets the precedent that the project will have tests so that the team knows not to skip writing them. In *UserInfo.Container.test.tsx*, add this code:

```
import { afterEach, describe, expect, it, vi } from 'vitest'
import { act, render, screen } from '@testing-library/react'
import UserInfo from '.'

const ui = () => render(<UserInfo />)

describe('<UserInfo />', () => {
  afterEach(() => {
    vi.clearAllMocks()
  })

  it('should render the user info screen', async () => {
    ui()

    expect(screen.getByText('Search bar')).toBeDefined()
  })
})
```

This is something to get you and the team going on actual development, so don't worry about making this pretty or super functional at this point. You'll follow this pattern of writing code for every part of the app, so all the components will have this structure and these three files as the minimum.

Set Up Routing

Based on the architecture diagram we made earlier, the main container is composed of two parts: the navbar and the current screen. Let's set up the initial routing for the current screen. You'll need to install React Router (*https://oreil.ly/jU8Ao*). There are a couple of alternatives to this: TanStack Router (*https://oreil.ly/fRkcc*) and Next.js (*https://nextjs.org*). To install React Router, run this command:

```
npm i react-router-dom
```

This is where you'll handle what the app renders based on the URL. Remember, at this point in the app you aren't trying to get everything feature-complete. You're trying to set up the skeleton to enable everyone to work on different parts. It can be tempting to try to do everything yourself and dive into the details, but you have to know when you have enough in place to let the team do their magic, too.

Now you need to create a new file in the *src* directory called *routes.tsx*. This will give you two routes that direct users to the different screens available. The reason you want to implement routing now is because the project will have different URLs for the pages you're making so that you can set up some initial linking. Add this code to the file:

```
import { createBrowserRouter } from 'react-router-dom'
import UserInfo from './screens/UserInfo'

const router = createBrowserRouter([
  {
    path: '/',
    element: <UserInfo />,
  },
  {
    path: '/actions',
    element: <div>Actions go burr</div>,
  },
])

export default router
```

Update the Root of the App

Now you can update *App.tsx* to have the base UI layout with the following code:

```
import { ThemeProvider } from '@mui/material/styles'
import Box from '@mui/material/Box'
import { RouterProvider } from 'react-router-dom'
import styled from 'styled-components'
import theme from './theme'
import router from './routes'

const AppContainer = styled(Box)`
```

```
  display: flex;
`

const CurrentScreen = styled(Box)`
  width: calc(100% - 240px);
  margin-left: 240px;
`

const App = () => {
  // Do some stuff here
  return (
    <ThemeProvider theme={theme}>
      <AppContainer component="main">
        <CurrentScreen component="section">
          <RouterProvider router={router} />
        </CurrentScreen>
      </AppContainer>
    </ThemeProvider>
  )
}

export default App
```

Now you should run the app to make sure everything is still working as expected. You should see something like Figure 14-2.

Figure 14-2. Skeleton of the app with the user info screen

You can check the code for this chapter in this PR (*https://oreil.ly/guxuc*) to make sure you have everything set up correctly. Now you have more code that you can commit to the repo. This can be the example the other devs use to start building more of the core functionality of the project. These first components give you a chance to really try out the new repo and see if any adjustments need to be made to the tools or the configs.

Remember to make commits often and keep them small. It will help with code reviews as well as make sure you don't lose a huge number of changes. Encourage the team to do the same and include it in your conventions for PR reviews.

Also remember that at this point in the project, you aren't responsible for single-handedly creating everything. That's why these components are essentially placeholders and you haven't dived into the designs yet. I know I've said this a few times, but it's important not to get hung up on making one part perfect before the team has a chance to actually look at the project structure, understand it, ask questions, and give their own input. Things will change.

All your scripts should still run without errors. This is a good time to test any pipeline things the DevOps team has in place, such as deploying to different environments. That way, the DevOps team can address any issues as early as possible so that development flows smoothly as the team ramps up. I'll get into the CI things you can handle for the frontend and backend in Chapters 25 and 27 because once the infrastructure is in place, you and the team will likely handle more of that.

Conclusion

In this chapter, you set up all the initial tools and configs for the React app. You worked on the first components to make sure the project works as expected. The code you have so far is going to enable the rest of your team to get started on other functionality. You don't have *all* the core functionality in place, like state management and data handling, but that's something other devs can add as they go.

You and the team will install more packages and set up more config files as you need different functionality. As you and the team dive deeper into the designs and functionality, you need to have conversations and maybe even small demos to compare packages. With the repo in this state, you should definitely have a meeting to go over how everything works so that there isn't confusion once everyone starts working on different pieces.

## CHAPTER 15

State Management

With the repo established and the app ready to be developed, it's time to start building views based on the Figma designs (*https://oreil.ly/6WcoC*) and your architecture diagram. You already have the header container mostly filled out, so you can see where you start to juggle multiple things like state, API calls, and conditional rendering.

Managing your state is going to determine how you handle dynamic data and values that change based on user actions. There are a few ways to approach state management, and most apps use a combination of the approaches to keep the code as simple as possible.

In this chapter, I'll cover:

- Different ways to manage state and when you might use them
- The state lifecycle in React
- How to share state between components
- Prop drilling management

Understanding how state works, when it's updated, and why you use different approaches is important. You need to have a deeper knowledge of this so that you can coach others on your team and you can write the most optimal code possible. When states aren't managed correctly, that can lead to some strange side effects in the UI. So let's start by diving into how component state works.

How Component State Works

In React, there is one method that controls how things are initially rendered on the page: the `render` method, which is usually in the *main.tsx* file. It looks like this:

```
ReactDOM.createRoot(document.getElementById('root')!).render(
  <React.StrictMode>
    <App />
  </React.StrictMode>
)
```

The argument in `createRoot` is the `domNode`, which is where you manage the Document Object Model (DOM) inside it. The `render` method is where you display a React component, typically the `<App />` component.

The `render` method alone won't show any updates to the UI when the user interacts with it. State is how React handles rendering based on user interactions like button clicks, form events, and data changes. You can think of the state as a component's memory, as described in the official docs (*https://oreil.ly/rRX5Y*). After the initial render, components rerender in response to state updates.

React uses a virtual DOM (*https://oreil.ly/-bZdl*) to try to make the rerenders as efficient as possible by updating only the affected parts of the page. So when your state updates, only the components with the state changes will rerender. For example, that's what happens when a user clicks a button and an API call is made to fetch data that updates on the page or if a button is clicked and a modal pops up.

That's where the different React hooks (*https://oreil.ly/LV1N_*) come into play. A *hook* is a piece of code in the React framework that lets you work with the React lifecycle methods. Hooks are only usable in React functional components since they replaced the original class methods (*https://oreil.ly/wt-jN*) that came in older versions of React. They are meant to simplify the process of sharing states between components and the process of maintaining a component throughout its lifecycle. A few are specifically used to handle state in your components as the project increases in complexity: `useState`, `useContext`, and `useReducer`.

useState

This is the hook you'll probably use the most in any React app. The `useState` hook provides the "memory" for an individual component. So when a user is entering values in a form, for example, `useState` stores those values until they change. Component state is isolated to a specific instance of a component, so you don't have to worry about states accidentally overlapping. You might have multiple search bars on the screen for different parts of the page, such as one in the header and one in the footer, like in this small example:

```
import SearchBar from './SearchBar.tsx';

const UserInfo = () => {
  // Fetch user info from the backend here

  return (
    <Container>
      <div>
        <header>
          <SearchBar />
        </header>
        <footer>
          <SearchBar />
        </footer>
      </div>
    </Container>
  )
}
```

Each SearchBar component has its own local state that is updated independently of the other. So any user actions in the first search bar won't affect the way the second search bar works. The Container component doesn't know anything that's happening in either of the search bar components to render correctly because the states are completely isolated from it. If you needed to have a state that affects both search bars in some way, then you would raise the state from the search bar components to the higher-level Container component.

When you raise the state (*https://oreil.ly/x-EIT*) of a component, you take the state from a child component and move it to the parent component. In this case, that would mean you move the useState hook from the SearchBar component and have it in the Container component.

The useState hook works by giving you access to both a value and an update method for that value. That's why you always see the state being declared in a format like this:

```
const [userInfo, setUserInfo] = useState<UserInfo>(initialUserInfo)
```

userInfo is the current value, and setUserInfo is the function you can use to update the current value; it triggers a rerender in React. initialUserInfo is the initial state value that gets used by the hook. The useState hook is great for whenever you have some state that's specific only to a component and doesn't need to be shared, such as forms, inputs, styled elements, and other small pieces of functionality that get reused a lot throughout the app. It can also be the starting point for testing out state in your app before you move on to a more complex state-management tool.

useReducer

Before you decide to use Redux, you should check out the useReducer hook (*https://oreil.ly/93rNA*) because it works similarly. This is React's built-in way of creating a more structured representation of your state in components and using actions and dispatchers. You can have predefined ways to update the state instead of updating it all at once, like with useState. An example of this is when you need to update a state that has a lot of interrelationships. Maybe you have several filters on a page that change when other filters are used. This would be a good place to try the useReducer hook.

Once you have functionality like that, your app state is at a higher complexity—this is something you want to look out for. When you recognize that handling states in your components involves several state changes across multiple user events or you're doing a lot of state management by passing props between components, it's time to research how to make that more efficient and maintainable.

When you use the reducer, you're able to manage a complex state as a single object instead of having multiple state variables. Many of the pros and cons of choosing between useState and useReducer come down to team preference. This is a great time to do a little demo to go over the differences and decide what to do together. You'll find that a mix of useReducer and useState can be nice for handling more complex scenarios as the app grows.

useContext

As the app grows in complexity and size, you will tend to raise the state higher and higher in the code. Over time, that leads to *prop drilling*, where you pass values through layers of components that don't need them. That leads to inefficient rerendering, and the code can get messier. You can use the useContext hook (*https://oreil.ly/tJoaW*) to extract your state and remove some prop drilling.

The <ThemeProvider /> component is an example of context being used for providing styles for all the descendant components in the DOM tree. Anything that requests the values from the <ThemeProvider /> component with the useContext hook will have direct access to them instead of having to pass them down the context tree.

It might be good to set up a context in the beginning if you know a certain value will get passed to deeply nested child components—although this is something that will likely be added over time because you can find real use cases for it when you need to refactor code. Understanding when to pivot to a different approach is one of those things that you'll have to use your skills to bring up. When you find prop drilling happening, document the values being passed and why. Then take that back to the team and discuss what everyone thinks about making the switch to useContext.

Larger apps will have many context providers at the top level of the app to manage values and state.

More Details About useContext

The `useContext` hook is a great tool, but there are some nuances to it that Ethan Brown was able to comment on. First, check out this example in his GitHub repo (*https://oreil.ly/BDGhQ*). He also had a bit more to say about how this hook affects performance:

> When state is lifted to the top level in larger apps, it's a common performance killer when people don't understand what `useContext` does and doesn't do for you. If you read through the example repo above, you'll see that context does not do anything for performance. I've seen far too many instances where someone says, "We use this piece of state everywhere, and I'm tired of passing it down. So let's switch to using context, and it will improve performance, too!"
>
> The problem is that context doesn't inherently do anything at all to improve performance and can even result in much worse performance if you're not considering how often the state in question is changing. For example, something like theme, language (for i18n), light/dark mode, or "current user" are all pretty reasonable uses for context as they change seldom, and when they do, you expect them to substantially change the entire component tree. Another reasonable use is a significant application context switch. For example, if you're building some kind of document editor, and users edit document X and work on that for a long time before switching to document Y, context makes sense.
>
> On the other hand, an example of a poor use of context is a sort or filter setting on a table. Such a setting is likely to change frequently, and every time it changes, the entire component tree has to re-rerender. This would have significant negative performance consequences, which would outweigh any benefit that context brings.

Knowing What App Level to Manage State In

When you have state that needs to be shared between components, then it's time to lift that state higher in the app. For example, you might have two filter inputs that display on the same page, and you want to update the page only when both have been changed. To do that, you would remove the state from the individual filters to the page level and then toggle the state for both filter inputs there. That way, you have a single source of truth that determines when both filters have been updated.

As you run into props that are getting passed down over 10 levels, you might bring up using context with the team. Larger apps can pass more than 10 props down 20 levels, which gets unwieldy over time. So when you notice the depth of the props getting farther away from the parent component, stay aware of that over time. Just because props are being passed a few levels doesn't mean it's time to use context. When it becomes a notable hindrance to development, then it's time to discuss it.

Take notes as you work on the code and add new features. It's a great idea to track observations you have in the codebase. It doesn't have to be a formal process or anything that gets shared with the team immediately. I usually keep a note with a bulleted list of potential refactors just so I remember where I saw room for improvements. During retrospective meetings or other team meetings, I'll bring up some of those things and try to get them on the sprint as tech cleanup.

Different Approaches to State Management

Before you move on to other tools, I highly encourage you to go through the React docs (*https://oreil.ly/kIlpT*) and learn more details about how the hooks work to manage state. You might find out that all you need are the built-in state-management hooks. If you've gotten to a point in your app where you need something more powerful than the built-in hooks, it's time to evaluate other tools.

There are a few approaches you should keep in mind as you and the team choose the state-management tools you'll work with. Three approaches to state management are reducer, atom, and mutable.

The *reducer* approach is the one that has a centralized source of truth. This is when you dispatch actions from all the components to the central source. Some strengths of this approach include having that central source and devtool support if you're using Redux (*https://redux.js.org*) or Zustand (*https://oreil.ly/k6W7c*). Some challenges include a number of new terms and concepts to understand and they may not be the absolute fastest tools compared to the built-in hooks.

The *atom* approach is where the state is split into smaller parts and can be managed through hooks. It's like creating your state as shareable components because you can derive states from these smaller parts. Packages like Recoil (*https://recoiljs.org*) and Jotai (*https://jotai.org*) are commonly used in this approach. Some of the pros to managing state like this are that it integrates really well with React features and it uses a similar format to what you already do with the useState hook. The main drawback is that you may need to create a graph representation of state instead of a linear one, and that can confuse more junior devs on your team.

The last approach I'll talk about is the *mutable* approach. This is when you work with tools that have proxies under the hood to create mutable data sources that can be directly written to and read from. Some of the packages you can use for this include MobX (*https://oreil.ly/p0ElX*) and Valtio (*https://valtio.pmnd.rs*). Some useful things about this approach are how flexible it is, how your dependencies are automatically updated when the state changes, and how it helps decrease the number of rerenders with the proxy. A drawback is that you aren't able to easily see when and how your data is being updated, making it harder to track changes through the code. The mixture of mutable and immutable data can also lead to unclarity in the code.

Proxies are just objects or functions for other objects or functions. It's like when you have an endpoint that handles the calls for your third-party services instead of calling them directly. With regard to state management, a proxy tracks changes to the original object and triggers listener functions when an object is updated. Check out the MDN docs on proxies (*https://oreil.ly/viUyD*) to learn more about what's built into JavaScript.

One of these approaches is typically used in addition to the built-in React state hooks. You'll want to discuss this heavily with the team because the choices you all make now will affect the bundle size, the user and developer experience, and how scalable the code is that you're working on.

A great way to make the choice of what approach to use is to figure out what the team's expertise is and then make a few small prototypes using different packages. You could do a comparison of state management using Redux, Jotai, and Valtio with a simple demo app and do your own benchmark tests. This will show you how fast the app will perform, the difference in bundle size, and what it's like to actually work with the package in the context of your app. Keep in mind that performance differences are complex and usually don't show until the app is much larger.

Once you've gone through this process with the team, you can add more functionality to the `UserInfo.Container` component you started work on in Chapter 14. For this project, you can assume it is of medium complexity, so you will use Valtio as the state-management tool. While it's an underdog, it can use existing devtools like Redux Toolkit (*https://redux-toolkit.js.org*), unlike MobX. It's also compatible with Node and Next.js and doesn't solely work in React.

It's important that you try out new things so that you can have a good toolbox to select from. It's a good exercise for you to try approaches you're unfamiliar with so that when you run into a relevant use case, you know where you can start. Don't worry about becoming an expert on every tool and methodology out there. Just having some awareness of what's possible will help you kick off conversations and spark ideas in other devs on the team.

Setting Up the State Manager

This won't be a tutorial on the details of how Valtio works, but it will show you how to implement it in your project. If you want to learn more about the inner workings behind the functions and variables we use, check out the Valtio docs (*https://oreil.ly/ZJeCC*) for more code examples and explanations. The purpose of this section is to give you a hands-on example of how you would work with a new tool and integrate it into your app. You'll need to install Valtio with the following command:

```
npm i valtio
```

Now you need to create a new file in *src/pages/UserInfo* called *UserInfo.State.tsx*. This is where you'll define some types, the proxy (*https://oreil.ly/AD9Gd*) that Valtio will use to keep track of state variables, and the actions that will be used to update the state based on user interactions. In this new file, add the following code:

```
import { proxy } from 'valtio'

const OrderStatus = {
  Pending: 'pending',
  Shipped: 'shipped',
  OutOfStock: 'out_of_stock',
} as const

export type OrderStatusKeys = (typeof OrderStatus)[keyof typeof OrderStatus]

export interface Order {
  id: string
  productName: string
  status: OrderStatusKeys
  orderedDate: string
  deliveryDate: string
  totalAmount: number
  hasBeenReviewed: boolean
}

export const orderStore = proxy<{
  filter: OrderStatusKeys | undefined
  orders: Order[]
}>({
  filter: undefined,
  orders: [],
})
```

It's important to note the `orderStore`. The `orderStore` is the actual proxy that stores the state as it's updated across different components. So this will hold the values you would normally set in a component with the `useState` hook. With the state-management functionality and variables in place, you need to use them in your components. Here's a snippet from the *UserInfo.Container.tsx* file:

```
...
import { useSnapshot } from 'valtio'
import { orderStore } from './UserInfo.State'

...

const UserInfo = () => {
  const orderSnap = useSnapshot(orderStore)

  const [userInfo, setUserInfo] = useState<UserInfo>(initialUserInfo)

  useEffect(() => {
```

```
  // Fetch user info and orders from the backend here

  setUserInfo(userResponseData)
  orderSnap.orders = orderResponseData
}, [])

return (
  <Container>
    <div>
      <div>{userInfo.name}</div>
      <div>Search bar</div>
      <div>
        {orderSnap.orders.map((order) => (
          <div key={order.id}>{order.productName}</div>
        ))}
      </div>
    </div>
  </Container>
)
}
…
```

This is where you need to import useSnapshot and orderStore so that you can work with the state in the component. The first thing to notice is the orderSnap variable because it's how you're able to access the current state in orderStore. When the page initially renders or rerenders from a state change, you'll have access to all the latest state values by calling useSnapshot with orderStore.

In the useEffect hook, you can see the mixture of local state and state from the proxy. orderSnap.orders is how you update the state in the proxy; that state will come from some API call. Depending on the component and app, you might do a hybrid approach like this to manage state as efficiently as possible. This is where some of the art in tech comes in as well as your developer experiences. For example, you might choose to handle form state locally and other states with the proxy. It mostly depends on what you and the team agree on; just stay consistent with the approach.

The JSX of the component that gets rendered uses orderSnap to map all the orders that are currently held in the proxy state. Once you start adding more components to this page, such as filtering orders, you'll start adding more actions to *User-Info.State.tsx* and use them throughout the app. This is a super-simple example of using a state-management tool. You could do all this with the built-in React hooks, but hopefully, you get an idea of how this can grow with the app and expand to handle complex features and state that needs to be updated on a deeper level than what's in the local component.

With the state extracted outside of any component, you can use it anywhere in the app. That's the power of a state-management tool and why they're typically used on larger apps. Many times, you don't need to lift the state outside the components until you have an established app and it becomes a need. Implementing a state-management tool too early can slow development and add more complexity than needed.

Conclusion

In this chapter, you dived into some of the details behind state management in React. Many of the built-in hooks will be more than enough to handle your application as it grows over time, but you can add a more powerful or versatile tool if the need arises. It's important to talk through these decisions with your team because their expertise and opinions will drive the future development and maintainability of the app.

Something you can do to help facilitate these conversations is set up little demos where the team can see how different tools work. State management can get messy when you have multiple actions updating multiple states across several components, so getting everyone to weigh in on the direction you all will take is crucial. Remember, as you build the app and the product grows, you and the team will have to decide the best way to handle state going forward and make sure it's well documented.

## CHAPTER 16

Data Management

You already have some state management in place, so now it's time to fetch and update data. Talk with the devs who are working on the backend so that you can communicate expectations around API calls. Since you're a full stack dev, you can also note any changes that need to be made and write tickets to do that work yourself. For now, you and the backend devs have agreed on expected endpoints and data schema, so you can get started.

It's a good practice to limit the number of API calls that the frontend needs to make for performance reasons. So you really need to understand how the data will affect the page layout and when it needs to show in the UX flow. Users need a consistent experience or else they think something is wrong with the product or some data they need is missing or incorrect. Considering this will help you figure out how data should flow.

In this chapter, I'll cover:

- API calls
- Async handling
- When to check on backend functionality
- Tools you can use

There are some nuances to calling data endpoints because you have to think about latency and what happens when your backend requests don't return what you expect. You also have to think about when data should be requested and why calls are being made. This is going to show you if the backend returns data in the format you need. You will likely need to make minor adjustments on the backend as you put together the interface.

Before you jump into the code and request data, it's good to evaluate the tools you have available and review them with the team.

Potential Tools for Fetching Data

The ecosystem for JavaScript tools is constantly changing, so you have to do research to make sure you're staying up to date with the latest tools. There are currently several you should mention in the discussion with the other devs to make the selection: Tan-Stack Query (*https://oreil.ly/4CDZJ*), SWR (*https://swr.vercel.app*), RTK Query (*https://oreil.ly/Y7JZf*), and React Router (*https://oreil.ly/3zx6h*). You'll find that some of these tools work well together and pair nicely with Axios (*https://oreil.ly/mqrK1*) or the built-in Fetch API (*https://oreil.ly/hiMro*).

Some specific metrics you want to look at for data-fetching libraries include:

- Cache management
- Devtools
- Retry handling
- Error handling
- Query and mutation capabilities
- Supported protocols
- API definitions
- How well it integrates into the front-end framework

You also need to consider standard package metrics like:

- Bundle size
- Community support
- Documentation
- Examples

The team's experience is going to help drive the decisions here because each dev will be able to highlight some of the practical aspects of the tools they've worked with. If you already have Redux in your app, then RTK Query will be a great option because it's part of the Redux suite. Having caching, memoization, or refetching implemented out of the box could lead you to choose a full-feature tool, like TanStack Query or SWR.

 Memoization is when functions that are time or computationally expensive have their results cached. When you pass a function the same argument values, it will return the same result. In these cases, memoization will return a cached result when the same arguments are passed to the function without running the function again.

It's important to have discussions and demos for all the options you all come up with. The packages you choose at this point will greatly affect speed and user experience as the app grows and functionality becomes more dependent on data updates. As with state management, you *can* switch tools later, but that will be a large refactor that you and the team will have to do gradually.

If there's a reason to switch to GraphQL or tRPC (*https://trpc.io*) on the backend—for instance, you have very complex data relationships or deeply nested values—then your frontend tool will also likely change to be compatible with the response you'll get. That's when you might consider something more specific like urql (*https://oreil.ly/9kcjK*) or Apollo Client (*https://oreil.ly/VrF-i*). You can find comparisons (*https://oreil.ly/g7gJB*) of a number of tools (*https://oreil.ly/dAwyt*) that have been done by different people (*https://oreil.ly/TKJ0f*), but it's good to do your own benchmark testing for at least the top three choices from the team.

Once you've figured out the tools and combinations you want to use to get the best metrics, you can install and set up the tools that you and the team agreed to use for data handling. Then you'll get into some of the details, like loading states and configuring headers. We'll take a deeper dive into error handling in Chapter 18 because that will involve more than just API errors.

Handling API Calls with Axios and TanStack Query

You'll use Axios for your API requests because it comes with many built-in configs, so the syntax you'll use is a little more straightforward than with the standard Fetch API. You'll also use TanStack Query as the tool to handle your API responses because it's very feature rich. Caching responses, pagination, and reducing the number of requests you need to make are just a few of the huge tasks this package handles for you out of the box.

> One quick thing to take note of is that the Fetch API can do essentially the same things as Axios. So it might not be necessary to install the package. Axios does offer a streamlined developer experience, though. This is another thing you'll want to check in with your team on because some devs have a preference for one tool over the other.

Install Axios, TanStack Query, and the TanStack Query plug-in to help with debugging and catching potential issues with these commands:

```
npm i @tanstack/react-query axios
npm i -D @tanstack/eslint-plugin-query
```

TanStack Query works like a context, so you'll need to create the query client (*https://oreil.ly/YjwLI*) and wrap the entire app in the query client provider (*https://oreil.ly/mMogL*). In the *App.tsx* file, make the following updates to initialize and use the query client and provider:

```
…
import { QueryClient, QueryClientProvider } from '@tanstack/react-query'
…

const queryClient = new QueryClient()
…
const App = () => {
  // Do some stuff here
  return (
    <QueryClientProvider client={queryClient}>
      <ThemeProvider theme={theme}>
        <AppContainer component="main">
          <NavBar />
          <CurrentScreen component="section">
            <RouterProvider router={router} />
          </CurrentScreen>
        </AppContainer>
      </ThemeProvider>
    </QueryClientProvider>
  )
}
```

The whole app is wrapped in the `QueryClientProvider` component, and it has access to everything in the `queryClient` cache. You can do more advanced things, like set options for the cache on the query client. It has a lot of methods that you can use to interact with the cache as well, so make sure to read through the docs as you go through the initial setup to see if there's anything you need up front. Some of these options will come up organically as the app grows and user needs change.

Before you move on to updating the `UserInfo` component to fetch data with Axios and store it with TanSatack Query, there's a dev task you need to do. In the root of the project, add a new file called *.env*.

The .env File

On the backend, Node introduced first-class support for *.env* files in Node 20 (*https://oreil.ly/OxTw4*). Before that, devs used the dotenv package. As with the backend, you can use environment variables (env vars) on the frontend. One big reason to use env vars is that they are more secure because they live in memory, not on disk. This means that it's generally harder for an attacker to get sensitive data because it gets reset instead of persisting somewhere like a database, which is true for the backend.

On the backend, you can use env vars liberally to provide secrets or sensitive configs. You just have to make sure you don't pass anything to the frontend accidentally. On the frontend, env vars are simulated and should *never* contain sensitive info. When you build the code, your env vars will be present in the compiled output in plain text. So frontend env vars are only good for things you don't mind being public, like end-point URLs or public API keys.

This is a very extensive topic, and it's not something you need to dig too deep into unless you want to get into the details of security mechanisms and hardware. Just know that when you use env vars, your secrets are typically not stored in your repo (check the *.gitignore* file for more details) and get pulled from your CI/CD pipeline based on the environment the app gets deployed to.

When you're developing locally or working in a develop environment, it's OK to load environment variables from disk in an *.env* file because the values here shouldn't affect your production data or billing for services. Depending on the tool you choose to build your app, you'll access env vars similarly to how you do on the backend with code like the following:

```
const apiUrl = process.env.VITE_API_URL
```

Since you're using Vite on the frontend in this example app, you'll access env vars (*https://oreil.ly/-U0gV*) with this code:

```
const apiUrl = import.meta.env.VITE_API_URL
```

So go to your *.env* file because this is where you'll put the URL to call your API. The reason you define the API URL in this file is because the value might change depending on what environment the app gets deployed to. Some teams have a develop environment for the backend that's used for testing both backend and frontend functionality. This environment is separate from production, so the API URL will be different. In that new *.env* file, add this line:

```
VITE_API_URL=http://localhost:3000
```

For local feature development, it's good to run the backend code locally from the state it's in at Chapter 11. That way, you can just connect to the local API instead of a deployed API and make adjustments to the backend as needed.

Now you can create a new file in *src/page/UserInfo* called *useUserInfo.tsx*. This is a custom hook (*https://oreil.ly/7NSvt*) that will handle the API calls for you. You'll add the code to make the backend calls using the VITE_API_URL you just defined. The reasons you're making a custom hook are to have a clear separation of concerns, to make testing easier, and to keep your component code readable. So add the following code to your custom hook:

```
import { useQuery } from '@tanstack/react-query'
import axios from 'axios'

function useUserInfo() {
  const {
    isLoading: ordersAreLoading,
    error: ordersErrors,
    data: orderData,
  } = useQuery({
    queryKey: ['orderData'],
    queryFn: () =>
```

```
    axios.get(`${import.meta.env.VITE_API_URL}/v1/orders`)
      .then((res) => res.data),
  })

  const {
    isLoading: userIsLoading,
    error: userErrors,
    data: userData,
  } = useQuery({
    queryKey: ['userData'],
    queryFn: () =>
      axios.get(`${import.meta.env.VITE_API_URL}/v1/users`)
        .then((res) => res.data),
  })

  return {
    ordersAreLoading,
    ordersErrors,
    orderData,
    userIsLoading,
    userErrors,
    userData,
  }
}

export default useUserInfo
```

The first thing to note is the useQuery hook (*https://oreil.ly/eos-F*) being called to fetch the data with Axios and cache the response. The useQuery hook includes a number of values you can use to make the app more responsive, but for now you need only the loading states (ordersAreLoading, userIsLoading), the error states (ordersErrors, userErrors), and the data from the requests (orderData, userData). The API URL you defined is being used in the requests. All of these are returned as values from your custom hook in *UserInfo.Container.tsx*.

In *UserInfo.Container.tsx,* you'll need to do the following refactors to your code to use this hook and render the component based on the values returned from it:

```
...
const UserInfo = () => {
  const {
    orderData,
    ordersAreLoading,
    ordersErrors,
    userData,
    userIsLoading,
    userErrors,
  } = useUserInfo()

  const { showBoundary } = useErrorBoundary()
```

```
useEffect(() => {
  orderStore.orders = orderData
}, [orderData])

useEffect(() => {
  userStore.user = userData
}, [userData])

if (userIsLoading || ordersAreLoading)
  return <div>Data is loading...</div>

if (userErrors || ordersErrors) <div>Something went wrong</div>
...

return (
  <Container component="section">
    <Header
      userName={userStore.user.name}
      joinedDate={userStore.user.joinedDate}
      onSubmitSearch={onSubmitProductSearch}
    />
    <OrderForm />
    <OrdersTable orders={orderStore.orders} />
  </Container>
)
}
```

You can note where the states get updated in the useEffect hooks based on their individual dependencies. So whenever the value for orderData or userData changes, the respective state will get updated as well. Finally, there are two conditionally rendered components for the loading and error states. This provides a better UX, so users aren't left wondering why they can't interact with the page.

Handling Loading States

Something you should create are actual components for your loading states. You can have different loading states for each component on the page that receives data dynamically. This is where your component library can help. You should discuss this with the Design and Product teams. MUI has different loading state components (*https://oreil.ly/xnv_f*) that you can customize for your app, which can give you a starting point for the discussion.

For example, you will have separate calls for your orders search in the table on the user info page and the general user data that gets loaded. You could block the whole page and wait for all the responses to return, but this will negatively affect the UX because users won't be able to do anything on the page. One of these responses will likely return before the other, and you'll need to show a slightly different loading state for each.

As a simple example, you can have two different loading components for the user header and the orders table that get conditionally rendered instead of one check for both loading states, as in the following example and Figure 16-1:

```
// UserInfo.Container.tsx
...
  return (
    <Container>
      {userIsLoading ? (
          <CircularProgress />
        ) : (
          <Header
            userName={userStore.user.name}
            joinedDate={userStore.user.joinedDate}
            onSubmitSearch={onSubmitProductSearch}
          />
        )}
      <div>Search bar</div>
      {ordersAreLoading ? (
        <CircularProgress color="secondary" />
      ) : (
        orderSnap.orders.map((order) => (
          <div key={order.id}>{order.productName}</div>
        ))
      )}
    </Container>
  )
...
```

Figure 16-1. Screenshot of the multiple loading components in the code

This removes that shared component that returned when both data requests were loading and gives you more flexibility with what users see and experience. Your loading state helps you take care of the asynchronous way API calls are made from the frontend. You can chain promises (*https://oreil.ly/P3SN3*), use `Promise.all` (*https://oreil.ly/L34oM*), or manually create a loading state to handle data. TanStack Query handles that with the `isLoading` value that gets returned until you get a response. You can combine multiple requests into one, depending on how you configure TanStack Query options.

Handling Error States

We'll go into much more detail on error handling in Chapter 18 because it's a huge discussion, but you can add a bit to your component now to cover it initially. Think of this implementation as scaffolding to unblock the team for now. When you get an error from any of your API requests, you want to handle it gracefully so that the app doesn't crash for the user. Having a simple error message that lets the user know something happened is better than nothing:

```
...
useEffect(() => {
  orderStore.orders = orderData
}, [orderData])

useEffect(() => {
  userStore.user = userData
}, [userData])

if (userErrors || ordersErrors)
  return (
    <Alert icon={<CheckIcon fontSize="inherit" />} severity="error">
      Something went wrong
    </Alert>
  )
...
```

Now the users will see this message whenever there's an error from either request. In Chapter 18, you'll see how to split these into separate messages for different error levels and how to handle them across components.

Configuring Request Headers

As you see in this example, you will get to the point where you need to make multiple requests to provide the functionality the user expects. This will involve sending requests to the backend that need specific values in the header, like access tokens or expected data types. So you need to configure your data-fetching tools to handle headers to avoid things like CORS errors (*https://oreil.ly/Z3Ztj*) or sending data in invalid formats. You can configure the headers on each request, or you can do it on a global level in the app to ensure consistency across all your requests.

For this app, you can assume that you and the team decided to configure the headers with Axios (*https://oreil.ly/ucot2*) at the global level for better maintainability and easier debugging. One of the most common headers to configure globally is for authorization, although you can configure headers for endpoint patterns as well. You'll do this by creating a new file called *axios.config.ts* in the *src* directory. In this file, you'll define the base URL for all the requests being made, the content type, and the authorization:

```
import axios from 'axios'

const AUTH_TOKEN = localStorage.getItem('dashboard_web_auth')

axios.defaults.baseURL = import.meta.env.VITE_API_URL

axios.defaults.headers.common['Authorization'] = AUTH_TOKEN
axios.defaults.headers.post['Content-Type'] = 'application/json'
```

For now, the AUTH_TOKEN is a placeholder value that may or may not come from the localStorage. That's something I'll get into in Chapter 19 as we cover more security concerns. Since the base URL is defined at the global level, it will be used for every request you make in the app. If you need to make requests for different base URLs, you can make those per request, or you can have different instances of Axios that you use.

After you talk it over with the team, you may choose an approach like making hooks for your requests or making an SDK for the backend. An *SDK* is when you make a package that exports methods that make the API requests along with types for the methods and parameters and any documentation for the methods. This is an approach you might take if you're making these API requests in multiple frontend apps or other backend apps. SendGrid (*https://oreil.ly/vqiOo*) and Google Maps (*https://oreil.ly/ND8MA*) are examples of widely used SDKs.

You also need to discuss the caching strategy your app will use, which I'll go over in Chapter 20. As you set up the rest of the frontend requests, you'll need to make sure the frontend isn't handling backend functionality.

When to Check on Backend Functionality

Anytime you start doing calculations on the frontend, it's time to examine the backend more closely. While the frontend can handle calculations, doing them on the backend provides more consistency across browsers and client machines. So when you get to a point where you need to do calculations with the data on the frontend, double-check if it would make more sense to move that logic to the backend. That way, you can do all the calculations directly on the server one time instead of thousands of times across clients, or you could cache the result and send it to the client.

If you do a lot of data formatting on the frontend, you should check if there's a reason for this. If you have other services that are calling this endpoint and that's a reason, consider making a different endpoint. Split the business reasons so that the user functionality doesn't get affected by changes meant for other services.

Another thing to look for is when the frontend receives large payloads. This might be for pagination, sorting, or filtering if it wasn't included in the original API specs. Go over this with the team because it could be something that needs to be added to the

---

backend for multiple endpoints. Having a standard format to request data for different pages is going to help with code quality as the app grows, so really discuss this with the team.

Something else to note is when you need to make multiple requests to fetch data and then merge it on the frontend. Talk it over with the team and decide if there is a way to make a single endpoint for this data or if you really do need the separate endpoints. It's not always a bad thing to make multiple requests if it makes sense for long-term development. There might be optimization reasons to have separate endpoints, like keeping a separation of concerns on the backend.

Conclusion

In this chapter, you learned more about handling the data requests and responses with tools that can make the process easier to manage. Caching is a huge undertaking on the frontend, so having a package that handles that for you out of the box with a few configs is very helpful. Also having tools that automatically tell you the status of your request helps you show the user meaningful messages on the page. When this is paired with state management, you've created a large part of your frontend.

Establishing consistent, well-thought-out data-management strategies now will help keep any future code secure. You have the core functionality in place, and you've enabled your team to really dive into feature development. There will be options that you'll update and add or even remove as the product becomes feature rich. This is when you'll need to be stricter in your code reviews so that the quality of the code remains high.

## CHAPTER 17

Custom Styles

You already have designs to work with to get the initial app built, but this will go through multiple iterations as you build out features and the Product team gets feedback from users. You will be working with the Design team constantly to ensure that the styling of the app remains consistent as new features are added and new designers are brought onto their team.

Fonts, sizes, spacing, colors, and custom components like steppers, modals, and containers are going to be reused throughout the app. Sometimes the Design team will introduce inconsistencies because there is a lot to manage. As this happens, make sure to mention it immediately so that you all can decide which is the best design for both the users and the devs. If you notice a design will decrease accessibility, mention that, too.

In this chapter, I'll cover:

- Accessibility
- Consistency in designs
- Custom themes
- Responsive design

You'll need to use your experience to know when designs are becoming too complex in the codebase and work with the Design team to find a good balance. You already have the structure set up for custom theming, so now you'll expand on that with the organization style guide. Let's start by covering accessibility because that should be built into the designs from the beginning.

Accessibility

The reason I'm bringing up accessibility first is because it can be an afterthought when you are trying to get a minimum viable product (MVP) ready and you and the team are churning out features as quickly as possible. Accessibility isn't a secondary part of the app design. It's just as important, if not more important, than concerns like mobile design. Not only does accessibility give fair access to information for those who have disabilities, but it's also a legal requirement under the Americans with Disabilities Act (ADA) (*https://oreil.ly/7piF5*).

While MUI has many accessibility features, it's your responsibility to ensure you use things like aria labels, alt text on images, semantic HTML for screen readers, and keyboard commands for navigating the page. Here are some example code snippets of these:

```
<!-- aria label example -->
<button aria-label="Cancel" onClick={onCancel}>Cancel</button>

<!-- alt text for image example -->
<img src="https://images.unsplash.com/photo-1497531551184-06b252e1bee1"
  alt="Multi-colored hot air balloon with three people in the basket
    in the sky" />

<!-- semantic html example -->
<h1>Welcome to the Test Store</h1>
```

As you build out forms, make sure you have clear instructions and you give useful feedback with error and success messages. While you should highlight any poor color contrasts you notice, the Design team should be aware of that and manage it. Make sure that static content is easy for users to find with their screen readers because it usually has important info they shouldn't miss.

Use Semantic Elements More than <div> Tags

If you notice that your components are made of a bunch of <div> tags, update them to use semantic elements like <section>, <article>, <aside>, or any of the others (*https://oreil.ly/uFlOr*). Developers have the habit of reaching for one or two elements and none of the others. Since you're going to have to implement custom styles anyway, using different elements isn't going to affect the way the page renders visually.

Each of the HTML elements has a meaning to accessible devices, and they will help give users an exponentially better experience. So when you type a <div> element, see how easy it would be for you to navigate the app with a screen reader and keyboard buttons alone. You can try it out with a tool like Polypane (*https://polypane.app/docs*) or Responsively (*https://responsively.app*). This doesn't mean that <div> elements are bad, but you should consider whether there's a better element before using them.

Making an Accessible Form

It's important that forms are accessible because they allow users to take action. If someone can't use or understand a form, they won't be able to handle critical tasks like submitting payments, updating personal information, or requesting services. Don't forget about making your informational content accessible as well, or else a differently abled user may not even get to your forms.

You're going to create a reusable, styled form in the app, and it will be added to the user info page for the first search bar with accessibility in mind. You can assume you've talked this over with the team and decided to go with React Hook Form (*https://oreil.ly/H1lqR*) as the package that will be used throughout the app. Install it with this command:

```
npm install react-hook-form
```

Once it's installed, create a new component under *src/elements* called *SearchBar.tsx*. This will be used for all the search bars in the app. Here's the code for the search bar:

```
import { Input, InputAdornment, InputLabel } from '@mui/material'
import SearchIcon from '@mui/icons-material/Search'
import { useForm } from 'react-hook-form'
import styled from 'styled-components'

export type SearchBarProps = {
  name: string
  onSubmitSearch: (searchText: string) => void
}

const FullWidthForm = styled.form`
  width: 450px;
  @media (max-width: 500px) {
    width: 100%;
  }
`

const SearchBar = (props: SearchBarProps) => {
  const { onSubmitSearch } = props
  const {
    register,
    handleSubmit,
    formState: { errors },
  } = useForm()

  const searchFieldInputProps = {
    maxLength: 15,
    minLength: 3,
  }

  return (
    <FullWidthForm
      aria-label={`${props.name} search form`}
      onSubmit={handleSubmit(onSubmitSearch)}
    >
      <InputLabel htmlFor="search">Search Input</InputLabel>
      <Input
```

```
            placeholder={`Search ${props.name}...`}
            type="search"
            fullWidth
            inputProps={searchFieldInputProps}
            startAdornment={
              <InputAdornment position="start">
                <SearchIcon />
              </InputAdornment>
            }
            {...register('search', { required: true, maxLength: 15, minLength: 3 })}
            aria-invalid={errors.search ? 'true' : 'false'}
          />
          {errors && errors.search && (
            <span>Search text doesn't meet requirements</span>
          )}
        </FullWidthForm>
      )
    }

export default SearchBar
```

 Don't forget to create the *index.tsx* and *SearchBar.test.tsx* files! I won't explicitly say that each time, but the pattern for new components will always have these files in addition to the core component file.

MUI combined with React Hook Form will give you forms that are easy to style, have accessibility out of the box, and allow you to handle your fields with a lightweight API. You'll have to read through the MUI docs to fully understand the props being passed to the <Input /> component (*https://oreil.ly/iQOBE*), but a few things need to be called out in terms of accessibility.

All of the aria-labels (*https://oreil.ly/YFXGI*) are there to help users on screen readers keep track of where they are on the page. Not every element on the page needs an aria-label, so use it only on interactive elements. Most of the elements should be intuitive enough with the visible text, and that typically translates well to assistive devices. Something else to note is that there isn't a Submit button on the search bar. This is per the design and also helps with accessibility because the default behavior for a form is to submit when the Enter key is pressed.

The type="search" prop is one way to introduce semantic HTML with your component because it calls out that this element is going to be used to perform a search. Another thing doing a lot of work here is the inputProps (*https://oreil.ly/8XKA5*) prop. This is one way MUI lets you handle errors in your forms.

Errors are an essential part of accessibility because they help a user figure out where they need to fix something and how they can do that. This input requires a value for submission, and there's a minimum number of characters. If a user enters an invalid value, they will get a friendly alert next to the input with the problem. Chapter 18 will focus on all the different errors that happen on the frontend and how you can account for them.

Checking Your Accessibility Implementations

Once you are ready to check how well your accessibility work has been implemented, the first place you can turn to is the browser devtools. Chrome in particular has some good devtools for evaluating how accessible your app is. You can do a quick audit by checking how things are grouped and any labels or functionality attached to them, as shown in Figure 17-1. You can check the order that users will tab through as they navigate the page with a keyboard only.

Figure 17-1. Accessibility tab in Chrome DevTools

You can also run an audit using Lighthouse (*https://oreil.ly/YNKNW*) to get more insights into how you can improve your accessibility, as shown in Figure 17-2. Lighthouse is an open source tool that audits your web app for performance, accessibility, and a number of other metrics. If you aren't sure of what to improve, this can give you a great list of things to do. Run your findings by the Product and Design teams because there may be legal implications that they deal with in the background. This won't necessarily tell you the exact components that need to be improved, but it'll give you a general idea of what to look for.

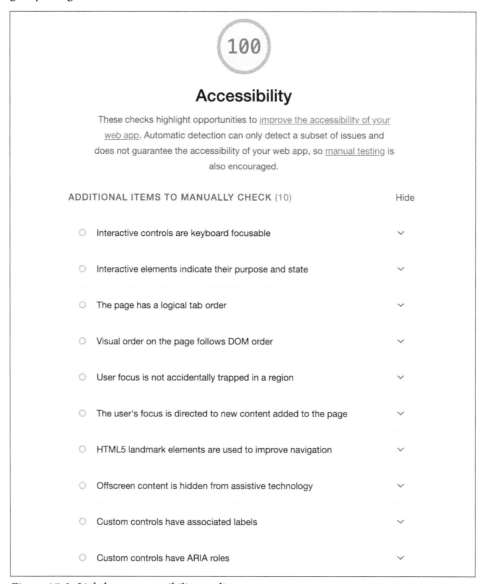

Figure 17-2. Lighthouse accessibility audit

Another tool I've used on enterprise apps is axe-core (*https://oreil.ly/xI21p*). This is a great lightweight tool to add an extra layer of accessibility testing. You can install it in your app and add it as part of your testing during development. It will help you and the team find commonly missed accessibility rules. It's a valuable tool when you want to add more automated testing to your deployment pipeline, which we'll go over in Chapter 24. Here's an example of how you can add it to your code:

```
axe.run(document, function (err, results) {
  if (err) throw err;
  console.log(results);
});
```

This will show all accessibility issues in the console when you run the app. You can configure axe to run only for specific Web Content Accessibility Guidelines (WCAG) rules (*https://oreil.ly/Br9Qd*) or to target specific components of the app if you need to focus on a complex area. This can be used to help you with compliance audits before new releases.

More Accessibility Considerations

Most apps will be used by people who speak languages other than English, so it's important to keep them in mind. One great tool for doing this type of localization is i18n (*https://oreil.ly/DPdXw*). You can create files for each language that you need translations in. If a user toggles the app to another language, all the text will be updated immediately. You will have to keep the design in mind as you add translations because some languages require more space for the text, so that can cause variations in spacing.

Consistent Designs

After you've addressed accessibility for the app to meet the current designs and specs, there will be continuous iterations on the designs. The hard part comes when the designs get scattered across different platforms like Figma, Miro, or even screenshots. It becomes difficult to keep track of the current versions of the designs. Differences in common components start to slip in, and the next thing you know, there are four designs for the same modal.

While the management and versioning of designs often falls on the Design team, you are the one who has to meet the requirements for new features. When you start noticing inconsistencies, you have to bring them up. It doesn't matter if it's as "small" as a change in padding on buttons or the colors being used in certain parts of the app. Changes like these can influence the way you and the team work on the app.

Something else you want to cover within the dev team is how you will implement styles and make sure that you document them. There will be a lot of opinions on how the code should be written. Some devs consider inline styles to be harder to maintain and feel that every element should be some sort of styled component. Others will disagree and say that CSS classes should be used to define styles. Then there are others who will want to have files for styles on the component level. None of these are wrong, and usually a combination of strategies will be implemented.

The main thing is to keep your codebase consistent. When you're doing PR reviews, call out anything that goes against the convention everyone agreed on. It's inevitable for changes to happen as the app grows and the team changes, but it should be understood and documented when something deviates from the norm. Over time, the code will become a form of version control for the designs, so you want to make sure that everyone is able to understand and explain where things are changing.

Custom Themes

You've already implemented custom theming with MUI in the *theme.tsx,* and you'll keep this file updated with any changes that affect the MUI components you use. Buttons are a good example of a commonly customized component. You'll have the same buttons throughout the app, and they will need to align with the company branding. In the styles for this app, several buttons have the branded green color. This is where you can update *theme.tsx* to something like this:

```
...
const theme = createTheme({
...
  components: {
    MuiButton: {
      styleOverrides: {
        root: {
          color: '#4C4C4C',
          borderRadius: '4px',
          background: '#B4CD93',
        },
      },
    },
  },
})
```

MUI has good support for custom theming, but it's not without issues. You can run into some conflicts with MUI. This happens with any component library that you choose, but there inevitably comes a time where your designs will get tricky to implement. You'll run into some situations where you'll have something in your custom themes and will still need inline styles for a specific page.

This leads to a mixture of CSS rules in your theme and in local components, making it hard to figure out where to add new styles. So anytime the Design team comes to you with global changes that already have custom styles, just ask about it. These usually create more work than Design anticipates and can unexpectedly change other parts of the design.

It's important to remember that there isn't a perfect component library or styling solution. There are other options like Tailwind CSS (*https://oreil.ly/MpJ_z*) or CSS Modules (*https://oreil.ly/Cmr34*), but implementing styles is more of an art than a science.

Every developer who works on the frontend will have an opinion, and the Design team may also have opinions on what they think will work best. You even run into situations where a new dev on the team isn't aware of existing components.

Tools like Storybook (*https://oreil.ly/UsfYM*), Ladle (*https://ladle.dev*), or React Cosmos (*https://oreil.ly/g5r_h*) help you with documentation so that finding existing components becomes easier. This will also help keep the Design team up to date with components that have been implemented. And these tools are good for prototyping components, especially when one component has several variations. You can think of this like the developer-design bridge for shared components, and it can be like a brand book for the overall organization.

Responsive Design

Mobile-first design is a common concept, but it doesn't always happen first. Sometimes you will be working on apps that only have desktop designs and you have to add responsiveness later. Before you jump into the design work for desktop only, double-check with Product and Design if there should be a mobile version, too.

There are a few ways to handle responsive implementation later in a project, but it's going to require a large amount of refactoring no matter how you try to get around it. If you're using a component library, like we are with MUI here, then you do get some responsiveness out of the box. The rest will depend on the layout you develop. One way to handle that is with *breakpoints*, where you switch to styles or components that have been developed for a subset of devices like tablets and phones. Here's an example of how you might implement that with the `Header` component:

```
const StyledHeader = styled.header`
  display: flex;
  justify-content: space-between;

  @media (max-width: 500px) {
    flex-direction: column-reverse;
    width: 100%;
  }
`
```

Using media queries (*https://oreil.ly/iKwQk*) like this is a common approach to building responsiveness. It generally works well regardless of the other style implementations you have, and you can add these at any point in the project. Or you might create separate components for the mobile view because the functionality is arranged differently enough that it's easier to read and maintain code this way. You and the team could even go with custom layout structures and create stylesheets because the page changes so drastically.

Create Your Components with Responsiveness in Mind

I've worked on apps where the company truly believed it wouldn't need a mobile or responsive version and that everyone would *have* to use the product on a desktop. Responsive versions of those apps were never created. While it's rare, this does still happen.

More often than not, though, many apps reach a point where they need to be responsive. Remember, this covers more than just mobile and desktop. Your users could have the window at less than full-screen size, they could be using any number of smaller screen sizes, and their resolution could be different. You should also consider adaptive design where you have fixed layouts for specific device types.

If you can, create your components with this in mind. It doesn't have to be perfect if you aren't styling according to designs. But if you have some responsiveness in mind from the beginning, that will make everything easier for development later.

Be aware of UX with responsive designs. You might have parts of the app that slide in and out on the page, or you might hide content completely on smaller views. This can make content inaccessible to users, or the product may become unintuitive to work with, especially when you consider going from cursor-based interactions to touchscreen interactions. Things like hover states aren't as easy for a user to figure out on a touchscreen device.

Images are something else you have to be careful with in responsive design. You may want to stretch or shrink an image to fit into a certain box, within a reasonable range. The aspect ratio should be maintained across all screen sizes to keep the image as clear as possible. With raster images like PNGs and JPGs, your images could get grainy when they're stretched. When you have images like graphics or illustrations, you can use Scalable Vector Graphics (SVG) to keep image quality across all device sizes. Here's an example of how you might implement a responsive image with srcset (*https://oreil.ly/Pksox*):

```
<img
  srcset="tulip-field-320w.jpg, tulip-field-480w.jpg 1.5x,
    tulip-field-640w.jpg 2x"
  src="tulip-field-640w.jpg"
  alt="A field of tulips blooming" />
```

Make sure you pay attention to browser support for the CSS you use to implement designs with a tool like CanIUse (*http://caniuse.com*). Not every browser version will support the latest CSS features, and some features aren't backward compatible. You'll need to work with Product to decide which browsers to support and which versions of those browsers you should support. Otherwise, you can end up with some very messy CSS styles just to support Internet Explorer 11 for a handful of users.

Also consider working with Web Components (*https://oreil.ly/GPwzx*). These are custom elements you can create with the JavaScript API. These elements are part of the shadow DOM, which keeps the styles and functionality of the elements separate from the main DOM so that you don't have to worry about them clashing with each other. This is a newer option that's growing in adaptation across JavaScript frameworks, so it's something that could come up in the discussions about the best way to handle responsive design.

Conclusion

In this chapter, you dived into some of the concepts behind implementing designs in your project. Of all the things on the frontend, this is probably the one that brings in the most opinions. There really isn't a standard way to implement designs because every team has its own expertise and ideas for what is maintainable. As the app grows, the organization expands, and new members of the Design team are added, even the core themes can change drastically.

The main thing here is to strive for consistency in user and developer experience. Whether you decide to use a prebuilt component library, implement styles based on class names, or do some combination of everything, as long as it doesn't interfere with the UX, you've reached the goal. And as long as the team can figure out where styles are coming from and how they are connected, then the DX is manageable. Just keep the communication flowing among your team, the Product team, and the Design team to avoid confusion as much as possible.

## CHAPTER 18

Frontend Error Handling

You've already implemented much of the functionality that is common to all frontend apps. Up to this point, you have created an infrastructure that should allow the app to be expanded to accommodate any new features that the Product team can throw at you. Now you can dive into more of the details on the frontend that make the app more user-friendly.

I've briefly mentioned errors in other chapters of the book, but we'll finally take a closer look here. Error handling was left out before so that you could focus on best practices for the other parts of the frontend. In practice, though, error handling should be included in the requirements for your tasks. You have to deal with all the errors that could potentially happen to the user. Error handling needs to be thorough so that you don't leak any sensitive information to users or malicious parties who are trying to attack your app and so that the app keeps a consistent UX.

In this chapter, I'll cover:

- Error components
- User validation errors
- API errors

These are all standard errors that will eventually come up, so I'll go over common ways to handle them. You'll need to work with the Product and Design teams to define and create useful error states that will lead the user down the path they need to take. As you and the team build the app, take note of any edge cases you run into during development, which could bring up things no one had considered before.

Error Boundary Approaches

Error boundaries (https://oreil.ly/BYtEd) are components that display a fallback UI, such as an error message, when errors are caught in your component tree. These error boundaries are unique to React, but it's generally a good practice to have something like them. If you don't have an error boundary, users will typically see a blank screen in production, and you'll see the React error overlay that tells you what the error is during development. This will happen anytime there's an issue with a component rendering or with any runtime errors. Usually, it's because of issues with API calls or something the user is doing that the app hasn't been tested for. This can also cause network errors if you're depending on a value to make a request.

You might think that using `try/catch` blocks like you would on the backend will work, but they don't capture errors like you might expect. That's because unlike on the backend, React is calling the functions instead of you, which is a more declarative approach. This type of error handling is fine for functionality that is imperatively implemented, but it's not the safest option for rendering errors.

The Difference Between Declarative and Imperative Programming

When `try/catch` blocks are discussed in terms of error handling, you'll hear about declarative and imperative programming. *Declarative programming* is when you tell the code what you want it to do without getting into the details of how it happens. *Imperative programming* is when you tell the code how to do what you want. To make sure the difference is clear, let's look at array handling as an example. With declarative programming, you would use the built-in array methods like this:

```
const filteredOrders = orders.filter(order => order.totalAmount >= 100);
```

With imperative programming, you would do something like this:

```
let filteredOrders = [];

for (let i = 0; i < orders.length; i++) {
    const order = orders[i];

    if (order.totalAmount >= 100) {
        filteredOrders.push(order);
    }
}
```

We usually do declarative programming in React because it's easier to read as you gain experience and it's faster to develop.

To address this restriction with `try/catch`, you can apply several common strategies to your app to create error boundaries. This includes boundaries at the:

- App level
- Layout level
- Component level

Regardless of what level you implement the boundary on, one thing to keep in mind is that the error boundary won't handle things like async errors, errors that happen in event handlers, and errors thrown in the boundary itself. You'll end up using a combination of these strategies to manage errors throughout the app.

The *app-level* boundary is at the top of the component tree in the project and wraps everything. This should be in place in every project so that you know that all errors from any level of your component tree are handled. This is also how you can keep your app from crashing. App-level boundaries aren't granular, so they really are a catchall for anything that happens. This is similar to having a `try/catch` at the top level of the app with additional `try/catch` statements for more specific errors.

Next are *layout-level* boundaries. When you have a group of components, like on the user page in this project, you might want to show more specific messaging to the user. If you have a subset of components that have a shared state, consider adding a boundary at this level. Note that if anything happens in one component, then the error boundary shows for all the components in that layout.

Finally, there's the *component-level* boundary. This is the most granular level because you have an error state for an individual component that doesn't affect anything else on the page. When you build components that are more isolated from the others—they have separate states or make their own API calls, for example—consider creating a boundary on that component.

When you implement the error boundary in a React app, you can build it from scratch (*https://oreil.ly/NW692*), or you can use a package like react-error-boundary (*https://oreil.ly/95Yyd*). In this project, you'll use the react-error-boundary package because it's lightweight and gives you a nice wrapper so that you don't have to use class components with your functional components. Install this in your repo, and then in the *App.tsx* file, import it and make the following updates:

```
...
import { RouterProvider } from 'react-router-dom'
import { ErrorBoundary } from 'react-error-boundary'
import styled from 'styled-components'
...
const App = () => {
  // Do some stuff here
  return (
```

```
    <ErrorBoundary
      FallbackComponent={ErrorFallback}
      onError={logError}
      onReset={() => window.location.reload()}
    >
      <QueryClientProvider client={queryClient}>
        ...
      </QueryClientProvider>
    </ErrorBoundary>
  )
}
...
```

This wraps the entire app in the error boundary. That way, any unexpected errors that occur will bubble up to the top of the app and be caught. You need to create the Error Fallback component and the logError function that are being used in the boundary. You'll also use the useErrorBoundary hook (*https://oreil.ly/j_bs5*) when the error occurs in async code or lifecycle management hooks, such as useEffect.

The onReset function handles retries from the error state. This will vary based on the level where you have the boundary. Often, it will reset the state of a component to trigger a rerender. If an error occurs at the app level, you can use this function to refresh the whole page. This way of doing a refresh will fetch data from the cache, so if the issue was with an API call, you need to implement a lower-level boundary with that state being captured.

Error Components

You'll have to work closely with Design and Product to decide what the errors should look like. Some teams like to use modals with retry buttons, full-screen error messages that direct the user to take a different action, toast components to temporarily alert the user of an error, or a combination of things. For this project, you're going to make dedicated components that display on the page in place of the expected layout.

You'll build components for a few specific cases, including when a value is undefined, when an error is returned from the backend, and generic mishaps. It's good to start with the generic "Something went wrong" component so that you know the app has something for anything that comes up. To accommodate the way React Router v6 currently handles errors, you need to do a refactor in *routes.tsx*.

 Double-check the React Router docs to see if this is still the case. Since packages change so frequently, there's a chance the behavior could be different by the time you read this.

Right now, *routes.tsx* looks like this:

```
const router = createBrowserRouter([
  {
    path: '/',
    element: <UserInfo />,
  },
  {
    path: '/actions',
    element: <div>Actions go burr</div>,
  },
])
```

You'll update it to the following where you use `useRoutes` instead of `createBrowser Router`:

```
import { useRoutes } from 'react-router-dom'
import UserInfo from './screens/UserInfo'

const Router = () => {
  const routes = useRoutes([
    {
      path: '/',
      element: <UserInfo />,
    },
    {
      path: '/actions',
      element: <div>Actions are here</div>,
    },
  ])

  return routes
}

export default Router
```

Then, you'll have to update *App.tsx* and replace:

```
import router from './routes'
import { RouterProvider } from 'react-router-dom'
...
<RouterProvider router={router} />
```

with:

```
import Router from './routes'
import { BrowserRouter } from 'react-router-dom'
...
<BrowserRouter>
  <Router />
</BrowserRouter>
```

It's important to be aware if any of the packages you use have built-in error boundaries that will prevent the errors from being caught at the app level or the level you're expecting. For example, React Router currently catches errors at the <RouteProvider> level. So if you notice during development that the error screen you're getting isn't right, start looking at the parts of the code that can trigger errors to see if anything is blocking them.

Now that you have the error boundary in place and you've refactored the code to handle it, you can build the generic ErrorFallback component. In *src/components*, create a new directory called *ErrorFallbacks*. In the new directory, add three new files: *index.tsx, ErrorFallback.tsx,* and *ErrorFallback.test.tsx*. In *ErrorFallback.tsx,* add the following code:

```
import { Box, Typography } from '@mui/material'
import { ErrorFallbackProps } from '../../types/errorTypes'

const ErrorFallback = ({ error, resetErrorBoundary }: ErrorFallbackProps) => {
  return (
    <Box
      margin="24px auto"
      role="alert"
      display="flex"
      flexDirection="column"
      gap="24px"
      textAlign="center"
    >
      <Typography variant="h2">Something weird happened</Typography>
      <Typography variant="h3">This is what it was:</Typography>
      <Typography color="tomato" variant="body1">
        {error.message}
      </Typography>
      <Button variant="contained" onClick={resetErrorBoundary}>
        Refresh the page to try again
      </Button>
    </Box>
  )
}

export default ErrorFallback
```

Remember that you will need to update the *index.tsx* file to use this component as a module. It's the same as you've done for every other component file. Tests should be written at the same time as the component, but we're going to come back to that in Chapter 21 so that we can go over all testing best practices together.

You now have a component that will show any time an error is caught at the component or layout level. It takes the error object and displays the message on the page so that developers can know what happened. It will look similar to Figure 18-1 when a runtime error is caught.

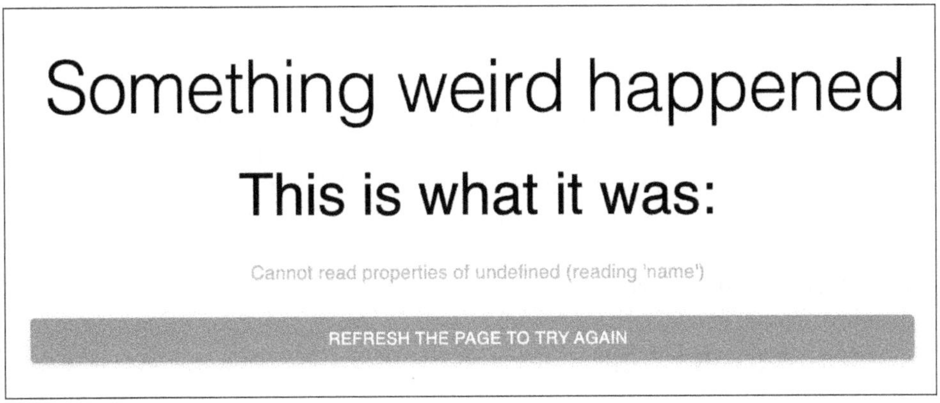

Figure 18-1. Generic error component with the error message

Logging Errors

The second part of handling errors is logging them so that you have a record of what's going on with the app when you need to debug production issues. A third-party service like Sentry, LogRocket, or Datadog or using a monitoring tool from your cloud provider, such as Amazon CloudWatch, will help out here. You can create a small helper function to do this. In the *src* folder, make a new directory called *utils,* and in that folder, make a new file called *helpers.tsx.* Add the following function to this file:

```
import { ErrorFallbackProps } from '../types/errorTypes'

export const logError = (error: ErrorFallbackProps['error']) => {
  // you should really be logging to some external tool
  // do not log real errors to the console
  console.log(error.message)
}
```

Keep a Consistent Frontend Folder Structure

The frontend has arguably reached a point where deciding on the architecture and folder structure is more complex and opinionated than the backend. Some teams will use something like a *utils* folder, or it might be called *helpers* or something else. You can choose to have a separate folder for your types or include them in the same folder as the component. It can get very convoluted and difficult to find functionality if the team doesn't remain consistent as the app grows.

While you are using a specific folder structure for this project, and it's a good starting point for any greenfield app, that doesn't mean it's the one you should use for every project. Just keep in mind that as you get exposure to more projects and products, you'll see vastly different structures and develop your own preferences. There isn't a right or wrong way as long as the whole team agrees to enforce the structure you all put in place.

This logging functionality can be as robust as you and the team want to make it. The better your logs are, the faster it will be for you to track down the root causes of the errors. You can also use a logging tool to give you metrics around which errors happen most often. That can point out places that need to be refactored or that don't give a good UX. One area this comes up with is when users need to enter information with ambiguous instructions.

User Validation Errors

When your users interact with your app, you need a way to give them feedback on their input. You can show inline errors as soon as the user focuses on an input. You can wait to show any errors until the user tries to submit the form or changes focus from an input. You can show errors in one block. You'll likely use a combination to give the user the most useful information.

You also have to account for the component library you're using. Since you're using MUI in this project, there's already validation on your input fields, and you may have noticed that when building the search form. With MUI, you can make a field required and pass the validation requirements to it like this:

```
const searchFieldInputProps = {
  maxLength: 15,
  minLength: 3,
  required: true,
}

<Input
  placeholder={`Search ${props.name}...`}
  type="search"
  fullWidth
  inputProps={searchFieldInputProps}
  startAdornment={
    <InputAdornment position="start">
      <SearchIcon />
    </InputAdornment>
  }
  {...register('search', { required: true, maxLength: 15, minLength: 3 })}
  aria-invalid={errors.search ? 'true' : 'false'}
/>
```

Now the user can't submit the request without entering at least three characters in the field, and the input is restricted to 15 characters, so the user won't be able to type in more than that. If they try to submit the form and the input doesn't meet the validation requirements, then they will see a specific message for their error, such as in Figures 18-2 and 18-3.

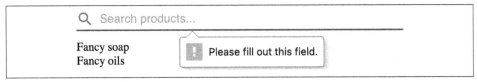

Figure 18-2. Required input error message

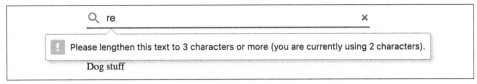

Figure 18-3. Required character-length error message

These messages come straight from the default Chrome HTML validation on input fields. You can take advantage of the other error message formats (*https://oreil.ly/ KenbN*), such as highlighting the input within a form with a customized message. The way you handle error messages will vary quite a bit depending on which components you use to accept inputs.

Another widely used approach to handling user input validation is at the form level with something like React Hook Form. You can add validation that will check all the fields when the Submit button is clicked. The implementation might look similar to this:

```
<Input
  placeholder={`Search ${props.name}...`}
  type="search"
  fullWidth
  inputProps={searchFieldInputProps}
  startAdornment={
    <InputAdornment position="start">
      <SearchIcon />
    </InputAdornment>
  }
  {...register('search', {
    required: true,
    maxLength: 15,
    minLength: 3,
    pattern: /^[A-Za-z]+$/i,
  })}
```

```
    aria-invalid={errors.search ? 'true' : 'false'}
  />
```

Or you can use a validation schema with a tool like Zod (*https://oreil.ly/HCRqv*), joi (*https://oreil.ly/dhDMH*), or Yup (*https://oreil.ly/3FHJz*) with React Hook Forms to pass a schema to useForm as an option. It will validate the inputs against the schema and show the errors. Here's an example of that with the search form using Yup:

```
import { useForm } from "react-hook-form";
import { yupResolver } from '@hookform/resolvers/yup';
import * as yup from "yup";

const schema = yup
  .object({
    searchText: yup.string().min(3).max(15).required(),
  })
  .required()

const SearchBar = (props: SearchBarProps) => {
  const { onSubmitSearch } = props
  const {
    register,
    handleSubmit,
    formState: { errors },
  } = useForm({
    resolver: yupResolver(schema),
  })
```

Having validations written as functions or schemas makes them more reusable across different components and gives you more control over customization. As part of the React Hook Form package, any <input /> that is registered with validations will be checked when the onSubmit function is triggered. When you show the user messages at this point in their flow, it can be easier to make them understand that they need to make changes before clicking the button again. The advantage of this is that the user won't see errors until they make the submission action.

There are varying views on what is the clearest way to show validation messages, which is why it's essential to work with the Design team because they should have a stronger idea of what the user expects from the app. That leaves you to help them figure out what errors might come from the backend and what that means to a user.

API Errors

React Query, which you're using to fetch your data, already comes with built-in error handling, which makes it easier to deal with any errors that come from the backend. Depending on the API design, the status codes can be used to show meaningful error messages to both the user and the developers. These errors might not have anything to do with an action a user took, but the user may need to refresh the page or do something else to try the request again. Your error components should guide them to the corrective action without revealing exactly what happened on the backend.

For example, if the API responds with a 422 status code, that could be an issue with how the code was written to format user input for the request. The frontend could have an incorrect parameter name that it submits to the backend. Or if the API server is down, the frontend might receive a 500 status code. There's nothing for the user to do in either of these scenarios, but they still need to be shown something. This is also where your logging will come in handy for any developers debugging the issues. You and the dev team might even tie log messages to each API error screen. Figure 18-4 is an example of a 404 being returned from a backend request in the browser tools.

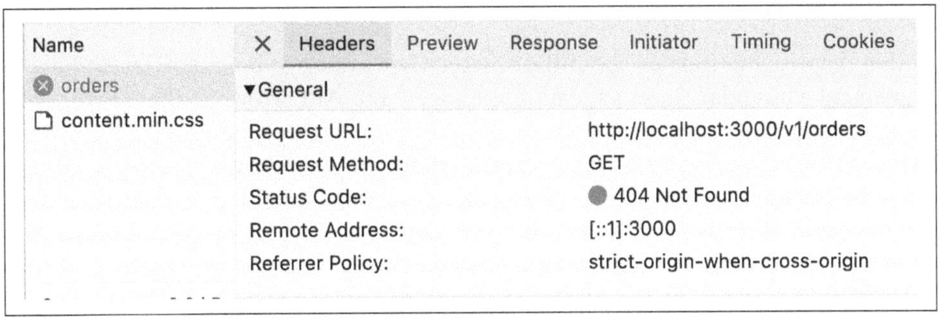

Name	✕ Headers Preview Response Initiator Timing Cookies
❌ orders	▼General
🗋 content.min.css	Request URL: http://localhost:3000/v1/orders
	Request Method: GET
	Status Code: ● 404 Not Found
	Remote Address: [::1]:3000
	Referrer Policy: strict-origin-when-cross-origin

Figure 18-4. Example of a 404 error from an API request

Here's what the JSON response from that request looks like:

```
{
    "statusCode": 404,
    "message": "Not found"
}
```

These screens or components will be similar to what you've already built for the generic error component. They will be modified versions of this with different wording and maybe even action buttons. The main differences are that they will show only under the specified conditions and they will happen at the component or layout level in the app. Some common ways to handle the content in these components include showing the error message that's coming from the backend or showing a custom message directly from the frontend strictly based on the status code and having the specifics in the logs.

Just to make sure you are handling the API errors appropriately, you can use a tool like httpstat.us (*https://httpstat.us*) or the tweak browser extension (*https://oreil.ly/ Vrxdi*). You can also mock errors from your server with a tool like Mock Service Worker (*https://oreil.ly/Qv-ea*), or you can add a property to your requests that forces a certain error and payload. An example of that additional property could be called responseStatus, such as the following:

```
GET /order/72?responseStatus=404
```

This goes back to your API design. The error messages sent in the responses might only apply to the developers debugging the issue, and you don't need users or malicious parties having access to the exact error. One strategy is to log the error message from the backend and display something different to the user. Be cautious with this approach because a malicious or curious user will be able to see the response in the browser tools. You typically want to send a redacted version of the error to the frontend so that this situation doesn't come up and you can focus on giving the users friendly and useful messaging.

Conclusion

In this chapter, you learned about the different types of error boundary levels, how to implement a boundary, user validation messages, and API error handling. Error handling is important for user experience, developer debugging, and ensuring app security. Once you have your app in a stable state and there are discussions around releasing it to production, double-check that you have something in place even if it's just the generic error component. This part can get overlooked as you focus on feature development unless Product, Design, or you bring it up.

Add this to your app fitness checklist. You may have to dig into the React docs and the docs for the packages in the app to fully understand how errors are handled. Understanding where errors are triggered from, how they bubble up in the app, and where they will be displayed on the page will affect the way the entire team writes code. This is another good time to have a demo or explainer meeting with the team to bring up any considerations that others have encountered. Error handling can be a little tricky, but once you have it implemented in the app, you and the team can iron out any ambiguities.

## CHAPTER 19

Frontend Security Considerations

Security is another area of the frontend that should be top of mind as you implement new features. Security is extremely important and encompasses such detail as to warrant its own book, but this chapter will cover enough for you to know what to be aware of.

You've already learned about some of the vulnerabilities and remedies for security on the backend in Chapter 8. The frontend is usually the most accessible part of a product and can act as a gateway for server attacks. Now you have to consider things like browser vulnerabilities and ways malicious users can manipulate the flow of how the app should work to gain more access than they should have. Think about how you store and transmit data on the frontend because everything that loads in the browser is accessible by users if they just open the developer tools. You and the team need to find a balance between user convenience and security.

In this chapter, I'll cover:

- More of the OWASP Top 10
- Common vulnerability vectors
- How to attack an app
- Ways attackers can get information directly from the browser
- Strategies to reduce the number of attack possibilities

You'll need to check with any local or regional data-privacy and compliance laws and rules that your product is governed by as well, such as PCI DSS (*https://oreil.ly/ wAXSU*), HIPAA (*https://oreil.ly/ve3RM*), and GDPR (*https://gdpr.eu/checklist*) (all mentioned previously in Chapter 8). These regulations can be more strict than regular best practices, so keep that in mind.

An overlooked skill is knowing how to do some basic attacks. You don't need to go into cybersecurity or learn a bunch of tools, but understanding what to look for will help you understand how attacks work and how you can prevent them.

Common Vulnerabilities

Many frontend vulnerabilities can be categorized as *insecure design* (*https://oreil.ly/ PVscX*). You know from Chapter 8 that the backend is more responsible for things like authentication, authorization, and the majority of security configurations. Insecure design happens *accidentally*. You and the team will do your best to ensure that the app is as secure as possible, but sometimes tight deadlines or unclear requirements can leave unexpected gaps. Let's go through some of the commonly overlooked areas.

Business Logic Validation

Sometimes the way an app's user flow is designed opens it to vulnerabilities. Even the *golden path*, or the path that you and the organization behind the app would like the user to take, can leave a lot of edge cases open for someone to exploit.

In your app, one area like this could be the ordering process. What happens if a user tries to place several orders for the same product within a few minutes? Or if they cancel an order as soon as it has shipped? While these scenarios are unlikely, ignoring the possibility leaves the organization exposed to these unexpected situations.

Imagine your customers can book a customer support call on an online calendar on your app. Are there limits to how many sessions a single user can book? If not, someone could build a bot that books all the sessions, costing the organization time and money. As you go through designs and specs, look for these kinds of openings and think about how they could be exploited.

Form submission flows are common areas for attacks. It can be tempting to tell users how many attempts they have remaining or what was wrong with their submission, but be cautious with the info you provide. A malicious user could use it to build bots to automate attacks on your site. These attacks can be prevented with strategies like an unannounced limit on retries or an extra manual step, such as a CAPTCHA.

Any data that gets passed in backend requests, like the URL query string or in the body of a request, can be an attack vector (*https://oreil.ly/EiiOe*). Such data can reveal some of the parameters used in API requests. (That isn't necessarily a bad thing, as long as there isn't any sensitive data in the string and the backend has its security validations in place.) Using query strings is a way you can make links shareable so that the same data can be fetched from a different tab or browser. Just be aware of what information about the API appears in the URL.

This also brings up how much data is shared with the frontend. Try to limit requested data to returning only what the user needs and be mindful of any potentially sensitive data like PII. That can include data the user doesn't see right away but that you expect them to need soon after the request has been made to help with performance. Just because data doesn't load on the page, that doesn't stop people from checking network requests in the browser devtools. As you work on the frontend and add more API calls, check that they return only the data you need and that any sensitive data is provided only *after* authentication and authorization are confirmed.

Session Management

Session management (*https://oreil.ly/A7qho*) deals with how you handle and store access tokens on the frontend, which can also be an attack vector (*https://oreil.ly/ejtRk*). Not all attacks happen from someone running bots or typing complex code into a terminal to execute remote commands. An attack can be as simple as someone checking your browser to see if there's any authorization information in the URL or if you're still logged in on an old device. Think about the last time *you* had to log in to your favorite website or tool.

When you're handling users' PII data, you need to implement session timeouts. With idle session timeouts (*https://oreil.ly/BPo4U*), the user is automatically logged out after a certain amount of time has passed and the page hasn't triggered any new API requests. This helps prevent attackers from taking and using a session ID. The downside is that if an attacker *does* get a valid session ID, they can keep that session active and do whatever they want. You shouldn't store the session time on the browser because an attacker can easily modify the values. It will require some work on the backend to make sure session IDs are really invalid after the time has expired.

You should also have in place *absolute session timeouts* (*https://oreil.ly/Tn230*): no matter where the user is logged in, after a set amount of time, they are forcibly logged out and must log in and reauthenticate to use the app. This improves on the idle session timeouts because even if a valid session ID has been hijacked, it won't last forever. This limits how long an attacker has access to a user's identity.

Don't forget to have a Logout button for users to terminate their own sessions. Security-conscious users will want the ability to log out manually. With automated timeouts in place, it can be easy to overlook this. This functionality can also be added to events like the user closing the browser or page, if you want to add logout reminders.

Another option is session renewal timeout (*https://oreil.ly/4BHRx*). This is when a session ID expires and a new one is generated in the background and replaced on the frontend, without any action from the user. This allows users to stay logged in longer without giving attackers access to the same session ID. (If you're logged into any apps where you haven't had to reauthenticate in a while, hopefully this is what's happening in the background.)

One more decision you have to make is if users should be able to be logged into the app on different devices at the same time. Allowing users to log in on multiple devices can potentially let an attacker log in at the same time as the user and go unnoticed for a while. If you allow this, set up monitoring and alerts to specifically identify unusual activity across sessions. On the other hand, if you allow only one login across all devices, that will require some backend work to make sure that session IDs are invalidated and that you have a mechanism to let users decide which device to stay logged in on.

Package Version Maintenance

Package versions falling out of date is a common vulnerability (*https://oreil.ly/EwZ87*) on both the frontend and the backend. If a package has had security patches, each vulnerability in the outdated, unpatched version is well documented and publicly available on any number of Common Weakness Enumeration (CWE) lists (*https://oreil.ly/k9vgY*). Some attackers just go to the OWASP Top 10 itself and build a list of attacks based on those findings.

Package version maintenance gets put off for many reasons, from not wanting to deal with breaking changes to needing to replace packages completely. I suggest having a ticket at least once a month to go through and update all your packages to the latest stable version. Ideally, you and the team can update packages as you work on new features or on eliminating other tech debt.

You can use tools like Dependabot (*https://oreil.ly/OyWhx*) to flag packages with vulnerabilities directly in your repo. Other code scanner tools like npm-audit (*https://oreil.ly/Lzce_*), Snyk (*https://snyk.io*), or retire.js (*https://oreil.ly/8XXHN*) tell you which packages are out of date. Not all packages need to be maintained. You'll find plenty that do a certain task very well but that haven't been updated in years. With experience, you'll learn to balance your package choices.

> Some of the tools mentioned here are great to integrate into your CI/CD pipeline. We'll dive into detail on this in Chapter 27.

Figure 19-1 is an example of what a report will look like if there are any vulnerabilities when you run npm-audit on your projects.

```
# npm audit report

axios  1.3.2 - 1.7.3
Severity: high
Server-Side Request Forgery in axios - https://github.com/advisories/GHSA-8hc4-vh64-cxmj
fix available via `npm audit fix`
node_modules/axios

body-parser  <1.20.3
Severity: high
body-parser vulnerable to denial of service when url encoding is enabled - https://github.com/advisories/GHSA-qwcr-r2fm-qrc7
fix available via `npm audit fix`
node_modules/body-parser
  express  <=4.19.2 || 5.0.0-alpha.1 - 5.0.0-beta.3
  Depends on vulnerable versions of body-parser
  Depends on vulnerable versions of path-to-regexp
  Depends on vulnerable versions of send
  Depends on vulnerable versions of serve-static
  node_modules/express

braces  <3.0.3
Severity: high
Uncontrolled resource consumption in braces - https://github.com/advisories/GHSA-grv7-fg5c-xmjg
fix available via `npm audit fix`
node_modules/braces

follow-redirects  <=1.15.5
Severity: moderate
follow-redirects' Proxy-Authorization header kept across hosts - https://github.com/advisories/GHSA-cxjh-pqwp-8mfp
fix available via `npm audit fix`
node_modules/follow-redirects

micromatch  <4.0.8
Severity: moderate
Regular Expression Denial of Service (ReDoS) in micromatch - https://github.com/advisories/GHSA-952p-6rrq-rcjv
fix available via `npm audit fix`
node_modules/micromatch

path-to-regexp  <=0.1.9 || 4.0.0 - 6.2.2
Severity: high
path-to-regexp outputs backtracking regular expressions - https://github.com/advisories/GHSA-9wv6-86v2-598j
path-to-regexp outputs backtracking regular expressions - https://github.com/advisories/GHSA-9wv6-86v2-598j
fix available via `npm audit fix`
node_modules/msw/node_modules/path-to-regexp
```

Figure 19-1. Vulnerability report snippet

It's important to vet the packages you choose from the beginning. This is code that you don't directly maintain, so you need to be able to trust that others are. If you find that one of the packages you use is no longer maintained, that could allow a vulnerability into your app. Look for replacements or consider building the functionality in house.

Input Validation

This discussion of input validation will be slightly different from what we talked about in Chapter 18 because now you aren't worried about what the user sees. Now you care about how the code handles what it gets from inputs. You have to programmatically validate and sanitize (*https://oreil.ly/Np82L*) the data you receive from users. Making sure the user has entered the correct data type is handled by any validation schemas and functions you implement in your inputs and forms.

What you need to check for is if the user is trying to force values into a certain format to get the app to do something they don't have access to. That can include SQL injection attacks (*https://oreil.ly/20NJU*) and cross-site scripting (XSS) attacks (*https://oreil.ly/x5UHO*). These kinds of attacks (*https://oreil.ly/VSu9E*) are common because forcing values is a straightforward avenue. Your backend already has input validation and sanitization in place, but it's nice to have some validation on the frontend to provide instant user feedback without putting any load on the server.

Anyone can type things into a form and click Submit just to see what will happen. Frontend validation and sanitization are great for UX and can slow down some basic attacks. Just always remember that they can easily be bypassed.

You can do form validation with the built-in field attributes, such as `required`, `type`, `min`, and `max`. This is one of the methods you used in your project. Here's an example of a form using this type of validation, which you can add to your project as a form to clean up later in *src/elements/Forms/OrderForm.tsx*:

```tsx
const OrderForm = () => (
  <form
    style={{
      display: 'flex',
      flexDirection: 'column',
      gap: '12px',
      alignItems: 'stretch',
      padding: '32px',
      width: '350px',
    }}
  >
    <div>
      <label>First Name: </label>
      <input type="text" required />
    </div>
    <div>
      <label>Last Name: </label>
      <input type="text" required />
    </div>
    <div>
      <label>Quantity: </label>
      <input type="number" min={0} max={12} />
    </div>
    <div>
      <label>Email: </label>
      <input type="email" />
    </div>
    <div>
      <label>Password: </label>
      <input type="password" />
    </div>
    <div>
      <label>Best Contact Time: </label>
      <input type="datetime-local" />
    </div>
    <button onSubmit={() => {}}>Submit</button>
  </form>
)
```

This will require your user to enter certain values in the different input fields before they can submit the form. You can also take a more programmatic approach to validation by using a form-handling package like React Hook Form. Here are a couple of examples of using this package with your `SearchBar` component:

```
const schema = yup
  .object({
    searchText: yup.string().min(3).max(15).required(),
  })
  .required()

  {...register('search', {
    required: true,
    maxLength: 15,
    minLength: 3,
    pattern: /^[A-Za-z]+$/i,
  })}
  …
```

You can use a validation schema for all of your inputs for more versatility and customization, or you can put the validations directly in the input's props.

Other Principles

There's a phrase that you might hear in the cybersecurity world: "security through obscurity (*https://oreil.ly/uAd8Q*)." It means that only the people who work on certain parts of the system have any knowledge about it. For example, the Security team probably knows more about roles and how authorization is implemented than you do. Keeping information about mechanisms to a need-to-know basis helps keep vulnerabilities secure. Another example of security through obscurity is having an organization-wide password tool set up so that only certain members have access to specific passwords. Everything is technically available, but it's more secure since only the people who need access to passwords will have them.

I said this in the section on session management, but I can't emphasize it enough: *anything* sent from the server to the client that provides clues about your infrastructure can provide clues for malicious users looking to exploit vulnerabilities. Things you might not even think of, such as `X-Powered-By` headers and URLs that expose the hosting provider (like using default AWS API endpoints instead of using custom domains), can give away enough information to help build an attack. Be very intentional with every piece of data that is sent to the frontend because it can be easily found.

How to Check Your Own App

Learning how to do some basic ethical hacking on your own apps will help you see security from the other side. You'll start to see how vulnerabilities leave paths open for anyone looking. One resource I highly recommend is the PortSwigger Web Security Academy (*https://oreil.ly/VdUzs*). The site has a ton of in-depth articles, examples, and labs for you to play around with some common attacks. I encourage you to go through some of the labs, such as the one on bypassing two-factor authentication (2FA) (*https://oreil.ly/Vc41o*) or one of the business logic labs, like the one on a low-level logic flaw (*https://oreil.ly/C7f9d*).

Doing labs is just one way you can start to understand how attackers think and what they watch for when they poke around for vulnerabilities. This isn't something you can write straightforward code for; it takes some strong observational skills, pattern finding, and a lot of creativity. That's one of the fun parts of ethical hacking: it stretches your mind in new directions. Learning more about it will help you grow in your career.

If you decide to go even deeper into learning how to attack the apps you develop, look into the Kali Linux OS (*https://oreil.ly/Ie5c1*). It comes with just about every tool you could need to attack any number of systems. You can even run it on a virtual machine if you want to play around with it without setting up an entire operating system. One of the best ways to know how to secure your app is understanding the tools and methods attackers will use to find and exploit any vulnerabilities that may exist in your app. You can even see what organizations are looking for by checking out bug bounties on sites like HackerOne (*https://oreil.ly/BJbAF*) and Bugcrowd (*https://oreil.ly/HRka-*) as well as directly on organization's sites, such as Microsoft (*https://oreil.ly/2VDU5*) and Apple (*https://oreil.ly/4KGS4*).

Always know the laws and keep legal restrictions in mind if you decide to try attacking a real application. You don't want to accidentally access some organization's database and get the attack traced to your IP address when you don't have permission to perform that attack.

Conclusion

In this chapter, you learned more about security on the frontend and where attackers can learn how to access user data and escalate their permissions in your systems. Attackers study the frontend systematically to figure out if there's something they can exploit. Don't think that your app is so small that no one will care to attack it or that it's so well established and secure that it's impervious to attacks. Just because not everyone knows how certain parts of the system work doesn't mean an outside party can't observe enough detail to figure it out. Work with the Security team to make sure the frontend is just as protected as the backend since it's your first line of defense. Because you and your team are responsible for the full stack, you need to understand how the systems work together to keep user data safe.

## CHAPTER 20

Frontend Performance

Now you have your frontend in a good place, and you've probably done at least a beta release of this product to customers. Going forward, you'll be adding more features, doing maintenance, and looking for ways to improve the app for both the developer and the user experiences. One way to do both is by improving performance. The faster and more smoothly the app runs, the more the UX improves, and the more streamlined the process becomes for devs to make updates as they develop locally.

It's frustrating to encounter apps that load slowly, have a jumpy interface as data becomes available, and are difficult for your dev team to update. Once your app is stable and you have all of the main architecture in place, you can start focusing on these concerns. This is your chance to really optimize the code based on patterns you've seen from logs and feedback from the dev team and other stakeholders.

In this chapter, I'll go over:

- Common causes of performance issues
- How to measure and improve your performance metrics
- Tools to improve your app's performance
- How to keep the code clean for better performance

Performance is a topic that tends to come up once an app has been in production for a while. One of the devs on the team will bring up how slow development is because the pages take forever to load code changes. This is something that should be in your mind from the beginning because it directly affects how the app is maintained and developed over time. While many performance issues can be addressed at later phases in the project, the sooner you bring them up, the better.

Benchmark Metrics

Before you dive into optimizations, you need to know what metrics your optimizations are based on. If you aren't sure which metrics to measure, a good place to start is with the Core Web Vitals (*https://oreil.ly/y3YK4*). Then you can research the particular metrics that are most applicable to your app. Is bundle size affecting load times? How are the response times on slow networks? What about the *largest contentful paint* (*https://oreil.ly/zuIuG*) (LCP)? It's OK to focus on a few metrics at a time and incrementally make changes to your app. Some of the main metrics to start with are LCP, *first input delay* (FID), and *cumulative layout shift* (CLS).

LCP measures how long it takes the largest image or content block to render relative to when the user navigated to the page. The goal is to have an LCP within 2.5 seconds of when the page first starts loading. It's recommended to keep it at least under 4 seconds. Anything longer than that provides poor UX and is something the team should improve.

FID measures how long it takes the browser to process event handlers that get triggered from a user interaction—in other words, how long it takes something to happen on the page in response to a click or type from a user. The optimal score for this metric is 100 ms or less; anything over 300 ms needs to be improved. Nobody wants to click on something and then experience nothing.

CLS is very important for layout development. This metric measures how jumpy the page is while it's loading. You want to limit how much the layout of a page shifts while the user interacts with the page. That's where things like skeleton loading components come in handy because they preserve the layout as content is loaded. A good score is less than 0.1, while anything over 0.25 needs improvement. Keep an eye out for this metric in particular because it's something that the dev team has direct control over.

You can use performance-testing tools to give you insights into other metrics to consider as well as to find out where your app is already doing well. If you're curious about any of the sites you visit regularly, WebPageTest (*https://webpagetest.org*) and Google PageSpeed Insights (*https://oreil.ly/WlGbs*) will let you enter the URL for the website you want to test and return a performance report. The rest of this section will introduce you to two more tools: Lighthouse (*https://oreil.ly/IG2He*) and sitespeed.io (*https://oreil.ly/WnBxy*).

Lighthouse Tools

You may have already used Lighthouse in your Chrome DevTools while doing local development. This audit doesn't take long to run, so do it periodically. That way, you can give a little report to the dev team about things they should watch out for as they make decisions. This is one way you can mentor everyone with real examples that have impactful solutions. You can also demonstrate the results to the Product team and any other stakeholders so that they understand when you ask for time to work on tech debt.

 While it's fine to check your Lighthouse results locally, keep in mind that the results in development can be drastically different than in production for reasons such as assets not being compressed, code not being minified (*https://oreil.ly/YBoJ3*), and less optimal configs. One way to handle this is to do a production build locally and then run Lighthouse on that build.

If you run the current project locally and open the Chrome DevTools, you can run a Lighthouse performance test. Your results will look similar to Figures 20-1 and 20-2.

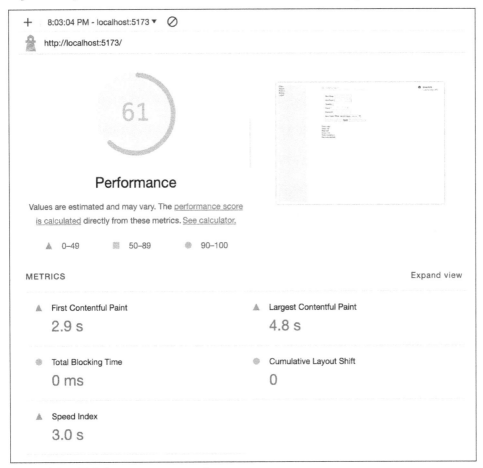

Figure 20-1. Lighthouse report overview

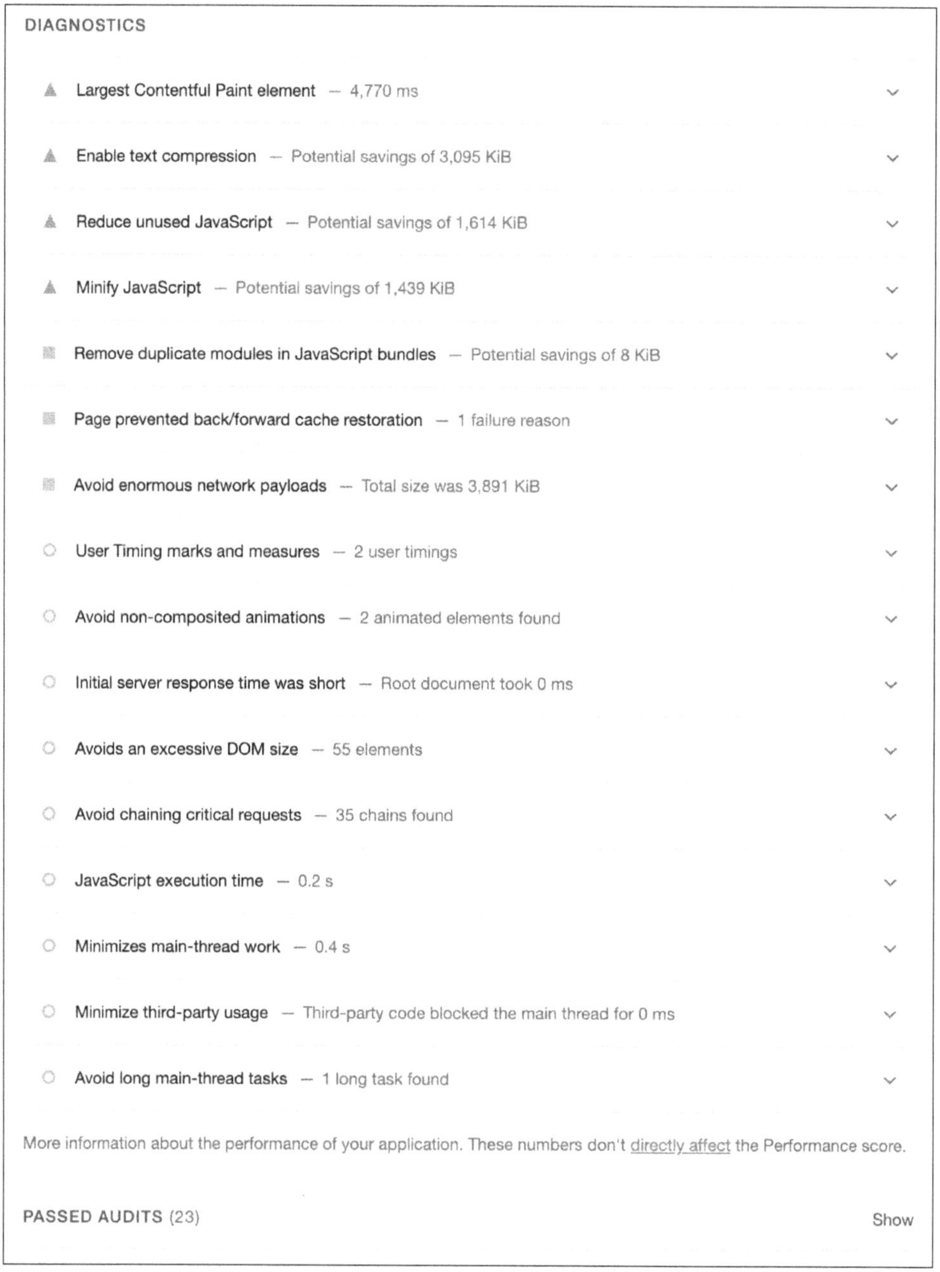

DIAGNOSTICS

⚠ Largest Contentful Paint element — 4,770 ms   ⌄

⚠ Enable text compression — Potential savings of 3,095 KiB   ⌄

⚠ Reduce unused JavaScript — Potential savings of 1,614 KiB   ⌄

⚠ Minify JavaScript — Potential savings of 1,439 KiB   ⌄

▦ Remove duplicate modules in JavaScript bundles — Potential savings of 8 KiB   ⌄

▦ Page prevented back/forward cache restoration — 1 failure reason   ⌄

▦ Avoid enormous network payloads — Total size was 3,891 KiB   ⌄

○ User Timing marks and measures — 2 user timings   ⌄

○ Avoid non-composited animations — 2 animated elements found   ⌄

○ Initial server response time was short — Root document took 0 ms   ⌄

○ Avoids an excessive DOM size — 55 elements   ⌄

○ Avoid chaining critical requests — 35 chains found   ⌄

○ JavaScript execution time — 0.2 s   ⌄

○ Minimizes main-thread work — 0.4 s   ⌄

○ Minimize third-party usage — Third-party code blocked the main thread for 0 ms   ⌄

○ Avoid long main-thread tasks — 1 long task found   ⌄

More information about the performance of your application. These numbers don't directly affect the Performance score.

PASSED AUDITS (23)   Show

Figure 20-2. Lighthouse report details

Now you have a list of metrics that you can focus on improving, and you'll also get some suggestions for improvements in the report.

You can use the Lighthouse npm package (*https://oreil.ly/AN-nL*) to create automated performance reports as part of your CI/CD testing. There are a number of configs you can set to generate the reports and save them in JSON or HTML format. Just to check it out, you can install and run Lighthouse on your project locally and save the results in JSON format with the following commands:

```
npm install -g lighthouse
lighthouse http://localhost:5173/ --output-path=./report.json --output json
```

You can find the full JSON report in the project GitHub repo (*https://oreil.ly/C8omi*), but here's a snippet of what the results look like:

```
"first-contentful-paint": {
    "id": "first-contentful-paint",
    "title": "First Contentful Paint",
    "description": "First Contentful Paint marks the time at which the first
        text or image is painted. [Learn more about the First Contentful Paint
        metric](https://developer.chrome.com/docs/lighthouse/performance/
        first-contentful-paint/).",
    "score": 0,
    "scoreDisplayMode": "numeric",
    "numericValue": 14375.424124999987,
    "numericUnit": "millisecond",
    "displayValue": "14.4 s",
    "scoringOptions": {
      "p10": 1800,
      "median": 3000
    }
},
"largest-contentful-paint": {
    "id": "largest-contentful-paint",
    "title": "Largest Contentful Paint",
    "description": "Largest Contentful Paint marks the time at which the
        largest text or image is painted. [Learn more about the Largest
        Contentful Paint metric](https://developer.chrome.com/docs/lighthouse/
        performance/lighthouse-largest-contentful-paint/)",
    "score": 0,
    "scoreDisplayMode": "numeric",
    "numericValue": 25557.863749999982,
    "numericUnit": "millisecond",
    "displayValue": "25.6 s",
    "scoringOptions": {
      "p10": 2500,
      "median": 4000
    }
},
```

They're the same results you'd see on the HTML page, but now you can do more with the results programmatically. Maybe there are some metrics that you want to pay close attention to, so you configure the system to throw some kind of error if the metric isn't above a specified threshold. That might include core web vitals like LCP, FID, and CLS since these have a huge impact on user experience.

Sitespeed.io

Let's look at an open source tool you can use for more flexibility over what you can modify and test during performance testing. Sitespeed.io is a really versatile option because you can create dashboards (*https://oreil.ly/xCa6-*) to monitor your app's performance over time, get reports for individual pages, and test with different browsers. It has lots of configs you can customize to test for almost any performance metric you want as well as accessibility testing. You can even run sitespeed.io in a standalone Docker container.

If you want, you can have sitespeed.io send messages to a Slack channel to alert the team when any thresholds have been exceeded. It can record videos for your performance tests. You can easily integrate it into your CI/CD pipelines. I recommend reading the sitespeed.io docs (*https://oreil.ly/wtM7-*) to learn all this package can do, but here's an example of what a test can look like with this tool:

```
npm i -g sitespeed.io
sitespeed.io http://localhost:5173/ --browser safari -n 2 --summary-detail


[2024-02-17 19:32:04] INFO: Versions OS: darwin 23.1.0 nodejs: v21.2.0
sitespeed.io: 33.0.0 browsertime: 21.2.1 coach: 8.0.2
[2024-02-17 19:32:05] INFO: Running tests using Safari - 2 iteration(s)
[2024-02-17 19:32:06] INFO: Testing url http://localhost:5173/ iteration 1
[2024-02-17 19:32:12] INFO: Take after page complete check screenshot
[2024-02-17 19:32:15] INFO: http://localhost:5173/ TTFB: 3ms DOMContentLoaded:
196ms FCP: 243ms Load: 197ms
[2024-02-17 19:32:16] INFO: Testing url http://localhost:5173/ iteration 2
[2024-02-17 19:32:23] INFO: Take after page complete check screenshot
[2024-02-17 19:32:26] INFO: http://localhost:5173/ TTFB: 3ms DOMContentLoaded:
201ms FCP: 248ms Load: 201ms
[2024-02-17 19:32:26] INFO: http://localhost:5173/ TTFB: 3ms (σ0.00ms 0%), FCP:
246ms (σ3.00ms 1.0%), DOMContentLoaded: 199ms (σ3.00ms 1.3%), CPUBenchmark:
61.5ms (σ13.50ms 22.0%), Load: 199ms (σ2.00ms 1.0%) (2 runs)
[2024-02-17 19:32:27] INFO: HTML stored in /Repos/dashboard-ui/sitespeed-result/
localhost/2024-02-17-19-32-04
1 page analysed for http://localhost:5173/ (2 runs, Safari/desktop/
[Object object])
    Score / Metric          Median
    ------------            ------
 √  First Contentful Paint  246 ms
    Page Load Time          199 ms
    TTFB                    3 ms
 !  Coach Overall Score     84
 ✗  Coach Best Practice Score  68
 !  Coach Privacy Score     80
 √  Coach Performance Score 99
```

Figure 20-3 summarizes the results.

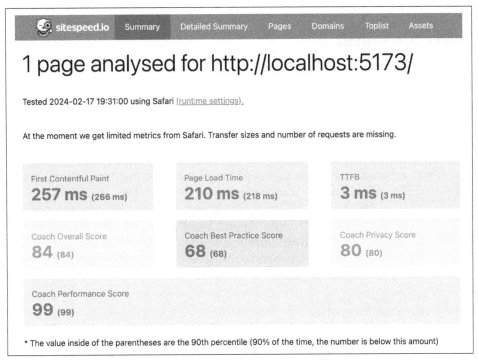

Figure 20-3. Siteseped.io results

Click on any of these metrics to get more detail about them and suggestions for how to improve them. If you want to check out the reports more, go to the project GitHub repo (*https://oreil.ly/Fjn7S*) and open the HTML files in your browser.

There are also commercial products available for performance measuring, such as Sentry and New Relic. I discussed those in Chapter 12.

Now that you know some of the tools you can use to analyze your site, it's time to look at areas where you can improve your app and actively guide the rest of the team to watch. You can include these as items in your PR review process or quarterly audits. Some will fundamentally change the way that you and the team develop code, so make sure to review them with the team—and don't forget about demos.

Areas for Improvement

After you've run the tests, you need to decide how to fix any performance issues. There are a few ways to update the frontend to speed things up. Some of these can be incrementally updated as you add new features; others will be a larger undertaking because they fundamentally change the way the app works. Let's start by looking at the packages you have in your project.

Bundle Size Analysis

Bundle size is one of the less obvious things that can slow your app down. There's a package for just about any functionality you can think of, but that doesn't mean you should reach for packages immediately. Every package you install increases your bundle size, which increases the page load and response times. Many packages also depend on other packages, so you might have things in your bundle that you don't directly use.

One way to determine which packages add the most to your bundle size is by analyzing your build with a tool like source-map-explorer (*https://oreil.ly/Oh8Nd*) or vite-bundle-visualizer (*https://oreil.ly/PjWjs*). These analysis tools will help you find out which project files are adding the most to your bundle size and where to trim things. I'll use vite-bundle-visualizer here, since you're using the Vite tool for your project. Figure 20-4 shows what the vite-bundle-visualizer results will look like for your project if you run these commands:

```
npm i vite-bundle-visualizer
npx vite-bundle-visualizer
```

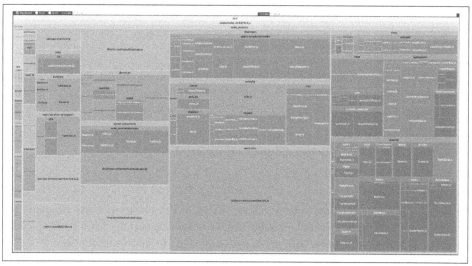

Figure 20-4. Source map for bundle size with vite-bundle-visualizer

You can click on each of the squares to see more detail about which file is adding the most to the size. This can help you decide if it's time to choose an alternative package or if you need to refactor certain files in your repo.

One project I worked on relied on a micro frontend architecture (*https://oreil.ly/Jrm-H*). The different micro frontend projects often bloated the consuming app, and source-map-explorer made it easy to clearly see which one was causing a given issue. You may sometimes be surprised to find that it isn't a package that's increasing your bundle size, but rather a component you and the team have written.

After you've analyzed your build to see where anything can be decreased in size, it's time to turn your attention to the build itself.

Build Configurations

Fine-tuning your build configs isn't easy, but it's a skill that you should have and that can really let you shine as a senior dev. Take the time to learn some of the ins and outs of the concept. Sometimes you can optimize your build configurations to decrease bundle size or even optimize the artifact you deploy to production. You might find yourself working on a project that was built on Webpack and need to update those configs (*https://oreil.ly/29o0o*).

Thankfully, for this project you started from scratch with a modern tool, Vite. If you're on a real-world app that is a Create React App (CRA) project, a tool like CRACO (*https://oreil.ly/CKnaI*) can help you access configuration settings that improve performance. Since this project is written in TypeScript, what you have in your *tsconfig.json* (*https://oreil.ly/jmaLT*) file will determine how your app is compiled: which files are included in the production artifact, where the files are located, how they are minimized or compressed, and with which browsers your app will be most compatible. Since browsers don't use TypeScript, your *.ts* files will get compiled to JavaScript at some point.

When you're trying to speed up your app, check your configs for files that *don't* need to be included in your deployment. Tests, reports, and any files used strictly for development can probably be left out of the production artifact. You should also check to see which JavaScript modules (*https://oreil.ly/grMgR*) you are targeting because this will affect how you handle polyfills (*https://oreil.ly/JcQh6*) for functionality that isn't supported in certain browser versions.

JavaScript's functionality has changed over the years, leading to modules like ES2016 and ES8 that have allowed it to include things like async functions (*https://oreil.ly/x0S0V*), the spread operator (*https://oreil.ly/twb1Q*), optional chaining (*https://oreil.ly/UygLk*), and nullish coalescing (*https://oreil.ly/sLRqn*). To stay up to date with changes, visit the TC39 GitHub repo (*https://oreil.ly/0nNLf*) occasionally to read the latest proposals.

Browsers don't make updates in sync with JavaScript updates, so your code might need polyfills to work with older browsers, depending on your build configs. That can slow the app by bloating the code with conditions and packages to get it to work for specific browser versions.

Build configs in general can get tricky. Honestly, it can be one of the more frustrating parts of development because there aren't always straightforward answers or strategies. It takes some experimentation to figure out what works the best. You just have to keep a level of grit that won't let you give up. I've definitely been there a few times.

Caching Configuration

Trying out different caching strategies can drastically improve performance. *Caching* is when you decide what resources and data should be stored in the browser to improve loading times. After a certain period of time, data in the cache is considered *stale,* which means that it needs to be refreshed from the server. You get to set that time period, so you have to balance between improving performance (by keeping data in cache longer) and consistency (cached data is out of date with respect to the server). Fonts and images tend to be stored in the browser cache for longer periods because they don't change often.

There's an art to deciding how long to cache data before making a new request for the most current data. You should research how often your data should be updated. Some data, like bank account info or order info, should be fetched with every page load. Other data, like product lists and event calendars, doesn't need to be updated as often. Work with your team to figure out what to do here.

The tricky thing about caching is that it can make debugging harder. When the user (or even the developer) has data cached locally, the app can appear to be having issues that may or may not exist. When you run into any issues where data isn't showing as expected, make sure you suggest that people clear their cache or try with a different browser. If the app is using outdated data from the cache that has values that don't exist anymore, that could crash the app.

You can implement any number of strategies (*https://oreil.ly/r1A8n*) to customize how caching works on the frontend. You can target certain endpoints to become stale after a specific amount of time, or you can select endpoints that should never be cached. Just make sure you clearly document how the cache is being handled. That documentation could be as simple as commenting the code so that the dev team understands what's happening for each cache implementation.

There are so many tools available now that have made this better. You're working with React Query, which handles caching out of the box, so take some time to read through the default configs (*https://oreil.ly/gwO1l*) and the React docs (*https://oreil.ly/bwiB5*) before you start changing things. Even the built-in React hooks like

useContext (*https://oreil.ly/fMq42*), useMemo (*https://oreil.ly/0FzC8*), and useCall
back (*https://oreil.ly/gOfCK*) can help cache some data for you. You have many
options to choose from, so I suggest you read through the documentation.

You also need a mechanism to perform *cache busting*, where you force-reload pages
or delete the user's current cached data. You might need to do that if API updates
change the response in ways that break the frontend or if you need to push updated
data to your users to meet some third-party upgrade deadline. You can do this by
writing code that force-reloads the page and changes the cache strategy temporarily,
or you might use a content delivery network (CDN) (*https://oreil.ly/3Cm0C*) that lets
you push changes to all users.

> CDNs can boost your app's performance. They essentially cache
> snapshots of your app on servers that are geographically closer to
> the user so that the user gets the page content faster. This can add a
> wrinkle to debugging production issues, so if you get reports that
> some but not all users have issues and you're using a CDN, that
> could be the cause. Clear out the CDN using the service provider's
> dashboard or CLI and see if that fixes the problem.

With React Query, the code implementation for caching will involve setting a few
parameters on your endpoint requests. Here's an example of setting a stale time for a
particular endpoint in your project to clear the cache and refetch the data:

```
const {
  isLoading: ordersIsLoading,
  error: ordersErrors,
  data: orderData,
} = useQuery({
  // data stays in cache for 1 hour (in milliseconds) and is
  // garbage collected afterwards
  gcTime: 3600000,
  // data is refetched after 1 hour (in milliseconds)
  refetchInterval: 3600000,
  // data becomes stale after 30 minutes (in milliseconds)
  staleTime: 1800000,
  queryKey: ['orderData'],
  queryFn: () =>
    axios.get(`${import.meta.env.API_URL}/v1/orders`).then((res) => res.data),
})
```

The main thing you and the team have to understand is what config values actually
do with your data. This is when you should turn to the docs (*https://oreil.ly/se6sB*)
and get a good understanding of the package you're using. Once you've got a caching
strategy in place, users will notice the difference in their experience. Just remember to
watch out for the cache when it's time to debug issues.

Lazy Loading

Lazy loading is a way to speed up your page load times by having the app load important content first and the remaining content when the user needs it. That way, the user doesn't have to wait for all the page content before they see any content at all. You can use this technique on any page that implements some type of load-on-scroll functionality.

As the user needs to see more content, lazy loading makes it available; in the meantime, they see some type of loading element. This can have a huge impact on your CLS score because if you don't style the loading elements correctly, lazy loading can cause drastic page shifts.

Fortunately, there are a couple of built-in ways to handle this in React. You can lazy load with the <Suspense /> component (*https://oreil.ly/uVQmO*) or the lazy (*https://oreil.ly/gZWtk*) method. This lets you create a loading state for any components that depend on data loading with the flexibility to create things like page scroll loading, and it lets you handle different components on the page with custom loading components. These custom loading components are sometimes referred to as "skeleton components" because they have the same dimensions as the component that will eventually load.

For example, you might have a <div /> that's styled to match the order table in your app. It doesn't have to be fancy, but it will help you avoid that content layout shift issue. Here's what that might look like when it's implemented with <Suspense />:

```
...
const TableLoadingSkeleton = () => (
  <table>
    <thead>
      <tr>
        <td>Product</td>
        <td>Description</td>
        <td>Price</td>
      </tr>
    </thead>
    <tbody>
      <tr>
        <td colSpan={3}>Loading...</td>
      </tr>
    </tbody>
  </table>
)
...
<Suspense
  fallback={<TableLoadingSkeleton data-testid="orders-loading-circle" />}
>
  <OrdersTable orders={orders} />
```

```
</Suspense>
...
```

Figure 20-5 shows the resulting page.

| Q Search products... |

First Name: [   ]

Last Name: [   ]

Quantity: [   ]

Email: [   ]

Password: [   ]

Best Contact Time: [mm/dd/yyyy, --:-- 📅]

[Submit]

Product Description Price
Loading...

Figure 20-5. Skeleton loading component in `Suspense fallback`

Now if there's any delay with the component loading, you can target it specifically with its own loading component. Remember to keep at least the height and width of the loading component about the same as the real component. An added benefit of this method is that you might see ways to make your components smaller, so you can manage the code better over time and even improve testability.

 You can do something similar to lazy loading by conditionally rendering components based on loading state, but this is an alternative to that if you want to keep the code in a certain format. This is another decision to discuss with the team because it can come down to preference.

You might also want to try lazy loading packages or imported components. That way, you call even less content until you need it on the page. Here's an example of how you can do a lazy import of the **Header** component in the *UserInfo.Container* file:

```
...
const Header = lazy(() => import('../../components/Header'))
...
<Suspense
    fallback={
      <CircularProgress
        color="secondary"
        size={100}
```

```
        data-testid="header-loading-circle"
      />
    }
  >
    <Header
      userName={userInfo.name}
      joinedDate={userInfo.joinedDate}
      onSubmitSearch={onSubmitProductSearch}
    />
</Suspense>
  ...
```

These are a few ways to improve your page load time and your CLS score at the same time.

Prefetching

Prefetching is when you get the data or components that you expect the user to need next and have them waiting in the cache. React Query helps you do this with the prefetchQuery (*https://oreil.ly/68Nje*) method. *Server-side rendering* (*https://oreil.ly/XZPYj*) (SSR) also comes up when you bring up prefetching data because you can prefetch entire pages from the server if you're working with something like Next.js or React Server Components (*https://oreil.ly/yjn1-*), which is relatively new to the framework.

SSR is a completely different paradigm than what's currently used on the frontend, and not every app will implement it. I recommend reading up on SSR (*https://oreil.ly/c3WWl*) before you try to use it. It's an effective tool that can speed up your app a lot, but it has its own drawbacks: for example, the server-side-rendered components never rerender. If you aren't expecting that, it can be hard to debug. These components won't update when useState or useEffect hooks are called, and the code likely won't compile anyway. The upside to using server components is that you can write backend functionality the same way you write your frontend code, like database queries, and it isn't exposed to users.

Scenarios where you would want to use SSR include any static content that doesn't change when a page is loaded or functionality that isn't user specific, such as shared event calendars or product lists. The performance benefits may be limited if all the content is specific to a user, as with user account info or dashboards with specific user data. I encourage you to look through the docs (*https://oreil.ly/4_f-3*) and form your own opinion. Every technology has its uses, but you have to discern when and why.

CSS, Images, and Fonts

The last thing I'll cover in this chapter is optimizing your assets. Images in particular have a huge effect on how fast your pages load because they can be large and take time to download. Doing things like compressing images, using images with the

---

correct dimensions from the server, and using formats like SVG can improve those load speeds. There are also the WebP (*https://oreil.ly/QKgCo*) or AVIF (*https://oreil.ly/rkc4P*) formats for images, but there isn't wide browser support for these formats yet, so you might still have to fall back on SVGs or PNGs. Remember, you can always check browser support with CanIUse (*http://caniuse.com*).

When it comes to CSS files, whether you're using a package or your own custom CSS, you need to minify it and check for unused styles, which contribute to your bundle size and page speed. CSS can handle quite a few things you might be doing with Java-Script, like dark mode, gradient animations, and parallax effects. Make sure you check out the latest CSS rules (*https://oreil.ly/NQSMl*) before you jump into a Java-Script solution because CSS is constantly changing, especially for responsive layouts and animations.

Fonts are often overlooked because they tend to come from some other service, like the Google Fonts CDN (*https://fonts.google.com*). Make sure you're loading only the fonts you need and remove any unused fonts or icons. If you can, self-hosting your fonts can speed up your pages because you don't have to rely on a connection to a third-party CDN. This also goes for things like the MUI library. You can import the specific components you need on a page instead of the entire library, decreasing the amount of content the page needs to load.

Conclusion

In this chapter, you learned about testing your app's performance and how to spot where to make improvements. Never forget that poor performance leaves people out. People who live in rural areas, people who only use cell phones or older hardware, areas that have slow internet connections, and people who pay for cell plans by data use could be excluded if site performance is bad. Often, we as developers are used to having nice hardware with high-speed internet connections, so this can be easily overlooked. But don't forget that not all users have this access.

As you learn more about how users interact with your app, you'll be able to make these decisions with your team based on the data you see. It's great to keep best practices in mind early in the feature-development process, but you never know what users will do or ask for until you show them the app.

Watch those key performance metrics as they change over time, and you'll learn more about their behavior so that you can focus on the areas that really matter. The best ways to handle things like browser support and the cache will reveal themselves over time. Do your best in the beginning and don't hesitate to make changes when the data shows you it's time to do so. What's important to users will change over time, too. As long as you know the main areas to focus on improving, you can discuss how to do this with the team and make new decisions over the life of the product.

## CHAPTER 21

Frontend Testing

In previous chapters, I mentioned that the best practice for writing any tests is to write them at the same time as you write any new functionality or do any refactors. Testing deserves its own focus, and that's what I'll cover here.

When you're building this app, you need to make sure you aren't releasing regressions in existing functionality. A *regression* is when new code unintentionally causes errors in existing functionality anywhere in the app. The QA team, if there is one, won't have time to run regression testing on every single release, but as a developer, you can take the initiative to ensure your code is solid. Your tests for the new code can bring up questions about how something works or what happens when it doesn't.

In this chapter, I'll cover:

- How to determine which parts of the frontend to test
- Unit testing
- End-to-end (e2e) testing
- Useful testing tools

The two goals of test writing are preventing unexpected broken code from ending up in front of users and documenting the app so that everyone knows how it's supposed to work. Testing also gives you more confidence with future development because you aren't worried about your changes breaking something unexpectedly.

Testing will bring your dev team, the Product team, the Design team, and the QA team even closer together as you all come up with different scenarios. Always remember that QA is not the enemy. Their job is crucial to deploying with confidence. They aren't telling you that your code is bad, just that it doesn't work as expected compared to the feature specs.

Determining Test Scenarios

If you aren't sure where to start, look at your components closely. Here's a list of things to look for:

- Anything that is conditionally rendered should probably have a test.
- Anywhere you make API requests should probably have a test.
- If an error might occur, there should be a test for it.
- If you manipulate data in any way, a test should likely be written.
- Pretty much anything that causes a change in the way a component is rendered should have a test.

It's not unusual for a single component to have a large test file as the functionality changes. When you do PR reviews, look for new test cases to make sure as many lines of code have test coverage as reasonably possible. When Product brings you requirements, you should think about test cases.

There's also a balance to this. Some features will take longer to write tests for than to actually implement. This is where you need to consider trade-offs between the effort it will take to write the test, the time it takes to write the implementation, and any upcoming release dates. Personally, I've never seen a frontend app written in any framework with 100% test coverage. That's completely different from the backend, where I've seen very close to 100% coverage in some projects.

This difference happens because of the complex and changing nature of the tools we use. It's hard to get tests to work with the way apps are rendered because of things like timing inconsistencies, triggering events, and external dependencies, such as third-party services. As you start writing tests, you'll notice when a test is taking up more time than the value it will provide. There's no hard rule, so lean into your experience, intuition, and the team to make sure no one is getting stuck on putting up a PR because of a complicated test.

Unit Tests

Whether you decide to use BDD (*https://oreil.ly/acx5Y*) or TDD (*https://oreil.ly/7l5l2*), as long as you write testable code, write tests for it, and make sure the tests pass, you should be good. *Unit tests* are the core of the testing you'll do on the frontend. This is how you check if components work as expected and account for edge cases. These are small and targeted tests to catch things like conditional rendering in a programmatic way. They help ensure that your code works with every deployment and give everyone more confidence in doing small deployments frequently.

Jest and React Testing Library

If you want a more established library to work with, Jest (*https://jestjs.io*) and React Testing Library (*https://oreil.ly/VXJto*) (RTL) are solid choices with plenty of documentation, examples, and community support. You've already used Jest for testing on the backend: it's the underlying framework for the NestJS testing suite. Using it on the frontend is different, though. That's where RTL comes in.

Any projects that are initialized with CRA (*https://create-react-app.dev*) have RTL included out of the box. However, the React team deprecated CRA (*https://oreil.ly/6bFGa*) in early 2023, which is why you bootstrapped this project with Vite. Even though RTL doesn't come out of the box with some of the alternatives to CRA, it's still useful to initialize your project. The way you write tests won't be much different from the way you'll write them with the tool you'll actually use in this project.

Vitest

Because this project has been initialized with Vite, you'll go ahead and use Vitest (*https://vitest.dev*) for unit tests. It's compatible with Jest, so even if the team is more familiar with Jest and RTL, the transition will be pretty straightforward. This is a newer tool that has quickly growing support in the React ecosystem. It can dramatically speed up the time it takes to run your entire test suite compared with Jest.

> If you ever migrate from CRA to Vite or any other tool, check the benchmarks on how fast things run. You'll notice differences in test speeds, cold starts for the app, and maybe even response times. The differences in test speeds will help when it's time to deploy the app to different environments. We'll get into deployment pipelines in Chapter 27, but since you're working on them now, it's worth noting how long your unit tests take to run. Having fast tests will also speed up local development, so look at the options and see which is best.

Let's write some tests for the `UserInfo` component so that you can establish some examples for the team in your repo. This will give you an idea of how you can break down a component into different test cases. First, let's start with the mocks for the tests:

```
import { afterEach, beforeEach, describe, expect, it, vi } from 'vitest'
import { act, render, screen } from '@testing-library/react'
import UserInfo from '.'
import { orderResponseData } from '../../mocks/orders'
import { userResponseData } from '../../mocks/users'

const mocks = {
  useQuery: vi.fn(),
```

```
    useErrorBoundary: vi.fn(),
    showBoundary: vi.fn(),
  }

vi.mock('@tanstack/react-query', () => ({
  useQuery: () => mocks.useQuery(),
}))

vi.mock('react-error-boundary', () => ({
  useErrorBoundary: () => mocks.useErrorBoundary(),
}))

describe('<UserInfo />', () => {
  beforeEach(() => {
    mocks.useQuery.mockReturnValue({
      isLoading: false,
      data: orderResponseData,
    })
    mocks.useQuery.mockReturnValue({
      isLoading: false,
      data: userResponseData,
    })
    mocks.useErrorBoundary.mockReturnValue({ showBoundary: mocks.showBoundary })
  })

  afterEach(() => {
    vi.clearAllMocks()
  })
})
```

Setting up all the mocks for your tests is going to make writing them easier as you run into more complex scenarios. In this example, you've set up mocks for the useQuery hook, which fetches your data, and some mocks to handle the error boundary functions. These mocks will allow you to return different values or responses as you write tests without having to call the real method in the component. This is important so that you don't have to test the functionality of the method you're calling—you can just focus on the way the code works.

If you check the imports, you'll find the orderResponseData and the userResponse Data in separate files. These are the mock responses you have defined for the API requests you make in the component. The reason they're not in the test file directly is because they might get used in other test files for different components. Keeping them in separate files makes them more maintainable because you can keep one source up to date, as opposed to having to update duplicate data across multiple files.

Inside the describe block, initialize the mocks to the state the component expects. That means making API requests, returning the mock data as responses, and setting any other values. You do this in the beforeEach block, which executes before every test in the describe block. At some point, you'll modify responses or data, and you don't want those to carry over to the next test case. That's why it's common to reset the values in the afterEach block.

Finally, you'll get into the test cases where you check for rendering states. It's a good practice to at least have a test that renders the component correctly. When you're deciding what values to check for in your test, make sure they reflect what should be rendered based on data or user interactions. Testing for static text can be misleading because it doesn't change regardless of what state the component is in. Here are a couple of tests you can write for this component inside the describe block, just to get you started:

```
it('should render the user info screen', async () => {
    render(<UserInfo />)

    expect(screen.getByPlaceholderText('Search products...')).toBeDefined()
    expect(screen.getByText('Dog stuff')).toBeDefined()
    expect(screen.getByText('Customer since 2002')).toBeDefined()

})

it('should render the loading circle when user data is loading', async () => {
    mocks.useQuery.mockReturnValue({
        isLoading: true,
    })

    render(<UserInfo />)

    expect(screen.getByTestId('user-loading-circle')).toBeDefined()
})
```

In the first test, you can see that the component gets rendered and then you check for values that come from the API requests as well as one of the interactive components. Change the values slightly and you'll find that the test fails. That's how you can check that your test works. The second test checks that the loading spinner shows when the API response is still loading.

 To make sure I've covered all the test scenarios, I like to have the component file open right next to the test file in a split-screen view. That way, I can go line by line and add things to my test file to match what's in my component. Doing this has led me to understand features in a better way and to work through some confusing rendering logic.

Another type of test you might consider is a snapshot (*https://oreil.ly/MdzF1*). *Snapshot tests* compare the output of your code to a snapshot file that has the exact expected HTML or values that should be rendered on the page. This can be useful to make sure the UI isn't changing unexpectedly or to confirm updates. Snapshot tests are usually easy to maintain since you don't have to write code for them: you just run a command (*https://oreil.ly/Le0Xr*) to update the snapshot file when needed.

After you've been in the details of writing tests for a while, it's normal to notice areas where the code can be written more clearly. Refactoring code to be more testable is a good thing. You can show the team areas that can be simplified or abstracted to helper functions or hooks that make the code more reusable and maintainable.

Sometimes a test can be difficult to write because the implementation is hard to understand. Unit tests will help you find those areas and improve them. Here's an example of some code that's a little hard to test although very straightforward to implement:

```
const updateDate = () => {
  const now = new Date()

  const formattedDate = new Intl.DateTimeFormat('en-US').format(now)

  return formattedDate
}
```

When you try to test this, it gets tricky because you're working with the current date every time. That can lead to situations where your tests are flaky and can fail by a number of milliseconds. Here's how that code can be refactored to make testing easier and the code give consistent results:

```
const updateDate = (date?: string) => {
  const now = date ? new Date(date) : new Date()

  const formattedDate = new Intl.DateTimeFormat('en-US').format(now)

  return formattedDate
}
```

Now you can pass a specific date to get a reproducible result. After you and the team get into the practice of including unit tests for everything you add to the project, you'll find that it catches regressions in development and leads to other conversations about how code should be broken down.

Mock Service Worker

There are a lot of other testing tools that can optimize your flow across the team and across other processes in the development lifecycle. One of those tools is Mock Service Worker (*https://oreil.ly/H6Y9g*) (MSW), which can mimic your endpoints. When you need to check that an endpoint is being called with the correct parameters and returning the expected data, having mock data helps; this tool takes it to the next level. This is great if you need to deploy the app to a develop or feature environment for dev testing or for the Product team to play around and see how the app works in different scenarios. Alternatives like Nock (*https://oreil.ly/1eKG7*) or JSON Server (*https://oreil.ly/oOABB*) are also worth researching.

 I've seen tools like MSW used in organizations where the backend and frontend are separate teams: the frontend team develops against MSW based on the expected data. Be careful here, though. Sometimes the frontend can be developed before the backend is ready, which isn't a great practice if you aren't in close contact with the backend team. It can lead to redundant work if the backend team makes changes to the data structure.

MSW works by creating a service worker in your public directory. You then wrap the `<App />` component in a function (*https://oreil.ly/5hfUQ*) to determine whether the app will use real APIs or the mock ones you'll create. So the *main.tsx* file in your project will look like this:

```
export async function shouldEnableMocking() {
  if (import.meta.env.MODE !== 'development') {
    return
  }

  const { worker } = await import('./mocks/browser')

  // `worker.start()` returns a Promise that resolves
  // once the Service Worker is up and ready to intercept requests.
  return worker.start()
}

shouldEnableMocking()

ReactDOM.createRoot(document.getElementById('root')!).render(
  <React.StrictMode>
    <App />
  </React.StrictMode>
)
```

Now anytime you're running the app in `development` mode, you'll get the responses from MSW. The only thing left to finish the implementation of this tool is to create the handlers that will be called instead of the actual API. In *src/mocks*, create a new file called *handlers.ts* and add this code to it:

```
import { http, HttpResponse } from 'msw'
import { userResponseData } from './users'
import { orderResponseData } from './orders'

export const handlers = [
  http.get(`${import.meta.env.VITE_API_URL}/v1/users`, () => {
    return HttpResponse.json(userResponseData)
  }),
```

```
http.get(`${import.meta.env.VITE_API_URL}/v1/orders`, () => {
  return HttpResponse.json(orderResponseData)
}),
]
```

This is how you establish mock endpoints and their responses (*https://oreil.ly/esMrR*). Can you see how having the mock responses in their own files comes in handy now? From here, you can add more endpoints and more conditions to handle auth tokens and parameters.

E2E Testing with Cypress

The last type of testing I'll go over is *e2e testing*, which you can use to test the full user flow of an app in an automated way. With a tool like Cypress (*https://oreil.ly/-McxR*), you can run automated tests from the user's perspective. Cypress will open its own browser and perform actions in the way a user would. It will click buttons, type values into forms, and determine if the expected changes appear on the page.

Collaborate with the Product team to get all of the scenarios. Using tools like Cucumber (*https://oreil.ly/AoLzZ*) and Gherkin (*https://oreil.ly/p1wmc*) will help the Product team understand the purpose of testing and get them more involved. Gherkin and Cucumber let you write test scenarios in the given-when-then format, which can help you get Product to define requirements with less ambiguity as you work through specs and mocks together.

Depending on the organization, e2e tests might be work for the QA team. This is especially true if you have any *software development engineer in test* (SDET) members on the team: people who are dedicated to writing automated test suites with tools like Cypress. SDETs are typically found at larger organizations, although it's possible to work with them at startups.

Here's an example of what a Cypress test can look like:

```
describe('User Info', () => {
  it('Navigates to the TestStore home page', () => {
    cy.visit('http://localhost:5173/')
    cy.contains('Actions')

    cy.contains('Actions').click()
    cy.url().should('include', '/actions')
  })
})
```

When you run this with Cypress, you'll see the process exactly as a user would. The tool will run in a separate window, as shown in Figure 21-1.

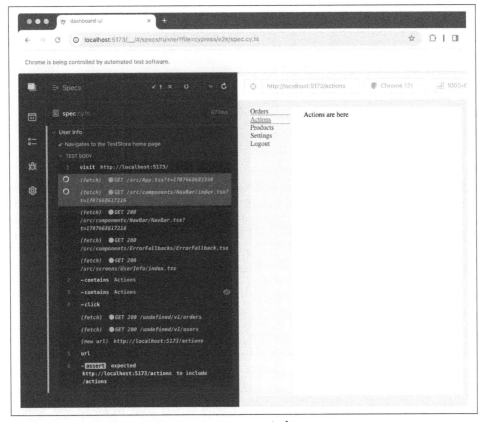

Figure 21-1. A Cypress test running in separate window

Now look at an example using Gherkin and Cucumber. You can request that the Product team write requirements in the Gherkin format:

```
// cypress > e2e > user-info.feature
Feature: User Info functionality

    Scenario: Navigate to user actions screen
        Given I am on the user info screen
        When I click the Actions nav link
        Then I should be redirected to the user actions screen
```

This code will be in a file called *user-info.feature,* and it will go in the *cypress/e2e* folder. You can take this feature and use the keywords Given...When...Then to define the steps in your e2e test, in a new file called *user-info.ts,* which you'll also store in the *cypress/e2e* folder. It will have this code:

```
// cypress > e2e > user-info.ts
import { When, Then, Given } from '@badeball/cypress-cucumber-preprocessor'
```

```
Given('I am on the user info screen', () => {
  cy.visit('http://localhost:5173/')
})

When('I click the Actions nav link', () => {
  cy.contains('Actions')
  cy.contains('Actions').click()
})

Then('I should be redirected to the user actions screen', () => {
  cy.url().should('include', '/actions')
})
```

These are a few ways you can implement e2e tests. You don't need to use Gherkin and Cucumber to get the most use out of Cypress, but these integral components can be effective if the teams agree. Some developers will say that using Gherkin and Cucumber actually make it *harder* to write and maintain Cypress tests because Cypress is pretty expressive out of the box; however, at enterprise organizations, they can be a useful way to include the Product team in more technical discussions.

There's no right or wrong answer to this. It just depends on what you and your team, along with the other teams and leadership, decide is the best approach. Personally, I prefer just writing e2e tests with Cypress directly because setting up Gherkin and Cucumber to work in a deployment pipeline can get a little tricky with configs.

Conclusion

In this chapter, you learned about different ways to test your frontend app. Sometimes pushing for technical work to be included as part of the feature requirements is a skill you'll need. Tests are one of those things, even in crunch times. Unless production is on fire and you need to release a hotfix immediately, make the argument for writing tests as part of your postmortem checklist. (We covered what that is in Chapter 12.)

It's easy to write tickets and say you'll come back to them, but there's never time, so it often doesn't happen. Not all organizations or developers value tests equally, so encourage the practice as early as possible. Even if you're working on an existing app, it's better to have some coverage than none at all. Tests don't speed up new feature development, but they definitely help keep the code stable from a technical perspective.

## CHAPTER 22

Frontend Debugging

You're finally at the point in your frontend app where you have everything ready for production. You've had to debug issues during development, so you already have some strategies or approaches to take. Now that everything's integrated and your app is in production, you need a more systematic approach to finding and resolving bugs.

Although there isn't a single strategy that will guarantee you find a bug the exact same way every time, there are some common things you can do to give yourself and the team a good starting point. So as you and other teams start to work together with the app on production, you can help everyone by learning how to quickly track down root causes.

In this chapter, I'll go over:

- Places to start your debugging journey
- Tools you can use to help
- Other areas to consider when you get stuck
- What to do when a bug is happening because of another team

Debugging is an art that takes time and exposure to numerous projects to get better at. It's one of the most underrated and valuable skills you can have because it will be applicable to any app you ever work on and across all programming languages. Even though we try our best not to introduce bugs to the code, it happens. As you encounter more causes of bugs in your work, you'll be able to add more debugging approaches to your toolbox.

The Debugging Process

One of the first things you need to do is become aware that a bug exists. Someone from the Support team could bring it up because they're getting a lot of users writing in about it. You could also find out something is happening in production based on your monitoring and alert tools. You might even be debugging a separate issue and notice a lot of the same errors happening in the logs. There's also the chance that you, someone on the dev team, or someone in QA notices something as you're testing other things.

Once you're aware that a bug is in production, it's time for you to start collecting information about it from different sources. That includes talking to Support to figure out the steps to reproduce the bugs users are seeing, looking through the logs more thoroughly, and going through the most recent changes that have been deployed to production. After you have enough info to reproduce the bug, then you can jump to the next step in the process, which is figuring out how to fix the bug and write tests for it.

You'll find that in many cases the bug fix can be a simple one-liner or a quick code change. It's the process of finding where that code change needs to happen that takes the most time. After you've made the fix, you can finish writing test cases to make sure you have coverage for this scenario. Finally, you deploy the fix to production and validate that it works there.

This is a typical debugging process that you might follow. Now we're going to go through how you might find and reproduce the issue once you're aware of it.

Looking Through Logs

After you've become aware of the bug, checking logs is one way you can start searching for the root cause. You can find what triggers the errors and look for the records in the logs that match with that. You should also check the backend logs to see if any API errors occurred that may have caused the frontend errors.

Depending on the logging tool you use, you should be able to search through the logs. If you know what page the error happened on, you may be able to find a root cause by searching for that specific page. There can be a lot of data to sift through in the logs, so keep your search very specific. You want to focus on things like:

- Patterns in the errors
- Certain events that cause errors each time
- Data being captured
- Users who experienced the errors

This is an area where you can really shine because going through logs can be a daunting task. Something to keep in mind as you go through logs is that having more logs from the app would be useful. Go ahead and add that to the code and deploy it! Your backend logs should be inaccessible by outside parties for security reasons anyway, so you can log more of the user data that you have available to get even more details about what's happening. If the error involves an API request, you can add more logs on the backend to see if it's getting the request and the response you expect.

Your logs can tell you if a certain component sent the correct parameters for a request. You can make the log message even more specific and include things like the user's auth token to check their permissions. Or if you notice the error messages aren't completely showing in the logs, you might need to update that specific logger. For example, if your log says something like `"error from orders.createOrder"`, that doesn't tell you what happened. It can also mean that the underlying error is being suppressed by custom error handling that you and the team have implemented on either the frontend or backend. Go into the code, search for that error message, and see what you have for the logger and why.

 A small thing to keep in mind when you are looking at logs is how you handle objects. If your log messages have in them, that probably means the data needs to be stringified.

This is especially true for third-party service errors. You might call a function directly from a third-party service, such as Okta (*https://oreil.ly/FnSom*), on the frontend. You don't have control over what info you receive if that package throws an error, but you can pass the info along in the raw format. That can help you trace bugs back to some settings you created in the dashboard for a service.

When you're reproducing the bug locally, don't hesitate to add loggers all over your code if they will help you track down a difficult bug. If you think they are crowding the code, you can always remove them once you've found a bug. Sometimes bugs won't occur when you run the app locally because you aren't connected to certain services or the environment has special configs.

Another thing is that you don't have to strictly log errors. You can have debug, info, and warn logs, like we discussed in Chapter 9. These will help you identify patterns in how the app typically behaves so that you can target deviations from normal behavior. That's why you can take the lead and create a log checklist for the team to go through and amend as they learn new things.

Here's a little checklist I use when I'm looking through the logs to find a bug:

- Figure out what time the bug was reported and filter the logs based on that.
- Look for specific messages that are related to the issue. That might be a page, a component, an API call, or a user ID.
- Read the full log object to see what's included in the message.
- Go through the call stack if it's included in the log object because this helps find a specific file where the error is coming from.
- Look for other logs that are happening around the related issue. Check if there are logs before or after the issue to get more info.
- Go to the code and see if you can find the problem area.
- If you can't figure it out, add more logs around the problem area in the code and recheck the logs.

> To trace an error through the call stack, you'll need to have your source maps (*https://oreil.ly/K5RIL*) configured correctly. This isn't typically enabled by default in many modern tools, like Vite (*https://oreil.ly/K8eSN*), Rollup (*https://oreil.ly/rYeih*), and esbuild (*https://oreil.ly/ybP_o*). They have a specific config value to enable source mapping.

This is just a starting point. When you get into your app's logs, you have to see where they lead you. There's no normal for what should show in the logs for an error, and the error might not even get logged. But understanding what you're looking for will help you figure that out faster so that you can move on to other debugging options.

Checking the Code

As you do your due diligence and check the logs, you'll end up in your code. This is when you can run the app locally and see if you can reproduce the bug. Keep in mind that as you debug, you'll jump across all the different debugging methods in this chapter. So if your logs immediately lead you to the problem in the code, don't hesitate to get right into some of those suggestions. You may also prefer to start in the code and then check the logs. Any approach that gets you to the root cause of the bug is the right one.

If you're just coming to the code with an error message, you can search the project for that message. If the message is in the code, this should show where it is. Then you can go to that file and start tracing what causes that error. This is where you have to keep track of where you've been in the code because it's easy to lose your place as you switch between files. Something that might be useful is opening a split view of files so you can do side-by-side comparisons.

Using console.log Messages

As you go through the code with the app running locally, toss in some `console.log` calls around areas that you think might help. This is similar to the logs you looked at earlier except it happens in the browser console, so you don't want to leave these in after you find the bug. You can have `console.log`s to help you figure out when a component gets rendered and what data it's rendered with. These programmatic checks can show you when you're getting data in a format you weren't expecting or when you aren't getting data at all.

For example, you might notice that your component isn't rendering. By using `console.log`, you can check in real time if the conditions for that component to render are being met. With a `console.log`, you might find that a response is stuck in a loading state, it's returning an empty array, or you aren't accessing an object value correctly. You might even catch a side effect happening where the component loads correctly on the initial render but something with a `useEffect` hook is making the component rerender incorrectly.

The best part about your `console.log`s is that you don't have to format them in a certain way because they're going to get deleted after you find the problem. Tools like missionlog (*https://oreil.ly/uq2qv*), pino (*https://oreil.ly/Vjak7*), and winston (*https://oreil.ly/1UAdr*) are also good frontend debugging packages. Here's an example of how you could mark up your component for debugging with `console.log`

```
useEffect(() => {
  console.log('userResponseData', userResponseData)
  console.log('orderResponseData', orderResponseData)
  setUserInfo(userResponseData)
  setOrders(orderResponseData)
}, [orderData, userData])

if (userIsLoading)
  return <CircularProgress data-testid="user-loading-circle" />
console.log('successfully completed the user loading state')
if (userErrors || ordersErrors) showBoundary(userErrors || ordersErrors)
console.log('successfully completed made it past the error states')
```

This is a small example of how `console.log` can be used to help you debug code locally. These are temporary checks that don't need to be logged in production. This is also how you can validate incremental changes in the code. When you get into a debugging flow, changing one line of code at a time can help you pin down the changes you need to make.

For example, maybe you need to update the URL with query string parameters that change based on drop-down selections users make. You notice that the query string doesn't update like you expect, but the page reloads anyway. You can change one of the drop-down values to use a state variable and see if that helps. If it does, then you can change another in the same way and see if the update still works. When you're debugging, you don't want to get to a point where you've fixed the bug but you have no idea how. Or worse, you fix the original bug and introduce a new one. Unit tests help to protect against this, but they aren't foolproof. That's why you want to do the changes incrementally and see what effect they have. If it means changing one line of code at a time, that's fine.

Using Breakpoints

Now that you've seen how you can use `console.log` to debug your code incrementally, you can take it a step further with breakpoints. When using a debugger like we will in the Chrome DevTools, a *breakpoint* is a place where code execution is stopped. This is how you can check values in real time without having `console.log`s everywhere. Breakpoints also allow you to see the call stack up to the point where the code execution stops, which may reveal where the real problem is.

You'll be able to step through the code line by line until you trigger the bug. That means you can see what data is getting passed as it's generated, and you can see the order that functions are being called in. If a function is called, you can usually step into it to see what values it receives and the output it returns. A caveat to stepping into functions is when you have async tasks, like API calls. You'll need to put the breakpoint in the callback itself because you can't directly step into that function.

This usually ends up being very efficient and succinct because you can keep track of what new code does. For example, maybe you refactor a function parameter to be an object instead of an array. Now you know what the real fix for the bug was, and you can clean up any code related to it. Next, you can start making incremental Git commits so that you don't lose your progress. Something that feels worse than fixing a bug and making a new one is fixing a bug and deleting the code.

Using Unit Tests

Because you already have tests in place like we covered in Chapter 21, you can use these to help you debug as well. Try running the unit tests and see if they pass to start. Then try changing the conditions for your tests and see if they still pass. If you notice a test is passing even though it shouldn't be, this is a sign that you need to take a closer look at the code for it. In some cases, there could be an issue with an async function, or you might not be rendering components as expected.

This is a good time to add more tests. Sometimes the exercise of going through the code line by line to look for new areas to test can highlight conditions. You can use this line-by-line review to try some refactors to simplify the code and reveal issues.

Using Git

Git can be your friend during any debugging session. Not only can it help you keep track of the changes you're making to fix the bug, but it can also help you quickly find the commit that introduced the bug. This is where a command like `git bisect` (*https://oreil.ly/zVafD*) comes in; we'll look at that more in Chapter 28. Looking through the Git history to see what changes were pushed before a bug started happening can take you right to the change that created it. You can look at the PRs that have been merged or use your IDE to see a comparison between the current code and the last commit, as in Figure 22-1.

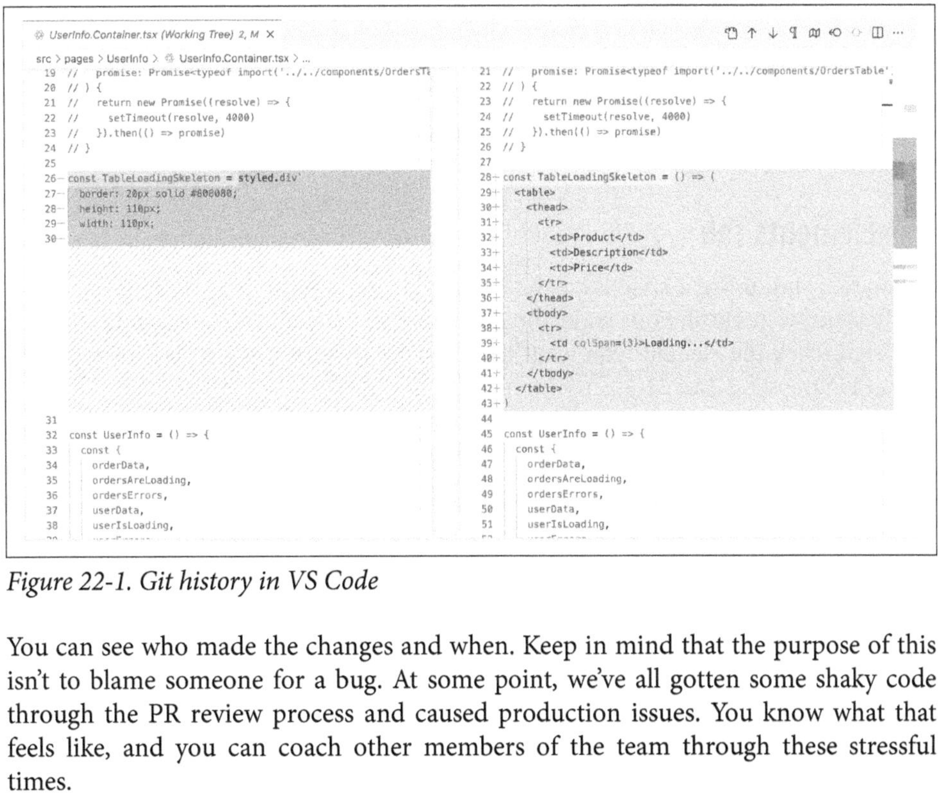

Figure 22-1. Git history in VS Code

You can see who made the changes and when. Keep in mind that the purpose of this isn't to blame someone for a bug. At some point, we've all gotten some shaky code through the PR review process and caused production issues. You know what that feels like, and you can coach other members of the team through these stressful times.

Once you know who wrote the buggy code, you can get on a call with them to figure out what they were trying to do and come up with a better solution. Some of the best debugging sessions come from a pair-programming session. Having two people looking at the issue lets you "rubber-duck" with each other to figure out what could have happened and the best approach going forward. As a rule of thumb, if you've been debugging for more than 30 minutes, see if you can bounce ideas off another dev.

Even typing out the question can help bring you out of the depths of the code. This is where an AI tool like ChatGPT (*https://openai.com/chatgpt*) can come in handy. When you have to explain the problem to someone else, you might find that *you* get a different view. You never know what someone else on the team has experience with. You might have an issue with datetime conversions, and that's what one of your fellow devs worked on in their last role. It can be tempting to get caught up in the idea that you should know how to fix everything quickly, but nobody knows everything, no matter how long they've been programming. So if you get stumped, reach out to others.

Using the Browser Devtools

When you're trying to narrow down why a bug is happening, use the browser devtools to see what's happening directly on the page. I'll be referencing the Chrome DevTools, but all the browsers have similar tools. You've already looked at the browser tools for performance and accessibility reasons, so we'll focus on four tabs: Elements, Sources, Network, and Application.

The Elements Tab

If you're trying to fix a style issue, but you're having a hard time finding the incorrectly styled element in your code, the Elements tab can help. You can go to the page and right-click the element you want to check the styles for, which will open a view like in Figures 22-2 and 22-3.

In the panel on the right in Figure 22-3, you'll see all the styles applied to the highlighted element. You can edit the styles live in the browser by changing values in the right panel. If you're dealing with deeply nested elements that have styles applied from parent components or third-party packages, such as MUI, this can really help you get to the root of the styles and what needs to be updated. You can even check for hover states and mobile views in the Elements tab.

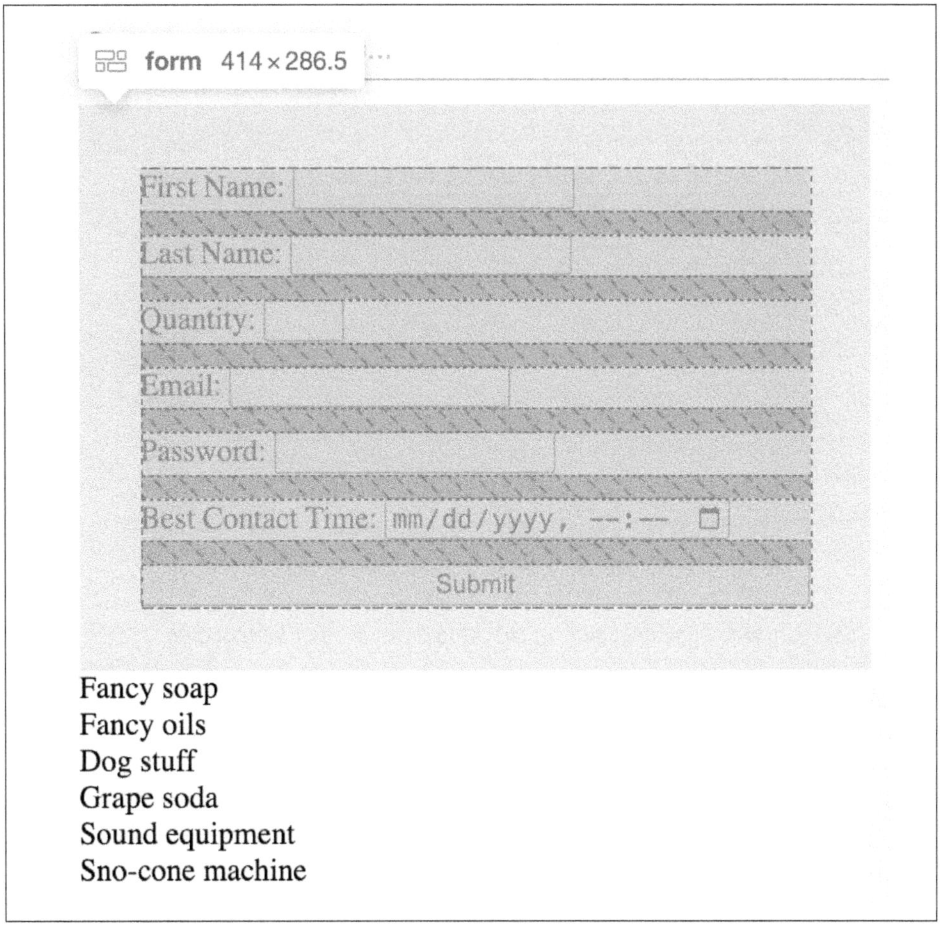

Figure 22-2. Page view of checking styles in the Elements tab of the Chrome DevTools

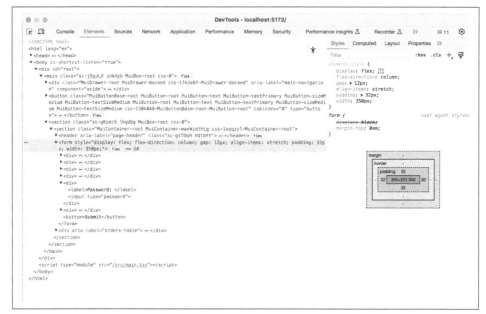

Figure 22-3. Chrome DevTools view of checking styles in the Elements tab

To check mobile views, you can click the second icon on the left in the header nav of the DevTools as shown in Figure 22-4. Then your browser will update the app to display in a mobile or responsive view that you can change based on the options in the drop-down, as shown in Figure 22-5.

Figure 22-4. Access mobile views in Chrome DevTools

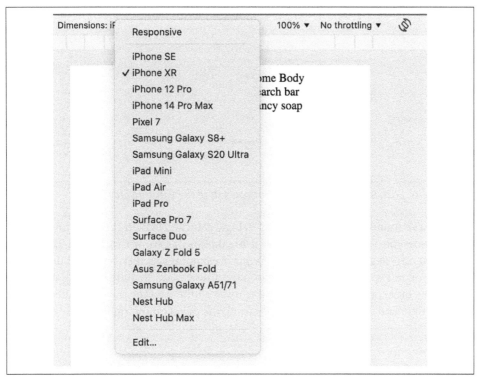

Figure 22-5. Responsive options in mobile view

The Sources Tab

If you need to check for things like states and rendering or even when values get set, the Sources tab is going to be helpful. This lets you go through the files in the app and set breakpoints so that you can step through the file execution. You can push Cmd–P on Mac or Ctrl+P on Windows in the Sources tab to search for the file you want to step through. Any file that's in your repo should be accessible in the Sources tab when you run the app locally, as shown in Figure 22-6. When the app is in another environment, like production, you might not be able to find the exact file because the code has been bundled and minimized.

Figure 22-6. Searching for a file in the Sources tab of the Chrome DevTools

After you've found the file you want to debug, you can click on the line number next to the code you want to check to set a breakpoint, as shown in Figure 22-7. Now when you refresh the page, you'll see if your breakpoint gets hit or not. If it doesn't get hit and you're expecting it to, then you have a new place to start tracking down the bug. If the breakpoint does get hit, you can see all the data for the component at that point in time and step through the code using the panel on the right.

Figure 22-7. Applying a breakpoint in the Sources tab of the Chrome DevTools

Figure 22-7 shows how to check if something unexpected is happening with your state variables, API calls, or any other functions that get called. Maybe you need to see what's causing a bug when a user tries to submit a form. Then you discover the input isn't being parsed correctly by stepping through the process with breakpoints. If you have a breakpoint enabled and refresh the page, it might initially show that no data is available. That's where your loading states will keep the app from crashing. If you continue to trigger the breakpoints, you'll get to a point in the lifecycle where the data is loaded. Then you'll be able to check what the issue might be, such as something directly with the data or a function getting called incorrectly.

The Network Tab

If you've narrowed the problem down to an issue with the data, you should use the Network tab to check your backend requests and responses. This is where you can see all the requests the app makes when a page loads, including components, packages, and API calls. If your API request is a place of concern, you can check the headers that were sent with the request and make sure that you have all the correct parameters. You can see an example of what an API request might look like in the Network tab in Figure 22-8.

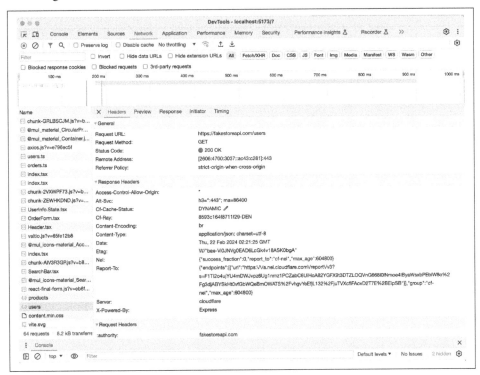

Figure 22-8. Checking the API request in the Network tab

If you see that the bug is an authorization error, like a 403 status code (*https://oreil.ly/IGQmx*), then you can check the credentials being sent in the request. You might notice that the URL being called isn't the right one because something should be in camel case or another format. You can see if the API is called or if there's a status code being returned that the app doesn't have a way to handle. The Network tab is going to show you all the traffic for a page.

> The DevTools work on any website, so I highly encourage you to go to a site you frequent and look at what's happening in the Network tab. It'll probably look like a jumble of indecipherable chunks and calls, and that's what you want to see on production in most cases. That's because of performance considerations. If anybody can access the APIs and their data the same way you do locally, that's a huge problem. That's why I've tried to bring up security throughout this book so that your app isn't in production with everything transparent for anybody to see.

Once you find the API request you're curious about, you can look at the response in either the Preview or the Response window. The Preview window will let you see the response in JSON format. The Response window also displays the data in JSON, but in a more expanded view. This will let you look at the data straight from the API response without ever touching your app code. You can see if the data comes in the format you expect or if fields have changed.

That can happen unexpectedly when you're depending on third-party services. They don't always announce when they've pushed a change to the API, so you might find out at the same time the users do. Figure 22-9 is an example of what a response from a third-party API might look like.

When you're debugging and you notice that a component gets stuck in a loading state or consistently throws the same error, try checking the Network tab. It might take you in a new direction or at least rule out a hypothesis. The last tab that you should look at usually ties in with the Network tab; that's the Application tab.

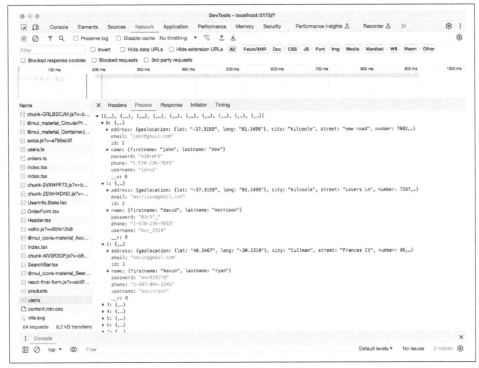

Figure 22-9. Checking the API response in the Network tab

The Application Tab

The Application tab is where you'll find your cookies, localStorage, and session Storage values. localStorage and sessionStorage hold key-value pairs for things like access tokens, user language preferences, app IDs, and any other info that helps customize an app for a user. If your bug is showing that you constantly get 403 errors, check this tab to see if some kind of token is set. If it's in JSON Web Token (JWT) format, you can copy it and decode it with a tool like jwt.io (*https://jwt.io*). Sometimes the bug is as simple as a user not having the right permissions to get a response from an endpoint.

Or you might find that a required value is missing from one of the storage options. Keep in mind that localStorage can persist even when a tab is closed, but session Storage is cleared when the tab is closed or the user ends a session by logging out. That could also be the cause of your bug. Things like user preference settings are kept in localStorage while things like whether or not to show a pop-up on a page or other state-tracking variables are kept in sessionStorage. The reason a user can have multiple tabs for the same website open at the same time and have different interactions is likely due to sessionStorage being used, so keep that in mind for bugs.

Figure 22-10 is an example of what `localStorage` might look like in a production app in the Application tab.

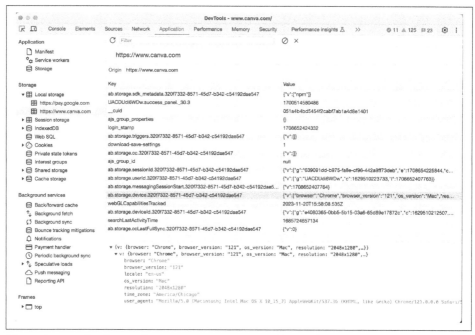

Figure 22-10. Checking values in `localStorage` in the Application tab

The browser devtools are an incredible debugging option, and they can tell you more about your app than you might find in logs or even in the code. They help you see what's happening at runtime when everything's been bundled and minimized. Sometimes it's the only way you can catch what's happening, especially with style issues. Once you have located a few places that might be causing the bug, you can start homing in on the details you may find in the logs.

Debugging in Other Environments

After you've checked all the tabs in the DevTools and checked out the mobile view of your app, it's a good idea to test your app in other environments. Maybe you couldn't reproduce the bug locally, so see what happens in the develop environment or in staging. If the bug is dependent on production resources, like connections to third-party services, you may need to debug there. If you're debugging in production, make sure you're using a test account and not a real user's account. That way, if you change settings or values, it doesn't affect anyone.

You could also recruit other devs to help you take a look at the bug in these shared environments. Using other environments like staging can help you loop in the

Product team so that you can confirm the expected behavior of the app. Something else you can do is have people on your team check the shared environment in different browsers and at different responsive sizes. That's definitely helped me uncover some hard-to-find bugs when I get overly focused on a desktop view in Chrome. Remember, your users aren't going to always use the app like you do. So try to debug from the user perspective when you find bugs.

Debugging in Unexpected Places

Bugs don't always come from the code, the data, or even feature specs. Sometimes, the most unexpected places are the source of the issue, and it can take longer than expected to find the bug. This is where you'll bring in people from other teams and start looking outside the application your team is responsible for.

You're going to be exposed to many issues like these. These are the bugs you'll remember and tell stories about because no one suspected the true source of the issue. Here are a few that I've run into at several companies over the years.

Users will always find new ways to interact with your apps that you weren't planning on. There was an instance where a user was accessing the site on an older tablet, and the page didn't render parts of the view because our responsive breakpoints didn't account for that screen size. It took days for us to figure that out and make an update for it. One other case was a user who was trying to interact with the app in the Safari browser and the styles on the page weren't rendering correctly.

Another time, users weren't able to see their data because a third-party update had revoked our app permissions without warning and they all had to give us access again. Another case was when certain users were experiencing inconsistent updates when they ordered products because the app server, the server our inventory system was on, and the server for our third-party payments were all configured with different time zones.

A different case was when our CI/CD pipeline was showing that deployments were completing successfully, but the app wasn't being updated for users. After a ton of digging, we found that the file hash where the artifact was stored wasn't being updated. That meant something was silently failing in our pipeline.

You might run into things as unexpected as the files not loading in one environment because of an issue with the filenames. One time, production was brought down because a server needed files to start with a capital letter and use underscores compared to the same files working in the development environment.

Don't forget to clear the cache and check if the issue is happening in other browsers. Also make sure your UI isn't being rendered server-side. That can make debugging tricky because SSR components don't rerender.

If you have an issue where an old version of the app runs fine and the new one doesn't, check the build artifact. Or if you notice that the changes you just released aren't showing in production, check that build artifact. Going through artifact hashes can be tedious, but if you know there's nothing wrong with the code, it's worth checking. There might be some underlying issue where the artifact is cached or it gets uploaded to a different location.

You might also check the CI/CD pipeline to see if anything in the deployment scripts changed. Maybe a new version of Node or your runtime of choice has been installed. Or some packages could have been upgraded in the pipeline. I'll go over some of the scripts you might have in your CI/CD pipeline in Chapter 27, but this is an area that can go overlooked and unmaintained until something breaks. If the bug crosses over into the infrastructure, you should check with the team responsible for maintaining it. We discussed handling critical bugs in Chapter 12, so if you run into them, you can refer to your incident playbook with more insight from the frontend.

While we used the Chrome browser as an example of debugging, make sure to check your app in other browsers. Sometimes your app will behave differently in other browsers because of the support they offer for things like new CSS rules or web technology updates. You also need to be comfortable debugging across window sizes because there is a huge range of devices that users will access your app with. By checking these areas, you'll find some of those trickier bugs.

Conclusion

In this chapter, I covered a few ways you can debug code. One thing I want to mention is that sometimes stepping away from the bug is the best solution. Go take a walk or eat lunch or do literally anything else. When you've been focused on an issue or a piece of code for too long, it's easy to get stuck on one aspect of the problem. I can't count the number of times a 30-minute walk has helped me come back and fix a bug in the fastest and simplest way possible after I've been at it for hours or days.

Reach out to others when you've tried everything you can think of. Many times, the bug and the solution end up being simple, but finding the bug source is the hard part. When you work with your team and others, you bring together a lot of different experiences and exposure. While you may have never seen a particular bug or worked with a certain tool, someone else on the team could have expertise in that area. Debugging isn't always a solo journey, especially when you need to get a fix to production because the bug is affecting customers. Don't feel like you have to figure it out on your own.

## PART IV

Deploying the Full Stack App

## CHAPTER 23

Full Stack Deployment Setup

Congratulations! You've made it through the initial challenges of setting up a backend and frontend app from scratch! Once the app is in a stable place with architecture decisions, third-party services, code conventions, package choices, and all the other pieces you've implemented throughout the rest of this book, you and the team are finally in a place where you can churn out features quickly and efficiently. Anything you do from here on will be to help the product grow and accommodate user needs over time.

Now it's time to shift your focus to setting up your deployment pipelines and making sure everything connects correctly from the database to the backend to the frontend and all the jobs in between. This is where the Security team will do more testing because the complete full stack app is ready. Before I jump into topics like CI/CD pipelines and integration concerns, it's important for you to take a step back and see how you and the team performed as full stack devs.

In this chapter, I'll go over:

- Other teams involved in the deployment process
- Checks for the frontend and backend
- Demos and team retrospectives

Although you've made it through this greenfield project, it's essential that you do some self-reflection and encourage the rest of the dev team to do the same. After working on getting a full stack app deployed, you may have some notes on what could be done better on your future projects. Let's start by discussing the other teams you'll work with to handle all your deployments.

Teams Involved in Deploys

There's usually at least one other team you'll work with to get all the infrastructure built in your cloud, but sometimes there are multiple teams. These teams commonly include Infrastructure, DevOps, and site reliability engineering (SRE).

The Infrastructure team typically manages the cloud platform itself. This team handles things like hardware, networking, storage, and server resources. They choose the best service options based on conversations they have with you and the DevOps team. The Infrastructure team has more experience managing Linux-based systems, and they help implement security practices at that level.

The DevOps team focuses on automating manual tasks like moving artifacts around or writing scripts to execute repetitive processes. This team works on implementing CI/CD pipelines with tools like CircleCI (*https://circleci.com*) or GitHub Actions (*https://oreil.ly/sCSGO*); we'll discuss this more in Chapter 27. DevOps also tries to foster collaboration across development and operations teams. When it comes to infrastructure automation, configuration management, and tooling for fast and reliable software delivery, you'll reach out to the DevOps team.

If you're at a bigger organization, you may have an SRE team. SRE teams focus on the reliability, performance, and availability of your applications. They work with monitoring tools, incident responses, and performance optimization. When you hear about service-level objectives (SLOs), it's usually with respect to metrics that this team measures and tries to maintain.

All these teams work with the dev team to ensure that apps have adequate resources to run reliably. They each manage different parts of the deployment process. It usually starts with the Infrastructure team setting up the foundation in the cloud platform. Then the DevOps team adds automations and pipelines to get the app to the correct services in the infrastructure. Finally, the SRE team monitors the deployed apps and makes sure that any changes to ensure uptime, performance, and incidents are handled.

Fully Understand the Deployment Process

Here's some advice for all devs about deployments from Jeff Graham:

> I encourage all engineers to learn and own their app's deployment process. While Infrastructure or DevOps teams might help (depending on company size), it's important that you fully understand every detail. You best know your code, tests, dependencies, build commands, etc. and can therefore make the best decisions. Besides improving your ability to troubleshoot, it will also increase your knowledge about DevOps, cloud services, and more.

These teams help you and the dev team deploy apps without worrying about the underlying systems. You'll have discussions with all these teams many times as you deploy to production while you slowly expose the app for more users to access it.

 If you're at a small organization, all of these tasks (DevOps, Infrastructure, and SRE) could become part of your workload, and you'll have to do your best to figure it all out. This can seem like an overwhelming undertaking, but take your time, read through docs, and reach out to people who work on these systems. Be clear with your organization that these are not areas you specialize in so that they have the correct expectations.

Backend and Frontend Connection Steps

At this point, you have the backend built, it's been tested, and you've been adding calls to it from the frontend. What you're doing now is double-checking everything you have in place to make sure the rollout to all the users goes smoothly. This is when you really put the infrastructure to the test and iron out the remaining wrinkles. You already have some stuff deployed to a staging environment and maybe even production, but with limited traffic.

Everything might be working perfectly, but as soon as you get more users and add more features, you'll notice some unexpected behavior. To help make this process as smooth as possible, here are some steps I use when I'm doing any full stack connections.

Backend Steps

Some devs will argue that you can start with the frontend, but I've found it much easier to have all the layers that support the frontend in place first. You can start with the frontend if it's more comfortable for you, but you'll likely end up doing some redundant work. There isn't a concrete rule about what should be handled first, and it's going to vary depending on the nature of the app.

Check your database connection with a database tool, such as pgAdmin (*https:// www.pgadmin.org*). It's one thing to develop against something locally or in a develop or staging environment. But when it's time to go to production, you need to make sure you have the right connection string, credentials, and data schema. Make sure the product you're using is configured correctly so that it doesn't return errors. If you expect this app to work at scale, this is a good time to consider connection pooling (*https://oreil.ly/h--Gq*). You might need to involve the Infrastructure or DevOps team here because they usually provision these resources.

Seed the production database to make sure data is populated correctly. It doesn't have to be a lot of data, but it should be enough to check that all your relations, tables, indexes, and values write how you expect. Since you've already done this in the initial setup, you should be able to run the same script with maybe a few modifications to the data you add.

Query the seeded data. Try out a few queries just to make sure you fetch the data you expect. Also try to update the data to check that any constraints are applied correctly and that invalid data types throw errors.

Set up the production database connection in your backend app. Once you've tested with the database tool directly, you know the database is stable and shouldn't be the source of issues. So you can confidently connect the app to the production database with the environment variables you set.

Double-check that the environment variables are set to the right values in the production environment. This is easy to miss when you're excited about everything working during a manual test.

Work with the Infrastructure team to get the backend server configured correctly. That will include setting the security for accessing the backend, handling SSL certificates, determining where parameters for scripts are stored and the regions the app will get deployed to, and invalidating your cache if you have one in place. This will also include setting up any user roles and permissions you'll need for cloud service access, which is separate from the roles and permissions in the app.

Set up logging, monitoring, and alerts for the database and backend API. You want to have these in place before you open the app to users so that you can adequately support them. Understanding how your app works in production by monitoring it is going to help you and the team find the places where the app can be improved over time. You can trigger alerts based on certain errors in the logs or based on monitoring things like CPU usage and memory usage. That will keep the team ahead of potential attacks or let the SRE and DevOps teams know it's time to scale the resources.

Check that the backend API is working with a tool like Postman (*https://www.post man.com*). At this point, your backend should be deployed to its production environment, so make sure that requests are returning the expected responses. Look for things like header configurations, permissions, and any encoding and decoding that should happen. This part can be automated with tests so that you have an established baseline for the expected behavior.

Check that your third-party services are working correctly. This is a critical point because you're switching from test credentials, which might have limits on your access to the third-party functionality. Take your time and go through as many scenarios as possible with the Product team to make sure you've got everything configured in the app and in the service dashboard. You'll also want to check the environment variables again to make sure you're using production credentials now.

Don't forget about your background jobs and cron jobs because when they are running in production, they can cause a lot of issues and shouldn't be an afterthought. Trigger each job and see if it updates data how you expect. Some jobs may not be easy to test if they depend on external services, so write a ticket to come back and check them as soon as data or events are happening in the external services.

Make a plan for when things go wrong. We'll go over this in more depth in Chapters 25 and 26, but you should have an incident plan ready for when deployments go wrong. The plan will include some type of rollback strategy and communicating time frames to customers and stakeholders. You'll want a plan ready because in the midst of an incident, everyone wants to put the fire out as quickly as possible, so it's hard to do things systematically.

Document all the steps for the database and backend. When it's time to do more deployments, having a detailed document that outlines what needs to be done will keep everyone on the same page. While a lot of this process will be automated, sometimes automations break. Having a detailed document of steps in place ensures you have a backup available for all the teams. You should consider making a backend-specific architecture diagram to highlight the connections you have between the app and the infrastructure services. An example of this is shown in Figure 23-1.

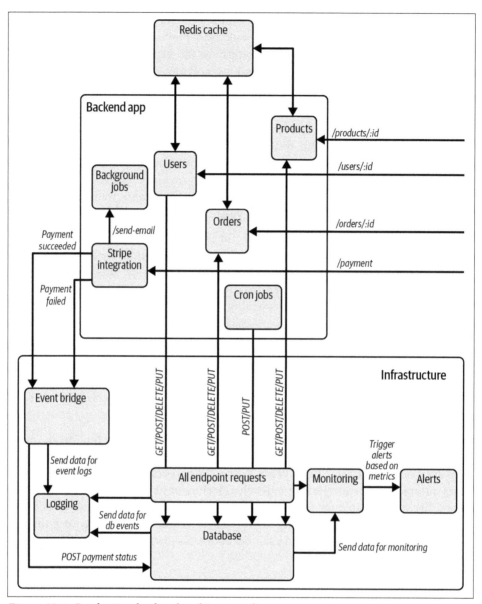

Figure 23-1. Production backend architecture diagram

Frontend Steps

With the backend in production, you can really get to work on connecting the frontend. All the data should be available for you via the API, so let's go through the steps to deploy the frontend to production. Some of them will be similar to what you did on the backend.

Work with the DevOps team to get the location for the frontend app configured correctly. This may be a little different from your backend, and DevOps may do both at the same time. It just depends on how they like to work. You still have the same considerations as the backend in terms of environment variables, regions, and cache busting. The cache might be handled differently because you'll probably want a CDN on top of the frontend for performance and uptime.

Implement a CDN to improve page load times, as discussed in Chapter 20. Since you're already working with the DevOps team, you might as well get this in place. Cloudflare (*https://oreil.ly/Thqer*) is a popular CDN service that lets you manage your frontend apps securely, and it comes with a lot of built-in functionality to make it easier to handle any issues that come up. Another popular one is CloudFront (*https://oreil.ly/gxU9o*) if you're working with AWS.

Optimize your bundle. Make sure the code is minimized and the assets are compressed. This will likely happen in your CI/CD pipeline, which we'll build in Chapter 27. This is the artifact that will sit on the frontend server and is the code that users will interact with. That's why you want to make sure to have a small bundle size.

Check that logging, monitoring, and alerts work. The frontend is what represents the product to many users, so you want to be just as aware of what's going on with it as you are on the backend. You may find it helpful to keep separate logging and monitoring dashboards for the frontend so that you can quickly find information. Same with the alerts because different people may need to be notified so that issues can be handled as efficiently as possible.

Verify that the frontend works on all the browsers you plan to support. We often focus on the browser that we develop in and don't check the others. CanIUse (*https://oreil.ly/HCY93*) lists the most commonly used browsers and the features they support, so check out the app in these other browsers once the app is deployed. You should also use tools like SauceLabs (*https://saucelabs.com*) to make sure the app works across different devices and browsers. This should be part of your testing and debugging during development, similar to what we discussed in Chapter 22, but if it got overlooked, you definitely need to do it now.

Check that all your forms work as expected. You'll get edge cases, but you need to make sure the core functionality is working. The UI should update accordingly, and you can use tools like the Network and Application tabs to see if your requests and responses are what you need them to be.

Use your app from the frontend and see the database changes in production. Go through several of the user flows with the Product team to make sure everything's working. This is another key time to have demos. Have Product sit on a call with you as you go through the app. Then have them take over and go through the user flows as well. Your app should be usable by anyone who hasn't been involved in the development process. As developers, sometimes we get so used to our workarounds that we forget nobody else will do that.

Create the documentation for the frontend. You can go as deep as getting into the details of how the app is structured and how it works on the component level or have a high-level diagram depending on what is useful for the actual integration visualization. Creating a diagram of your component tree might be a task you did earlier, or it could be something you help someone else on your team do. Keeping it at a higher level at this phase can make things clearer as you integrate so that you don't start mixing in things like component state with infrastructure. Figure 23-2 is an example of a high-level diagram.

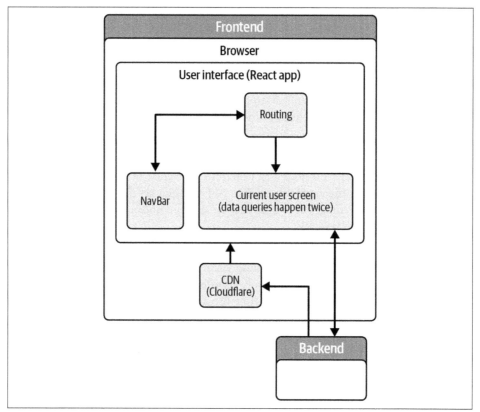

Figure 23-2. Production frontend architecture diagram

Cleanup Steps

After you've gone through all the steps of getting the entire stack deployed, there are still a few more things you need to check just to make sure you've accounted for as much as you can. After everything has been deployed, take a little break. Those 30-minute walks or just time away from the computer will give you a chance to come back with a fresh mind.

Now that the full app is in production, you want to make sure you can support it. One way to do this is to check the logs and see if your connection tests are showing there. Hopefully, you don't have any errors yet, but you should see some activity. Check if your monitoring is working correctly by looking for the traffic from your connection tests. Trigger those alerts to make sure they're going to the right emails and channels. You should also test your incident and rollback plans to see how they really work.

You don't actually know if your rollback plan works until you've tested it, but this can be a disruptive process. In the disaster recovery (DR) world, there's a saying that you don't have a backup plan if you haven't restored anything. Until you've tested your DR measures, you can't have any confidence in them. Incident response and rollbacks can be disruptive in production.

Something else that will help you is to familiarize yourself with the services you use. It can be easy to leave things up to the DevOps team and not really understand how they work—in this case, learning just enough to do basic tasks is a good thing. At least know where to go in the cloud provider to look at configs and then go through the cloud provider docs to get a high-level understanding of what's being set up.

The cleanup steps in this section should help you with the bulk of what you need to connect and what you should look out for. Every project is different, so add your own steps to this list based on your experience. Many devs have their own checklists that they've developed over their careers and that they take with them to new jobs or projects.

Documentation and Maintenance Steps

At this point, you should update the architecture diagram to its production state because you know how everything works together. Figure 23-3 is an example of what that can look like for this app.

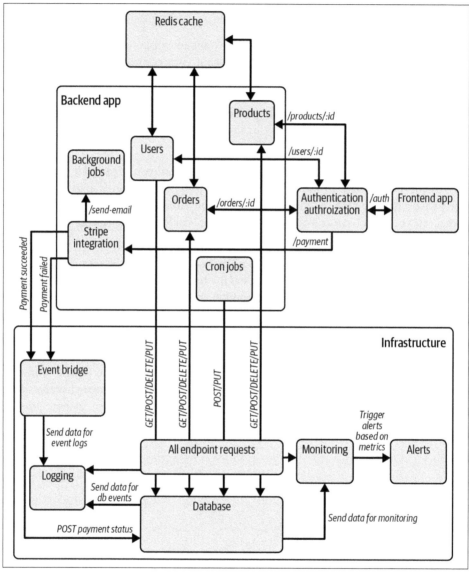

Figure 23-3. Production architecture diagram

Now that you have the diagram for production, keep it up to date as things change. You can add as much detail to the diagram as you like, even having lines that represent all the endpoints you have available and including the database schema. After you've taken these steps and made your own checklist, document it for the team and see what gaps they find to fill in.

Remember that your app might be in the production environment, but it's only public once you have users working with it. Until there are actual users, production may not be much different than your other environments. Go through the release process to move the team's changes from the other environments to production numerous times and involve every dev on the team so that they're comfortable with it. By the time you have users, it should be a routine thing to deploy to the production environment. You should also test your incident plans while there is minimal traffic to make sure they actually work.

Even though you've gone through this process from scratch, as you do this more, you'll learn new ways that things can go wrong. This is a constant learning process, and you will encounter scenarios that leave you surprised.

Conclusion

In this chapter, I gave you an overview of some general steps you should take as you get everything ready for production. There are a lot of moving parts after the code is written and tested in your preproduction environments. Whether this is the first time your full stack app is going to production or the hundredth time, be ready for issues. It's usually smoother after the deployment process has completed several times, but stuff happens. Test out the changes you've deployed before you announce to everyone that they're ready and stay ready to do rollbacks or handle incidents.

The main thing is that you've had exposure to the different areas, so you know how they work together and understand the process behind connecting them. At this point, you've coordinated across several teams, including the dev team. Now you can clean up the process, document it, and help others on the dev team go through production deploys. The more comfortable everyone gets with production deploys, the more smoothly they'll go over time.

## CHAPTER 24

Integration Testing

One of the best things you can do for the long-term maintainability of your apps is to write integration tests. When I discussed backend and frontend testing in Chapters 7 and 21, I mentioned how we would go into greater details on these tests. E2e tests are a great way to ensure that the changes you make don't break the full stack functionality. This is incredibly helpful when you do things like upgrade packages and make changes to global components so that you can catch unintended side effects. That saves QA time on regression testing, and it helps prevent bugs in unexpected places from getting to users.

These tests also help document how features should work as the app grows. If you change something, such as what happens when a button gets clicked, these tests are more robust than unit tests. E2e tests can be used to perform actions like a user so that you get the real flow consistently. That's the biggest difference between unit tests and e2e tests and why they give you more assurance that functionality hasn't changed.

The e2e tools that I'll talk about in this chapter are generally stack agnostic, so they aren't limited to just React projects. I'll go over writing the same tests using three of these packages so that you can compare how they work:

- Cypress
- Nightwatch
- Playwright

E2e tests typically take more time to write than unit tests, so while they offer more thorough flow testing, they are more expensive to develop and maintain. To keep the e2e test cases manageable, it helps to define them during feature development or product roadmapping.

The Test Cases

Before we jump into the code, let's start by defining the three test cases we'll write with each of the tools.

The first test case is making sure the order table loads. This functionality will require a few responses from different endpoints, waiting on a loading state to change, and waiting for the data to load in the table component. This feature has a lot of moving pieces, so the Product team will likely help you write out the scenarios. Maybe they'll use Gherkin (*https://oreil.ly/olEOS*), as we discussed in Chapter 21.

The second test case is to check if an order has been submitted correctly. In this case, you'll check that the inputs have valid values, the endpoint is called correctly, and you get the expected status code once the endpoint sends the response. This will help ensure that when users try to submit orders, they can do so successfully.

The third test case is making sure a user can't submit an incomplete order request. Now you're checking that the correct error message shows on the page if one of the inputs has an invalid value. This scenario helps ensure that users are provided with relevant, actionable feedback if they type in something wrong.

Now that we have the test cases, let's write the tests for them with the different e2e tools.

End-to-End Tests with Cypress

The first e2e tool I'll cover is Cypress (*https://oreil.ly/vLJ1h*). This is one of the most widely used tools for e2e testing, and it uses your app in a real browser the same way a user would. Think of it as like giving a person instructions on how to do something in your app. It has methods that let you target components on the page, and it will call your real APIs. You can also mock the API calls if you have dummy data that will be returned to keep consistency in the tests, but remember that takes away from the e2e part of these tests. To get started, go ahead and install Cypress if you didn't in Chapter 21.

```
npm install cypress --save-dev
```

You'll also need to add some configs to your *cypress* directory by updating your *tsconfig.json* file. Take a look at the Cypress docs (*https://oreil.ly/wyNnf*) to determine what you need to add because these configs tend to change often.

You already have some tests in *cypress/e2e/user-info.cy.ts,* and we'll add on to them. The first thing you need to do is refactor the tests with a beforeEach hook because this will automatically run repetitive code for you instead of having it in each test. You'll be making three API calls to get orders, get users, and post an order, so those can be mocked and intercepted for each test. Here's how you implement that:

```
// user-info.cy.ts
describe('User Info', () => {
  beforeEach(function () {
    cy.intercept('GET', '/v1/orders').as('getOrders')
    cy.intercept('GET', '/v1/users').as('getUser')
    cy.intercept('POST', '/v1/orders').as('createOrder')
  })
  ...
```

Next, you can add the first new test to the *user-info.cy.ts* file below the one where you click the "Actions" link. This test will check that your orders table is loading correctly, that you've called the correct endpoint, and that the data has finished loading. Keep in mind that the way I'm showing is just one of many ways to write any of these tests:

```
it('loads the orders table', function () {
  cy.visit('http://localhost:8080/')
  cy.wait('@getOrders')

  cy.get('[aria-label="orders-table"]')
    .contains('Dog stuff')
    .should('be.visible')

    cy.get(`[data-testid="orders-loading-circle"]`)
      .should('not.be.visible')
})
```

This uses the getOrders intercept you defined in the beforeEach hook. You get the orders table based on its aria-label and check it for one of the expected product names to make sure the data was returned from the response. Then you double-check that the loading icon for the table isn't visible on the page. Just a reminder: we added the data-testid (*https://oreil.ly/tBdEe*) attribute earlier.

Now you can run the test to make sure it passes and you're getting the expected results. If it runs and passes successfully, go in and change one of the assertions to make sure it's not a false pass. Purposely make the test fail by changing the check for the loading circle to be visible to make sure the test is correct.

The next test is a little more involved because you get to fill in a form programmatically. You have to target all the inputs and then type valid values into them. After that, you have to find the Submit button and click it. Then you can check that the API requests return successfully by using the createOrder mock intercept you defined earlier. You also check to make sure the success message is rendered on the page. Here's how you can write this test:

```
it('submits a successful order request', function () {
  cy.visit('http://localhost:8080/')
  cy.wait('@getOrders')

  cy.get('input[name="firstName"]').type('Ernest')
  cy.get('input[name="lastName"]').type('Abcde')
```

```
cy.get('input[name="quantity"]').type('3')
cy.get('input[name="email"]').type('e.abcde@ern.com')
cy.get('input[name="password"]').type('B1gt3sTAcc0un!')
cy.get('input[name="contactTime"]').type('2024-07-09T12:00')

cy.get('form').find('Submit').click()

cy.wait('@createOrder').its('response.statusCode').should('equal', 204)

cy.find('Order submitted successfully').should('be.visible')
})
```

The last test is to make sure your form validation works correctly and doesn't allow invalid form submissions. This will fill out all the form fields and keep the email in an incorrect format, which should display the form error on the page:

```
it('does not submit an incomplete order request', function () {
    cy.visit('http://localhost:8080/')
    cy.wait('@getOrders')

    cy.get('input[name="firstName"]').type('Ernest')
    cy.get('input[name="lastName"]').type('Abcde')
    cy.get('input[name="quantity"]').type('3')
    cy.get('input[name="email"]').type('e.abcde')
    cy.get('input[name="password"]').type('B1gt3sTAcc0un!')
    cy.get('input[name="contactTime"]').type('2024-07-09T12:00')

    cy.get('form').find('Submit').click()

    cy.get('.email-errors').should('be.visible')
})
```

Now you have a set of test cases you can expand on. Try running these tests to see if they pass. If they don't, take a look at the component code, the test code, and the Cypress docs to figure out where the issue is. Also try running these tests in your CI/CD pipeline to see how long they take.

End-to-End Tests with Playwright

The next e2e tool we'll implement is Playwright (*https://oreil.ly/9VJ0j*), another popular testing package. It has some similarities with Testing Library (*https://oreil.ly/yDJWm*); Playwright has a migration guide (*https://oreil.ly/fUDub*) that shows you how they implement similar functionality. It automatically runs tests in Chromium, Firefox, and WebKit, so you have three browsers covered. The configs are a little different from Cypress. It's all set up when you install and initialize the package with the following command:

```
npm init playwright@latest
```

You'll see multiple prompts, and there will be a list of options you need to go through to set the appropriate configs (*https://oreil.ly/Yk4-8*). Using the default values is fine for this example, but experiment with the other values to see what they change. With the initial setup done, you can go to the Playwright test file and rename it: *user-info.spec.ts*. Then add the following code to start your test file:

```
import { test, expect } from '@playwright/test'
import { orderResponseData } from '../src/mocks/orders'

let apiContext

test.beforeEach(async ({ page, playwright }) => {
  await page.goto('http://localhost:8080/')

  apiContext = await playwright.request.newContext({
    baseURL: 'https://api.teststore.com',
    extraHTTPHeaders: {
      Authorization: `token ${process.env.API_TOKEN}`,
    },
  })
})

test.afterEach(async () => {
  await apiContext.dispose()
})
```

Similar to what you did in the Cypress test, you have a `beforeEach` and an `afterEach` hook that navigate to the local URL and set up your API mock. With Playwright, you use the built-in context for API testing (*https://oreil.ly/VMyJR*). You can add specific headers and make this a utility object that you expand on for things like authorization and token validation. The *https://api.teststore.com* URL is the domain for the backend, but you can replace this with your own backend URL, especially if you're running the e2e tests locally.

There's one test case we wrote in Cypress in Chapter 21 that we'll add to our tests just for thoroughness. The case is to check basic navigation to make sure a link works:

```
test.describe('User Info', () => {
  test('navigates to the TestStore actions page', async ({ page }) => {
    const actionsButton = page.getByText('Actions')

    await actionsButton.click()

    expect(page.url().includes('/actions'))
  })
```

Then you'll add the same three test cases in this file that you wrote for your Cypress tests:

```
test('loads the orders table', async ({ page }) => {
  const ordersData = await apiContext.get(`/v1/orders`, {
    data: {
      orderResponseData,
    },
  })

  expect(ordersData.ok()).toBeTruthy()

  const orderRow = page.getByText('Dog stuff')

  expect(orderRow).toBeVisible()
})
```

Here, you set the context to return the mock response from the orders endpoint and then make sure the page loads with it. Next is an example of making a POST request with a form submission:

```
test('submits a successful order request', async ({ page }) => {
  page.getByLabel('First Name').fill('Ernest')
  page.getByLabel('Last Name').fill('Abcde')
  page.getByLabel('Quantity').fill('3')
  page.getByLabel('Email')
      .fill('e.abcde@ern.com')
  page.getByLabel('Password')
      .fill('B1gt3sTAcc0un!')
  page.getByLabel('Contact Time').fill('2024-07-09T12:00')

  const submitButton = page.getByText('Submit')

  await submitButton.click()

  const ordersData = await apiContext.post(`/v1/orders`, {
    data: {
      firstName: 'Ernest',
      lastName: 'Abcde',
      quantity: 3,
      email: 'e.abcde@ern.com',
      password: 'B1gt3sTAcc0un!',
      contactTime: '2024-07-09T12:00',
    },
  })

  expect(ordersData.ok()).toBeTruthy()

  expect(page.getByText('Order submitted successfully')).toBeVisible

})
```

The form field inputs are similar to what you did in Cypress where you get the field and type the value you want. How you make the POST request and determine if the request was successful are a little different than Cypress.

The final test case is checking for the form field validation error on the email input:

```
test('does not submit an incomplete order request', async ({ page }) => {
  page.getByLabel('First Name').fill('Ernest')
  page.getByLabel('Last Name').fill('Abcde')
  page.getByLabel('Quantity').fill('3')
  page.getByLabel('Email').fill('e.abcde')
  page.getByLabel('Password')
    .fill('B1gt3sTAcc0un!')
  page.getByLabel('Contact Time').fill('2024-07-09T12:00')

  const submitButton = page.getByText('Submit')

  await submitButton.click()

  const formError = page.getByText(
    "Please include an '@' in the email address."
  )

  expect(formError).toBeTruthy()
})
```

This is the same assertion you made in the Cypress test with different syntax. Now you can run the tests with the following command and see if the tests are passing:

```
npx playwright test
```

Figure 24-1 is an example screenshot of the test results in the browser. Playwright generates an *index.html* file that you can commit in your repo, or you can exclude it from the repo and still show it in your CI/CD pipeline.

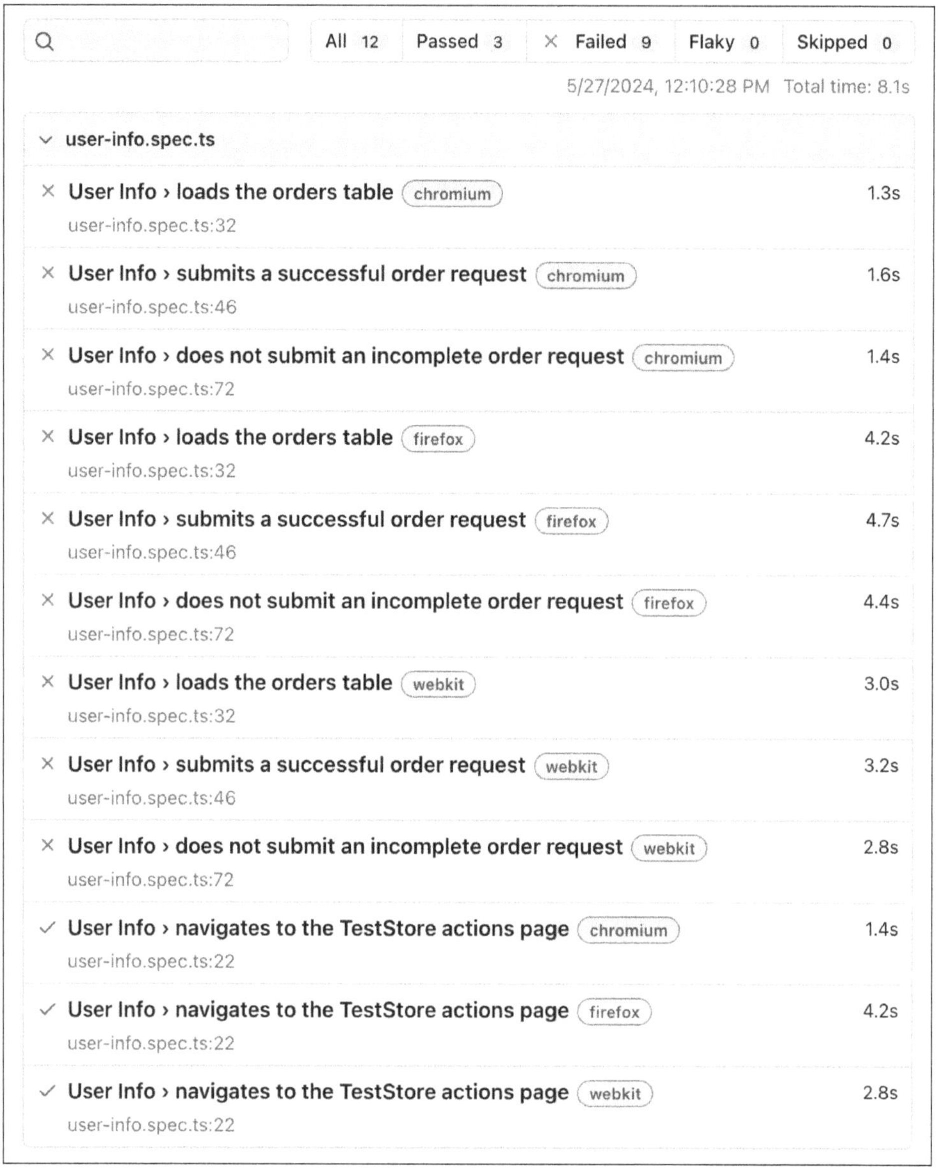

| Q | | All 12 | Passed 3 | ✕ Failed 9 | Flaky 0 | Skipped 0 |

5/27/2024, 12:10:28 PM Total time: 8.1s

∨ **user-info.spec.ts**

| ✕ **User Info › loads the orders table** (chromium) | 1.3s |
| user-info.spec.ts:32 | |

| ✕ **User Info › submits a successful order request** (chromium) | 1.6s |
| user-info.spec.ts:46 | |

| ✕ **User Info › does not submit an incomplete order request** (chromium) | 1.4s |
| user-info.spec.ts:72 | |

| ✕ **User Info › loads the orders table** (firefox) | 4.2s |
| user-info.spec.ts:32 | |

| ✕ **User Info › submits a successful order request** (firefox) | 4.7s |
| user-info.spec.ts:46 | |

| ✕ **User Info › does not submit an incomplete order request** (firefox) | 4.4s |
| user-info.spec.ts:72 | |

| ✕ **User Info › loads the orders table** (webkit) | 3.0s |
| user-info.spec.ts:32 | |

| ✕ **User Info › submits a successful order request** (webkit) | 3.2s |
| user-info.spec.ts:46 | |

| ✕ **User Info › does not submit an incomplete order request** (webkit) | 2.8s |
| user-info.spec.ts:72 | |

| ✓ **User Info › navigates to the TestStore actions page** (chromium) | 1.4s |
| user-info.spec.ts:22 | |

| ✓ **User Info › navigates to the TestStore actions page** (firefox) | 4.2s |
| user-info.spec.ts:22 | |

| ✓ **User Info › navigates to the TestStore actions page** (webkit) | 2.8s |
| user-info.spec.ts:22 | |

Figure 24-1. Overview of test results from Playwright

The test results show you which ones passed and failed and the browsers they were tested in. If you click one of the test results, you'll get a detailed view of why it failed or passed. Figure 24-2 is an example of what the details for a failed test might look like.

Figure 24-2. Detailed view of a failed test

Now you can go to the part of the test that's failing and start debugging. Playwright has some good debugging tools you can find in the docs (*https://oreil.ly/e8kyy*), such as breakpoints and verbose API logs. The breakpoints are similar to what you see in the browser.

End-to-End Tests with Nightwatch

The last tool you'll implement is Nightwatch (*https://oreil.ly/vqctm*). This tool is based on Selenium WebDriver (*https://oreil.ly/Ky66A*), which is one of the oldest browser-automation packages around. Many testing tools are based on Selenium for multiple types of projects. You also have the option to run your tests on a remote Selenium server, similar to Cypress Cloud (*https://www.cypress.io/cloud*). So if you or anyone on your team is familiar with Selenium, this is a good choice because those skills transfer. Another thing Nightwatch does well is integrate with SauceLabs (*https://saucelabs.com*) and other cross-platform tools if you need to test on a wider range of devices.

This command will install Nightwatch and take you through some setup questions:

```
npm init nightwatch
```

It's fine to accept the default values for the setup question in your terminal. Again, take some time to explore the config options (*https://oreil.ly/MW3hd*) in the Nightwatch documentation.

After you have the initial setup ready, you'll have to install the following Nightwatch package so that you can test the API requests as with the other e2e tools:

```
npm i @nightwatch/apitesting --save-dev
```

Unlike the other tools, Nightwatch has a separate package to keep the package focused on one task because often you'll want your e2e tests to hit your actual endpoints. In our case though, we're using mock data.

Now you have to update the *nightwatch.conf.cjs* file with a new plug-in and the `api_testing` object as described in the Nightwatch docs (*https://oreil.ly/rN84U*). This was the last bit of setup you needed to do before starting on your test cases. You'll create the same four test cases as you did in the previous examples with Cypress and Playwright and do some initial setup that will cover all the cases. Start with setting up the mock API server, the requests, and the data:

```
import { ExtendDescribeThis } from 'nightwatch'
import { orderResponseData } from '../src/mocks/orders'

interface CustomThis {
  customerPortalUrl: string
  submitButton: string
}

describe('User Info', function (this: ExtendDescribeThis<CustomThis>) {
  this.customerPortalUrl = 'http://localhost:8080/'
```

```
this.submitButton = '*[type=submit]'

let server

beforeEach(async function (
  this: ExtendDescribeThis<CustomThis>,
  browser,
  client
) {
  server = await client.mockserver.create()

  server.setup((app) => {
    app.get('/v1/orders/', function (_, res) {
      res.status(204).data(orderResponseData)
    }),
    app.post('/v1/orders/', function (_, res) {
      res.status(204).data([])
    })
  })

  await server.start(3000)

  browser.navigateTo(this.customerPortalUrl!)
})

afterEach(() => {
  server.close()
})
```

This does the same as the other test packages but with a different syntax and system under the hood. If you're familiar with Express (*https://oreil.ly/6Asmr*), this is similar to the way you would write API endpoints. That could be handy if you have team members who are stronger on the backend but do some frontend work and need to maintain code coverage for their changes. Then you can dive into the first test case of navigating to another page:

```
it('navigates to the TestStore actions page', (browser) => {
  browser
    .click('Actions')
    .assert.visible('Actions are here')
    .assert.urlContains('/actions')
})
```

This syntax is similar to what you would write with a Selenium test because Nightwatch is also based on the W3C WebDriver specification (*https://oreil.ly/HgVYS*). This spec is what lets you write code across all browsers, which is great for an e2e tool because you need to test on multiple browsers. WebDriver doesn't need to be compiled with your code, so just like with the other e2e tools, your automated tests run the same way as if a user were performing the actions.

The next test checks that the endpoint to get the orders data is being called correctly:

```
it('loads the orders table', async (browser, client) => {
  client.assert.strictEqual(
    server.route.get('/v1/orders').calledOnce,
    true,
    'called once'
  )

  expect(browser.element.findByText('Dog stuff')).to.exist
})
```

This accesses your mock API by checking if the client made a call to the route you've defined, and it checks the screen to determine if one of the ordered products has loaded.

The next test is for the form submission request:

```
it('submits a successful order request', (browser, client) => {
  browser.element.findByLabelText('First Name').setValue('Ernest')
  browser.element.findByLabelText('Last Name').setValue('Abcde')
  browser.element.findByLabelText('Quantity').setValue('3')
  browser.element.findByLabelText('Email').setValue('e.abcde@ern.com')
  browser.element.findByLabelText('Password').setValue('B1gt3sTAcc0un!')
  browser.element.findByLabelText('Contact Time').setValue('2024-07-09T12:00')

  browser.element.findByText('Submit').click()

  client.assert.strictEqual(
    server.route.post('/v1/orders').calledOnce,
    true,
    'called once'
  )

  expect(browser.element.findByText('Order submitted successfully')).to.exist

})
```

You can see that the format is similar to the other two tools because you find an input and set a value to it. Then you find the Submit button and click it to check if the POST request was made successfully.

The last test is the invalid email submission to check if the error message is on the screen:

```
it('does not submit an incomplete order request', (browser) => {
  browser.element.findByLabelText('First Name').setValue('Ernest')
  browser.element.findByLabelText('Last Name').setValue('Abcde')
  browser.element.findByLabelText('Quantity').setValue('3')
  browser.element.findByLabelText('Email').setValue('e.abcde')
  browser.element.findByLabelText('Password').setValue('B1gt3sTAcc0un!')
  browser.element.findByLabelText('Contact Time').setValue('2024-07-09T12:00')
```

```
browser.element.findByText('Submit').click()

const errorMessage = browser.element.findByText(
  "Please include an '@' in the email address."
)

expect(errorMessage).to.exist
})
```

Now you're ready to run these tests to see how they look when they pass or fail. One unique thing about running Nightwatch tests is that you have to specify the location of the tests in your command by default. You can set up a script in your *package.json* to help automate the process for you and the team locally and in the CI/CD pipeline. Here's the command that you can run to get the results from your test suite:

```
npx nightwatch nightwatch-tests
```

Then you'll get messages in your terminal and an HTML version of the test report saved in your repo. Now you're done trying out all these testing tools, and since you have written the same four tests with all of them, you can do some comparisons between them.

 One thing to note is that all of these e2e packages have been installed as dev dependencies. This is important so that your testing tools don't get bundled into the code that gets served in production. Remember, having unnecessary packages in your bundle makes your app run more slowly on the server and in the browser, and it opens the app for more malicious attacks. You can use any of these tools to perform API testing if you want to use the same testing tools across the frontend and backend.

Comparison Between Packages

Now you see how you can run e2e tests using different packages, how you set up the environment, how they run in your CI/CD pipeline, and how they help you check functionality from a user perspective. This is where you can really work with Product to nail down requirements and how to handle edge cases. A good rule of thumb is that if you struggle coming up with good names for tests, that means you might not be writing the best test cases. That's something to keep in mind as you review PRs from other devs and continue adding more test cases.

When you compare Cypress, Playwright, and Nightwatch, a key metric you should look at is how long it takes the developers to write and maintain the tests. Sometimes one package is easier for the team to pick up than the others, and that's a strong reason to choose it. If the team can write tests with one tool 10% faster than with another, that will save time over the long term as you have to update tests to address code and feature changes.

The time for the tests to complete in your CI/CD pipeline is another metric you should look at. That could be affected by the package size because the package will have to be installed before tests are run. Although if you notice that the test runtime for your app is similar across all the packages, then you should look at other metrics.

As with other packages, you need to decide which one of these has the best documentation for you and the team. Community support is also an important factor because that will determine how quickly issues are resolved and if you can find help when you run into the quirky aspects of any package. Take a look through the GitHub issues on these packages and see how well they were handled.

The Testing Pyramid

The "testing pyramid" is a cool concept that helps you decide how and when to implement different types of tests, such as unit tests compared to e2e tests. Here's a brief explanation from Ethan Brown:

> The conventional wisdom is that you have the fewest e2e tests because they're so expensive. I think tools like Cypress are slowly changing this conventional wisdom, but I think it's a valid big-picture framework all the same: invest in a technology in proportion to its cost (in either dollars or person-hours) and value. We could argue about how Cypress is changing the cost-value ratio of e2e tools, but it's harder to argue that the principle isn't correct.

Cypress is arguably the most established e2e testing package in the JavaScript ecosystem, so it's usually the first choice because more devs have had exposure to it. But if you and the team agree that you would rather use Playwright or Nightwatch, they are also widespread. Consider the long-term use of the package you choose. That will affect how quickly new devs can get ramped up on the project as the package you choose becomes a standard in your development process.

Conclusion

Now you have everything you need to test the full stack of the app from the frontend to the backend and maybe a little bit of the database. This is something that QA engineers will usually handle, but if you're working on a team without QA, now you can use your skills to get something in place. You should have an opinion on how to write tests, what tools to use, and why spending time on e2e tests along with unit tests is helpful. Remember, unit tests are more focused on the code handling specific scenarios whereas e2e tests are simulating scripted user interactions to make sure parts of

---

your app are working as expected. This is a holistic look at your processes, and you aren't concerned about the code behind it here.

Something else you can do with e2e tests is demo them for Product and stakeholders so that they can see how the tests run and the value they add. This can bring up more conversations for future work on the roadmap once the stakeholders see the automations run. Keep in mind that these tests are more time-consuming to write and maintain, so this might not be something you do immediately. But don't wait too long because then you'll end up with lots of features that need to be tested.

## CHAPTER 25

Making Deployments

Now that you have integration testing in place, it's time to decide when you want to do deployments and what the strategy behind them should be. Every deployment you do is meaningful to someone, whether it's the dev working on a change, a QA engineer doing feature and regression testing, stakeholders taking a look at things, or your end users. Each deployment also affects something else. When you push changes to the backend, it's going to affect the frontend even if it's indirectly. Pushing frontend changes affects anyone who works with the product through that part of the app.

Having a strategy and understanding the timing around deployments are essential to avoiding surprises. When you roll out changes, that affects the organization and your team's reputation for quality and reliability. These are some of the things you have to think about. It can be easy to consider your job done as soon as all of the code changes have been merged, but this is the beginning of one of your more visible jobs.

In this chapter, I'll cover:

- Frontend-only or backend-only updates
- Blue-green deploys
- Canary deploys
- Strategies for doing rollbacks

Just like you had to consider a lot of "behind the scenes" things for the initial development across the full stack, you have to do that with deployments, too. This is the planning part of the deployments from a holistic view. When you were building the app, you made sure everything worked with your tools and technology. Now you need to think about the overall impact on the product, the teams involved, and the users. You have to find the balance between speed and risk.

Deploying Frontend-Only or Backend-Only Updates

Something that's going to happen regularly is that the backend and frontend will release on different schedules. Not every change will require deployments of both apps while others will take some coordination across the stack. The thing to consider is how the parts of the stack affect each other and the services they interact with. The timing of the deployments is important, especially when you know that you need to wait for an update on one side of the stack or the other.

When you are working on backend features, you need to understand what impact the changes you make will have on other parts of the system. One task is to check if the updates will change the data that the frontend expects. If that's the case, then you're introducing a breaking change that will need to be accounted for. Another task is to check if you are changing data being sent to a third-party service. This could be because of an update from the service or because you're refactoring code to be more manageable. You also need to review if the changes will affect how the app works with infrastructure tools, such as the database.

Determine if your jobs will be affected by the changes. Sometimes a task like refactoring can lead to unexpected side effects. Updating the types or restructuring the folders can break things you aren't testing for. Unit and integration tests can help you catch many regressions, but sometimes things slip through. The backend usually touches more pieces of the system than the frontend, and that's when your documentation and architecture diagrams become really useful. So when you make updates, you know exactly how everything connects and what will be impacted.

The frontend can usually be deployed without affecting other parts of the system. What you need to watch for when deploying the frontend is that the backend and other services are ready. If you deploy a frontend change before the backend is deployed, then you risk breaking part of the app for the users. You also have to be aware of potential overlaps with changes from other devs, especially when multiple people are working in the same files. That could lead to functionality or designs getting overwritten.

Sometimes the designs change for one part of the app, and it looks inconsistent with the rest of the app. So you and the team have to be aware of the effects of changing shared components. Updating a component to match designs for one part of the app might break the layout for another part. Check any references for shared components to make sure that your changes don't have unwanted side effects before you deploy them to users.

When you do separate deployments, always check that the frontend and backend work as expected in the develop environment first. It will help if you version your frontend and backend releases and use slightly different numbers. For example, the backend could be a number ahead on version 2.0.0 while the frontend is on version 1.0.0. Those version numbers go in the *package.json file (https://oreil.ly/HMP5q)* for each project. It also helps to specify the version of the backend that the frontend depends on.

You and the dev team are the first line of QA, which makes it crucial that you are paying attention to these details. This is especially true when you've been focused on one aspect of the app for a while. Have a checklist or automation in place to help everyone catch things they might not see because they've been in the details of one side of the stack.

Deploy Strategies

As you work on projects across different teams at different organizations, you'll get exposed to numerous ways of handling deployments. What you do at an enterprise-level organization will be vastly different from what you do at a mid-size organization or a startup. There will be considerations like when to scale up infrastructure resources, how to plan work for new features, and what the priorities are for the dev team. This is another time when you'll be less focused on code and technical implementations and you'll be working closer with the Product team.

Release Dates

One important thing you and the Product team have to coordinate will be actual release dates. These are the deadlines that the dev team needs to meet to have features and fixes in production. Usually, the Product team has talked with a number of stakeholders to come up with a release date, and then they'll bring it back to your dev team. This is when you need to make sure you and the team have a good understanding of everything needed for the release.

Ask for designs and specs and take some time to discuss them as a team so that you can bring up any questions from a technical standpoint. If there's anything missing from the Product side, push back and let them know you can't commit to a release date until you have all the details you need to do the work. Show Product what's missing and work with them to fill in the missing pieces. Committing to work that hasn't been thoroughly laid out will set the team up for unnecessary stress because they'll try to squeeze in a lot of code at the last minute to meet a deadline.

Keep Constant Communication Between the Dev Team and the Product Team

Now part of your role becomes more about how you communicate with technical and nontechnical teams. That includes considering the reputation of the dev team. That should mostly be handled by your manager or tech lead, but sometimes the responsibility falls on you. That's especially true if your manager isn't technical. You don't want your team to become thought of as always missing deadlines or constantly pushing bad changes or incomplete requirements to production, even if it's not your fault.

When you're building your deployment strategy, remember to include some breathing room for the team in case things go wrong for reasons out of your control. Take an optimistically cautious approach to approving the deployment PRs and really test them as much as you can before they get to QA. It is an extra step for you, but it's one that pays off tremendously when you catch things before anyone else.

The Product team will lean on the dev team heavily to understand what's needed on the technical side so that they can communicate that to stakeholders. When you discuss the requirements with your team, a good strategy is to have a dev deadline that only you all know about. Always remember that the release date is when Product needs to have the features in production. That means all the code needs to be merged, tested, and working without bugs before then. It can be a good exercise to take the release date and work backward from it to see if you and the team can get all the changes in and tested, as shown in Figure 25-1.

The goal is to have a continuous release cycle where every small change goes to production as quickly as it can get through QA. That way, you aren't as worried about doing large releases at the same time. The size of the organization will affect production release schedules because you'll have a varied number of teams that need to handle different parts. Larger organizations may involve legal teams in their releases to make sure terms and conditions are well defined for new features. There might be bigger DevOps teams you need to work with to get support for your release date.

So you might end up doing only three to four production releases a year, even though you've been working on features and making lots of releases to your staging environment. If you're at a smaller organization, production releases can happen as often as every few days or weeks. At mid-size organizations and startups, you'll be able to do a lot more yourself and have considerably fewer teams to talk to. That will speed up the time it takes to release features. But even in these organizations, you'll reach a point where you might release to production only every few months just because there aren't enough people to get through all the work as the organization grows.

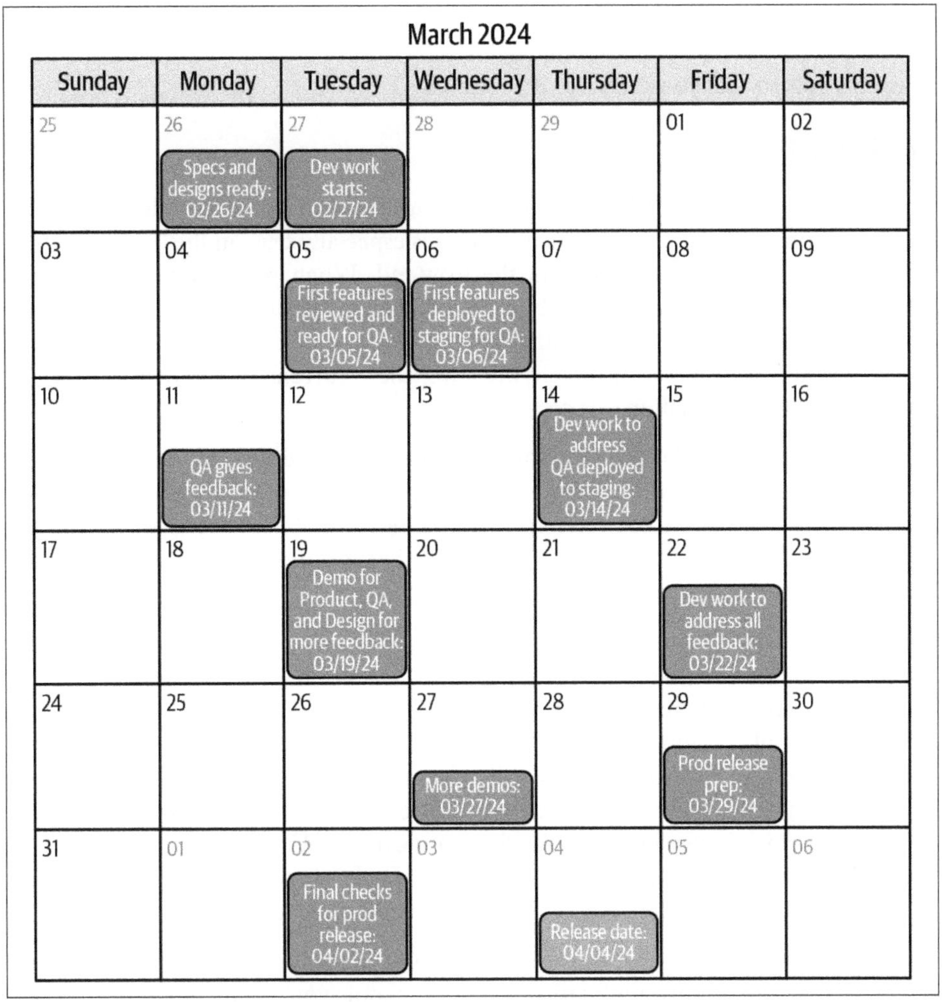

March 2024						
Sunday	Monday	Tuesday	Wednesday	Thursday	Friday	Saturday
25	26 **Specs and designs ready: 02/26/24**	27 **Dev work starts: 02/27/24**	28	29	01	02
03	04	05 **First features reviewed and ready for QA: 03/05/24**	06 **First features deployed to staging for QA: 03/06/24**	07	08	09
10	11 **QA gives feedback: 03/11/24**	12	13	14 **Dev work to address QA deployed to staging: 03/14/24**	15	16
17	18	19 **Demo for Product, QA, and Design for more feedback: 03/19/24**	20	21	22 **Dev work to address all feedback: 03/22/24**	23
24	25	26	27 **More demos: 03/27/24**	28	29 **Prod release prep: 03/29/24**	30
31	01	02 **Final checks for prod release: 04/02/24**	03	04 **Release date: 04/04/24**	05	06

Figure 25-1. Release timeline example

As you go through the requirements for features, update your dev docs with any conditions that the app needs to account for. This is something that will help you when you're discussing more features in the future. Also find out what's on the Product roadmap so that you can work with the team to prioritize tasks. The Product team should stay on top of prioritization, but it's important for you to check in with them and see if timelines have shifted based on info you've given them from the technical side.

Some industries, like advertising and finance, will have certain parts of the year where no releases to production can happen because that's when customers are spending the most money. These are referred to as "freeze periods," and they usually happen around major holidays. If you know there's some tech debt that needs to get worked on and you have feature work to implement, you can try to shift the tech debt to these freeze periods so that you can focus on releases.

Version Releases

Another strategy that will help you debug issues is versioning the releases of your apps, as mentioned earlier in the chapter. This is especially true on the backend where API changes could break more than the frontend. When you're doing a versioned release on the backend, you typically keep the current version for a period of time. That gives the frontend and any other consuming apps a chance to upgrade to the newest version without immediately breaking their current functionality. This is a form of graceful degradation.

Once the degradation date comes, you can choose to leave the old version available with a note saying that it's no longer supported and users need to upgrade. Or you can completely delete the old version. This is a decision you'll have to work with the Product team and stakeholders on, especially if it causes more work for the dev team outside the normal feature development flow.

Following semantic versioning (*https://semver.org*) is a way to help everyone understand the types of changes they can expect in a new version. Semantic versioning shows when breaking changes, reverse-compatible changes, or bug fixes are released with just a number. Honestly, I've seen this followed very loosely around organizations to the point that some teams will release v0.193.36 without ever releasing a v1.0.0 version. Since you want to use best practices and make things better for everyone, follow semantic versioning as much as you can. CHANGELOGs become crucial when you do versioned releases. They provide a quick way to see what the differences between versions are and are one of the ways others can debug their own apps.

There are plenty of tools you can add to your Git hooks or release process to make semantic versioning more automatic. Some of the tools you can use are release-please (*https://oreil.ly/U_3Xi*), commit-and-tag-version (*https://oreil.ly/O5zze*), and release-it (*https://oreil.ly/H1GhV*). By doing conventional commits (*https://oreil.ly/kIuoy*), like you'll do in your Git hooks in Chapter 27, you set your team up for an easy transition into semantic versioning. Something else you can do is run the npm-version (*https://oreil.ly/rQ3te*) command to update the package version. All of these update the package version in your *package.json* and *package-lock.json*. You can also use Git tags (*https://oreil.ly/Hexzf*) so that you have artifacts for each version of your app.

On the frontend, versioning the UI can be a tool for debugging and handling production issues. Sometimes deployments fail silently, and your changes don't make it to the server like you expected. Without having a version in the UI, it can take a while to figure out that the root cause is a failed deployment. This is also a great tool for the Support team when they have users contact them about issues. The frontend usually doesn't follow graceful degradation because there should be only one version of the UI for all users.

Frontend versioning usually means showing the app version in a component on the page that is always rendered. In the example app you built, that would be the nav bar for the app. In other apps, you might find a version number in the footer or somewhere else inconspicuous. This isn't something the user will have to be aware of normally. It should just be easy for them to find if they need to contact Support. One thing to consider is that the version number should be available in the UI regardless of whether a user is logged in.

You'll see all this versioning done in the wild with third-party services. Many third-party services use semantic versioning and degradation for releasing changes. They announce a deadline to make the upgrades so that users have a chance to do what they need to work with the new version. For example, say the current version of your service is v1.3 and the new version is v2.0. You know this version number means there are breaking changes, so you'll want to update the service version in your apps and test as soon as you can.

Blue-Green Deploys

When you know that your app receives a lot of traffic and you can't risk downtime for all your users, blue-green deployment is a good strategy. "Blue" and "green" refer to the environments the app will run in. For example, the blue environment may run the older version of the app, and the green environment runs the new version, but the color you use for each can switch. This lets you gradually move traffic from the old version of an app to the new one. That means you'll have two versions of the same app running in production at the same time with different amounts of traffic hitting them.

If one of your key metrics for your apps is uptime, you should discuss this approach with everyone because it will require more effort. You might start by transferring 10% of the traffic to the green environment and see how well your changes work. As you get confirmation that everything works as expected, you can gradually increase the amount of traffic to the green environment. Each time you increase the traffic, take a look at your monitoring tools to see how error rates are doing and how resource usage is adjusting.

Eventually, you'll reach a point where all your traffic is in the green environment. Then the blue environment can be on standby in case something happens and you need to quickly switch traffic back over. Once you are sure the green environment is really providing the uptime you need, then you can shut off the blue environment to save on costs. Your DevOps team might decide to use this as a template for the next update. That means the blue and green environments switch roles after each deploy, but that's more for their convenience.

Blue-green deployments are useful for a number of reasons other than uptime. You can do A/B testing easily to see how a percentage of users interact with new features before doing a widespread release. That can give the Product team research data that guides the future of the roadmap. You can monitor your key metrics to see if there's a significant difference between the two versions of the app. Blue-green deployments also let you test changes in production. All of the teams can do last-minute testing to verify that everything works as expected and then switch the traffic over because the changes are already in production.

As with any strategy, there are downsides to this approach. Setting up environments and resources for blue-green deployments takes a lot of time and effort. It's a costly strategy because you are working with two production-level environments that have to be provisioned with the same resources. It takes a lot of testing to ensure that both environments really do work the exact same. You can run into issues with keeping data in sync across the environments. That's especially true if one environment has schema changes that the other doesn't. Containerization can help with this; we'll talk about that in Chapter 26.

This is true for any external services because you'll be using the same credentials to connect from different environments. You have to check the license agreements with your services to see if that's possible. Check for any indirect interactions between the environments through the external services. That can lead to unexpected data or config changes that make both environments unreliable. There's sometimes a risk that data leaks between the two environments. For example, you might have some cached DNS records that point the blue frontend to the green backend, and that can get even crazier if the DNS records get updated at different times because of geographic location. Blue-green deployments work for both backend and frontend apps, but just be aware of the risks compared with the value.

Canary Deploys

Canary deployments are similar to blue-green deployments with slight differences. With canary deployments, you don't need two full production environments. Canary deployments take advantage of a feature-flagged approach of releasing new changes. That way, you can deploy the changes to the production environment, but they are hidden from users until you give them access. This requires some additional setup in your app to handle toggling on and off pieces of code, so you'll have to work with the team to think through the best way to do that.

Canary deployments allow you to have the new features running in parallel with the existing features instead of separated in a different environment. You can think about these deployments as slowly unveiling a feature in production instead of having the new version in one environment and the old version in another. This is like doing progressive delivery (*https://oreil.ly/QqVSi*) or staged rollout (*https://oreil.ly/X6kZx*).

The dev team will have to make more architectural decisions to handle the feature-flagging functionality. You need a way to be able to manage feature flags by user groups in a way that is sustainable.

It's easy to forget to fully enable a feature, and then the Support team starts getting issue reports. Or you might deprecate a feature flag too soon and open new features to users before they are fully complete. You can choose to create your own feature-flag management tool, or you can use a tool like FeatureFlags (*https://featureflags.io*), LaunchDarkly (*https://oreil.ly/-f37f*), Unleash (*https://getunleash.io*), and PostHog (*https://oreil.ly/n9BV8*). No matter which option you choose, make sure you document all the flags you have in the app, the state of rollout they're in, and the user groups that have access to them.

Consider having a ticket as a reminder to clean up feature flags as time goes on so that you and the team don't lose track of what's still relevant. Using feature flags provides a few advantages, such as more visibility of upcoming features to everyone and getting the dev team used to creating stable PRs, and it encourages more consideration around how you implement a robust feature-flag system.

Canary deployments shouldn't be confused with canary releases. A *canary release* is how you can test an early version of an app with users who like to adopt tools early. You'll see this a lot with open source projects when they have nonstable versions. These will have separate version numbers than normal stable releases. You can also see this with larger organizations, such as Chrome canary releases.

These are a few strategies you can use to get your frontend and backend changes out to users. Once the changes have been deployed, you still have to account for things going wrong and have plans to handle that.

Strategies for Doing Rollbacks

Despite all your planning and testing, there will be times when things go wrong in production. If everything was working fine before your last deployment, one assumption you can make is that it's something wrong with the code. While that may not always be the case, this is the area you have the most control over. With that in mind, you need to have contingency plans to be as ready as you can for anything that comes up.

Deploying Older Versions

A strategy for rolling back a deployment is to redeploy the previous app artifact. This becomes simpler if you use Git tags for your release versions or you have somewhere in the cloud where all your previous versioned builds are stored. If you follow blue-green deployments or canary deployments, that also simplifies this rollback strategy for you. You don't have to do anything to your code or open new PRs to trigger your pipeline.

This is where you'll have to work more with the DevOps team. They can do this for you, or maybe there's a user interface where you can select which version you want to run on production. Either way, this is a fast rollback strategy that can take the pressure off the dev team while they track down the root cause of the issue.

Reverting or Resetting PRs

Another strategy is to revert the release PR. For our example, this means you remove the code that was merged into the main branch that triggered the deployment in your pipeline. You'll have to open a new PR that targets the main branch, and that will trigger a new deployment in your pipeline to go back to the previous working version of your code. There are a few ways to do this with some Git commands. The Git commands are only briefly covered here because Chapter 28 is an in-depth discussion of Git and commands you can use.

One way is to use the `git revert` (*https://oreil.ly/So9W5*) command with a specific commit ID, as in Figure 25-2. You may be tempted to use this command, but unless you understand what this doc on reverts (*https://oreil.ly/5kxdh*) is talking about, don't use this. Check out the book *Version Control with Git* by Prem Kumar Ponuthorai and Jon Loeliger (O'Reilly) if you really want to become a Git expert. A very simple explanation of what happens when you run `git revert`, is that it removes only the changes in your workspace, not the Git history. It's like hitting an undo button locally. But again, unless you're a Git expert, it's probably best to avoid this command.

```
milecia@Milecias-MacBook-Pro-2 dashboard-ui % git log -3
commit 0cb0ca536ad7304e0709324f8a160e05ac1d0c79 (HEAD -> ch-15, origin/ch-15)
Author: flippedcoder <milecia.mcgregor@aol.com>
Date:   Mon Jan 15 09:48:16 2024 -0600

    added backend requests and axios config

commit 1e6e69456dac007cd32ebe71b75e62b6011fb286
Author: flippedcoder <milecia.mcgregor@aol.com>
Date:   Sun Jan 7 20:25:31 2024 -0600

    created .env file

commit feb094644379986dfc3cbd540fa4f3e49eb9acf7
Author: flippedcoder <milecia.mcgregor@aol.com>
Date:   Sun Jan 7 20:17:48 2024 -0600

    wrapped App in QueryClientProvider
● milecia@Milecias-MacBook-Pro-2 dashboard-ui % git revert 0cb0ca536ad7304e0709324f8a160e05ac1d0c79
Removing src/axios.config.ts
[ch-15 f32745b] Revert "added backend requests and axios config"
 2 files changed, 29 insertions(+), 43 deletions(-)
 delete mode 100644 src/axios.config.ts
```

Figure 25-2. Example of `git revert`

If you need to undo multiple commits, you should consider using the `git reset` (*https://oreil.ly/HvFAn*) command. This will undo all the changes that happened after the commit you specify. So this command resets commits cumulatively, not just the commit you specify. The reset option you choose is very important here. If you run `git reset -soft`, this will uncommit your changes and leave them as staged, like in Figure 25-3. That way, you can review them one more time and decide how to handle them.

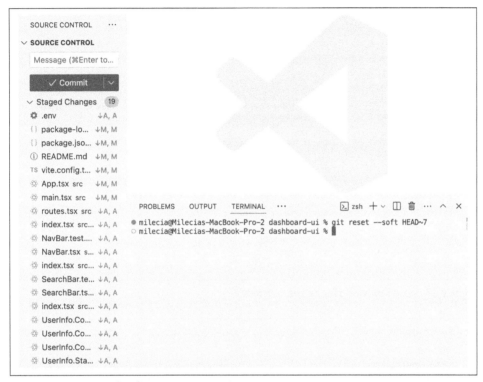

Figure 25-3. Example of `git reset -soft`

If you run `git reset -mixed`, this will uncommit your changes and move them out of the staged state, as shown in Figure 25-4. So the reset commits will look like changes you just made locally. The other option you have is running `git reset -hard`. This will uncommit your changes, move them from the staged state, and delete them, as in Figure 25-5. Be careful when you do a hard reset because you completely lose those changes.

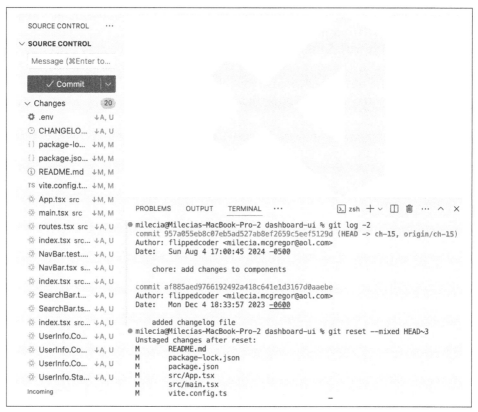

Figure 25-4. Example of `git reset -mixed`

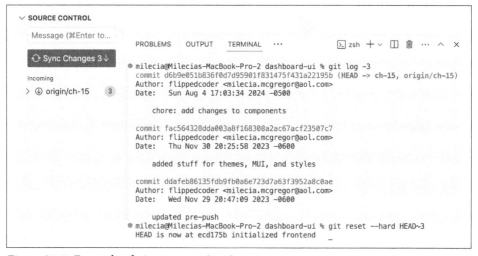

Figure 25-5. Example of `git reset -hard`

Many developers confuse the `revert` and `reset` commands because you often only have to undo the most recent commit. Both commands work fine in this scenario. But as soon as you need to undo more than one commit, the difference between the commands and the options you use becomes important to understand.

The easiest and simplest approaches are to redeploy an older artifact, switch traffic to your blue or green environment, or rerelease a previous tagged version. You need to be very comfortable with Git commands and the reasons for using them or else you can introduce even more issues. Take some time to play with these commands and see how they change the code.

Deploying a Hotfix

This is more of a roll-forward strategy because you don't undo anything. The dev team works as quickly as possible to find the root cause, patch the code, and make a new PR to the main branch. Sometimes this approach makes sense because the infrastructure isn't set up to handle rollbacks and the repo isn't set up to handle reverts. So your only choice is to move forward. This can place stress on the team, especially if downtime or bugs are costing users and the organization money.

If you have to work with a hotfix strategy, start by looking at the logs and the last commit because this is likely where the issue is. This is one of those times when your experience will really come in handy. Stay calm and go through the same debugging process you would in any other environment. A hotfix will not go through the same QA process as your normal bug fixes and feature deployments. At this point, it's up to you and the dev team to test the specific issue that's happening. You should get on a group call so that several people can verify the fix together. Including QA and Product in that group call will help you verify other functionality so that you have full confidence that the hotfix you're about to push doesn't cause more issues.

Have a Realistic Approach to Hotfixes

Ethan Brown made this additional comment on hotfixes:

> It's reasonable and realistic to create a "hotfix protocol" that may include lowered review, test, and check requirements as long as the last step in the process is "do all the review, test, and check that are part of the normal process as soon as the crisis is over." In the meantime, getting the hotfix out takes precedence over all other work. When pressures get high, there are two types of people: people who confess to cutting corners and liars. So let's not shame the corner cutters or let the liars get away with their lies. Make a process that fits the situation and include in that process a way to "uncut" those corners when the fire is out.

Conclusion

In this chapter, I covered some strategies you can use for your deployments. These are just a few approaches you can take, so feel free to get more creative with them. You may find that a combination of strategies will help your situation the best. Make sure to partner with the DevOps and QA teams closely here. The success of your releases is only as good as the infrastructure the code is run on and the thoroughness of your testing. Reach out to them to make sure everyone knows the plan and is aware of release dates.

Doing deployments shouldn't be a stressful time for the team when you know that you've given yourself space to handle bugs and prep the cloud resources. Constant and frequent communication with the Product team and stakeholders will avoid surprises for everyone. Let them know when you run into issues, even if it doesn't seem like it will delay their timelines. Keeping everyone updated should be a part of any strategy you and the teams decide to implement, and that will pay off in the form of more trust and freedom for you and your team.

CHAPTER 26

Integration Concerns

You've gone through the process of getting the full stack app to production, and everything seems to be working smoothly. Getting the app to production isn't a small feat, and you now have a good baseline to work from, so you can start looking at areas that can be improved. This is when you can really stress-test the app to see how well the frontend and backend are connected and how the third-party services really behave.

As you and other teams start to poke at the app in production, a number of concerns will come up. Some will be surprises to everyone, no matter how much planning you do. Someone might notice they don't have access to a certain page or there's an unexpected glitch on the frontend. While you and the team have done all you can to test everything in a preproduction environment, some things will just behave differently. This is where you start to hammer out those things you couldn't test for in any other environment.

In this chapter, I'll go over:

- Frontend and backend concerns
- Things you should check for with your third-party services
- Data and security management in production
- Containerization of your app

This is a point in the development lifecycle that takes grit and perseverance because you're so close to being done! These last integration concerns are what will help you, the team, and everyone else know that you can automate your deployments with confidence that they will work consistently. Before, you were able to develop and test each layer in isolation to keep your development focused. Some of the issues that arise at this point will be trickier to pin down than any of the issues that came up before because they could be caused by anything in your environment.

Frontend and Backend Concerns

You've tested the frontend and backend separately, you have unit tests for them, and you have some e2e tests as well. Now you need to start picking at things that can help you maintain the best user experience possible. One of those things will be double-checking your error handling. Consider the case where you've tested everything in preproduction and now you have a missing environment variable in production. How does the app respond? Or what happens to the app when your frontend and backend deployments get out of sync because you have a new team member who doesn't understand the process yet?

Understanding your own deployment schedule will determine when and how features and bug fixes get released. Deploying the backend first is often a good move—unless there are breaking changes in the API. In that case, you need to coordinate the frontend and backend to ensure the least amount of downtime for users or do it during nonpeak hours.

Since the team works on features asynchronously, are there any changes in your code that come from another dev? Sometimes changes get merged into branches silently, which can cause issues for everyone. I'll go over some Git branching strategies in Chapter 27, but always make sure you know what code is on a branch before starting the deployment process. Multiple features might be getting merged to the same branch and have incompatibilities that take time to resolve. Talk to one another before deployments are scheduled so that everyone is aware of what's going on outside of their work.

Have you already factored in browser and device testing? Sometimes older browser versions can change the layout of the frontend because they don't support features you're depending on. This is something that may slip past preproduction testing because everyone gets tunnel vision on getting the change released. You also have to check that responsive or adaptive design has been implemented to account for users viewing the app on different screen sizes and devices. Really push the edge cases of what a user might do.

A subtle thing to check is time zone handling in production, especially with any scheduled jobs. Sometimes a different server can throw your timing off by milliseconds, and that can cause an issue with a job running today or tomorrow. It can also lead to confusing data being shown to the user. Figure out what time zones your servers are in and test that your code is running as expected. Checking jobs in production is something that can get overlooked, especially when they run on an interval instead of immediately when an event happens.

Wherever possible, use UTC in your application. This includes your databases, APIs, scheduled jobs, and so on. It will keep everything consistent and avoid bugs related to a server's local time.

Something else to do is clean up your config files. Go through your *tsconfig* files to make sure you're optimizing for production. You might have left some files for pre-production environments in your build, such as mock data or toggles to force switching between different views. You won't need those in production, and you especially don't want that kind of developer functionality accessible to users. They add unnecessary bloat to the build artifacts and potentially open attack vectors.

The key is to try to break the app in as many ways as possible before the user does. That's why it can be a good idea to do some testing in production right after a deployment to make sure the changes for both the frontend and the backend are there. You do have to plan for production testing so that it doesn't disrupt the users. That can be in the form of known fake user accounts and having fake data that is separated from real data. Be sure to communicate with everyone when you're testing in production so that weird occurrences aren't flagged as real issues. It can be uncomfortable admitting that there still could be bugs, even after your extensive testing and the team's hard work to write good code.

Third-Party Service Concerns

Not all of the concern is for your code because you'll be working with third-party services and packages that have code maintained by other organizations. When you switch to your production credentials and turn off test mode in the third-party service, the app may behave differently. This is when you have to verify that you have the service configured correctly.

I remember one case of working with Stripe where we spent so much time testing in preproduction that when we did the release, there weren't any products set up in production mode in Stripe. The errors we received in production were different from what we tested with, and we even noticed events we hadn't accounted for. It took a good two months of continuous testing in production before we were confident that users could be notified that the new feature was ready. It required a combined effort among the full stack devs, QA, DevOps, and Product to finally get the feature in a place where all the edge cases were addressed and we had enough documentation to feel confident that we could adequately support our users.

Just because a feature is in production doesn't mean users have to know about it immediately. You can have it behind a feature flag, like we discussed in Chapter 25, where only users with certain permissions have access to the new feature. A *feature flag* is a way to enable or disable a specific feature. Feature flags are commonly used on the frontend to hide functionality for users until the backend has been updated or more testing has been done. This can give you breathing room to test in production without it affecting current users. Don't forget to turn off the feature flag when you're ready for all users to see the feature! Not doing so can lead to issues with expected release dates.

External services introduce a different type of uncertainty to your app. One of the things you can do to stay ahead of changes is to scan the websites of the external services you use for announcements of upcoming changes. Pay attention to emails from the services on updates that have been made or new features they are working on. Look through the external service docs at least once a month to see if a beta or alpha version of the service has been released silently. This will help you stay ahead of anything that could break your app.

Remember that not all the breaking changes will depend on version updates to any packages you have installed on the frontend or backend. Sometimes they just change responses or events regardless of the version you have. That's why your logs and alerts are so important. They'll help you track down those unexpected changes. Some third-party services are better than others at letting you know updates are coming.

If you go through your logs and trace an error to an external service, make sure the error message isn't being suppressed by some log message you wrote in your code. You need the raw error from the service to figure out if the issue is on their end or yours. This is a key point when your third-party service requires some action from the user, such as giving your app permission to access their account in the external service. Google Analytics (*https://oreil.ly/nq3sj*) is a good example of an external service that does this.

You could end up getting errors in your app because a user hasn't given your app permission to access their data. This is another issue I've run into on projects, and it took three devs at least a full day to figure out that was the problem because we had custom error messages on the backend for everything. Or you might run into situations where your app uses services that depend on one another. If you don't get data from one service, then the other service won't execute as expected. Then you end up having to figure out what to do with the compound issues, and it can take days to make a workaround for it before you even consider how to handle it in the long term.

Even your cloud services will have updates that could potentially cause downtime. It's up to you to stay on top of these changes and decide how to handle them because users won't know or care why your app is down. The main thing is communicating with users that you know something's wrong and you're actively working on it. You can always work with the Support or Sales team to send out emails letting users know your app will be down for scheduled maintenance when you have to work through issues in production.

It may be hard to test your services in nonproduction environments because of limitations they have. Setting up test accounts or testing for new features with your services can be difficult to manage, especially if you need real user data. Keep that in mind as you prepare your production deployments. That's why it's essential to test things in production *before* you announce they are ready for users.

Setting regular maintenance schedules for external services will help you stay on top of many issues, but sometimes production just brings out the unexpected. So you have to do your best to minimize the impact of your external services and keep alternatives in mind, even if that means building your own solution at some point. It's an art of balancing flexibility, control, costs, and time. There are some things you can't do without an external service, like get specific user data. One of the other trade-offs that really comes up in production is that third-party services can expose your users to vulnerabilities and attacks you have no control over.

Data and Security in Production

Because attacks can come from anywhere at any time in production, you need to work with the Security team to see what they do for testing. Get the Product and Design teams and relevant stakeholders involved in production testing. The more everyone works with the app, the better the organization as a whole will understand it. Everyone being familiar with how the app works across the full stack is invaluable when you're discussing the roadmap and upcoming features.

Lean into testing for security vulnerabilities or loopholes in the business logic. If you didn't get a chance to add security testing tools (*https://oreil.ly/1LuB4*) like we discussed in Chapter 8, this is a great time to include them. Now that everything is connected, you can see exactly what any user is able to access. Try out different user roles on the frontend to see if the access token you get will allow you to access backend resources you shouldn't be able to. Check your tokens to see if they expire like you set them to. Take actions that go against the business rules you know should be in place and see if you can break them.

For example, in the app you built, it shouldn't be possible for a user to order an item that's out of stock. But can you find a way to bypass that rule? You have limited the number of products you show, but is there a way to break that filter and see all the products? These are the types of business logic loopholes you want to find. They can get more complex as you start thinking of ways to manipulate the app with things like values from the URL, local storage, and session storage.

You should check to see if there are any workarounds for backend logic through the UI. Are strings parsed and validated on both the frontend and backend? It's more critical on the backend because this is a layer that protects your database. In your forms, see if SQL queries can be submitted as string values and then check the backend to see what it does. This is one way to see if your app is vulnerable to SQL injection attacks (*https://oreil.ly/yXtsX*). Generally, check whether you can force any values that don't conform with what you have planned for on the backend.

When the user authenticates themselves in the app, are there any step-up authorization (*https://oreil.ly/ZipN6*) calls that need to be made for further access? If so, is there anything a user can deduce from the step-up process? Things like code verifier strings and encoded user permission strings can be added to the URL in these auth calls, even briefly. These usually won't be useful on their own, but depending on what you store in the browser, they could become useful info.

Double-check that your tokens expire how you planned and see if the database updates the status on those tokens. Also check that users are not able to manipulate tokens in API requests to give themselves different permissions. Anyone can decode your JWTs, see what the values are, and change them. Make sure they can't use the altered token to manually call endpoints through a tool like Postman.

This is also a good time to look at the responses that come through in the browser to double-check that you aren't revealing sensitive information. You don't want to send things like users' addresses or any other sensitive info in plain text. This should be handled through JWTs or by simply having HTTPS enabled on your server. Certain input fields, like passwords or Social Security numbers, should be masked so that people around the users can't easily see the details they type in. The `password` input element (*https://oreil.ly/S5rDr*) does this by default, and there are packages like @react-input/mask (*https://oreil.ly/2mdhT*) and react-input-mask (*https://oreil.ly/dE-Fo*) to help with other fields.

Containerization of Your App

Something that will come up, even during development, is that your app will run in certain environments (like your machine) but not others. Or you might notice the app doesn't run the same across preproduction and production servers. That's usually because there are configs somewhere in those systems that are slightly different. For example, you might run Node 21.2.0 locally, but the production server uses Node 18.19.1.

Differences like that can have a huge impact on the functionality of your app. That's why running the app in a container is an approach many teams take. *Containers* (*https://oreil.ly/kWXOn*) let you bundle all the dependencies you need to run an app, such as the version of the runtime you need and any libraries that need to be installed. Containerization is very similar to virtualization. The big difference is that containers don't fake the hardware they run on like virtual machines do. Containers just run in isolation on the existing hardware, but you can't do things like install device drivers or interact with USB hardware. So a container is like having the app run in a different world on the server.

The most commonly used tool for this is Docker (*https://oreil.ly/wSBYI*), although there are others, such as Podman (*https://oreil.ly/BOOFB*), Buildah (*https://oreil.ly/LtDmW*), or runc (*https://oreil.ly/WbC7O*). If you can set up containers at the beginning of your project, that will make a consistent development experience for everyone on the dev team. I'll walk you through the process of setting up containers for your frontend and backend apps using Docker.

Go ahead and install Docker Engine (*https://oreil.ly/_ClV-*) locally so that you can run it on your machine. This is how you can help get a consistent dev environment ready for the whole team. Understanding how you can unblock everyone is an essential skill. That's why knowing some basics of how to use this tool will come in handy. You don't have to be a pro at working with containers, but you might find that it's interesting, and you can dive as deep as you want.

For now, you'll need to make some updates to your *vite.config.ts* file. The values you have in this file and the *tsconfig* files are going to directly affect the build artifact you get for production. So if you run into issues with the build, check your config files first. Here are the updates for the *vite.config.ts* file:

```
...
export default defineConfig({
  base: "/",
...
  preview: {
    port: 8080,
    strictPort: true,
  },
  server: {
    port: 8080,
    strictPort: true,
    host: true,
    origin: "http://0.0.0.0:8080",
    watch: {
      usePolling: true,
    },
  },
})
```

We'll start by creating an image for the frontend app. An *image* is a template that has the instructions for creating a container with all the libraries and dependencies required for an application to run. You create images by writing a Dockerfile (*https://oreil.ly/XlTfg*) that has Docker commands to build the container the app will run in. These are similar to the commands you would run in a terminal on the server to set up a container. Here's a simple Dockerfile to run the production build of the app in a container:

```
FROM node:21-alpine

WORKDIR /dashboard-ui

COPY package.json .

RUN npm install

COPY . .

RUN npm run build

EXPOSE 8080

CMD [ "npm", "run", "preview" ]
```

Six instruction keywords followed by arguments are used in this Dockerfile. First, the FROM (*https://oreil.ly/X66as*) instruction is how you set the base image (*https://hub.docker.com*) that the container is built on. The argument for this instruction is commonly the runtime version you want to use. Next, the WORKDIR (*https://oreil.ly/tKFaO*) instruction sets the working directory in the container for the other instructions that are run in the Dockerfile. This is how you can set the location where your app files are copied to in the container.

An instruction that gets used a lot throughout a Dockerfile is COPY (*https://oreil.ly/Cy3Ml*). This is how you're able to move files from your computer's directory into the container. The RUN (*https://oreil.ly/kL80q*) instruction is how you execute commands that you would typically run in the terminal in the container. Next, the EXPOSE (*https://oreil.ly/aMQuT*) instruction lets Docker know how to expose the container's specified port to the host server. This is like the virtualization comparison earlier. The container is still isolated, but there's a way for the host server to interact with it. Finally, the CMD (*https://oreil.ly/qk_KW*) instruction sets the command that will be executed when the container is running from an image.

The `npm run preview` command is used here as an example since you're running the container locally. The Vite docs (*https://oreil.ly/FK1Ff*) don't recommend using this in production, so this is just for local development:

```
FROM node:21-alpine

WORKDIR /dashboard-ui

COPY package.json .

RUN npm install
RUN npm install serve -g

COPY . .

RUN npm run build

EXPOSE 8080

CMD [ "serve", "-s", "dist" ]
```

With your real production frontend, you should serve the app from an S3 bucket, Vercel, Cloudflare, or something similar.

To create an image from this Dockerfile, enter the following command in the terminal of your frontend app directory:

```
docker build . -t "dashboard-ui:v1.0"
```

This command is how you build the image defined in the Dockerfile. The `.` between `build` and `-t` is very important and also easy to miss. This is how you specify that the command runs in the current directory. The `-t` option is how you set the name and tag for the image, which are `dashboard-ui:v1.0` in this command. You don't have to name the image and can just use the generated ID, but I've found naming to be useful when you have a lot of images.

After this command finishes, you'll have an image that you can turn into a container. You can see your current Docker images with this command:

```
docker images
```

And you'll get an output like this:

```
REPOSITORY     TAG        IMAGE ID       CREATED         SIZE
dashboard-ui   v1.0       8179b8302716   21 seconds ago  1.43GB
```

Finally, you can run this command to start a container based on that image:

```
docker run -d -p 8080:8080 dashboard-ui:v1.0
```

The -d option is how you run the container in detached mode, which makes the container run in the background instead of displaying the process in your terminal. The -p option is how you map the host port (the port on the server) to the container port (the port inside the container) so that the app is exposed and running on the port you specified in the Dockerfile. Now you should be able to access your app via the container at *localhost:8080*.

You can also see this container running in your terminal with this command and output:

```
docker ps
```

This is similar to the ps (process) command for Unix systems (*https://oreil.ly/ wcWAW*). So you'll see the currently running processes in the container, as in Figure 26-1.

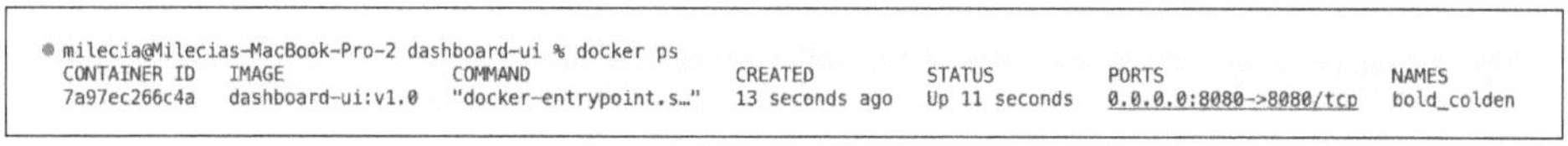

Figure 26-1. Docker container running

You'll have a similar Dockerfile on the backend. The main difference between this and the frontend will be the CMD instruction argument to run the app. Here's what that will look like:

```
FROM node:21-alpine

WORKDIR /dashboard-server

COPY package.json .
COPY package-lock.json .
RUN npm i -production

COPY src src
RUN npm run build

EXPOSE 3000

CMD ["node", "dist/main.js"]
```

As you create new images, you should be aware of golden images. A *golden image* is a template with the environment, tools, packages, and security settings predefined for all the other images you make. These are good to have because they are rebuilt to keep the latest security patches installed, they speed up app development because you and the team won't have to worry about configs, they maintain consistency across all your images, and they can be used to automate deployments for new apps. If you have a dedicated DevOps team, they will typically be responsible for keeping the golden image up to date.

Conclusion

In this chapter, I went over some of the integration concerns that will arise in production and some methods for solving them. Some of the more unpredictable issues will come from your third-party services. Since you don't have control over when they make changes or what those changes will be, you have to monitor them. Regularly go through their docs and announcements and do some testing in production to stay on top of changes. Many of the integration concerns can be managed with coordination between the developers and the other teams you work with.

Most of this chapter explained setting up Docker and creating containers to keep your production deploys consistent. You should partner with the DevOps team to keep those Dockerfiles up to date with both security and app needs—we'll talk more about that in the next chapter. It will benefit you to understand some of the basics of Docker so that you can help maintain the images for your apps. That way, when small updates need to be made, you can help your team stay unblocked because they won't need to rely on the DevOps team for things like version updates or changes to the scripts that are executed.

## CHAPTER 27

Building a CI/CD Pipeline

Now that you've gone through the process of integrating the frontend and backend along with all the infrastructure and services you need, you can automate your deployments with a CI/CD (continuous integration and continuous deployment) pipeline. That way, you can ensure that all your deployments to production or other environments run the same way each time. This is a standard for just about every organization you might work at.

Having an automated CI/CD pipeline will encourage your dev team to make small and frequent releases. You'll partner with the DevOps team to build and maintain this pipeline. Your contribution will be having a deep understanding of how the app works and how it should run. That way, you can help set environment variables and runtime versions, and you can make sure the correct commands are being executed to get the app in a deployable state.

In this chapter, I'll cover:

- Using CircleCI to set up a CI/CD pipeline
- Selecting tools to simplify your pipelines
- Setting up different environments and their purposes
- Using GitHub as part of your process

A lot of options and tools are available to set up your pipeline, and I'll go through some that will get you going quickly. This is another area that crosses over with DevOps quite a bit, so you don't have to be the expert here. Work with them to understand enough to keep your team unblocked; you can decide to go deeper from there or not. Once you've created your own pipeline, you can modify it as the project's needs change.

Creating Your Own Pipeline

Deploying an app to any environment involves running a number of commands in a terminal on the server. There are steps to download all the packages, build the app or the container, set environment variables, handle any other setup, and run the app on the server. There can be any number of steps to deploy the app smoothly. That's where automation comes in because it's easy to skip steps or run them out of order when the process is manual.

Your CI/CD pipeline will help you with automation because it ensures consistency throughout your process. Your pipeline will have steps and stages. A *step* is an individual command you run to do a task like create a build or invalidate a cache. A *stage* comprises multiple steps to complete a specific goal, such as doing testing or deploying an artifact to a service.

At a minimum, you will have a build stage, a test stage, and a deploy stage, although a number of others (*https://oreil.ly/lds1Q*) may be included. During the *build stage*, you'll have steps to get the current version of the code from the team repo. All the individual features and fixes you and the team have been working on will get combined during this stage of the pipeline.

Common steps in the build stage include:

- Spin up the environment
- Prepare your environment variables
- Check out the code from the repo
- Install all your packages
- Run the build command(s)

The *test stage* is when you run unit tests, integration tests, and maybe some security tests on the version of the app you're ready to deploy. Teams can be tempted to skip this stage in crunch time because it can take a while for the tests to run, depending on which tools you use. Fight the temptation to skip the test stage in favor of faster deployment times. Your tests have been written to save you from regressions, bugs, and security vulnerabilities getting to users.

Common steps in the test stage include:

- Run code-quality tests
- Run unit tests
- Run integration tests
- Run security tests
- Report test results to the devs

The last stage is the *deploy stage,* when you decide which environment the changes are released to. You can use the deploy stage to manage other things, like rollbacks, and you can set the stage to run on a schedule or trigger based on certain events. This stage differs greatly based on the organization where you work because the strategy you'll use depends on the industry, the size of the teams, and the agreements between engineering and business. Some organizations will never automate deployments to production while others expect that to happen once the pipeline has been triggered under the right conditions.

Common steps in the deploy stage include:

- Set up any secrets or connections to the cloud service that will serve the build artifact
- Upload the artifact to the cloud service
- Move the build artifact to the server location
- Reset the cache service for the app
- Send notification that the deploy has been successful or has failed

Although the steps in each stage will depend on the organization where you work and the tools being used, the steps listed are ones you can implement if you have to set up your own pipeline.

Speed Considerations

As you look at these stages, keep in mind that you want them to be fast without sacrificing quality. I've seen some CI/CD pipelines take more than an hour to get through all the stages. That slows your team substantially, leads to frustration for everyone involved, and creates a situation where you can't release small, incremental changes. Each of these stages can be broken down into smaller stages, with some of them running in parallel to speed up the pipeline.

Keep the execution time in mind as you build the pipeline. The first place to start and get instant feedback is in your PRs. One sign of a good pipeline is that you get failures as early in the pipeline as possible. That way, the dev team can address issues quickly, and you haven't wasted a lot of time watching scripts run just for something to fail at the last stage because of a code problem.

One strategy I've seen work is running the build and test stages on PRs that target certain branches. For example, you might open a draft PR before it's ready for review. It can be helpful to check that the tests are still passing and the build is successful at this point because you can address issues in the PR before you even get a review. It's a way to get feedback early in your development process so that it doesn't hold up reviews or releases later. You can get feedback even earlier in your development process when you have some of these checks implemented with Git hooks.

One of the purposes of automating deployments is to have confidence that the code will work consistently in any environment you use. That's why you should take time to think out the steps for each stage and document them. One of the best things you can do is stay on top of documentation for things like this. That way, you can get feedback and validate your ideas while making the strongest decisions based on everyone's experience. Documenting your CI/CD pipeline will also help you think through most of the process, so when it's time to write the code and use the tools, you aren't still figuring out the big picture.

Now that you know what your pipeline consists of, you can start adding some of the initial automation checks.

Git Hooks

Since your project uses Git, you can set a lot of checks to help you catch issues long before it's time for a deployment. You already have a couple of Git hooks (*https://oreil.ly/OMoGl*) in your frontend repo (*https://oreil.ly/ItaNR*) for pre-commit and pre-push actions using Husky (*https://oreil.ly/JZ2CO*). The commands you currently have are to enforce code quality before any changes leave a dev's machine. Right now in your repo, you have these commands in your pre-commit hook:

```
#!/usr/bin/env sh
. "$(dirname -- "$0")/_/husky.sh"

npm run lint
npm run format
```

You can add more code-quality and developer-hygiene checks here to watch for commit messages, merge conflicts with the target branch, and restrict commits to protected branches locally. Let's add a new hook to check the commit messages that developers write. Create a new file in the *.husky* directory called *commit-msg* in your frontend repo and write the following script to check the format of the commit messages:

```
#!/usr/bin/env bash
. "$(dirname -- "$0")/_/husky.sh"

commit_types="(build|chore|ci|docs|feat|fix|perf|refactor|revert|style|test|wip)"
conventional_commit_regex="^${commit_types}(\([a-z \-]+\))?!?: .+$"

commit_message=$(cat "$1")


if [[ "$commit_message" =~ $conventional_commit_regex ]]; then
    exit 0
fi

echo "The commit message does not meet commit standards"
echo "An example of a valid message is: "
echo "  feat: update modal fields"

exit 1
```

This will make it easier for you to quickly look through merged PRs and see what changes are present on the shared branches. This is particularly helpful when you're debugging issues that come up in your environments after a deployment. You and the team should decide what the commit messages should look like, but at the minimum, they should let anyone glance through the PRs and see what each one implements. You might go with ticket numbers or identifying code changes by type, such as fixes, bugs, features, and other types defined in the conventional commits spec (*https:// oreil.ly/3LWM-*). You might even look at using AI tools like ai-commit (*https://oreil.ly/ KduBa*) or aicommits (*https://oreil.ly/Fn2_G*) to further automate this task.

Another Git hook you can use is the `pre-push` hook. This runs a script any time a developer tries to push changes to a remote branch, even if it's just their own branch. Right now, you have this hook configured to run your unit tests before any code leaves a dev's computer. Here's the script you currently have:

```
#!/usr/bin/env sh
. "$(dirname -- "$0")/_/husky.sh"

npm test
```

 Be careful of the commands you run in the `pre-commit` and `pre-push` hooks because sometimes they can hinder the team from sharing work in progress. This could lead to a situation where the devs comment out all the `pre-push` checks, which results in lower-quality code getting to the shared branches. Be selective with the commands you run in these hooks to keep them useful. Remember, you still have plenty of checks that will happen in the pipeline.

I want to mention that you don't have to use a tool like Husky for Git hooks. When you're working in a repo that uses Git, you can look in the *.git/hooks* directory of the project and find examples for all the possible hooks you can use, as shown in Figure 27-1. Remember that the *.git* directory is probably hidden in your file explorer in case you don't find it immediately. The reason some devs prefer using Husky over the built-in hooks directory is because it handles much of the configuration for you in the background.

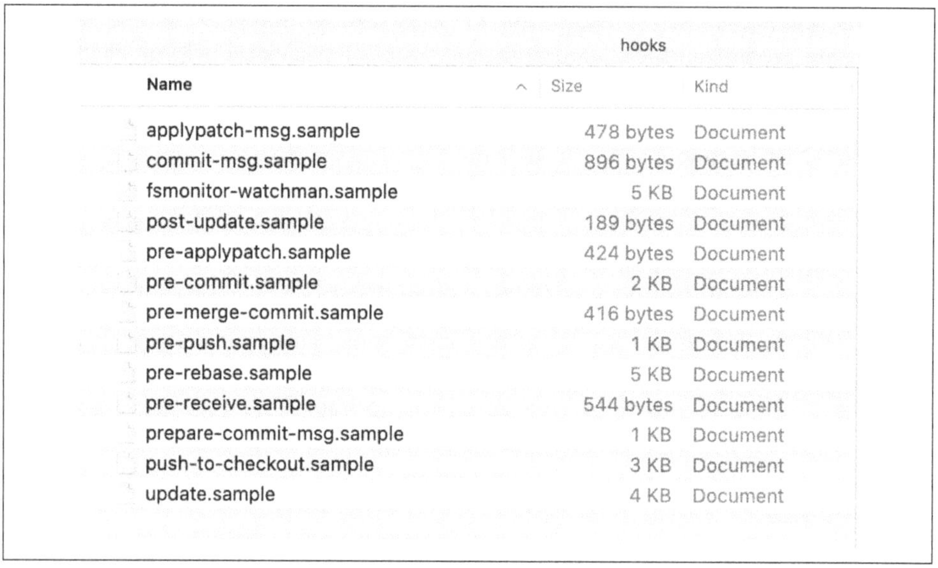

Figure 27-1. Git hooks in the .git/hooks directory

Here's an example of how you could implement `pre-commit` and `pre-push` hooks in pure Git. This script already exists; you just have to remove the *.sample* ending from the filename of the hook you want to use.

This is the `pre-commit` hook:

```
#!/bin/sh
# pre-commit hook
# An example hook script to verify what is about to be committed.
# Called by "git commit" with no arguments. The hook should
# exit with non-zero status after issuing an appropriate message if
# it wants to stop the commit.
#
# To enable this hook, rename this file to "pre-commit".

if git rev-parse --verify HEAD >/dev/null 2>&1
then
    against=HEAD
else
    # Initial commit: diff against an empty tree object
    against=$(git hash-object -t tree /dev/null)
fi

# If you want to allow non-ASCII filenames set this variable to true.
allownonascii=$(git config --type=bool hooks.allownonascii)

# Redirect output to stderr.
exec 1>&2
```

```
# Cross-platform projects tend to avoid non-ASCII filenames; prevent
# them from being added to the repository. We exploit the fact that the
# printable range starts at the space character and ends with tilde.
if [ "$allownonascii" != "true" ] &&
    # Note that the use of brackets around a tr range is ok here, (it's
    # even required, for portability to Solaris 10's /usr/bin/tr), since
    # the square bracket bytes happen to fall in the designated range.
    test $(git diff --cached --name-only --diff-filter=A -z $against |
      LC_ALL=C tr -d '[ -~]\0' | wc -c) != 0
then
    cat <<\EOF
```

This is the pre-push hook:

```
#!/bin/sh
# pre-push hook
# An example hook script to verify what is about to be pushed. Called by "git
# push" after it has checked the remote status, but before anything has been
# pushed.  If this script exits with a non-zero status nothing will be pushed.
#
# This hook is called with the following parameters:
#
# $1 -- Name of the remote to which the push is being done
# $2 -- URL to which the push is being done
#
# If pushing without using a named remote those arguments will be equal.
#
# Information about the commits which are being pushed is supplied as lines to
# the standard input in the form:
#
#   <local ref> <local oid> <remote ref> <remote oid>
#
# This sample shows how to prevent push of commits where the log message starts
# with "WIP" (work in progress).

remote="$1"
url="$2"

zero=$(git hash-object --stdin </dev/null | tr '[0-9a-f]' '0')

while read local_ref local_oid remote_ref remote_oid
do
    if test "$local_oid" = "$zero"
    then
        # Handle delete
        :
    else
        if test "$remote_oid" = "$zero"
        then
            # New branch, examine all commits
            range="$local_oid"
        else
            # Update to existing branch, examine new commits
```

```
                range="$remote_oid..$local_oid"
        fi

        # Check for WIP commit
        commit=$(git rev-list -n 1 --grep '^WIP' "$range")
        if test -n "$commit"
        then
                echo >&2 "Found WIP commit in $local_ref, not pushing"
                exit 1
        fi
    fi
done

exit 0
```

Now you're using the Git lifecycle to handle some common checks before anything gets to the CI/CD pipeline, which will save you a lot of time on PR reviews, triggering the pipeline, and waiting for it to report issues that could have been found much sooner. You can add more hooks if you and the team think it will help save time or keep things consistent.

GitHub Configs

You've added tools to make sure you catch as much as you can before the code moves from a developer's computer, so now it's time to move to the next layer. That's going to be on GitHub in your PRs. This is where you can do more to enforce code quality and do some initial testing to make sure the code works as expected and doesn't break anything obvious. The conventions you set early in the project are going to be great here because you've already accounted for what should be checked in the PR reviews.

There are a few things you should set up in your repo on GitHub to ensure that the branches are protected from less thorough reviews. Consider restricting direct pushes to your main and develop branches since these are the ones that all the devs typically branch and deploy from. You should also restrict which branches can be deleted and by whom as well as other actions that can be taken. You do this in the settings for the repo, which will look something like Figure 27-2.

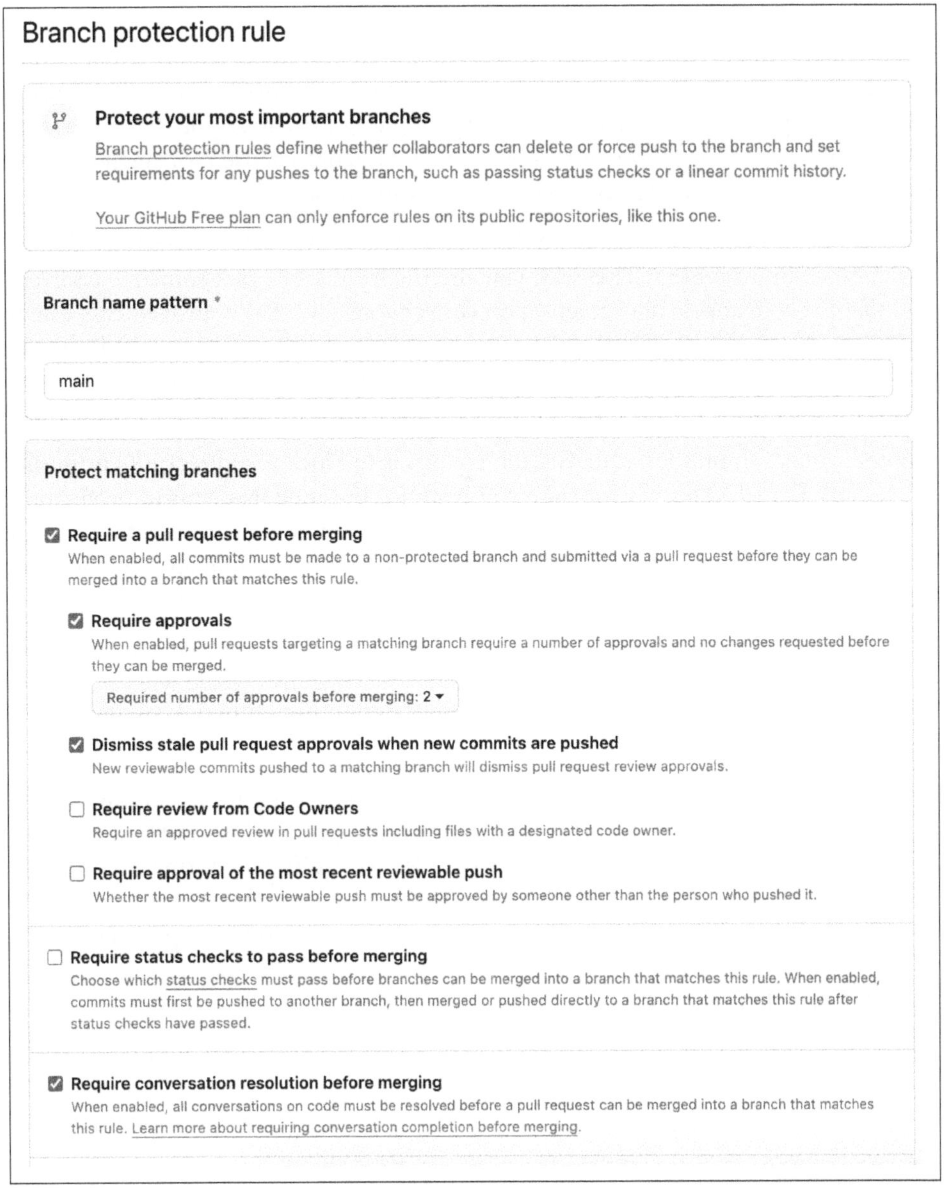

Branch protection rule

🔀 **Protect your most important branches**

Branch protection rules define whether collaborators can delete or force push to the branch and set requirements for any pushes to the branch, such as passing status checks or a linear commit history.

Your GitHub Free plan can only enforce rules on its public repositories, like this one.

Branch name pattern *

```
main
```

Protect matching branches

☑ **Require a pull request before merging**
When enabled, all commits must be made to a non-protected branch and submitted via a pull request before they can be merged into a branch that matches this rule.

　☑ **Require approvals**
　When enabled, pull requests targeting a matching branch require a number of approvals and no changes requested before they can be merged.

　　`Required number of approvals before merging: 2 ▾`

　☑ **Dismiss stale pull request approvals when new commits are pushed**
　New reviewable commits pushed to a matching branch will dismiss pull request review approvals.

　☐ **Require review from Code Owners**
　Require an approved review in pull requests including files with a designated code owner.

　☐ **Require approval of the most recent reviewable push**
　Whether the most recent reviewable push must be approved by someone other than the person who pushed it.

☐ **Require status checks to pass before merging**
Choose which status checks must pass before branches can be merged into a branch that matches this rule. When enabled, commits must first be pushed to another branch, then merged or pushed directly to a branch that matches this rule after status checks have passed.

☑ **Require conversation resolution before merging**
When enabled, all conversations on code must be resolved before a pull request can be merged into a branch that matches this rule. Learn more about requiring conversation completion before merging.

Figure 27-2. GitHub branch settings

Explore the settings you have available in GitHub, and you'll find something suitable for just about every rule you want to enforce. I'll go into more detail on Git branch strategies in Chapter 28 because this will hugely impact how you handle things in your dev, deploy, and incident processes. For now, we'll focus on having a `main` branch that is used for production deploys, a `develop` branch used for staging or pre-production deploys, and dev branches that the team works on.

A good rule of thumb is to require at least one PR approval before merging a developer's branch into `develop`. That way, you and the team know that someone else verified that the code meets the agreed-upon conventions and that improvements can be suggested and handled. A bare minimum check in any PR review is to pull the dev branch to your machine and make sure the app runs and meets the acceptance criteria for the ticket.

Another rule of thumb for your GitHub configs is to block any direct PRs or pushes to the `main` branch. This is your source of truth for the code that runs in production, and you don't want anyone to be able to directly change that code without going through the release process. Keep this in mind when hotfixes come up. Someone may need to temporarily disable that rule to get a fix to production quickly.

One more rule is to run some of your pipeline checks directly on the PR. For example, making sure that the tests pass and a build is successfully created will catch issues before the PR gets merged and potentially blocks the team while the dev figures out what's wrong.

With these rules and restrictions in place, you can have even more confidence that the code you and your team are writing will work in production, and you can keep better code hygiene so that you don't have files with different formatting or with methods and variables written differently. You've done everything to catch issues at the PR-review and code-merging levels, so now you can start on your pipeline.

CircleCI Configs

There are plenty of CI/CD pipeline tools, such as Jenkins (*https://jenkins.io*), CircleCI (*https://circleci.com*), Bamboo (*https://oreil.ly/IycNX*), GitHub Actions (*https://oreil.ly/uGb3g*), and TeamCity (*https://oreil.ly/YDmDC*). I'll use CircleCI to set up the pipeline for this app because it takes very little configuration and it integrates well with GitHub, Bitbucket, and others. To use CircleCI, you can sign up (*https://circleci.com/signup*) for a free account and connect it to the GitHub repo you want to set up a pipeline for. Once you are signed up, I encourage you to go through the Quickstart Guide to connect to your repo and create your initial CircleCI config file. You'll see something like Figure 27-3 once you're logged in and you have to choose which GitHub repo to set up a new pipeline project in.

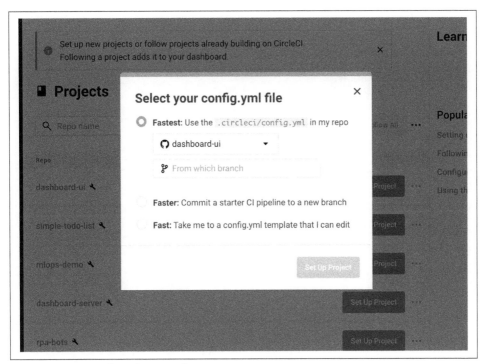

Figure 27-3. Initial CircleCI pipeline setup

I selected the `main` branch to set up the pipeline, and I chose the Fastest option. Your pipeline config file will be in the new *.circleci* directory at the root of your project in the *config.yml* file. Now if you go to your GitHub repo, you should see a new branch called `circleci-project-setup`, which will have your initial CI/CD pipeline config file. Open a PR to merge this to your `main` branch, and you'll see the new file, as in Figure 27-4.

Figure 27-4. GitHub PR to add CI/CD config generated by CircleCI

You'll make plenty of changes to this file to set up your own stages and steps, but for now, you want to make sure your pipeline works from your repo. Open a PR with any changes, even just an update to the README, and you should see something like Figure 27-5 in GitHub.

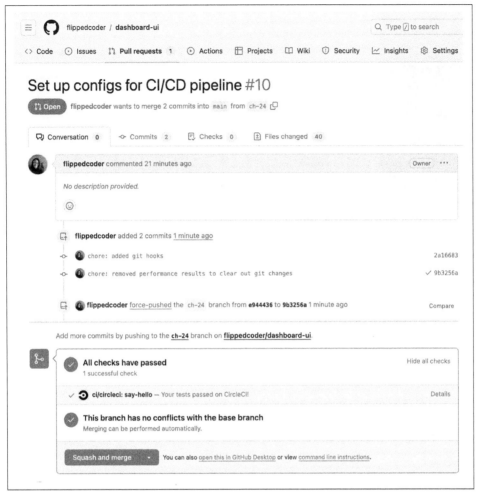

Figure 27-5. CircleCI status on GitHub PR

Now you have this check that will run on every PR you and the team create. To find out what exactly happens with the checks, go to your CircleCI dashboard, and you should see something like Figure 27-6.

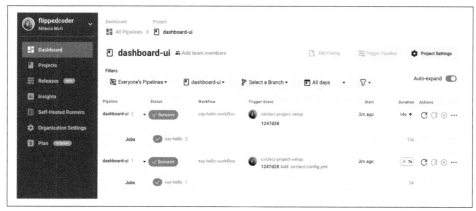

Figure 27-6. CircleCI dashboard

From here, you should click on the workflow called say-hello-workflow and then click the say-hello job within it. This will show you the steps that have been run for this job, as shown in Figure 27-7.

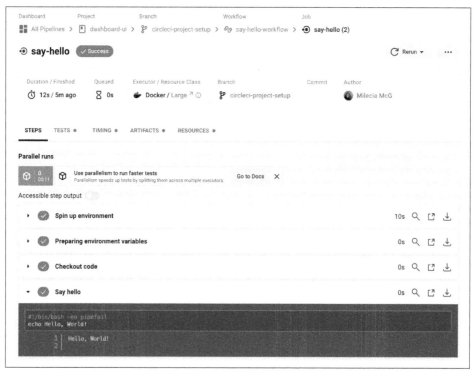

Figure 27-7. Say-hello job steps

Since you have confirmation that the pipeline is connected to your repo, you can start building your own stages and make a pipeline that deploys the code to production and other environments. It's a good idea to do this one stage at a time so that you can make sure each works like you expect. This will save you time on debugging your pipeline configs.

Let's start with the build and test stages we outlined earlier. In your *config.yml*, add the following code:

```
version: 2.1
orbs:
  node: circleci/node@5.1.1
  cypress: cypress-io/cypress@3
  snyk: snyk/snyk@2.1.0
jobs:
  unit-test:
    docker:
      - image: 'cimg/base:stable'
    steps:
      - checkout
      - node/install:
          node-version: '21.2'
      - node/install-packages
      - run:
          command: npm run lint
      - run:
          command: npm run test
  security-scan:
    docker:
      - image: 'cimg/base:stable'
    steps:
      - checkout
      - node/install:
          node-version: '21.2'
      - node/install-packages
      - snyk/scan
  integration-test:
    docker:
      - image: 'cimg/base:stable'
    steps:
      - checkout
      - node/install:
          node-version: '21.2'
      - node/install-packages
      - snyk/scan
  build:
    docker:
      - image: 'cimg/base:stable'
    steps:
      - checkout
      - node/install:
          node-version: '21.2'
```

```
    - node/install-packages
    - run:
        command: npm run build
workflows:
  build-and-tests:
    jobs:
      - build
      - unit-test:
          requires:
            - build
      - security-scan:
          requires:
            - unit-test
  integration-test:
    jobs:
      - cypress/run:
          start-command: npm run start
```

This is a very basic setup, and you should work with your DevOps team to make something more robust than this, but it's enough to get a pipeline in place to run a few checks. Since CircleCI is only one of the tools you might use, I'll give a brief overview of what the different parts of this file mean, but you should read about the concepts that CircleCI uses (*https://oreil.ly/pBwnc*) to get a deeper understanding. For example, you will likely have sequential jobs run based on the results of previous jobs, and there are a few of those present in this config.

The first thing you will notice in the config is the version. This is the version of CircleCI your pipeline will use, and it determines what keys (*https://oreil.ly/D_-0K*) you have available to use in your pipeline. Then there is the orbs section. Orbs (*https://oreil.ly/eIoZz*) are shared packages that can contain jobs and commands that simplify your config file. Many third-party services will have orbs available, so you don't have to write all of your commands from scratch. That's how you're using Cypress for your integration testing and Snyk for your security scan in the pipeline without having to set up anything.

Next, you have the jobs section. Jobs (*https://oreil.ly/refei*) contain all the steps you want to run at various stages in your pipeline. They will be one of the most detailed sections in your config because jobs are the building blocks for everything you do in the pipeline. Last, you have the workflows section. Workflows (*https://oreil.ly/YuOL3*) are how you put the jobs together in the order you want them to run in your pipeline based on the requirements you set.

All of these sections can be used in more advanced ways where you write custom scripts for jobs and have more granular requirements in your workflows. You can eventually get to a place where you have workflows and jobs for container orchestration with Kubernetes (*https://kubernetes.io/docs*), but that'll be something for the

DevOps team to handle. For now, if you push the changes to your config to your repo you'll see something like Figure 27-8 in CircleCI.

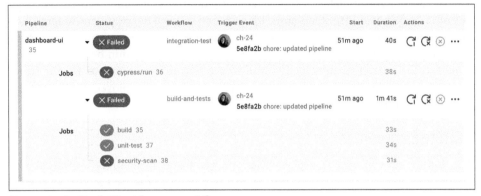

Figure 27-8. CircleCI with new workflows

You can go into the build-and-tests workflow to see the details of the jobs being run in it, as shown in Figure 27-9.

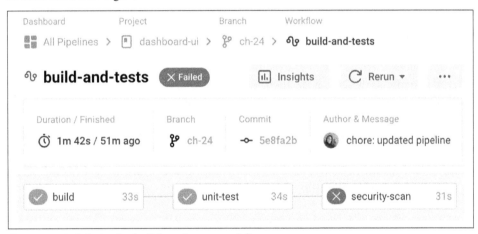

Figure 27-9. Jobs in the build-and-tests workflow

Take note of how long each workflow and their jobs take so that you're aware of how long your pipeline stages take to run as a whole. This information will help guide you as you add more jobs and steps. This is how you'll be able to find places to improve your pipeline.

You now have a CI pipeline in place, and the only thing left is to work with the DevOps team to handle the deploy stage where your build artifact is passed to your cloud services to run on the servers they've set up. This last bit with the DevOps team is the *CD* part of the CI/CD pipeline.

Environment Pipelines

The last part of your pipeline setup is handling multiple environments for your apps. For both backend and frontend apps, it's common to have development, staging, and production environments. There might be additional feature environments for the frontend because those changes may need to be tested in isolation before being promoted to the next environment. If you do have feature environments for the frontend, this is usually the first environment that changes get deployed to. Let's take a look at these different environments in a little more detail.

Feature Environment

The *feature environment* is a place where larger frontend changes get tested first before they are merged into the rest of the code. When you are refactoring a large piece of the frontend app and it changes views or data handling substantially, this is a good place to make sure the changes don't break everything. Having feature environments will keep the rest of the team unblocked as well because they can still merge their smaller changes to the development environment and do their testing in a larger system.

Development Environment

The *development environment* is usually a place where the dev team can do preliminary deployments to test how their changes work with the overall system. The deploys here can happen in an ad hoc manner as long as the team communicates with one another when changes are being deployed. You might even bring the QA team in here to do some quick tests or just to give them a demo of what to expect soon. The development environment for the frontend and backend are usually connected to each other so that you can test how your full stack changes will work. Often, the feature environments for the frontend are connected to the development environment for the backend. This is also a good place to make sure your feature flags are working as expected, like we discussed in Chapter 25.

Staging Environment

The *staging environment* is where you'll check that the changes you've made work as expected. You'll work with the QA team here to do their feature and regression testing. You can also give the Product and Design teams access to this environment so that they can do user acceptance testing and make any final requests. This is where your frontend and backend changes should be in sync and you are connected to any third-party services to test a fully integrated app. It should be as close to production as possible. You'll likely have test credentials for your services, and you may decide to use them only in the staging environment or in development as well.

Production Environment

The *production environment* is the one where users are interacting with the app. After all the testing in the previous environments, you should be fully aware of what to expect from a user's perspective. This is usually where the best server resources are, and it's where you want to make sure you update your environment variables for third-party services and cloud services.

Environment Variables

You can use *environment variables* to control the deployments to your different environments and set up connections in different environments. For example, it's very likely that your DevOps team will have an entirely separate infrastructure in place for the development environment compared to the production one. That includes things like separate databases and event managers.

There are a few approaches you can take to manage the env vars in your pipelines. You can set up variables for each environment in CircleCI in the Project Settings and then reference them in the *config.yml*. Now anywhere in your apps that reference the env var will use the value you've set. Here are the new jobs and workflow in the *config.yml*:

```
...
deploy-dev:
    docker:
      - image: 'cimg/base:stable'
    steps:
      - checkout
      - run:
          name: 'dev env vars'
          command: |
            echo $API_URL
  deploy-staging:
    docker:
      - image: 'cimg/base:stable'
    steps:
      - checkout
      - run:
          name: 'staging env vars'
          command: |
            echo $API_URL
  deploy-prod:
    docker:
      - image: 'cimg/base:stable'
    steps:
      - checkout
      - run:
          name: 'prod env vars'
          command: |
```

```
        echo $API_URL
...
deploy:
  jobs:
    - deploy-dev:
        filters:
          branches:
            only: develop
    - deploy-staging:
        filters:
          branches:
            only: staging
    - deploy-prod:
        requires:
          - build-and-tests
        filters:
          branches:
            only: main
```

Figure 27-10 shows what this will look like in CircleCI.

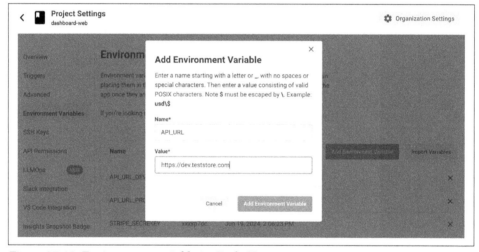

Figure 27-10. Environment variable in CircleCI

These new jobs will require close work with the DevOps team to make sure you connect to the infrastructure as expected. In this example, note that you connect the app to different versions of the API_URL environment variable and that your deploy workflow is dependent on which branch changes have been merged to. Another thing to note is that in this workflow, the build and test stages are required to pass first before you deploy to production, but not the other environments. This check is bypassed for the sake of the example, but it's something you should have in place in your real pipeline. The new pipeline is shown in Figure 27-11.

Figure 27-11. Production deployment in CircleCI

Another approach to handling env vars is to have separate *.env* files for each environment. This is a risker approach that can be done in a private repo or with a script that updates these values in memory when the app passes through the pipeline. Otherwise, you risk everyone having access to your production and test credentials. Keep in mind that one of the reasons env vars are considered a best practice is because there's no persistent record of them anywhere except in your cloud provider and they have a secure infrastructure to handle them. Any other time, your env vars are loaded in memory and don't persist outside of it.

With the different deployments you have in your pipeline, all that's left is working with your DevOps team to connect everything to services and infrastructure, and testing that the environments are working like you expect.

Conclusion

In this chapter, I went over building your own CI/CD pipeline. You learned about the different stages and jobs that are necessary for a simple pipeline. I encourage you to take a look at the pipelines at your organization. There are a number of environments that you'll deploy to, and you have to account for the differences between them in your pipelines.

You were able to build a pipeline with CircleCI, which is just one of the many tools you can use to deploy your code. I recommend checking out some of the other pipeline tools to learn how they work compared to what we did here. As long as you have the stages we've covered here, you can work with your DevOps team to create more advanced functionality.

## CHAPTER 28

Git Management

Understanding Git is one of the best skills you can cultivate. It doesn't matter if you work on the full stack, specialize on the frontend or backend, or decide to learn a different programming language. You need to know how to manage the changes that happen in the repo. The team will look to you for guidance on how to handle their branches and how changes are merged across the shared branches.

You've done a lot of good setup for your team by defining code conventions, using Git hooks to enforce standard commits, adding rules to your branches in GitHub, and following a consistent PR review process. Now you need to go a little further and understand various commands and strategies you can use to minimize conflicts as multiple developers push changes to the remote repo.

In this chapter, I'll cover:

- Branching strategies
- Managing merging with Git commands
- Handling merge conflicts

One of the trickiest things to do is untangle branches once changes have been merged because you have to make sure to keep the correct version of changes. It always helps to have a few techniques in mind for when conflicts happen, especially around deploy time. I'll go through some of the ways I normally manage branches and merges from different teams as well as some other methods I've been introduced to over the years. Hopefully, these options will help give you ideas for what you might do.

Branching Strategies

There are a number of ways to handle branches as you have changes being developed concurrently. A few things you want to keep in mind are overlapping file changes, package version updates, how large a feature is, when the feature is supposed to be released, and if there are any app-wide changes. These considerations will help you figure out how you and the team want to handle the changes that are coming in. Some of your branch strategy will be driven by how your deployment pipelines have been defined.

Common Branches and Merge Flow

As we discussed in Chapter 27, there will be different environments that your code gets deployed to. These environments are typically connected to certain branches. A common strategy is to call those branches main, staging, and develop. The names might vary at different organizations, but their uses will be similar. The main branch is for production deployments, the staging branch is for testing changes before they are released to production, and the develop branch is where the dev team will do its own validation before involving QA or other teams. Both the staging and develop branches are typically connected to a deployment environment.

When PRs (*https://oreil.ly/pmZvu*) are ready to be released to production, the typical flow is to merge a PR to develop. There will be some initial dev team checks once the changes are on develop. After develop has been cleared, the changes will go to staging for QA and Product approval. Once everything has been validated on staging, then the changes get merged to main, and the production deployment is triggered.

> Keep in mind that PRs are a feature of GitHub or Bitbucket, not Git itself. GitLab refers to the same concept as a *merge request.* You can merge changes using Git without ever creating a PR.

You can think of main as the source of truth for the app as the users are currently experiencing it. If there's ever a question about which features are available or what changes are the correct ones, main is usually the branch you want to refer to because of how it affects the users. The staging branch is the source of truth for all the changes that are ready to be released to users. It probably contains fewer changes than the develop branch, and it has functionality the main branch doesn't. The develop branch is usually the source of truth for the latest features that have been approved by the dev team. So when you're starting a new task, this is typically the branch you want to work from. Figure 28-1 is an example of this flow.

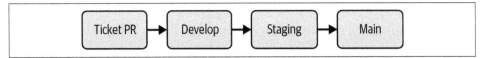

Figure 28-1. PR branch merging flow

You'll want to treat the `main` and `staging` branches carefully. They usually have rules around them to prevent any direct pushes except for in the case of hotfixes, which was discussed in Chapter 25. These branches are connected to environments that shouldn't experience downtime, especially `main` since it's connected to the production environment. You want to protect the `develop` branch as well, but maybe to a lesser degree.

Ensuring that the unit tests and build are successful is fine here because someone may need to validate their changes in a cloud environment before they're ready to get the code reviewed. There are times when you'll want to merge smaller changes to a shared branch to help unblock someone else's work. That can include adding new components to the frontend, like buttons or modals, or updating response values from an endpoint.

PR Reviews

The reasons we review each other's code include:

- Ensuring that quality code gets merged to the shared branches
- Checking that there aren't any obvious bugs getting to production
- Helping to share and spread knowledge across the team
- Fostering communication and collaboration on the team

Remember that the purpose of the code review isn't to criticize one another or make the comments personal. You won't have the same context for a code change as the person who made it, so be humble and ask questions if there's something that seems odd to you.

There are multiple things you'll want to check for when you do a PR review. Here's a checklist of items you may want to include:

- Require at least one approval from another dev to confirm that someone other than the author has seen the new code.
- Make sure the unit tests pass and the build is successful when pushing changes to `main` and `staging`.
- Check for anything that goes against the code conventions the team has in place, such as naming or function formatting.

- Pull down the branch and make sure the app runs.
- Run the app locally to see if the functionality works as expected.
- Go through the changes line by line and make sure you understand them.
- If there's something you don't understand, ask questions about it because you might not be the only one.
- Try not to impose your own coding style on another dev because there are always multiple ways to approach the same task.
- Be mindful of how conditions are written and how third-party services are called.
- Double-check that data is sent and returned as expected.

You can add any number of tasks (*https://oreil.ly/Y8VfS*) to the PR review, and you can make a PR template (*https://oreil.ly/1Ivga*) that's automatically available on all PRs. This checklist has a short number of items to check for, so work with your team to determine what's best for your reviews. One way to make reviews smoother is deciding how to handle branches.

Branches for Smaller Functionality

Often, each branch you create will be associated with a ticket, especially with bug fixes and smaller one-off tasks. Every time you need to make a new branch, you should pull down the latest changes from `develop`. I usually pull changes every day and sometimes multiple times throughout the day just to make sure I'm working with the latest code. This will ensure you aren't working with older code that could cause merge conflicts later.

With these branches, try to make small commits when you can. Let's take the user sign-up form task as an example. This will require new types, a new component, an API call, and maybe some new packages. Making each of these changes its own commit can help you during debugging, but you don't have to do this. Once you're ready to merge to `develop`, it's a good practice to squash all the commits for your individual branch; we'll talk about that in a bit.

Since you and the team already have conventions for branch names and commit messages from Chapter 27, the intent of your changes is clearer. Having that intent is really helpful when you need to update packages as part of a task because that's one of the changes that can lead to cascading issues once the branch is merged. You can pinpoint the exact feature or bug fix that holds the updates and undo that one if it starts blocking other developers. So if you've merged in multiple tickets and squashed the commits, you'll still have a flow that looks like Figure 28-2.

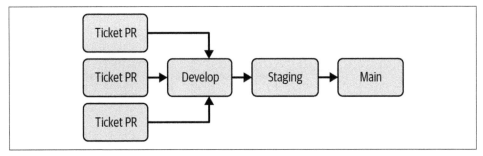

Figure 28-2. Multiple tickets merged to `develop`

As soon as these smaller branches are approved, they should be merged quickly. This will help keep changes flowing to the `develop` branch and prevent branches from becoming stale. A *stale branch* is one that has sat long enough for `develop` to have updates to after it's already been approved. Small, quick merges will help mitigate conflicts and keep the dev team in sync with changes.

Feature Branches for Larger Implementations

Sometimes a larger feature will be under development. This type of work will add significant new functionality to the app. It may or may not have anything to do with existing code, so this work can usually be implemented in isolation from other changes in progress.

 Remember that feature flags, which we discussed in Chapter 25, are also an option for this. You can use feature flags and feature branches if you want to do a more fine-grained rollout, or you can choose one over the other. When you're developing a large feature that needs multiple small parts to work, then a feature branch may be preferred. If you're developing a smaller, high-impact feature, then feature flags may be the way to go.

When the team is working on multiple large features, it's a good idea to consider creating separate branches for them that you merge smaller changes into as you build more of the functionality. That way, you aren't blocking the `develop` branch, and the team can review the feature in smaller chunks. When it's time to merge to `develop`, the individual pieces have been thoroughly reviewed, and the feature can be evaluated at a higher level. Having a separate feature branch also makes testing easier because you can focus on one particular feature without worrying about any other changes. The flow for this strategy is shown in Figure 28-3.

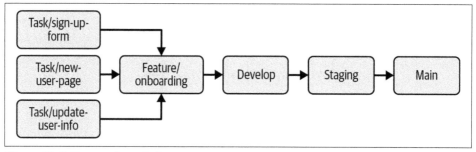

Figure 28-3. Feature branch flow

In this example, you're working on a feature called "onboarding," so you've created a feature branch called `feature/onboarding` based on the `develop` branch. After you create the `feature/onboarding` branch, then every task you work on related to onboarding will have its own branch based on it. The `task/sign-up-form` branch was based on `feature/onboarding` just like the other task branches. These smaller units of work will get reviewed and address any feedback, then get merged to `fea ture/onboarding`. That way, when you finish all the tasks related to onboarding, the feature branch PR review won't be as tedious for the team to go through.

This strategy helps you keep track of all the smaller development work needed to make the full feature, which will let you focus on one thing at a time and keep the code quality up with things like types and tests. It helps with release time because you have multiple steps of validation that the full feature is complete. Merging the task work directly into `develop` can lead to a weird user experience because all the functionality isn't available yet unless you use feature flags. Using a feature branch can give you more time to think through edge cases and ask questions that come up as you develop because you have to break things down into smaller pieces, which can reveal areas that don't have all the requirements defined.

Squashing Commits

The most important thing when you merge branches, big or small, is to communicate when things are merged. Most of the time, this will happen in the PR reviews, but when you know a change is going to affect shared parts of the app or core functionality, it helps to explicitly alert the team. That way, you all can work together to make sure there are minimal conflicts between changes.

There are a few ways you and the team might decide to merge branches. The first is by squashing commits from individual ticket branches that get merged to `develop`. When you squash the commits for a PR, that means you take all the commits you've made on that branch and roll them together under one commit. You usually don't need to see all the small commits that went into a bug fix or even a feature.

Something to remember is that your small commit messages can be informal, as in the example in Figure 28-4.

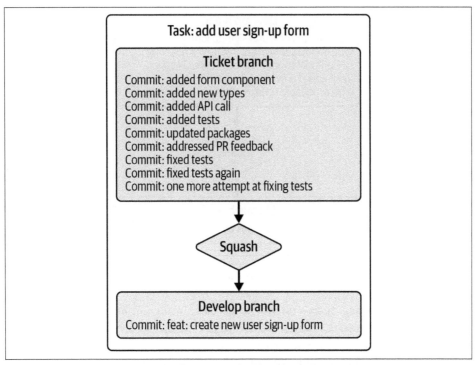

Figure 28-4. Squashing commits from an individual branch to `develop`

When you squash commits from individual branches to `develop`, it helps take the noise out of your Git history so that you can see the changes as an overall feature or bug fix. This is useful when you need to debug because it's unlikely you would undo a single commit without the context of the other changes associated with it. Squashing the small commits is like keeping the history organized by the tasks and features or by the ticket number, not by the work that went into them.

Usually, you want to merge commits that go from `develop` to `staging` and from `staging` to `main` without squashing them. Because you've already squashed the small commits from the individual branches to `develop`, you're left with the most relevant info in your Git history so that you don't lose track of those features and tickets that are being tested or released. Figure 28-5 is an example of what would happen if you squashed all your commits from `develop` to `staging` and why it makes it harder to know what features are included. You don't usually want to do this.

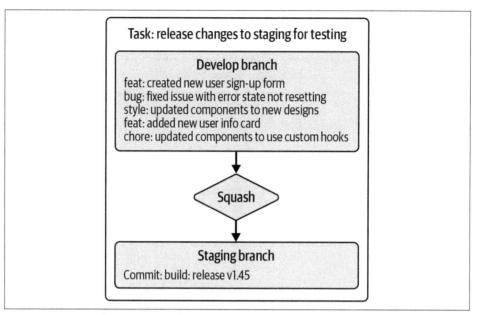

Figure 28-5. Squashing commits from develop *to* staging

Now if you have a bug, there's no way to go back in the Git history and figure out what feature introduced it. If you saw this entry in the history for the develop branch, the only way you could figure out what changes were included is to go back and look at the original PR. That might leave you with missing context. So when you're merging changes to the shared branches like develop, do not squash commits.

> A super important thing to note here is that you need to keep feature branches in sync with all changes that get merged to develop. Since feature branches indicate that the work being done is in progress, it's easy for these branches to get out of sync, depending on how often changes get merged to develop. Once your feature branch diverges from develop, you end up with merge conflicts that get messy to sort out. At least once a week, you should rebase your feature branch with the changes from develop. We'll go over how to handle that in the next section.

As an exercise, take some time to look through the current Git history at your organization. An example of what that might look like on GitHub is shown in Figure 28-6.

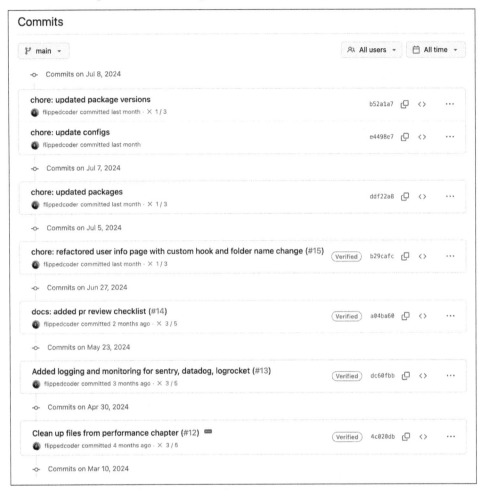

Figure 28-6. Project Git history in GitHub

You can use the `git rebase` command to handle squashing commits, and it would be great if you understood how that works (*https://oreil.ly/iMS8e*). Realistically though, you'll be using the buttons on your PRs to squash your commits. You can see what the button options look like in Figure 28-7.

Figure 28-7. Squash button in GitHub

By clicking the "Squash and merge" button, you can bundle all the commits in your PR into a single commit with a message that summarizes the changes. This cleans up your history and can help you focus during debugging efforts. Hopefully, this will also show you why you don't want to squash commits to your shared branches. It removes the ability to see separate commits. If you really need to get the original history, there are ways to do it, although it can be difficult.

Rebasing and Merging Branches

Since you know how to squash commits from your individual branches to make a develop-ready commit, you can turn your attention to how you keep feature branches up to date with an upstream branch like develop. This will make merging your changes easier when they're ready for testing. Any new changes on develop could introduce merge conflicts that are tedious to fix if you wait too long to update your feature branch. As a rule of thumb, I always pull down the latest changes from develop every day and rebase my local feature branches. That way, if there are any conflicts, they will be smaller and more manageable.

This does leave you and the team with a choice to make. Do you all agree on rebasing feature branches, or would you rather merge the changes from develop? Let's take a look at the difference between the two and how they affect your Git history.

When you rebase your branch, that means you are moving the beginning of the history of the feature branch to the end of a source branch, like develop. This results in the Git history for your feature branch starting where the latest changes from develop begin, as shown in Figures 28-8 and 28-9.

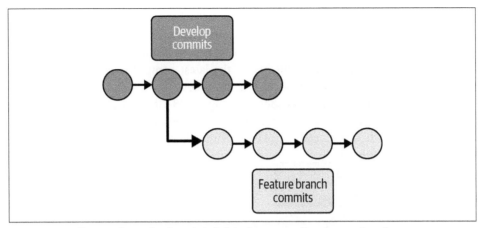

Figure 28-8. Feature branch when it is behind current changes on develop

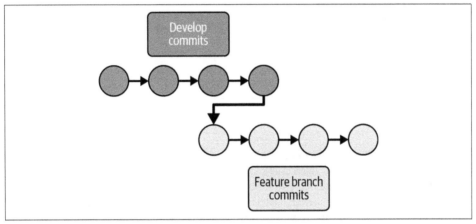

Figure 28-9. Feature branch after it has been rebased with current changes on develop

If you and the team go with the rebase option, be mindful that this can make revert-
ing changes difficult, it can lead to making similar but different commits during
merge conflict resolution, and it can break intermediate commits if you perform
them incorrectly. You never want to rebase a shared branch, like develop or main,
onto a feature branch for these reasons. Rebasing is very useful for your individual
branches because you're the only one working on them. But if you rebase a shared
branch, it can cause major problems, such as removing a number of existing commits. Only rebase the feature branches with the shared branches to avoid this
problem.

When you merge `develop` into your feature branch, that means you're making a commit of the changes from `develop` on your feature branch. That adds the full history of the changes from `develop` to the head of your feature branch instead of moving the beginning of the feature branch history to the latest commit on `develop` as with a rebase. So every time you merge a commit from `develop`, it gets added as the latest change of your feature branch, as shown in Figure 28-10. That can be nice because rebasing can be a more involved process whereas merging is just one step. It does become an issue when you need to roll back or revert changes, though.

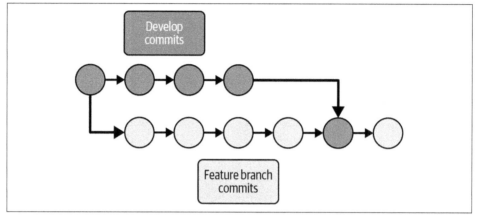

Figure 28-10. Merging a branch

 Something else to be mindful of is what you do with your branches after they've been merged. It's good technical hygiene to delete branches after they've been merged so that you and the team can manage Git better. Deleting merged branches removes a lot of noise from the repo, and it should be fine since all the changes are already in a shared branch and are recorded in the PR that got merged.

Merging is usually the easier option because it just adds the changes to the end of the feature branch, so you don't have to decide which parts of individual commits to keep in the history as with rebasing. I encourage you to get familiar with rebasing, though, because it can actually be easier to handle merge conflicts and it can produce better results. There are trade-offs for both approaches, and you might use a combination of both to manage all your branches. You will find a comparison of the methods in Table 28-1. If you want more details on how rebasing and merging compare with each other, check out this Atlassian tutorial (*https://oreil.ly/ddbHP*), the book *Version Control with Git* by Prem Kumar Ponuthorai and Jon Loeliger (O'Reilly), or this article on one of the revised ways of managing branching (*https://oreil.ly/kjJL3*).

Table 28-1. Comparison of rebase and merge

Rebase	Merge
More linear and less cluttered history	History cluttered with merge commits
Resolving conflicts can be a multistep process	Resolving conflicts is a single-step process
Not recommended for shared branches	Good for shared branches
Rewrites commit hashes	Preserves commit hashes

You'll want to work with your team to establish a pattern for when to merge and rebase. On most of the teams I've worked with, we used this general flow:

- If you're developing on an individual branch or a feature branch, you should *rebase* with develop to keep your code up to date.

- Once your individual or feature branch has been reviewed, the branch should be *merged* to develop.

- After a change is on develop, those changes should be *merged* to staging.

- From staging, the changes should be *merged* to main.

That way, you keep the Git process consistent and avoid situations where you may need to undo or cherry-pick changes, which can be a difficult process. The goal is to be able to understand which commits contain each feature. As long as you can go through the Git history and understand when features were deployed and what code was associated with them, you have a good strategy.

Handling Merge Conflicts

No matter what strategies you implement, eventually you will have to resolve merge conflicts. It's one of your skills that will be tested many times, and it will expand your knowledge of Git commands, communication, and the project itself. Some conflicts are simple, such as a couple of lines in a single file as shown in Figure 28-11. Others will span multiple files with large changes. It will require some creativity to handle them without losing important changes or breaking the app. I'll go over some ways you can approach merge conflicts, so you'll have a few more tools to work with.

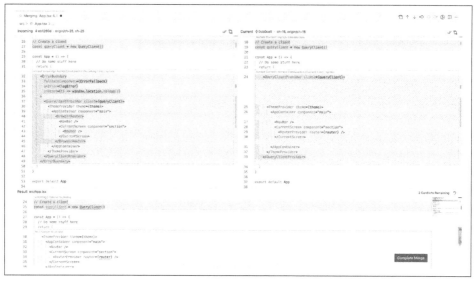

Figure 28-11. Merge conflict in the Git resolution tool

Discuss with the Dev Who Made Changes

Usually, the dev with the conflicted branch is the one who has to fix it. You should reach out to the dev and get them to try to fix the conflicts first because they are the ones who know how a feature is supposed to work. While you will probably be able to solve the conflicts, you may be missing context on which changes to keep. That's why it's important to encourage everyone to solve their own branch conflicts before they bring you in. You can make suggestions like merging changes from the shared branch into their branch or doing a rebase.

If it gets to the point where they are stuck, see if you can hop on a screen-sharing call with them and try to work through it. Something you can do to prevent large conflicts with feature branches is to encourage the team to update their branches every day with any changes from `develop`. The conflicts tend to be smaller or at least more focused when they do this. If the feature branch is very out of sync with `develop` and a rebase doesn't work, it may be a good idea to open a new branch with the latest changes and then re-add the feature code as an absolute last resort.

This is a great opportunity for you to mentor another dev on how to handle merge conflicts and the process you have to go through. Always try to include them in the process of cleaning up their branch so that this task doesn't turn into something only you do. If you find yourself going through each commit on a shared branch, loop in the dev who added the changes. Remember the goal isn't to blame them. You're just trying to get an understanding of what happened so that it can be fixed.

Use git bisect to Find the Affected Files

Sometimes a merge conflict can be hard to track through the Git history. You might check out a really early commit and see if the bad code is there. Then you check out the next commit in the history and look for the conflicting code there. And you do this process for a while until you find something.

That's where `git bisect` comes in. This is a tool that does this for you, allowing you to go through commits and mark them as good or bad until you narrow down to the commit that contains the conflict.

Let's go through an example of this. Start by looking through your Git history to find a good commit hash (one before the merge conflict) and a bad commit hash (one after the merge conflict). Now you can start the process with the following command:

```
git bisect start
```

Now you're in the interactive menu for the `bisect` process. Keep in mind that you can exit this menu at any time with the command `git bisect reset`. But to continue with the process, enter the following command with your good commit hash:

```
git bisect good b29cafce7
```

Then you need to enter the bad commit hash:

```
git bisect bad f0dd190b8
```

Based on what you've entered, `git bisect` will check out a commit halfway between these two, as in Figure 28-12. That's how this command works: it will continue checking out commits that are halfway between the ones you label good and bad until you find the bad one.

```
● milecia@Milecias-MacBook-Pro-2 dashboard-ui % git bisect start
● milecia@Milecias-MacBook-Pro-2 dashboard-ui % git bisect good b29cafce7
● milecia@Milecias-MacBook-Pro-2 dashboard-ui % git bisect bad f0dd190b8
  Bisecting: 1 revision left to test after this (roughly 1 step)
  [e4498e79aee00896b95d57323e503364c3f995d1] chore: update configs
○ milecia@Milecias-MacBook-Pro-2 dashboard-ui % ▮
```

Figure 28-12. Selecting a commit between the good and bad ones

At this point, you need to examine the files that have the merge conflicts to determine if the changes are what you expect. If they aren't, then you'll enter this command and get an output similar to what's shown in Figure 28-13:

```
git bisect bad
```

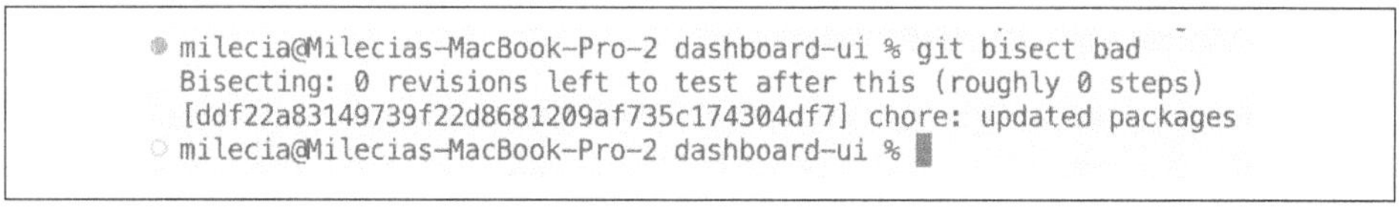

```
  milecia@Milecias-MacBook-Pro-2 dashboard-ui % git bisect bad
  Bisecting: 0 revisions left to test after this (roughly 0 steps)
  [ddf22a83149739f22d8681209af735c174304df7] chore: updated packages
  milecia@Milecias-MacBook-Pro-2 dashboard-ui %
```

Figure 28-13. Labeling the next bad commit

This will tell the `bisect` tool that the commit you currently have checked out is bad, and it will open a new one. This new commit will be halfway between your initial good commit and the latest bad commit. You'll continue this process until you find the next good commit. Once you have a good commit, you'll run this command:

```
git bisect good
```

Then the `bisect` tool will give you the hash for the bad commit, and you can do whatever you need to resolve it, as in Figure 28-14. Doing this can save you hours of time manually going through commits, and it'll pinpoint bad commits with more accuracy. I encourage you to try this out next time you run into a conflict!

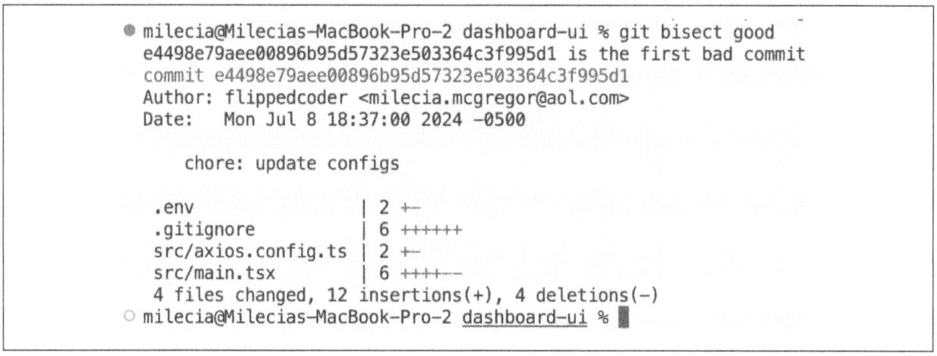

```
  milecia@Milecias-MacBook-Pro-2 dashboard-ui % git bisect good
  e4498e79aee00896b95d57323e503364c3f995d1 is the first bad commit
  commit e4498e79aee00896b95d57323e503364c3f995d1
  Author: flippedcoder <milecia.mcgregor@aol.com>
  Date:   Mon Jul 8 18:37:00 2024 -0500

      chore: update configs

  .env                 | 2 +-
  .gitignore           | 6 ++++++
  src/axios.config.ts  | 2 +-
  src/main.tsx         | 6 ++++--
  4 files changed, 12 insertions(+), 4 deletions(-)
  milecia@Milecias-MacBook-Pro-2 dashboard-ui %
```

Figure 28-14. Showing the bad commit and the files that were changed

Manually Compare File Changes

Sometimes merge conflicts are so big and complicated that you and the other devs can't figure out which changes need to stay and what effect they will have. This is when you might need to resort to a manual method of comparison. You can look at the code that's already on the `main` and `develop` branches to make sure you aren't breaking anything. Then you can start looking at changes that were introduced on the feature branches and add them.

This can involve making a separate branch and copying and pasting code from multiple branches into it. Sometimes you run into more confusion when you use the Git resolution tool if you're facing large conflicts with little context. Usually, when I see a conflict with more than five lines of code in a single file, that's when I start evaluating my options for resolving them.

When you fix complex merge conflicts like this, make sure to run the app locally. Sometimes things can look fine in the code, but there are still runtime issues. This is where your tests will come in handy because you'll be able to find some of those unexpectedly affected areas. All the tools and conventions you've implemented early in the project are going to start paying off when you get to issues like this. You'll also want to double-check that the features you've merged are still working as expected. This is when you should bring in the devs who worked on the features to get validation.

Conclusion

Understanding the ways you can use your Git skills to help the team is a subtle thing you should do. The branching strategy you help shape is going to affect everything from the CI/CD pipeline to the way the team does their everyday work. It's going to affect how you debug larger issues, and it will create the history for the entire project. You also have to be aware that as the team grows, there will be conflicts between branches, and the team will often turn to you to handle the complex ones.

Stay on top of the common Git commands like the ones I covered in this chapter, such as `rebase`, `merge`, and `bisect`. You'll find new commands as you go through merge conflicts and discover ways to more efficiently manage the team's branches. As you solve any conflicts, get creative with your approaches and document them. When you learn new things, try to document them and show them to the team, and encourage the rest of the team to do the same. That's one way you can help everyone learn more about how Git works so that you aren't the only dev who feels comfortable with any scenarios that come up.

## CHAPTER 29

Project Management

There's more to your dev career than doing all the technical work. You'll have to do some form of project management. This is how you start taking more ownership for what gets shipped to production for users. Now is when you start really asking questions about features and the roadmap and work closer with the Product team. Get comfortable asking about the validity of a feature and push back when new functionality will change or break something already in place.

As the project matures, Product is going to want to collaborate with you and get your opinions on how features should work and what that looks like from a technical perspective as they expand the roadmap. You'll be expected to chime in with things they haven't considered, such as how designs might take longer to implement than it seems or the difference between frontend and backend work. You're going to be an expert on how the app works and how changes might affect it, so you have to become comfortable communicating that openly and honestly.

In this chapter, I'll go over:

- Approaching sprint discussions
- Defining and managing tasks to keep the team at a steady pace
- Handling communication with Product

This process is going to vary at every organization you work with, but you can bring up points from your experience that will be valid almost everywhere. The key is understanding where the lines are between you and Product so that you can better perform your role. I've been in some organizations where I've crossed the Product line too often, and I've had instances where I wasn't speaking up enough in Product discussions. Work with your manager to get a grasp on what the expectations are and make sure everyone knows them. It avoids a lot of confusion and miscommunication later.

 In the cases where I was crossing the Product line, that usually involved defining acceptance criteria for a feature. The Product team does a ton of user research that the devs aren't involved in and may not be aware of. So things like this can be left up to them, and you can ask all the questions you need to get clarification. Try not to make too many assumptions about how the feature should work from a user perspective and collaborate with Product to make that definition clear.

Sprint Discussions

There are a few common themes that come up during sprint discussions, such as estimates, requirements, and division of tasks. This is a group effort and takes collaboration. It may feel tedious at times, but it's helpful to ask as much as you can initially so that you and the team have a smooth sprint once it's started.

Estimates

Something that will come up early and often is Product asking for estimates. They are trying to get an idea of how long it will take to develop, test, and deploy a feature to production so that they can communicate a timeline with sales, customer support, and any other stakeholders. This may come up during sprint planning, when you and the team are picking up work, and you might feel pressured to agree on a date. Until you have all the requirements and designs as well as time to do some research, resist the urge to throw out a date or agree to one.

It's easy to look at a ticket and think it's simple to add something like a new dropdown or a new endpoint, but then you get into the weeds of it and find out it's way more complex than you thought. Do not give your most optimistic estimates because development rarely goes perfectly. Give yourself and the team some breathing room with larger estimates. You'll be surprised at what you run into when you try to make small changes, even if it's something like updating copy or colors. The last thing you want to happen is you and the team coming in late on deadlines because you underestimated how much work something will take.

There's an old saying: "underpromise and overdeliver." Even if you know for a fact that you can finish a certain amount of work, it's usually better to agree to a little less just in case something comes up. If you end up having time to finish everything and then some, then everybody's happy and you're not stressed out. Either way, you still meet the commitment you originally made.

I want to stress how important it is to not give the most optimistic estimate. When you know the app and the codebase really well, you can come up with a solution pretty quickly on the fly, and that's fine. You can include the details in the ticket unless you're trying to help another dev have a chance to think through a solution themselves. Also, don't give an estimate on work the team has to do until you talk it over with them.

Dev Capacity

It will take time to establish a baseline for the number of points the dev team can handle. When you have a new team or a new team member, it may take two to three sprints to get an accurate measure of the number of points the team can complete. This should include your buffer for overdelivery. You can see how much other work gets finished outside the feature and bug tickets. Eventually, this will account for days off and holidays as well. Until you have a few sprints to set the baseline, it's hard to say how much the team can get done.

Remember that point values will vary across organizations. You may work at an organization where an entire feature is 5 points and other places where the same work would be 13 points. Points can be associated with a certain amount of time; for instance, 5 points might represent a half week of work. But points are supposed to be a representation of how complex a task is (*https://oreil.ly/BRp3z*). They should take into consideration all the supporting activities you need to do.

Remember this when you are choosing tickets to work on for the sprint and leave yourself some capacity for other things. You will still have to do PR reviews, address bugs that come up from QA, and handle the other random things that inevitably pop up. When you max out the number of points or tasks you can handle, you don't leave yourself room for these other little things. You'll want to look out for the other devs, too. During sprint planning, when tickets are assigned and pointed, double-check with everyone that they've taken on a reasonable load.

It's easy to fall into a cycle of taking on too much and working more hours as the team slowly gets stressed out. This is when your experiences will come out because you know how much you can handle without getting burned out. It's tempting to try to show how much you know or how fast you can get through tickets, but that will lead you to a rough spot that can take months to overcome.

 Burnout is a real problem. I've experienced it several times over the course of my career, and each time it took months to come out of it. For me, it always starts by taking on a little more and more until my whole existence is work. Then, everything piles up, and eventually, I crack under the pressure. Burnout is not easy to recover from, so take steps to prevent it (*https://oreil.ly/m5_Q7*) from happening.

Feature Requirements

Another thing that can't be emphasized enough is making sure you have everything you need before you agree on an estimate for a ticket. All the designs and requirements should be ready for you so that you can accurately determine how long a ticket will take. Agreeing to incomplete tickets usually leads to scope creep, which balloons the work well past what you estimated. Of course, questions will come up as you do development, but you shouldn't have questions about the core functionality of a ticket.

You should also consider having a research category of tickets when the details of a feature are still being created. Figure 29-1 is an example of what that ticket might look like.

If Product hasn't written up specs, work with them to get that documented but try not to write it for them. This is where that fine line between responsibilities comes in. The specs should be able to tell you how the product works, what it should do, when it should do it, and how it affects the user. You should be able to break that information down into the technical implementation and ask Product more detailed questions. That's the ideal partnership between Product and the dev team. All your sprint discussions should start based on some documentation they give you. Figure 29-2 is an example of how a good ticket could be written using the Gherkin format (*https://oreil.ly/ae66c*) we discussed in Chapter 21.

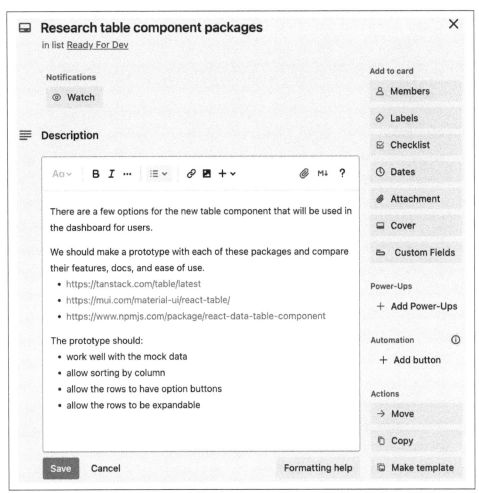

Figure 29-1. Example of a research ticket

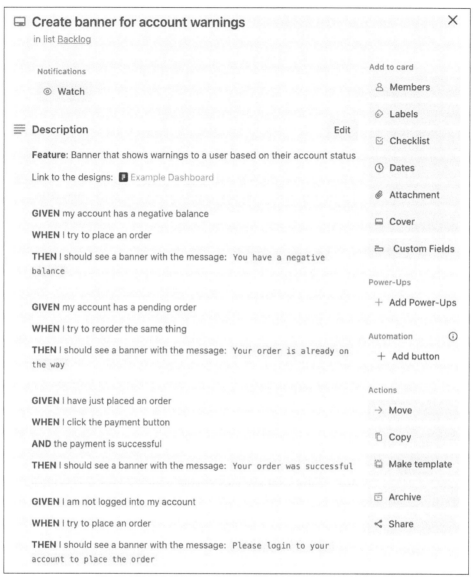

Figure 29-2. Example of a well-defined ticket

Push back hard on Product if the documentation is not ready for you and don't agree to any work that hasn't been properly defined. You might even push for things like epics to group a set of tickets under if the feature is large. An *epic* (*https://oreil.ly/ NlmPf*) is a large feature that can be broken into several stories. It likely has multiple components in a design and possibly involves backend updates. This requires multiple tickets to chunk that work into tasks a single dev can manage or for a few devs to work on independently. This is also how you can give better estimates for the overall feature because you know the smaller pieces that build it.

For medium features, you may have to work on a few components or make smaller backend updates. These tickets can also be grouped under an epic for better clarity, but that will be a decision for you and Product to make. Small features usually involve a few tickets and can generally be addressed by a single dev, so they don't need an epic. Work with your dev team to figure out how you need to break apart the feature to determine its size.

Dev Team Ticket Review

It's a good idea to review all the tickets or feature specs as a dev team so that everyone understands what's going on. This is how you can have more productive discussions with the Product team. While it does add another meeting to everyone's calendar, it will save you all time over the course of the sprint. By facilitating these dev meetings, you're taking more of a leadership role and showing your ability to juggle priorities outside the code.

When you have group dev discussions about tickets that haven't been thoroughly defined, more questions will come up. People on your team will have different experiences and perspectives that will help make the ticket and the work more complete. As an example of how this meeting might go, Figure 29-3 shows a poorly defined ticket.

Figure 29-3. Example of a poorly defined ticket before the dev meeting

Before the meeting, you should spend time going through tickets for the upcoming sprint to highlight the ones that need the most review. Set aside at least an hour to look over everything and start compiling a list of questions. Plan for the first 15–20 minutes of the meeting to be time for the team to review the tickets because it's likely they haven't had a chance. Send out reminders to the team a day before the meeting so that they can set aside time to review tickets. Sometimes it can be hard to get people to speak up during these meetings, so you can start with a question you have and then have everyone ask a question. It also helps to make a checklist of the things that should be defined in any ticket. Here's an example of some of the things I ask for in tickets:

- Where are the designs?
- What data do we need to display?
- What happens with different statuses?
- How should we handle missing values?
- Are there restrictions on the parameters a user inputs?

By the end of this process, you'll have a number of questions for the Product team. Send Product the team's questions ahead of sprint-planning meetings and make sure to follow up. By the time you get to sprint planning, the ticket will be refined and look similar to Figure 29-4.

As you get more comfortable with this process, you can start passing the responsibility to lead the dev meetings around so that others on the team can get that experience. Your sprint discussions will lead to discovering more about the feature than Product initially specified, and that's a great thing. It will help give everyone a more realistic view of how much work a feature will take, the approach that should be taken, and the context for why one approach is better than another.

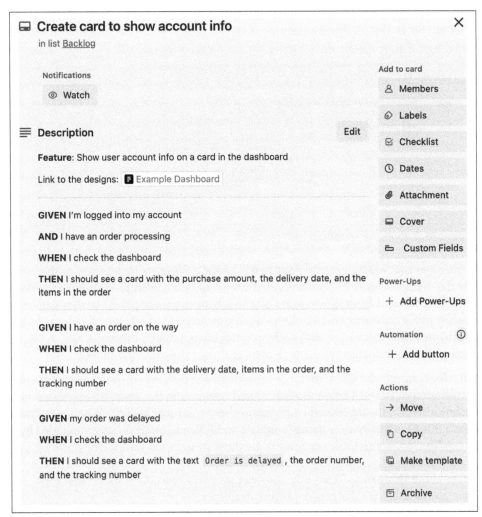

Figure 29-4. Example of the refined ticket after the dev meeting

Roadmaps

Whenever you have discussions about an upcoming sprint, you should review the Product roadmap. This will keep everyone up to date on what's coming and when the anticipated release dates are. That way, you aren't surprised by things the Product team has known about for a while. Reviewing the roadmap will keep everyone on track with priorities, and you can anticipate what you will focus on next. So if there's something you can do to help prepare the codebase for the next round of features in your current sprint, you can discuss it with the team to get early feedback. Figure 29-5 is an example of what a roadmap can look like.

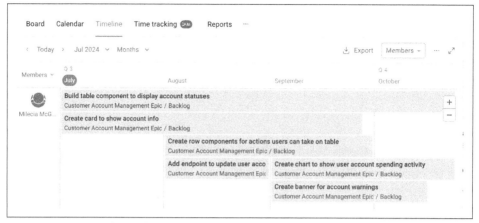

Figure 29-5. Example roadmap

Remember that roadmaps help your nontechnical colleagues make sense of the work the dev team is doing. This extends all the way up to leadership, such as VPs and C-suite executives. It keeps them aware of what's happening and when, so they can handle any public relations around all the work your team has been doing. It's easy to get lost in the code and forget about why the roadmap matters, but this helps the business present an informed message to users and any external stakeholders.

The dev team should also have some form of an engineering roadmap, even if it's just a collection of tickets related to updates and refactors in the code. It's important that technical concerns are brought up during these meetings as well. When you know that a third-party service is going to update an SDK, a package is being upgraded by a major version, some refactors need to be done to unblock future dev work, or you want some time to implement documentation or other DX tooling, Product needs to know about those tasks. That way, they can give you space to work on them without being pressed by stakeholders on feature deadlines.

A cool thing that happens when you start reviewing the Product and Engineering roadmaps together is you might find where new useful features can be added. Seeing the features expected for the year laid out in one place can generate some creative ideas. For example, Product might want to add email alerts to user actions, and you already have better event handling on the dev roadmap. That can lead to a new combination of the two tasks that gives you both what you need at the same time. Without that discussion, they would have been implemented separately and maybe at different times.

Defining and Managing Tasks

There are a lot of approaches to how you define and manage your tasks as a dev. Many of these will be based on personal preference, experience, and the way your organization works. A few things you may want to keep in mind are how your tasks fit into the roadmaps, how your work may overlap with other developers' work, feature priorities, and your own interests. These things will go into creating your own dev workflow, which will help you consistently finish all your tasks for a sprint and help out the rest of the team without too much stress.

Maintain Team Awareness

As you and the team work on features, keep yourself up to date on the roadmap and have a general idea of all the features that are currently in development. You'll be asked to help other team members with their tasks from time to time. Being aware of what everyone is working on is a great way to add value to the team. It doesn't mean you're responsible for tracking everything and making sure things get done on time. That's a job for the tech lead or engineering manager. This is for your own sanity, and it helps when discussions come up about how to shape some of your technical decisions.

Differences Between Tech Leads and Engineering Managers

A *tech lead* (*https://oreil.ly/MbEJi*) is a dev who has other responsibilities within a team with respect to their skills. For example, you might have a backend tech lead who handles some of the more difficult tasks with that part of the stack and becomes the go-to person for questions in that area. They're still individual contributors and don't have direct reports.

An *engineering manager* (*https://oreil.ly/zosvG*) is usually responsible for strategic planning in the department, budgeting, and hiring. They have direct reports and rarely get into the code. They may occasionally jump into the code, but they typically provide the resources for their reports to get their tasks finished.

For example, if someone on the team is implementing new shared components and you're also working on the frontend, you might find that there's some overlap in your work even if it's for a different feature. Or if someone is creating a new database table for the backend, you might be able to add your own fields to it instead of having conflicts when you try to create something they already made. Keeping mental notes of what others are doing will help you all avoid duplicate work. Even though you will have dev meetings throughout the week, it's useful to keep yourself aware of what's coming up.

Having a shared goal for the end of the sprint will keep the team focused. It brings a sense of unity to the tickets and clarifies with the team what they are building toward. As everyone works on their tickets, they will have a better idea of how what they are working on connects to the overall goal of the sprint and the work the rest of the team members are doing.

In some organizations, you'll find that Product puts tickets into the sprint based on the priority they have and the team's capacity. At other organizations, Engineering will have a more hands-on approach to deciding what tickets are in the sprint. Either way, tickets will be assigned to the team based on how much capacity an individual dev has and sometimes whether they are more focused on the frontend or backend. You might end up working on a large feature that spans a few months, or you might have a lot of smaller tickets that jump everywhere.

Write and Clarify Tickets

After you've done your research, created the smaller tickets, and discussed your findings with the relevant people, you can finally add details to the tickets you've created. Try to include as much as you can so that anyone on the team can pick up one of your tickets with few questions. Include links to feature specs, UI designs, and any other information that can help a dev get started. Also try to list some initial acceptance criteria so that when you do have those sprint discussions, there's a starting point.

If there's a specific feature or task that interests you, speak up! You don't want to be passive with the work you get to do. Keep in mind that you may not always get to do the stuff that interests you, but that will make you a better dev in the long run.

This may include researching tickets about something you've never worked with. When you're working on a research task, try to create smaller tickets as you discover functionality that needs to be added. You don't have to fill in all the details immediately, but having some initial placeholder tickets will help Product with planning deadlines and setting expectations early.

Figure 29-6 is an example of a large feature epic with smaller tickets.

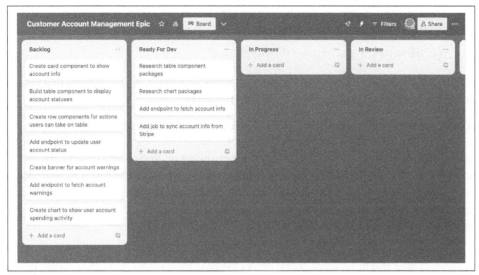

Figure 29-6. Feature epic with tickets in Trello

It's usually a good idea to have focused tickets for the frontend and backend work. Then you can have more details about the backend work by endpoints, resources that need to be created, and events that need to trigger actions in different systems. The frontend can be broken down into components that need to be added or updated, API requests that need to be made, and any hooks or other helper functions that need to be created. As you define these tasks, you want them to be as independent as you can make them.

As part of the focused tasks between the frontend and backend, it's helpful to have tickets to add mock data and tests. With this, the frontend devs know what to expect from the backend, and the backend devs understand what they need to do for the frontend. That will enable multiple devs to work on the same feature without having a lot of overlap. This really helps when someone has finished all their tickets for a sprint and is looking for small pieces of work to do to help keep the team moving forward. Again, it will be on your tech lead or engineering manager to coordinate who's working on what, but you can be a huge help by writing good tickets.

Consider Overhead Tasks

When it comes to managing your own tasks, you need to take a realistic look at your capacity:

- Are you going to be out a few days during the sprint?
- Do you anticipate working with QA to nail down bugs before a release?
- Is there a lot of dev work going on that will lead to a flood of PR reviews?

- Are any new team members joining? Are you integrating a new third-party service?

- Will there be any package version upgrades?

All of these will take away from your capacity for new work, and you have to account for them so that you don't end up taking on too much.

These are the subtle tasks that tend to be overlooked during sprint planning, so it's up to you to consider them for yourself. Bring up these tasks in your sprint discussions with Product so that they're aware of the other things on your plate. This helps set an example for the dev team because it will make others consider what they have to do as well. Then you all start making more accurate estimates for how much work you can get done. As your estimates become more accurate, Product can come up with more realistic deadlines for stakeholders.

Something else to keep in mind as you go through the tickets in your sprint is their priority. There might be some work you're looking forward to more than other parts, but stay focused on priorities. Work on the highest-priority tickets first, and then you can enjoy the end of your sprint as compared to rushing at the last minute. Things always come up when you're working on high-priority tickets that you don't expect or didn't account for. So it's better to start them as soon as you can.

Pace Yourself

You have to find a good balance between challenging yourself and taking on too much. The last thing you want to do is end up with more tasks in a sprint than you can handle. If Product wants you to switch your focus midway through a sprint, ask them what should be deprioritized. While it may be necessary to push through a heavy workload from time to time, that should not be the expectation every time. Be conscious of what you agree to because it will set a standard that will be hard to change as time goes on, and it may become part of the company culture if you agree each time the situation comes up.

You have probably experienced burnout a few times throughout your career. It's not the easiest thing to recover from, so it's best to try to avoid it. By keeping a reasonable workload, you set an example for the team to take care of themselves as well. As we discussed in Chapter 22 on debugging, make sure you take breaks from your work throughout the day. The Pomodoro technique (*https://oreil.ly/i71LF*) is a popular approach to balancing focused work time with regular breaks. It's easy to get hyperfocused on a task that you want to get finished, but take the break anyway.

Manage Context Shifting

Over the course of a day, you'll likely have multiple meetings, get messages from other devs, answer QA and Product questions, work on a few different tasks, and deal with any alerts or other miscellaneous happenings. This is a lot of context shifting. When you do that, it slows your workflow because you have to orient your mind to the new task on hand. Doing this multiple times throughout the day can cause mental fatigue and can even create some emotional overload.

When you're working on a feature and you're really focused, it can take a while to shift your thoughts to an unrelated meeting. So you have to do things to protect your flow state (*https://oreil.ly/070U1*) when you hit that groove. *Flow state* happens when you are completely focused on a single task and nothing else distracts you. One thing you can do is try a version of the Pomodoro technique where you won't respond to any messages or calls until your time is up. Unless production is on fire, most questions or tasks can wait 30 minutes or longer.

Another technique is to separate your day into discrete blocks. If you know you're more productive in the afternoons, block off a few hours then for the more difficult tasks. You can have a block of time in the morning just for meetings, impromptu pair-programming calls, and office hours when you're available for general questions. Later in the afternoon, you can make time for PR reviews or other meetings. The main thing is to have hours of time set aside for one specific type of work so that you aren't context switching every few minutes.

 I'll admit that it took me a while to learn how important protecting my time is. I used to think that when I received a message, I needed to respond immediately. Or if a team member reached out with a question, I thought I should drop everything and help them as soon as I could. This is not a sustainable way of working, and it led me to severe burnout several times. Blocking off time on my calendar to focus on coding, meetings, and other tasks really helped me become more efficient, and it keeps me from burning out. Remember, every message or alert you receive is not a fire. So it's fine to acknowledge someone's request and let them know you'll get back to them.

You can make a little game out of trying to combine contexts where you can. Maybe you're working on a feature with another dev, and you can include pair programming in your focus blocks of time. Or you can switch up your work environment to help make context switches faster. That could mean changing rooms, moving your monitor to a different angle on your desk, or changing the type of music you are playing. There are ways you can condition yourself to get in the flow state for all the tasks you're juggling.

Something that helps tremendously when you're trying to figure out how to organize your day is to record what you currently do for a few weeks. There are products that can help (*https://oreil.ly/jVsL-*) with that, such as WakaTime (*https://wakatime.com*) or even just a planner. You'll find patterns in your work routine that you can use to your advantage and optimize your schedule. It can be surprising when you really analyze what tasks you focus on and when you do them. As you go through your day, take notes on what you worked on and for how long. Record each time you shift contexts and what you switched between. You're creating your own personal time data that will help you determine what changes you should make.

If you don't use a time-management tool, this is the perfect time to start. When you have your tasks for the week laid out for you, it takes a bit of mental load off you because you aren't worried about what you need to do every day. My favorite time-management tool is a paper planner. Writing tasks down for the next two to four weeks helps me stay on top of everything from work to personal tasks. There's also a little satisfaction in physically crossing things off the list. But there are digital tools like Google Calendar (*https://oreil.ly/hMVt7*), Todoist (*https://todoist.com*), OneNote (*https://www.onenote.com*), Evernote (*https://evernote.com*), and Obsidian (*https://obsidian.md*) if you want something with more features.

A combination of these approaches will help you deal with context shifting more effectively and get more done with your time. Try out a few of them and feel free to use your creativity to come up with other techniques that work for you. Give each approach a few weeks to evaluate its effectiveness. Once you find what works for you, stick with it! You can experiment with new tools or different techniques from time to time, but you'll have a point of reference to come back to if things get really busy.

Keep Communication Open

One of the best things you can do is to foster a culture of communication for your team and others. If you see that a task is going to take longer than you thought, let the relevant people know as soon as you do so that there aren't any surprises. If you run into something in the code where you need to have a discussion with the team, bring it up. When you speak up about anything you encounter, that normalizes it for the team to do the same. You might find that others have the same questions.

 There are many environments, both professionally and culturally, where asking questions can be met with contempt even though no one knows the answer. Try to be the person who speaks up, no matter if you think it's a "stupid" question or not. I can't tell you how many times I've spent hours trying to find an answer for something I thought I should know just to find out that I've run into a larger-scale question that no one on my team can answer either.

It's better to overcommunicate and have people ask you to stop than to sit quietly and struggle for long periods of time. It helps if you mention things you've tried or ideas you have for solutions to get the conversation started. Your thoughts might reveal areas of the product that need more consideration, or you might find that some of the devs have expertise in areas you didn't know about. Always remember that no one knows everything, so don't pressure yourself to become an expert in everything. When you run into inconsistencies in requirements or things that shouldn't be allowed from a technical perspective, let Product and Design know.

Conclusion

This chapter went over some of the things you can do from a project management angle. There's always some overlap between your work and Product's work, so this will help you keep the division more equal. Don't be a passive listener in meetings because the things being discussed will directly affect your daily work. If it seems like Product has an overly ambitious roadmap and deadlines, point that out early. When you get tickets that don't have well-defined acceptance criteria, ask the detailed questions to get it.

It's your responsibility to manage your time efficiently, so do what you can to help yourself. This includes using time-management tools, taking breaks, and understanding the tasks that you have to do to keep feature development moving forward. If you have a hard time focusing or planning, consider reading *Getting Things Done* by David Allen (*https://oreil.ly/W0inR*). Reach out to the dev team to get help, suggestions, and feedback because everyone has different experience and they can all teach you something. This is how you grow into more leadership areas because you can be a multiplier for the team when you foster a better culture with your actions.

## CHAPTER 30

Understanding the Business Domain

One thing that will set you apart is deeply understanding the business domain you are developing an app for. Any dev can write software to meet requirements, but when you understand how a specific domain works, you'll be able to make better-informed decisions. The domains you may encounter could be industry specific, such as advertising and media, energy, government, financial services, health care, hospitality, manufacturing, logistics, retail, telecommunications, and travel. Domains could also include multiple industries or no industry at all.

A business domain expert is someone who deeply understands the industry they work in and many of the intricacies and problems in it. You'll find that often the domain experts aren't the people who create the product requirements or the devs who build the product. They're the people more on the business side who have seen a gap in the industry and are building a solution with help from others, like you. A good example of a domain expert is someone who has worked in health care for years and who has seen the problems that staff and patients deal with.

In this chapter, I'll go over:

- Domain-specific knowledge
- App needs for different business domains
- Architectural and system design decisions
- How to learn from other teams
- Documentation

You don't have to be that person who's worked in an industry for years to become a domain expert. But you do have to have a genuine interest in learning as much as you can about a specific domain. That means you'll have to step away from the developer world and talk to domain experts and people who currently work in that domain. Doing some research on what's currently happening in an industry will help you gain some of that knowledge. It's equally important to understand the history of an industry so that you know what has already been tried and the results. This is one of the fun things that many developers at all levels tend to overlook in favor of furthering their tech skills.

Make sure you don't assume you have all the answers, even with your new domain knowledge. Domain experts have more experience and understand the processes and systems better than you. They often have undocumented systems that accomplish specific tasks. We want to understand those steps to help automate them with software, but we can't do that without the experts' help validating that things are doing what they're supposed to.

Domain-Specific Knowledge

At this point, there are a lot of different paths you can take in your career and your skill development. Regardless of whether you want to stay on the individual-contributor path or move over to the management track, knowing how to learn about a business domain will be a huge asset.

Every product you work on is providing a service to the organization's customers. The organization is building this product because it's something that has a competitive advantage in some way. This advantage may not even be a technical one because its importance may be found in a nontechnical aspect. Maybe a logistics company has found a new way to organize inventory, and the software is just an aid to that. When you get into the business domain, unless the domain is technology, your technical knowledge isn't what you should lean on because it's secondary to the organization's focus. Remember, you are always building software to solve some kind of problem. The software is how you deliver a solution to the users, but it may not be the solution itself.

A quote from *Empowered* by Marty Cagan (Wiley) resonates with this topic:

> In strong product companies, technology is not an expense, it is the business. Technology enables and powers the products and services we provide to our customers. Technology allows us to solve problems for our customers in ways that are just now possible. Whether the product or service is an insurance policy, a bank account, or an overnight parcel delivery, that product now has enabling technology at its core.

There are a few strategies you can use to familiarize yourself with different domains. I'll go over three of them.

Learn from People Working Directly in the Domain

The first strategy is learning from domain experts where they are. It's always great to start with people who already work in the domain every day because they can tell you exactly what they do and how. These are the people who know what is really happening behind the scenes to keep everything moving. For example, if you're working on software for a manufacturing organization, go to the shop and talk to the machinists and mechanics who actually build the physical products.

You can also join online communities or go to meetups and conferences for that domain. It doesn't hurt to join some organizations that are focused on people in that specific domain. Professional trade associations and standards bodies will help you connect with the people doing this work every day. That could include local chapters of an engineering community or a casual get-together for people who work on CNC machines.

You're trying to figure out where these experts are and go to them. You can start internally at your organization by talking to some people in sales and marketing to see who they are targeting. The main thing is that you make an effort to show up where they are having discussions and listen to them. It's OK if you don't understand what they are talking about in the beginning or the actual meaning behind the changes you read about. Ask questions when you have them, and you'll find people who are happy to answer you.

It's good to learn about some of the history of the domain because that will give you a lot of context for the current state. You might start reading articles about the news in an industry and learn about how it's changed over time and who the leaders are. This might even help you understand the purpose of your organization's work. It also helps establish you as a domain expert because you will start to understand and speak the jargon for that domain. Then you can bring in your technical skills and show how they apply to that domain in a meaningful way. It will also give you more empathy when you're developing features for users because you really get what the use case is.

Take Courses

The second thing you can do to build domain knowledge is take courses. There are free online courses for just about anything now. With a few searches, you can find a course on logistics or hospitality. If you want a more structured approach, courses will typically give you that. It also gives you a chance to deeply learn about something not related to your technical skills. Some devs see this as a conflict with keeping technical skills up to date because it takes time away from the code and other technical decision making. I personally think it helps broaden your perspective with using the tools because you can focus more on what matters: the product.

Consider taking courses at a local community college or another type of institution and see if your organization will pay for it. These programs give you hands-on experience in what a domain is really about. You can get something from talking to people and reading on your own, but some domains benefit from a more structured introduction. I suggest selecting one domain and trying to find free courses to start with to decide if that's the domain you really want to do a deep dive into.

Work in the Domain

The third approach to gaining domain knowledge is to go work in that domain for a while! You might find a way to get the experience by volunteering with different organizations. For a while, I was interested in construction, and I was able to get involved with Habitat for Humanity, a nonprofit that builds or updates houses for people in the community. It was a great way to help people and learn a lot at the same time. You can also look for part-time opportunities so that you can stay in tech while you explore another domain. The best way I've found to get this exposure is to ask local business owners if they need help and explain to them what you're trying to do.

Maybe you've been thinking about what you would do if you didn't write software, and you've wanted to explore other options. If you are able to do so, working in a domain for a while will give you all kinds of new skills. This approach isn't for everyone, and it requires a much larger commitment than the others discussed so far, but it can be fun and give you more perspective on the technology industry as a whole.

This will open a whole new world to you, which might even inspire you to try the entrepreneur route. One way to come up with business ideas is to figure out what an industry is lacking, and the best way to do that is firsthand experience. Even if you don't take on a job or volunteer opportunity to learn more about a domain, listening to domain experts after you have some general understanding of how the domain operates will provide tidbits on the missing pieces or pain points. You can take those and expand further to figure out how your tech skills and domain knowledge can overlap, and that can give you a target to focus on in the domain.

Architectural and System Design Decisions

After you've gained more understanding about the business domain, you can use it to drive some architecture designs for the software. You can use clean architecture (*https://oreil.ly/QoDVj*), CRUD (create, read, update, and delete) architecture, or layered architecture, and these will work most of the time. But if you're working in a more complex domain, you might choose an architecture that better fits it. There is some overlap between the domain-based architectures and the others, so be mindful of the complexity that you introduce into the design pattern for the app.

Domain-Driven Design

Domain-driven design (DDD) is an architecture that involves designing the product to match the business domain. It takes more work to implement up front because you and the team have to work together with domain experts to come up with a shared language that describes the functionality consistently. This involves creating a domain model that reflects the rules, processes, and entities in the business domain. By having all of this in the beginning, you can set the code up to precisely meet the needs of the business.

There are several parts to the architecture that you have to define: bounded contexts, entities, value objects, aggregates, and events. Using this approach typically involves microservices that use *bounded contexts*, parts of the code that are separated by business functionality.

Entities in this architecture are objects with unique identities that aren't defined by their attributes. These are usually things that may have attributes that change over time and need to be tracked. An example of an entity is an order because it has a consistent identity, such as an order ID, that doesn't change based on the total price, the customer, or the products. But it will likely have a status attribute that needs to be tracked and updated over time. These are also called *reference objects* because while the attributes they have may change, what they represent in the business remains the same. Figure 30-1 shows what an order entity might look like.

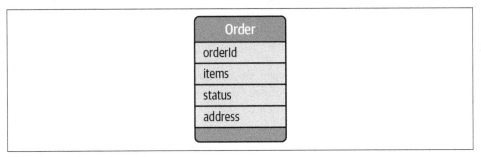

Figure 30-1. An order entity

You could have any values or types in the attributes for this order entity, and it will still represent an order to the business. Entities always have a specific ID, are mutable, and typically have a lifespan. So while an order will always be part of the organization's data, it's fine if the attributes change as long as the ID remains the same.

Value objects, on the other hand, are defined by their attributes, are typically immutable, and don't have unique IDs. This includes things like addresses, prices, and dates.

In our example, a value object might be the customer. Figure 30-2 shows what the address value object looks like.

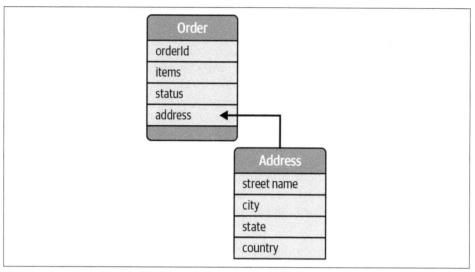

Figure 30-2. An address value object related to the order entity

You can think of a value object as a type for an attribute in the entity. If you change one of the attributes in the type, it makes a completely new object. For example, if someone updates their shipping address, we don't want to update the old one because it could be their billing address. So that would lead to a new instance of the address being passed to the order. You can usually think about the relationship between entities and value objects as the difference between a table and a row in a database. An entity could represent a table while a value object may represent some columns in a row of that table.

Aggregates show relationships between entities and values to represent how they are grouped together. For example, if you take an order and add more info to it, such as a whole customer entity, that could then be seen as an aggregate because it's grouping information.

Events are the triggers in the system that make different parts of the domain react based on changes that happen across the bounded contexts. For example, if a customer has enabled automatic ordering of a product by a certain time, when the date passes, it can trigger events to charge the customer and ship their products.

When the business domain is complex and has a lot of overlapping dependencies between parts of the system, it may be worth the effort to set all this up. This architecture does have a steep learning curve because of all the domain knowledge the team needs and the intentionality you need to have when creating the entities, values, events, and bounded contexts. All of these pieces will grow in complexity as the organization grows to have more offerings.

You have to make sure events are handled correctly so that your system doesn't end up in a broken state where data isn't being updated as expected or the events aren't being triggered at the right times. This takes special effort when you're working with third-party systems because data can get out of sync between what you have in your database and what they show users in their systems. Keeping bounded contexts clean can also become difficult as you start to need data from one context to trigger functionality in another context.

One of the best resources on DDD is *Domain-Driven Design: Tackling Complexity in the Heart of Software* by Eric Evans (Addison-Wesley). This was the book that established the DDD architecture in the early 2000s, so it has all the information about how DDD should work and be implemented by your team. You can also find some good information about DDD in this blog post (*https://oreil.ly/Nvnio*). DDD is such a huge topic that numerous books have been written about it with plenty of in-depth examples. Some of these books include *Implementing Domain-Driven Design* by Vaughn Vernon (Addison-Wesley), *What Is Domain-Driven Design?* by Vladik Khononov (O'Reilly), and *Learning Domain-Driven Design* by Vladik Khononov (O'Reilly). I highly encourage you to take a look at these resources because they have entire chapters dedicated to some of the concepts I've only briefly mentioned here.

C4 Design

The *C4 model* (*https://c4model.com*) is another type of architectural design that can be used when you understand the business domain of your product. You'll still need to work with domain experts to create a shared language and understand the relationships among the parts of the system. This breaks down the diagramming process into four parts: the system context, containers, components, and code. The system context is made up of multiple containers. Each container has multiple components, and each component has code in it. These take the high level of the software business domain and zoom into the individual parts at different levels.

The *system context* is where you typically start because it defines the product you're building. It's the most abstract of all the layers in this architecture. This is where you'll define how your product fits into the business domain and what problem you're solving. The containers in this architecture are defined as frontend apps, backend apps, databases, serverless functions, and content storage like S3 buckets.

This terminology takes time to adjust to because we call a lot of things *containers*. The same goes for *components* in this architecture. Containers are similar to what you might think of for a frontend architecture, but it applies to every part of the system. Your backend can be described in terms of components in this architecture when you group functionality together. For example, all the methods and endpoints that handle orders can be called a component in this context. *Code* refers to the software you'll write to make up the components.

You can organize the code into folders and files you'll write in the components. All of these pieces are connected in a diagram with lines that represent their relationships between one another, which lets you visualize how the smallest pieces of your software fit in the business domain. This will enable you to create an architecture that works like a map you can zoom in and out of when you need clarification on something in the domain. Tools that explicitly let you build C4 models include Miro (*https://oreil.ly/Vwzbs*), Lucidchart (*https://oreil.ly/-5z4n*), IcePanel (*https://oreil.ly/bRzlb*), and Mermaid (*https://oreil.ly/eyCyY*).

A good resource on the C4 model is *The C4 Model for Visualising Software Architecture* by Simon Brown (Leanpub). This helpful visual (*https://oreil.ly/hGrBC*) breaks down the different layers of the architecture. The main thing to remember is that the C4 model was made to help document how parts of the system work in an easy-to-read way.

Learning from Other Teams

To understand the business domain of your organization with more focus on what you're building, reach out to the internal teams that engineering doesn't commonly talk to, including sales, marketing, finance, and customers. This is where you have to take initiative because opportunities to talk to these other teams don't come up organically.

Get on Sales Calls

Developers don't usually interact much with the Sales team or the sales process. When we do, it's usually to bring technical validation to a call so that customers understand our product better. That's the perfect reason to jump on a call with a member of the Sales team. You can learn more about what customers need and what drives the revenue for the organization. Getting involved in this process is a great way to get insights to bring back to the Engineering and Product teams.

Something interesting that happens on these calls is understanding how the software you build fills a need in another organization. This is especially true when your product is for a nontech industry. Being able to see the real-world application makes a difference in how you think about features and how you implement them. It will also help you understand how the product is demonstrated by people who aren't involved in the development process. You'll be talking about technical implementation, and that might bring up some ideas you want to take back to the dev team.

At this phase, you aren't going to provide technical support or help the customer integrate anything. You could help with the sales demos and highlight functionality that the Sales team doesn't know about or show different ways the product can be used. Be careful about this and make sure you coordinate what you'll do with the salesperson. This is a great time to see how customers view the product you're building and get the perspective of stakeholders. It will also shed light on the importance of your role in the organization. You already know you're valued for your technical skills, but this will give you a new angle for looking at the software you build.

Join User Research Studies

Participate in or watch user research studies or user testing sessions. These are commonly led by user researchers, product owners, or UX designers, depending on your organization. This is one way the Product team comes up with the features that you work on. They reach out to existing customers to see if there's anything that could be improved in the app and then get on a call to walk through that with customers. Sometimes the best features come from a user just talking about what they do in the app and what they wish they had.

This is also how the Design team gains an understanding of how users actually interact with things. They might present the user with multiple designs for the same screen and watch how they navigate through different tasks. Then they can take the best from all the designs and make one user-refined experience.

Talk to Marketing

The Sales team might be closing the deal, but marketing helps generate the leads. Marketing's activities include creating social media campaigns, running booths at conferences, developing and researching customer personas to learn where they are and what they want, and raising awareness of what the organization does through networking and building relationships across the industry. Marketing creates the funnel of customers that leads to sales. So they have to understand the product well enough to talk about it at a high level.

Reach out to someone in marketing to see if you can occasionally sit in on their discussions just to better understand what they talk about in regard to the product. You might learn that parts of the app are unclear to them, so they describe it in an unexpected way. You can also learn about the customer personas they've made and figure out more about the target audience for the software you're building. This can help you think about accessibility, the location of tools, and even naming conventions.

You can review product screenshots, content copy, and videos to make sure they make sense with the capabilities of the app. This is another way you can get stakeholder feedback from the people who are trying to get others interested in the software you build. In all the meetings you go to, take notes and review them later. You could find out that something that was hard to implement is also hard for nontechnical users to understand.

Listen in on Customer Support Calls

This is something that is crucial to product development. Understanding the issues customers have while using the product will help you figure out where things can be improved. You could also help the Support team learn more about the features of the app. Or you can create features that help the Support team assist customers better. Sometimes people know they're having difficulties with something, but they can't explain what they need. When you come in with the knowledge of how the app works under the hood, you can see where improvements can be made more quickly than they can explain the problem.

This might be a small thing, like better documentation or naming conventions. Or it could be something larger, such as a clearer layout for a page, refactored features, or new tools. Working directly with customers will show you edge cases you didn't know could happen. This comes up a lot when users need to log in with another service like Google or Facebook. Understanding their struggles will give you more empathy for users as you build features, and it will lead you to ask more questions about requirements.

The things you'll learn on customer calls will help you consider internal stakeholder needs more as well. This is something that can get overlooked in favor of getting more features out to customers. But if the product can't be supported adequately, those new features will end up causing more customer frustration than they will solve. This will show you how you're an internal stakeholder, too, because you might find yourself doing hacky things in the code to figure out where a user's problem stems from.

Learn About Legal

This is an area you don't have to get super familiar with, but it helps to have a little knowledge about it. These are the people who make sure the organization doesn't get into legal trouble because laws, regulations, or compliances aren't met correctly. A few examples include PCI, HIPAA, GDPR, and international embargos. You might meet with them once or twice or even ask for a list of legal requirements for the software that you can review. This can help you do some technical auditing to make sure your systems can pass a legal audit.

Since you're likely using third-party services or open source tools in some capacity, you need to make sure they meet compliance rules with the country your product originates from. This can get tricky to pin down since software is developed by thousands of people all over the world, but once you have a list of rules, it's a little easier to know what you're looking for. Talking to the legal team can also bring out more of the business domain you didn't know about. It's unlikely that they use the software, but they can tell you the legal implications for it.

Documentation Considerations

While it's not solely your responsibility to document everything in the business domain for the Engineering and Product teams, it will help if you bring some considerations to them. You want to help everyone keep the documentation organized in a way that's easy to search through. When you're writing docs that are centered on the business domain, it can be easy to bloat them with all the info you've learned from domain experts, other teams in the organization, and even the notes you've taken. Here are some things you can do to maintain the docs.

Define Jargon

Since this is documentation for the business domain, there might be some acronyms or jargon that others are unfamiliar with. Don't assume that people know what words mean because this documentation could quickly become part of the onboarding material for new team members, both in Engineering and in other departments. This can help the dev team understand why parts of the architecture are divided like they are in the software and why you implement code a certain way.

You can distill some of the more common things you've learned about the domain here and work with Product to get more of the details. The Product team will likely have more domain knowledge, so collaborate with them by having them contribute to the docs. When they introduce new features that bring in another part of the domain, have them clearly define it in these shared docs.

Only Keep Relevant Info

It can be easy to try to cram everything you've learned about the business domain into the documentation, but try to highlight the main points and put the details in an appendix, asides, or footnotes. Focus on things that pertain to the architecture and features so that new devs can understand how the code fits together and why. You don't need to go into detail about the history of the domain or how the marketing department has different customer personas. Find a balance between giving enough context for the features and providing some background on how the domain operates. Keep in mind that if the info was useful to you, it will likely be useful to others.

Share Your Knowledge

Once you've compiled all your knowledge, share it with the team! You can do things like lunch-and-learn meetings to informally teach others about the domain. These can be quick 15- to 30-minute meetings where you talk about behind-the-scenes processes, takeaways you've gotten from professional organizations, and how the domain connects to the software. You can also help others start presenting on domain topics that interest them.

A more laid-back approach to sharing knowledge is posting the latest news or interesting tidbits you come across in your research to your dev team chats, such as part of a conversation you had at a meetup or an article you ran across. You could even introduce this as something the team takes turns with. Maybe every other day or at least once a week, someone shares a new thing they learned in the chat.

Show How the Product Affects the Organization

When you're talking about the business domain, show how the software you and the team are building fits into the way the organization generates revenue. This is an area where you can use diagrams to clearly illustrate the gap that the product is filling in the domain. Having this included in your documentation can give the entire Engineering department a better understanding of what they do and why. It can also show the rest of the organization how important the software work is.

Departments are frequently siloed, so it can be hard to describe what you do in the context of the whole organization. But when you have these kinds of docs to refer to, you can easily show the impact you're making every day. This is going to overlap some with any organizational charts that are in place, but keep it tailored to Engineering and perhaps your team specifically by including the details of your app in the diagram. Having diagrams and definitions like this might also make it easier to update your architecture and figure out which approaches are better for the long-term maintenance of the product along with the changes in the domain.

When you connect your team's work to the overall goals of the organization, that helps the dev team really feel the impact they make. It's easy for the team to become disconnected when they're focused on getting features finished for a sprint. Showing them how their work contributes to the direct growth of the organization can be a huge morale boost and help them see how valuable their skills and inputs are.

Conclusion

In this chapter, we went over some ways you can learn more about a business domain and why that's important. It will help you tremendously to have some knowledge about the domain you work in because it can change the tools you use or the approaches you take. It helps you to become more involved in the organization holistically. It's always good to remember that you aren't writing code just to build a technically sound product. You're writing code to create a product that meets the needs of its users and maybe entertains them a bit.

Domain knowledge coupled with relationship-building skills as you talk to other departments in the organization will make you invaluable to any organization you work with. It will also make you a more thoughtful developer because you'll be more likely to think about things like regulations and laws the app may fall under. You'll understand the impact your changes will have on customers and how that drives business as a whole. With this kind of domain knowledge, the relationships you create, and the technical skills you have, you'll be a more well-rounded senior dev in many aspects.

## CHAPTER 31

Working on Different Types of Projects over Your Career

Throughout this book, you've built a greenfield product, which means you built it from scratch and made all the initial decisions on how the code should be developed. While you'll get a chance to work on projects like these, it's a less common scenario. Often there is an existing codebase with established practices, and there are core functionalities that can't be easily changed.

As you go to different organizations over the course of your career, you'll pick up a lot of new skills and patterns from existing projects. You'll join teams of other senior devs and learn new paradigms and methods for building apps. When you get a chance to do something similar to what you've done throughout this book, you'll go in with even more experience. A greenfield project will stretch you in different ways after you've worked on legacy projects for a while.

In this chapter, I'll go over:

- Considerations for brand-new apps
- Considerations for existing apps
- How all of this affects your career

This is where you can explore your experience and how it differs between greenfield and legacy projects. I'll give you some key things to look for depending on what type of project you're working on.

Considerations for Brand-New Apps

You have to make a lot of decisions early that will determine the future maintainability of a greenfield codebase. You'll be able to refactor things and swap out components and packages for better ones in the future, but having a well-defined base is going to make this a smoother process. While you'll spend a lot of time and energy creating diagrams, writing docs, and developing processes in the beginning, it's effort well spent as the codebase evolves over the years and you aren't the only dev working on it.

Remember that you won't go in having thought out every possible scenario. You will discover some things as you go and get feedback on what you've built so far. But you can set up a strong foundation to help spark those conversations earlier rather than later. There's a balance you and the Product team will have to find between pre-planning and actually building something.

Working with a greenfield app is your chance to set up the codebase in a way you wish other projects you've worked on had been initialized. With all your knowledge, you've experienced some of the pitfalls and seen mistakes made in other organizations. Whether it's for a startup, a mid-sized organization, or an enterprise-level organization, a brand-new app has a lot of the same considerations. You'll need to consider the tools the organization favors as the starting point, and then you can start bringing in your experiences. Something that will help is having your own checklist that you've developed over the years.

I'll walk you through the things I do on every greenfield full stack app. This can be used as a lightweight checklist to get you started. Each of these points in the checklist involves many details that we've covered in the previous chapters of this book.

Understand the Problem You're Trying to Solve

Before you even set up a new repo, you need to understand the problem that the software you're building is trying to solve, like we did in Chapter 1. This will involve numerous calls with the Product team and senior leadership so that you can nail down the functional needs. You'll even need to talk to higher-level business colleagues to understand more about the business domain and how they foresee the software helping in that area, what the weaknesses of the software may be, and their plans for how the product solves a domain need. Then when you talk to Product, you'll have a clearer understanding of the roadmap.

At this point, you're trying to look at the roadmap and make technical decisions that will grow as the app grows. When you get a firm understanding of the problem, you can start choosing tools and services that will work best and require the least amount of refactoring years from now. It may help to create a software bill of materials (SBOM) to keep track of which tools solve which technical problems, their security implications, and how well they integrate with one another.

Generating a Simple SBOM with AuditJS

There are a number of tools (*https://oreil.ly/uzDfl*) you can use to generate SBOMs of different detail levels, but a quick one to use in your repos is AuditJS (*https://oreil.ly/6kOW3*). It will generate a list of all the dependencies in your repo, the current versions, and the vulnerabilities they have. Figure 31-1 is an example of what that will look like.

```
[383/486] - pkg:npm/resolve@1.22.8 - No vulnerabilities found!
[384/486] - pkg:npm/restore-cursor@3.1.0 - No vulnerabilities found!
[385/486] - pkg:npm/rfdc@1.4.1 - No vulnerabilities found!
[386/486] - pkg:npm/rollup-plugin-visualizer@5.12.0 - No vulnerabilities found!
[387/486] - pkg:npm/rollup@4.20.0 - 1 vulnerability found!

  Vulnerability Title:  [CVE-2024-47068] CWE-79: Improper Neutralization of Input During Web Page Generation ('Cross-site Scriptin
g')
  ID:  CVE-2024-47068
  Description:  Rollup is a module bundler for JavaScript. Versions prior to 2.79.2, 3.29.5, and 4.22.4 are susceptible to a DOM C
lobbering vulnerability when bundling scripts with properties from `import.meta` (e.g., `import.meta.url`) in `cjs`/`umd`/`iife` f
ormat. The DOM Clobbering gadget can lead to cross-site scripting (XSS) in web pages where scriptless attacker-controlled HTML ele
ments (e.g., an `img` tag with an unsanitized `name` attribute) are present. Versions 2.79.2, 3.29.5, and 4.22.4  contain a patch
for the vulnerability.
  CVSS Score:  6.1
  CVSS Vector:  CVSS:3.1/AV:N/AC:L/PR:N/UI:R/S:C/C:L/I:L/A:N
  CVE:  CVE-2024-47068
  Reference:  https://ossindex.sonatype.org/vulnerability/CVE-2024-47068?component-type=npm&component-name=rollup&utm_source=audit
js&utm_medium=integration&utm_content=4.0.45

[388/486] - pkg:npm/rxjs@7.8.1 - No vulnerabilities found!
[389/486] - pkg:npm/safe-buffer@5.2.1 - No vulnerabilities found!
[390/486] - pkg:npm/safer-buffer@2.1.2 - No vulnerabilities found!
[391/486] - pkg:npm/scheduler@0.23.0 - No vulnerabilities found!
[392/486] - pkg:npm/seed-random@2.2.0 - No vulnerabilities found!
[393/486] - pkg:npm/seedrandom@3.0.5 - No vulnerabilities found!
[394/486] - pkg:npm/semver@5.7.2 - No vulnerabilities found!
[395/486] - pkg:npm/semver@7.5.3 - No vulnerabilities found!
```

Figure 31-1. SBOM example

Build the Data Schema

In Chapter 3, you saw that deciding how to model the data is an important step because it will affect the tools you choose and the way the app can grow in the future. Some standard things you want to build into your schema, whether you use a SQL or noSQL database, are audit values such as a "created at" date, an "updated at" date, and a user ID for who made the update. Many ORM frameworks add these fields automatically. These are applicable to any table you create. You should also consider relationships between your data so that you can decide on the most performant way to store and reference values.

This is where tools like dbdiagram.io (*https://dbdiagram.io*) or Miro (*https://miro.com*) will help you organize and present your ideas for the data schema, data types, and relationships like you did in Chapter 3. Take your time and refer to the roadmap as you come up with your initial ideas for the data schema. Keep expandability in mind because this is going to need to scale over time, and it may eventually be integrated with other systems, such as a data warehouse or a data pipeline, to get insights directly from the tables. Keep naming conventions in mind as well because that will help clearly and accurately describe what data you're storing.

Decide on an Architecture

The system architecture is a huge decision because it's what the dev team will be locked into over time. That's why this was covered throughout the book, in Chapters 5, 6, 10, and 23. It's important for you to pick a simple but flexible architecture to get started with. Your options include any combination of backend monoliths, microservices, frontend monoliths, and micro frontends. Based on what you know about the business domain and the current roadmap, you can make some guesses for how the app will grow and let that drive your architecture. Make sure to create as many diagrams as you need to show how everything connects and then keep them up to date.

It's a tedious task to diagram the architecture, but including everything in this initial process will help you catch potential pitfalls early. Try to build out a full diagram and then make iterations to refine it. Include your background jobs, workers, events, endpoint connections to the frontend, and any third-party services you can think of. You don't have to have everything for the app figured out at this stage, but a good estimate will help give you and the team a strong starting point as more decisions come up.

Pick Your Cloud Provider

Your cloud provider is going to determine everything from the services you have available to the bill the organization has to pay every month. Do some cost analysis for three or four cloud providers and compare the costs to the services you need. Be realistic about your user base and how it's projected to grow. Look into other services that integrate into the cloud platforms. Creating a spreadsheet with your needs and doing a comparison between platforms will help you and the organization make a cost-effective selection.

You also need to consider what skills devs have or would be interested in developing because building a team requires people who can work with the tools you choose. Bring security considerations into this evaluation, especially if you're working in a heavily regulated domain. Think about how hard it would be to migrate to a different cloud provider if something were to happen. If you can, test out the services in a few cloud providers to determine how easy it is to find help with issues and how configuration will work.

Build the Backend

This is when you start implementing the architecture you've designed. You can begin choosing the tools you want to use in the codebase to make development smoother, like you did in Chapter 2. It helps to set up some scaffolding to have boilerplate folders and file structures that the team can get started with based on your architecture and data schema so that you have an idea of how you want to start adding features.

Connect the app to the database and create your seed script, like you did in Chapter 3. It will also help you to write an endpoint or two just to have something to test with. You can start with smaller features, such as an endpoint that gets an order from the database and one that updates a customer profile. The goal is to get something working so that you know you have all the key connections, permissions, and environment variables in place before the dev team starts focusing on the code.

Build the Frontend

Similar to the backend, you're going to implement your frontend architecture and spec out the app structure you want to go with. If you've decided on a monolithic frontend, you can start with the folder structure so that you organize components, utility methods, and API calls early. Or if you go with a micro-frontend architecture, as we discussed in Chapter 13, you can start making the different repos that will become the components for the overall frontend. This is where you want to choose frontend tools and decide how you call endpoints and how you handle styles.

Try to get a main container component and a smaller component created to test how the app runs. Then make an API request from the smaller component to make sure you can connect to the backend without problems. Check for some initial responsiveness with your designs and start scaffolding some of the shared functionality. Adding some tests at this phase will also set the foundation for a level of code coverage that the dev team agrees on.

Integrate the Backend and Frontend

After you've done the initial checks with the frontend setup, you and the team will start adding more features. Even with all the planning, documentation, and diagramming, there will still be weird connection issues, such as what we addressed in Chapter 23. You'll run into things like the API not having permissions enabled for the frontend, names and types not matching across the frontend and backend, and CORS (*https://oreil.ly/4Vcf4*) issues. This is likely when you'll start seeing areas of both sides that can be refactored.

A huge, very public incident (*https://oreil.ly/0sHJ6*) happened when the teams working on the FAFSA form didn't do these checks. There's only so much you can develop in isolation, and even then you should be talking to one another.

At this point, you're getting a full view of how the app will grow and the considerations the team needs to make going forward. Reference and update your architecture diagram as you find complex areas and new relationships between the frontend and backend. This is when you can start making more strict decisions and conventions for the project going forward. You can use this as a chance to refine your PR review and deployment processes, too.

Set Up Your CI/CD Pipeline

In Chapter 27, you built a simple CI/CD pipeline. This involves setting up any environments you want to deploy the frontend and backend to and figuring out where to store secrets and credentials. This will likely fall on the DevOps team to handle, but you're expected to help them check that the app is deployed and working as expected. That means you'll look at which endpoints are being called to make sure the environments are connected on the frontend and backend correctly. You'll do data checks to make sure data is coming from the right environment.

Check your cloud services to ensure that assets are in the correct locations and are configured with appropriate access levels. Set up any automations for your branches that will help get your changes out consistently. This is a good time to check the bundle size of your build to see if there's room for optimization. If you're going to run your apps in containers, check that the containers are configured for your environments.

Perform QA Testing

Work with the QA team to fully test the app and write test cases to cover all the functionality required by Product as well as any edge cases you have found. Get Product involved and do demos as you build and deploy features to get some user acceptance testing. This is also a good time to discuss automated testing as a task that can be shared between QA and the dev team.

If there isn't a dedicated QA team in the organization, you can perform testing based on the feature specs and designs you have. Check how the app works in different browsers, with different network speeds, and with multiple types of users. Force the app to throw errors and see how well it handles them. Look for discrepancies in values you get from the backend compared to what gets displayed. Check to see if data is being synced at the expected time and updating tables correctly.

Check Your App in Production

The first time you deploy your app to production, there will be things you need to adjust. You might find that there are some configs or resources that need to be updated to match the load in production. Or you might realize that you only have user roles set up in other environments and you need to add them. This is a time to check how secure your app is by looking at network responses to see if any PII is leaked. See if you can force the app to give you access to resources that should be protected.

Look at things from a user's perspective here because this is exactly what a user will interact with. As you fetch data from more third-party services, you'll notice that there is certain data you can test only in production. Try to have test accounts and test users or a way to toggle between user roles available in production to avoid using real user data. Check your logs to make sure they're recording events and your alerts are working.

Considerations for Existing Apps

Existing apps are sometimes called "legacy" apps. These are codebases that existed before you joined the team that originally created them, and they will make up the majority of the apps you'll work on. Most organizations will need you to come in and add new features, maintain the codebase, and make improvements where you can. This is where things become less clear because not every team has adequate documentation or a good understanding of the problem they're trying to solve. You can bring fresh ideas to something that everyone is used to working around.

Get Access to the Services You Need

Any existing app will already be connected to the relevant services, so you'll need access to all of them. This is something that gets overlooked until you realize you need to do something you can't. It's very common that this is how you end up determining what you need credentials for, but it's not very efficient. Ask for access to all the services when you're setting up the project for the first time and make sure you have access across all the environments.

Some of the services you'll need to log into include the cloud platform, logging, storage, monitoring, and any other third-party services, such as Stripe or Twilio. If you don't see these services and the steps for how to connect to them anywhere, update the onboarding docs to include them. It will be fresh in your mind, and you can document any tips that will make the process easier for the next dev.

Get a Dev Instance Running

This will be one of the first things you do when you join the team. There will be tools you need to install, services you need to configure, and quirks you need to know about to get the app running locally. After you've pulled down the code and installed all the packages, you should see if there's anything else in the app's documentation that will help you get started.

Once you've gotten as far as you can with the docs, reach out to others on the team to help you with any further setup. As I mentioned before, updating or creating these docs will help onboard any devs joining the team after you, so this work will be greatly appreciated. There will be things that have been forgotten for the initial setup that you'll bring up, such as local environment variables or commands that need to be run in a certain order. Make sure you have the frontend, backend, and database connected locally so that you can work every part of the app.

Look at the App in Production

The best way to learn what the app does when users work with it is by using the app in production. Since you'll be coming in with little context or knowledge of how things are supposed to work, this is a great time to ask the Product team about the product you're jumping into. Make sure you're working with test credentials in production because you should not use real user credentials and start clicking around on things.

You might reach out to the QA team here as well to get some of the test credentials they use for production. Taking a tour through the app in production is a quick way to find out if you have permission to access the functionality you'll need to debug things in the future. This will help the dev team get you anything you need that was overlooked in the onboarding documentation. This is a good time to ask about where and how user data is stored so that you can check there when you need to debug.

Look at the App in Nonproduction

At some point, you need to make sure you have access to the developer view of the app. This might be in staging, develop, other environments, or all of them. It's another checkpoint to make sure you have the right user roles to access all the systems and functionality you need to get work done. This is where you might reach out to another dev and get them to walk you through the different environments and the release process. Take notes here because there will likely be a few steps you need to go through to switch between environments.

See if there are small tickets you can finish quickly to make sure your changes will be reflected across these environments and that you're doing the release steps in the correct order. This is your chance to see how long it takes deployments to finish, the type of code coverage the app has, and any automated security checks that are in place. You should also see if there are any admin pages for internal users or if feature flags are used anywhere. This is an opportunity for you to learn about some of the hacks your team uses to test scenarios for Product validation or demos.

Read Through the Code

This will help you understand the folder structure and the architecture of the codebase. When you start going through the code, work backward from something you've seen in the UI. This will guide you from the frontend all the way through the database and other parts of the infrastructure. Do this with a few features to guide yourself through the code in a structured way. Some devs try to just look at the folders and their contents to get a sense of what's happening, but that doesn't always give you context.

Try reverse engineering some features to learn about the implementation and patterns the team uses. This will give you more targeted questions to ask as well as an idea of the debugging process. You can also try correlating the code to what you read in the technical and product docs. That can help you understand relationships between engineering teams and the expectations for the separate codebases they work on.

You can also get a code walkthrough from someone else on the team. Then you'll be able to ask questions in real time as you start to understand how things work. When you do get your first few tickets, consider pair programming with someone who has been on the team for a while. You might have an idea for how something should be implemented just to find out that it's already done a certain way.

Take Notes About Potential Refactors

As you become familiar with the code, you'll see areas that you might have implemented differently. If you see parts of the code that can be improved for performance or if there are packages that can handle some of the more complex functionality, point that out. As you work in different codebases, you may find they all have a lot of functionality in common. In that case, you could advocate for a new shared codebase to move that common functionality to. That's how internal UI libraries and SDKs are created.

When you notice things you would do differently, ask the team why they were implemented the current way. There could be a strong reason for using an older version of a package or a less popular programming pattern. You need the context for why decisions were made. So take notes on the things you would do differently and talk to the team about them. Once you have the context, then you can make your suggestions based on performance optimizations, DX improvements, or security enhancements.

You might come up with suggestions, such as a template codebase that all new projects can be created from to keep consistency between codebases. Or you could suggest new roles or permissions to streamline dev access across resources and tools. Adding more types to TypeScript projects is another place where you may find room for improvement. Something I've seen on projects that have consultant devs rotate on them is a need for a better folder structure and general code organization. It's OK to be the leader on bigger initiatives like that early on as you start taking your first features.

Ask Questions and Document the Answers

If you're having a hard time understanding how a certain part of the app works, that means you're not the only one. You'll find these questions come up while you're onboarding and getting your local environment set up to work on your first feature. When you have questions, start a doc and include the answers as you talk to team members about them. I've found that sometimes no one remembers how they set up, and it takes some looking through random Google Docs and people's local environment variables to figure it out.

One of the best things you can do for an existing app is to add documentation around these unclear parts of the app. That includes technical docs, product docs, and anything else that may help the next dev who joins after you. Don't hesitate to ask everyone questions throughout your onboarding time and after. You'll learn how the organization works much faster when you reach out instead of waiting for someone to ask you if you have any questions.

Improve the Code Quality

That means you do things like DRY (don't repeat yourself) the code out when you see repetition and make shared utility functions and components. You should feel comfortable asking the team about patterns in the code and why they were selected. Look for ways you can simplify files and folder structures. Remember, this type of work can be done incrementally, so you don't have to rewrite the app yourself. Use your review to open discussions with the team on best practices and approaches you've seen.

Don't Go Overboard with DRY

Here's a word of caution about DRY that came up from a discussion with Ethan Brown:

I used to be an enthusiastic proponent of DRY, but I've since moderated my advocacy. I've found that in practice, DRY has its downsides, and they can be big:

1. Adding layers of abstraction that may reduce the amount of code but at the expense of clarity: you can end up with code that ostensibly does something simple, but you have to step through half a dozen functions (for example) to understand what's really happening. As well intentioned as this can be, sometimes repeating yourself really is the best choice.

2. The time and effort spent creating a beautiful abstraction doesn't pay for itself, either because you spend a lot of time abstracting something that's only done a handful of times (and doesn't grow over time), or you miss the mark of the parameterization and you make ostensibly abstract code that has to be tweaked constantly for future use cases.

3. Not observing patterns for a sufficient amount of time to understand the most appropriate abstraction. I'm absolutely guilty of this…sometimes I see this shining cathedral of abstraction in my mind and I get excited about that…only to find later that there was a better way.

I still think DRY is a useful context, but I prefer to present it with some more nuance these days.

Also take this as a time to learn about different ways to implement an app. On the backend, you'll see microservices, monoliths, SQL, and noSQL, and all of them are valid as long as they can be justified. This helps you expand your toolbox more because you'll get the experience other devs have already brought to the team. There will be things you have opinions on and things you will adapt to. Just keep an open mind and open eyes as you move through the codebase and learn how the team has been working on the code.

Add Tests

Some existing apps were created without test coverage being a high priority. As you work on new features and refactor existing code, don't be afraid to add more test cases. This will be something you can bring to the team to improve development going forward. If you notice that coverage is low, you could take the initiative to lead the team in slowly increasing it. Writing tests for existing code is a great way to learn about how the software is supposed to work and understand the scenarios that the user may run into.

If there is already high test coverage, see if you can introduce e2e tests if they aren't in place. You can write tickets to add tests to existing functionality and see how well documented the app is. Working with Product here is going to give you insight into how the teams work together and what the expectations are around product ownership. We addressed tests in several chapters in this book, so you can use that skill to suggest improvements or new metrics to measure as a dev team.

There is a balance for adding tests to an existing project because it can be an expensive undertaking. There may have even been a well-reasoned and thorough argument for not writing tests. Tests take time to write and then take time to maintain as the code changes. So work with your team to figure out the reasoning behind having tests or not having them.

Learn What Different Alerts Mean

You might receive email alerts when an error happens in the apps and be unfamiliar with them. Take some time to understand how alerts work for the team, where errors stem from, and where the alerts are shared. Make sure you have access to any logging tools or the server where log files are stored.

As you become more comfortable with the apps, you'll be expected to look into errors and warnings. Go through existing logs and learn some preliminary stats on common errors. Then use the logs to see which part of the stack is producing them. You can add this to your notes as you learn the process for handing them. When an error comes up, see if you can pair with another dev to learn how they get to the root cause and take more notes. This will introduce you to systems that you may not work with regularly. You'll learn how communication is handled and how resolutions are made. Not every alert will be related to the code, and you'll learn how to decipher what's relevant to your team.

As you work on both greenfield and legacy apps, that will help you determine the direction you want to go in your career. You'll gain experience in many areas, and you'll start to gravitate toward certain areas. That's when you have to make decisions about where to add depth to your knowledge and figure out which career path suits you best for this point in your life.

Your Career

Over the course of this book, you've learned many things you need to do to set up a full stack app so that it's maintainable in the long term. You've learned how to communicate with almost every team in the organization and why it's important to do so. You've reviewed the Product roadmap and helped add a vision for the technical roadmap. You've helped lead your dev team in discussions and with feature implementation.

At this point in your career, you'll be adding more depth to your skills as you get exposure to more complex technical tasks and start mentoring devs who are earlier in their careers. This brings many senior developers to a crossroads with the path they want to take next. With all the knowledge you have about the frontend, backend, database, business domain, and the way the teams work together, you have a solid foundation for all the options ahead of you.

The Technical Path

Some devs like to stay on the technical path and move to roles with more responsibility, such as architect, staff engineer (*https://noidea.dog/staff*), and principal engineer. You'll still be able to write code, but you'll have a more prominent teaching impact. As you dive deeper into the technical side, you'll start working at more of a system level than at the code level. You may have some tickets to work through, but most of your tasks will focus on how parts of the system will work together.

For example, instead of implementing individual endpoints, you'll come up with how the endpoints should connect to the database, how they trigger other events, naming conventions based on the domain, and the data schema for them. You'll be the one generating and documenting the diagrams for how all these things fit together and then presenting it to the team for feedback. You'll be responsible for stepping in when others on the team get stuck on a debugging issue that involves multiple parts of the system and external services.

As you move farther along the technical path, you'll be responsible for keeping packages up to date and understanding how their dependencies affect the codebase. You'll bring more of a vision to unite multiple teams under the engineering department and help develop and drive a technical roadmap. This means you'll spend more time thinking about how the app will work in the future and what everyone can do to prepare for that. That includes things like building internal tools to unblock the dev teams, tracking key metrics like PR review time and how well estimates are made, and understanding how dev tasks fit into the overall strategy of the organization.

Another skill you'll develop is how you communicate. As you pass the senior dev level, how you communicate with others becomes more and more important. You'll be mentoring early career devs, helping Product manage risks when estimates are off, and helping other devs get acknowledged for the work they do. The farther you go on this path, the more your role becomes enabling the rest of the team to get through their tickets quickly and accurately. This typically means you spend less time writing code and more time thinking about how to improve every part of the system to keep everyone moving.

This can also take you to the tech lead role if you're more interested in the leadership side of the technical path. That usually involves more project management because you're working with the team to meet timelines and you're working with Product to deeply understand the goals and explain to them any technical blocks. At this point, you're working with an engineering manager to help maintain or improve the culture of the team. As a tech lead, you might also jump in and work on some tickets if it's necessary to meet a deadline.

If you choose to continue on the technical path, it will benefit you to stay on top of industry trends so that you can help the team implement the latest best practices. This will also give you awareness of new tools that may solve a problem the team has. Spend some time deepening your knowledge of the organization's structure as well. Knowing how the different teams and departments relate to one another will help you figure out who to talk to when questions arise.

The Management Path

The other path you can take is on the management side. This includes engineering manager, associate director, director, and vice president roles. These roles typically remove you from the code completely as you start to focus on the coaching, growth, and strategic sides of the engineering department. You may still write some code, but that depends on the size of your organization and how it defines the role. In these roles, you're usually involved in more meetings with the individual team members to understand how they are doing and how they'd like to progress.

You'll help create the culture for the engineering department and set up career levels that each developer can grow into. You'll do things like review how much the teams are spending on tools and if there are better alternatives. A large part of what you'll do is help everyone on your teams grow in their own careers. You'll be listening to them in your one-on-one meetings and taking notes on what they tell you. It's important that you give them good feedback on how they're performing.

When they're doing a good job, make sure you acknowledge them both in your one-on-ones and publicly. That will encourage them to keep up the good work as well as help them get the recognition they've earned, which is essential when it comes to promotions. On the other hand, it's also important for you to give them critical feedback. The only way people on your teams can improve is if you tell them the areas where they can strengthen.

If other team members have brought up concerns about their work, make sure you let them know as soon as you can. It's better to alert them long before reviews so that they have plenty of time to make changes. This is a great chance for you to coach them on ways they can improve and give them resources to teach them the skills they need. As you have one-on-ones with everyone, you should be asking for feedback on what you can do better for them. It can be hard to get your team to give you critical feedback, so try to lead this effort by example. A huge part of your job is understanding how you can better serve your teams, so the main way you can grow is to get feedback from them.

Some other good sources of critical feedback include exit interviews and anonymous surveys. The people on your team may feel uncomfortable directly telling you the ways you can improve, so this can take some of that pressure off.

If you move to a position where you're a manager of managers, create documentation to help guide them through their own one-on-ones and give them tips on how to have difficult conversations with their people. This is an interesting role to be in because you likely won't ever touch any code, but everything you document will serve as a starting point for other managers who report to you. So write docs on interview questions, things they can ask in one-on-ones, how they can keep people engaged in the organization's culture, and how they can help their people grow. All this is part of helping them grow into better managers.

Something else you'll do on this path is have more meetings with Product and stakeholders such as the VPs of other departments and maybe the C-suite executives to understand the plan for the business and how your teams and department fit into that. You'll be directly involved in mapping out the Product roadmap and keeping the technical roadmap in alignment with it. This is when you'll be involved in hiring decisions and help determine when it's time for the team to grow to support the organization's goals.

Communication is essential to success on the management path because that's almost exclusively what you'll do. You won't have tickets anymore, and your involvement with sprints and everyday development tasks will decrease substantially. The majority of your work will be meetings and documenting the outcomes from them in a way that translates into work for all your teams. You want to be the shield for your teams so that they aren't pulled into a lot of meetings for clarification.

You have to learn how to balance your personal views with organizational decisions and communicate what needs to be done effectively. You need to feel comfortable pushing back on decisions that will negatively affect your teams. Part of management is advocating for your teams and making sure that their needs are considered in large decisions. Speak up when something seems odd to you because that's one of the most valuable things you can do in your position.

 Here are some good resources when you're considering the management path:

- *The Manager's Path* by Camille Fournier (O'Reilly)
- *Engineering Management for the Rest of Us* by Sarah Drasner (Skill Recordings Inc.)
- *Resilient Management* by Lara Hogan (A Book Apart)

Professional Journal

Something I highly recommend is keeping your own personal documentation on what you see and do across the different projects you work on. That will be your template for how you approach anything. You can take some of the practices you learn at each organization along with you on your career. This is going to help you at every point because you'll start to run into similar scenarios everywhere.

You should take notes on situations you're the proudest of and situations where you struggled the most. This is invaluable when you're interviewing for new roles because you'll inevitably be asked some situational or behavioral questions. It's also good to have when it's time for reviews in your existing role. It can be hard to remember what you've done in the past six months or year, so write it down.

When you learn a cool new tech thing because it's a standard practice at an organization, add it to this journal. You may be surprised how often similar issues occur across teams, organizations, and industries. If you've ever had that feeling where you think you did something before, this journal will help you validate that. I've had this happen a number of times where I run into difficult bugs or feature specs and I added them to my journal. Then I was able to reference them when the same scenario happened elsewhere.

This journal should be on your personal computer, not a company one. You never know when you'll lose access or have the computer wiped when it's not your own. Keep in mind that this isn't a formal document. This is just for you, so it can be in any format you want. The following sidebar has the format most of my professional journal entries conform to. For tech issues, it tells me what happened and what I did to fix it. For situations I'm proud of or struggled with, I try to tell the story of what happened and how it played out.

Professional Journal Entries

Here are a few examples of entries from my personal journal:

Issue with finding a custom npm package in the CircleCI pipeline

An error was being returned saying that the specific package couldn't be found. The solution was:

- Delete the *package-lock.json*
- Reinstall all of the packages with `npm i`
- Push the changes in a PR to the branch with the pipeline issue
- Merge the updated *package-lock.json* and let the pipeline run again

---

Issue with unit test passing when run individually, failing when run with all the other tests

Data was being mutated each time a function was called, so the test would only pass sometimes. The solution was:

- Finding out there was an array method being used that was mutating the original array
- Using the spread operator on the original array to create a new instance of it
- Using the array method on that new instance

Proud moment: tracking down a two-year bug in the UI

On a project, there was a bug in the UI that was hard to track down because we used a micro-frontend architecture, so there were at least six teams responsible for small pieces of functionality, and they all did things differently. There was even one team that wrote their frontend in Vue while the other teams used React. I was able to manage a large number of dependency conflicts and found that one of the micro-frontend teams was force-installing their package into the container app because they didn't want to upgrade their internal dependencies. That led to all the other teams building workarounds for this one error. It took about 2.5 months to successfully fix the dependency conflicts between six apps, but that also fixed a bug that had existed for years. By the time I finished these upgrades, it allowed each team to refactor their code for higher quality, and it improved performance of the overall app because I was able to remove unused packages, decreasing the bundle sizes for the micro-frontend teams and the container app team.

Moving to Other Areas

After traveling farther down a path or going down another path entirely, you might decide that you need a complete change and you want to try something else. Maybe you've always been interested in data engineering, and you have some background in database management. Or you wanted to try being a DevOps engineer because you've done a little work with the infrastructure that sparked your interest. It's fine to take up a new specialty and work on that for a while.

If your organization has the capacity, you may be able to help out on different initiatives and improve your skills in the process. You could also choose to take a less senior role in a different area, such as becoming a junior data engineer. Your core software skills aren't going anywhere, and working in a different part of the tech world can improve your creativity because you can see how things work from another viewpoint. This is a time when you can get certifications or help work on smaller functionality your organization needs. There is a trade-off when you do this exploration because the current state of our tech stacks is constantly changing, so you might not stay up to date on the latest and greatest.

 Regardless of the path you choose, it will help you greatly if you take some form of leadership training. See if there's anything your organization recommends or has access to. Several books have helped me learn about leadership, even if some of them are unconventional:

- *How to Win Friends and Influence People* by Dale Carnegie (Simon & Schuster)

- *Thinkertoys: A Handbook of Creative-Thinking Techniques* by Michael Michalko (Ten Speed Press)

- *Spark: How to Lead Yourself and Others to Greater Success* by Angie Morgan, Courtney Lynch, and Sean Lynch (Houghton Mifflin Harcourt)

- *Wherever You Go, There You Are: Mindfulness Meditation in Everyday Life* by Jon Kabat-Zinn (Hachette Books)

You can always jump around to different specialties as well. Maybe you try data engineering and you don't like it. You can come back to software development until you figure out what the next thing is. You might find that there isn't a next thing and you're content with where you are. Not everyone wants to climb the ladder and get promoted as soon as they can, and that's fine. It's your career, and there is no such thing as "normal." You have to do what's best for you and your life because you're the only one living it.

Conclusion

Congratulations! You've made it to the end of this book. By now you've done everything on the frontend and backend that it takes to build a maintainable full stack app. You know what it takes to evaluate tools, handle cross-team communication, keep track of technical decisions, and help out your team members when you need to. You've learned about the subtle and unspoken skills that go into being a senior dev, such as writing solid documentation for everything and bringing your experience to the table.

I sincerely hope that you've found this book useful and you'll refer to it if you ever get stuck at any point in your development process. If you found any of this helpful, I'd love to hear from you about your experiences! Or if you thought something was off base or I missed something, I'd love to hear about that as well. While this book doesn't cover every potential consideration you'll run into, it does go over a lot of the standard ones. As you move on through the years and through your career, always keep in mind that there's something new to learn all the time. As software engineers, we never know everything, so keep an open mind and a sense of humility, and that will take you a long way.

Index

architectural and system design decisions, 402-406
C4 design, 405
domain-driven design, 403
atomic design methodology, 162
consistent designs in apps, 215
data-driven, 10-13
design considerations for ecommerce app, 8-10
effects of changing shared components, 316
frontend apps, 167
insecure, 98
insecure, frontend vulnerabilities as, 234
responsive, 217-219
separation of concerns, 163
user actions screen in Figma, 5, 7
user info screen in Figma, 4
components of, 7
Design team, 4
learning how users interact with things, 407
project kickoff meeting, 4
working with on building standard for components and terminology, 163
dev (development) dependencies, 43
e2e testing packages installed as, 311
dev branch
PR reviews of, making sure app runs and meets acceptance criteria, 350
Dev Containers (VS Code), 26
develop branch, 350, 364
caution with merging feature tasks directly to, 368
changes merged to, keeping feature branches in sync with, 370
merging commits to staging without squashing them, 369
merging flow to, 365
merging multiple tickets to, 366
pulling down latest changes from when making new branch, 366
rebases and merges with, 375
rebasing feature branch with changes from and merging develop with, 372-375
requiring PR approval before merging developer's branch into develop, 350
restricting direct pushes to, 348
source of truth for latest features approved by dev team, 364

squashing commits from develop to staging, 369
developers
advice about deployment process, 288
defining and managing tasks in project management, 391-397
developer surveys, 165
discussing merge conflicts with dev who made changes, 376
experience with AuthZ, testing, 100
helping other developers debug, 114-115
development
getting dev instance of existing application running, 420
running only frontend in container during, 337
development (dev) dependencies, 43
e2e testing packages installed as, 311
development environment, 358
development mode, app running in, 263
development team
capacity of, in sprint discussions, 383
coordinating with DevOps in scaling backend app, 141
going through deployment to production until process is routine, 297
keeping constant communication between Product team and, 318
reviewing all the tickets or feature specs, 387
devices
accessible, meaning of each HTML element to, 210
assistive, 212
checking that frontend works across different devices, 293
testing, integration concerns and, 330
using breakpoints to switch to styles or components developed for subset of, 217
DevOps
coordinating with DevOps team, 15
partnering with to build and maintain CI/CD pipeline, 341
partnering with to keep up Dockerfiles, 339
role of team in deployments, 288
role of team in frontend deployment, 293
working with on frontend development, 170
working with team on deploying older versions (rollback), 324
disaster recovery (DR), 295

updating README, 28
use in building REST API, 55
validations, handling with class-validator package, 58
Network tab (Chrome DevTools), 279
checking API requests in, 279
Preview or Response windows, viewing API response in, 280
New Relic, 247
Next.js, 183
prefetching pages from server, 254
Nightwatch
comparison with Cypress and Playwright, 311
end-to-end tests with, 308-311
Nock, 263
Node
different versions run locally and by production server, 334
Node 20.10.0, running React frontend app locally via, 180
nonrelational databases, 38
NoSQL databases, 423
npm run preview command, 337
npm-audit, 236
vulnerability report snippet taken from, 236
npm-version command, 320
nvm, 180

O

Object instances, 105
Object instances in log messages, 147
object-relational mapping tools (see ORM tools)
one-time password (OTP) authentication, 92
open authorization (OAuth), 92
optimizations, 132
(see also performance)
backend performance, 123
orbs section (CircleCI configs for CI/CD pipeline), 356
orderData, 202
orders
creating endpoints for, 56
order table in database schema, 39
testing orders table loading in e2e test with Cypress, 301
working on orders service, 58
orders endpoint, 33

ordersAreLoading, 202
orderSnap variable, 195
orderStore proxy, 194
ORM (object-relational mapping) tools, 42
deciding which to use, 43-46
migrations or SQL queries made by, 46
OTP (one-time password) authentication, 92
overhead tasks, 393
OWASP Top 10, 97, 236

P

P90 latency, 120, 121
pacing yourself, 394
package managers, 169
package.json file
updates of package version, 320
versions of frontend and backend in, 317
packages
bundle size and, 248
choosing for frontend, 167
lazy loading, 253
metrics to consider for data-fetching tools, 198
outdated versions of as attack vectors, 98
updating version of, 320
version maintenance, common frontend vulnerability, 236
pages folder, 181
password authentication, 92
enforcing stronger user passwords and adding MFA, 98
passwords, masking in input fields, 334
patterns (architecture), 162
Payment Card Industry Data Security Standard (PCI DSS) compliance, 65, 91
payment handlers, third-party services for, 63
integrating Stripe third-party service, 65-71
PBAC (policy-based access control), 96
questions to ask before choosing, 96
peak response time (PRT), 120, 121
peer dependencies, 43
penetration testing (pen testing), 99
Penpot, 6
performance
backend, 119-133
alerts and monitoring, 124
caching, 125-132
metrics on, 120-123
other ways to speed up your app, 132

professional journal, 428-429

progressive delivery or staged rollout, 322

project example for this book

    choosing approach for backend, 24

    kickoff, 3-20

projects

    creating new NestJS project, 25

    dashboard-web frontend app example, 172

    different types of, working on over your
        career, 413-430

        considerations for brand-new apps,
            414-419

        considerations for existing apps, 419-424

    Git history in GitHub, 371

    project management, 381-397

        defining and managing tasks, 391-397

        sprint discussions, 382-390

    React project folder structure, 181

promises, chaining, 204

prop drilling, 190

properties

    adding property to requests to force certain
        error and payload, 231

providers (in React), 177

provisioning resources, 137

proxies, 193

    orderStore storing state, 194

    Valtio proxy to keep track of state variables,
        194

PRs

    blocking direct PRs to main branch, 350

    branch merging flow, 364

    CircleCI status on GitHub PR, 352

    examining quickly for changes in shared
        branches, 345

    GitHub configs in, 348

    instant feedback on your CI/CD pipeline in,
        343

    merging to develop branch, 364

    opening PR to merge circleci-project-setup
        with main branch, 351

    PR reviews, 365

    requiring approval before merging develo-
        per's branch into develop, 350

    reverting or resetting in rollback strategy,
        324

    running some pipeline checks directly on
        the PR, 350

targeting certain branches, running build
    and test stages of CI/CD pipeline on, 343

PRT (peak response time), 120, 121

ps (process) command for Unix systems, 338

Q

QA (quality assurance)

    getting test credentials from QA team for
        production, 420

    performing QA testing for brand-new app,
        418

    working with QA team, 17

    working with QA team on frontend devel-
        opment, 170

queries

    basic SQL queries, 42

    querying seeded data in database, 290

query keyword (GraphQL), 34

query optimization (database), 123

questions, asking, 396

    about existing application, 422

quick wins, starting with, 67

R

raster images, getting grainy when stretched,
    218

RBAC (role-based access control), 94

    benefits and limitations of, 95

    trade-offs with, 96

React, 166, 170

    building first feature of frontend app,
        181-185

        project structure, 181

        setting up routing, 183

        updating root of the app, 183

    component state, how it works, 188-192

    declarative programming in, 222

    error boundaries, 222

    handling lazy loading in, 252

    setting up and building React app, 171

    setting up initial React app, 172-181

        build configs, 175

        CHANGELOG and README files, 179

        linters and formatters, 172-174

        running the app locally, 180

        styles, 176

        testing, 178

    state management, different approaches to,
        192-193

About the Author

Milecia McGregor is a staff software engineer who's worked with TypeScript, Angular, React, Node, Python, SQL, AWS, and many other tools to build web apps. She also has a master's degree in mechanical and aerospace engineering and has published research in machine learning and robotics. She's had her own businesses, spoken internationally at a number of tech conferences, and worked in roles ranging from frontend developer to associate engineering director. She publishes articles covering all aspects of software for several publications, including freeCodeCamp. In her free time, she spends time with her husband and dogs while practicing martial arts and working towards a pilot license.

Colophon

The animal on the cover of *Full Stack JavaScript Strategies* is a tawny frogmouth (*Podargus strigoides*), a species of frogmouth native to the forests and woodlands of Australia and Tasmania.

Despite their owl-like appearance, tawny frogmouths are more closely related to nightjars. They have a wide, frog-like mouth, large yellow eyes, and soft, mottled brown and gray plumage that provides excellent camouflage against tree bark.

Tawny frogmouths are primarily nocturnal and carnivorous, feeding on a variety of insects, spiders, worms, slugs, snails, small mammals, reptiles, and frogs. These birds are known for their exceptional camouflage and silent flight, making them highly effective hunters.

The tawny frogmouth is currently listed as of "Least Concern" by the International Union for Conservation of Nature (IUCN). However, habitat loss due to deforestation and urbanization poses a potential threat to their populations. Many of the animals on O'Reilly covers are endangered; all of them are important to the world.

The cover illustration is by Karen Montgomery, based on a black and white engraving from *Brehms Tierleben*. The series design is by Edie Freedman, Ellie Volckhausen, and Karen Montgomery. The cover fonts are Gilroy Semibold and Guardian Sans. The text font is Adobe Minion Pro; the heading font is Adobe Myriad Condensed; and the code font is Dalton Maag's Ubuntu Mono.

O'REILLY®

Learn from experts.
Become one yourself.

60,000+ titles | Live events with experts | Role-based courses
Interactive learning | Certification preparation

**Try the O'Reilly learning platform
free for 10 days.**

www.ingramcontent.com/pod-product-compliance
Ingram Content Group UK Ltd.
Pitfield, Milton Keynes, MK11 3LW, UK
UKHW011607140125
453572UK00003B/4

9 781098 122256